PSY★COMM

Psy-Comm Vol. 1
Written By Jason Henderson and Tony Salvaggio
Illustrated by Shane Granger

Inks - Jeremy Freeman
Tones - Chi Wang
Copy Editor - Hope Donovan
Production Artist - Gloria Wu
Cover Designer - Jorge Negrete

Editor - Bryce P. Coleman
Digital Imaging Manager - Chris Buford
Production Managers - Jennifer Miller and Mutsumi Miyazaki
Managing Editor - Lindsey Johnston
VP of Production - Ron Klamert
Publisher and E.I.C. - Mike Kiley
President and C.O.O. - John Parker
C.E.O. - Stuart Levy

A  Manga

TOKYOPOP Inc.
5900 Wilshire Blvd. Suite 2000
Los Angeles, CA 90036

E-mail: info@TOKYOPOP.com
Come visit us online at www.TOKYOPOP.com

ISBN: 1-59816-269-1
First TOKYOPOP printing: November 2005
10 9 8 7 6 5 4 3 2 1
Printed in the USA

PSY★COMM

[Vol. 1]

WRITTEN BY
JASON HENDERSON AND TONY SALVAGGIO

ILLUSTRATED BY
SHANE GRANGER

HAMBURG // LONDON // LOS ANGELES // TOKYO

PSY★COMM

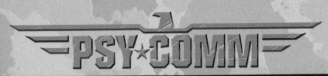

VOLUME [1]

CONTENTS

PSY★COMM

CHAPTER [1]

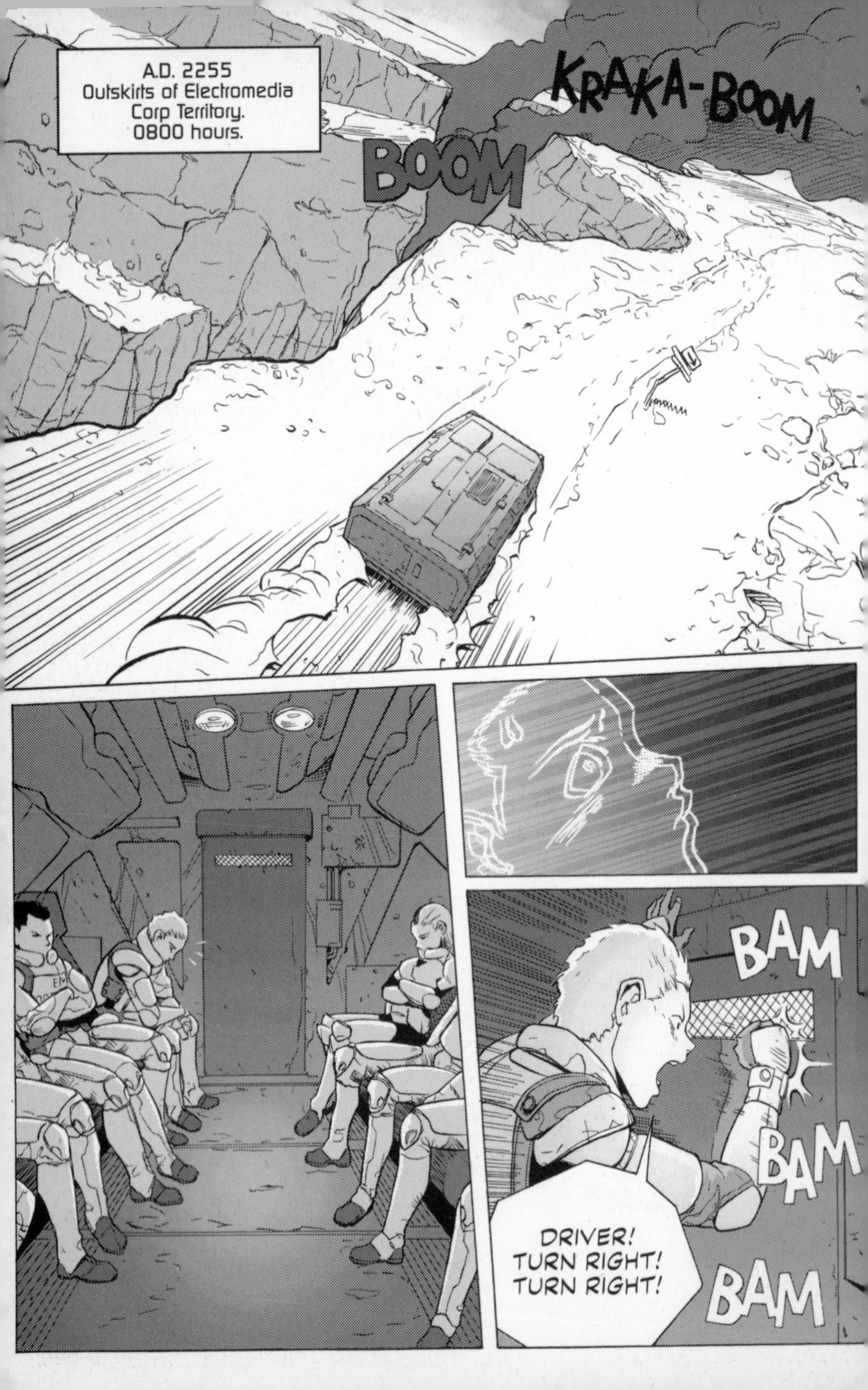
A.D. 2255
Outskirts of Electromedia
Corp Territory.
0800 hours.
BOOM
KRAKA-BOOM
BAM
BAM
BAM
DRIVER!
TURN RIGHT!
TURN RIGHT!

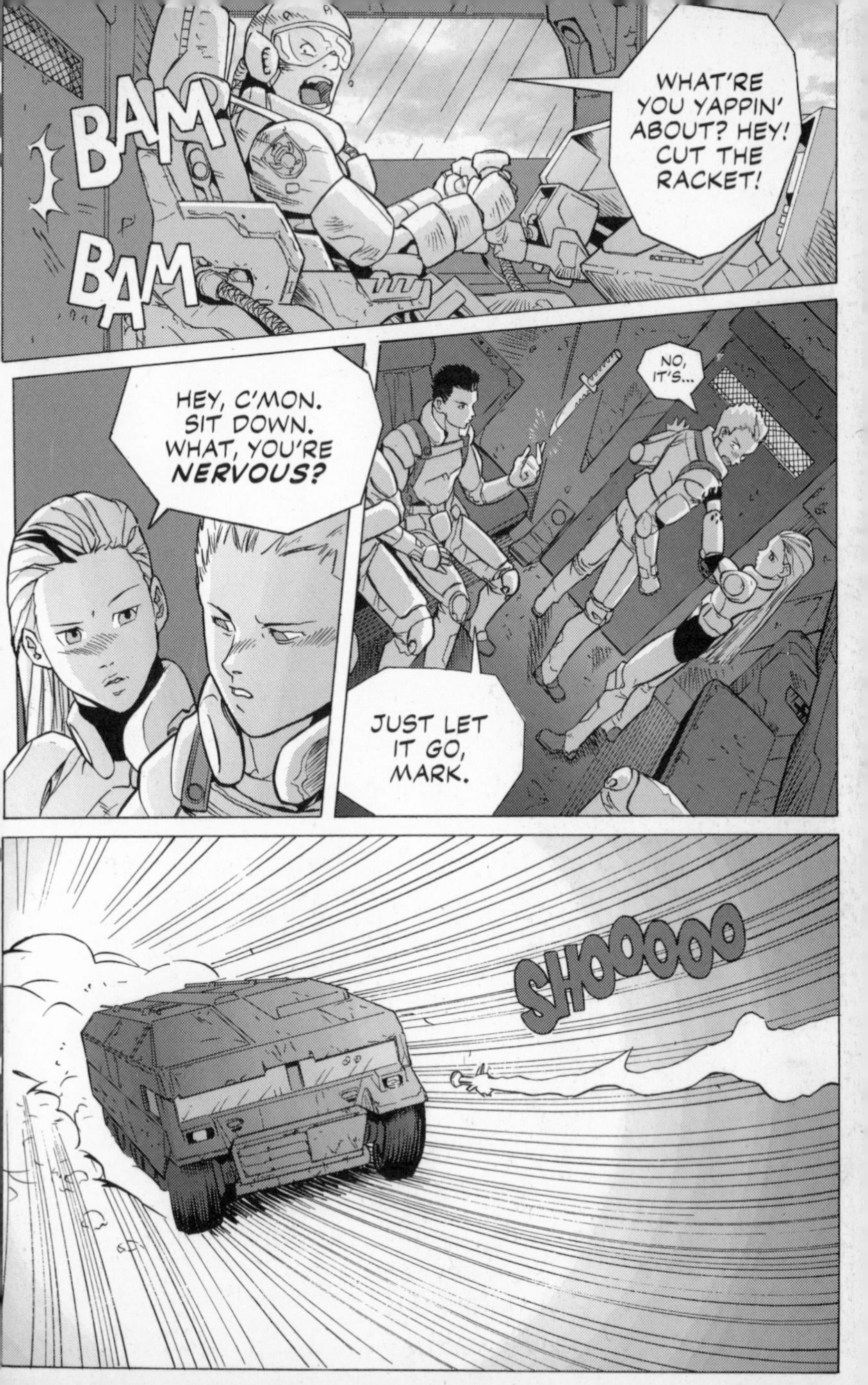
BAM
BAM
WHAT'RE YOU YAPPIN' ABOUT? HEY! CUT THE RACKET!
HEY, C'MON. SIT DOWN. WHAT, YOU'RE *NERVOUS?*
NO, IT'S...
JUST LET IT GO, MARK.
SHOOOOO

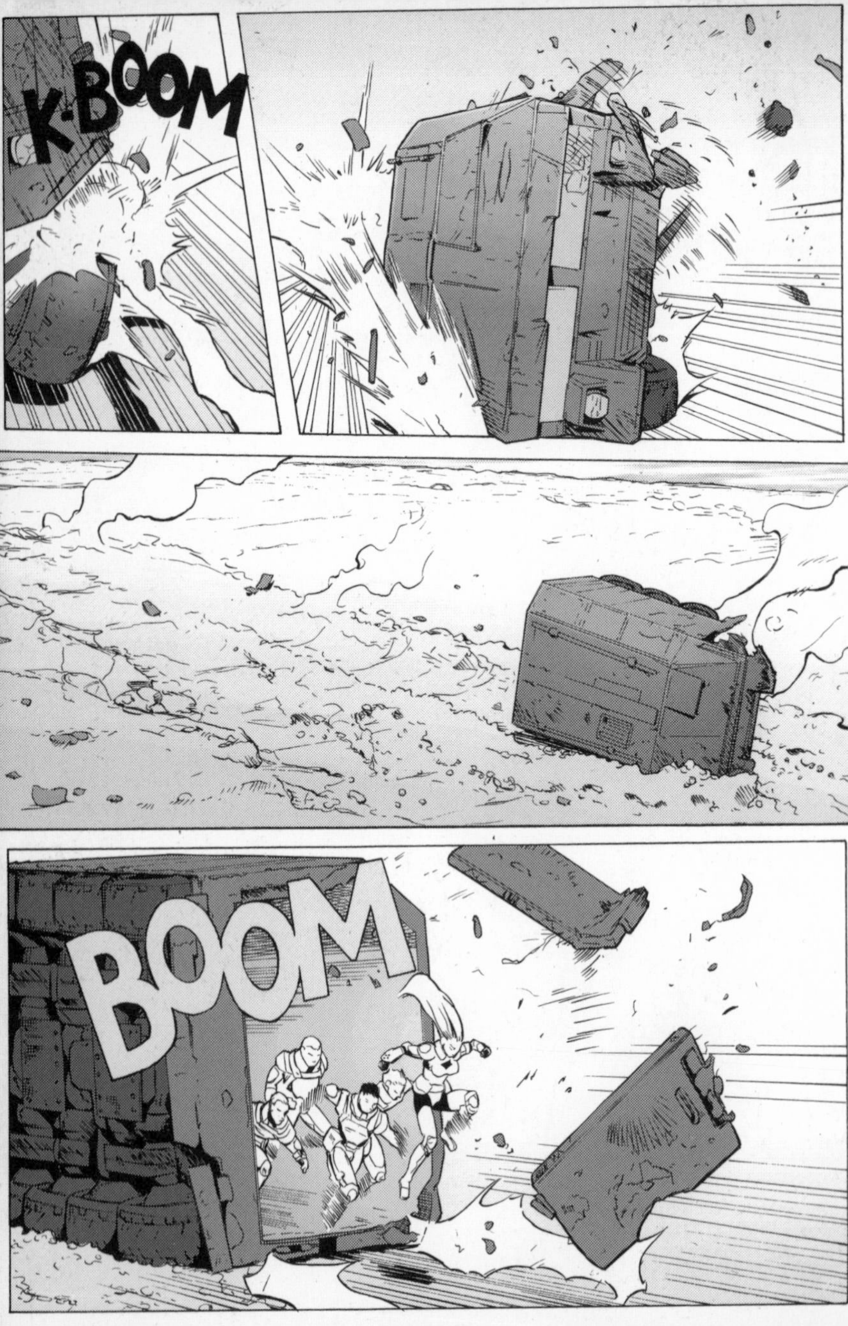
K-BOOM
BOOM

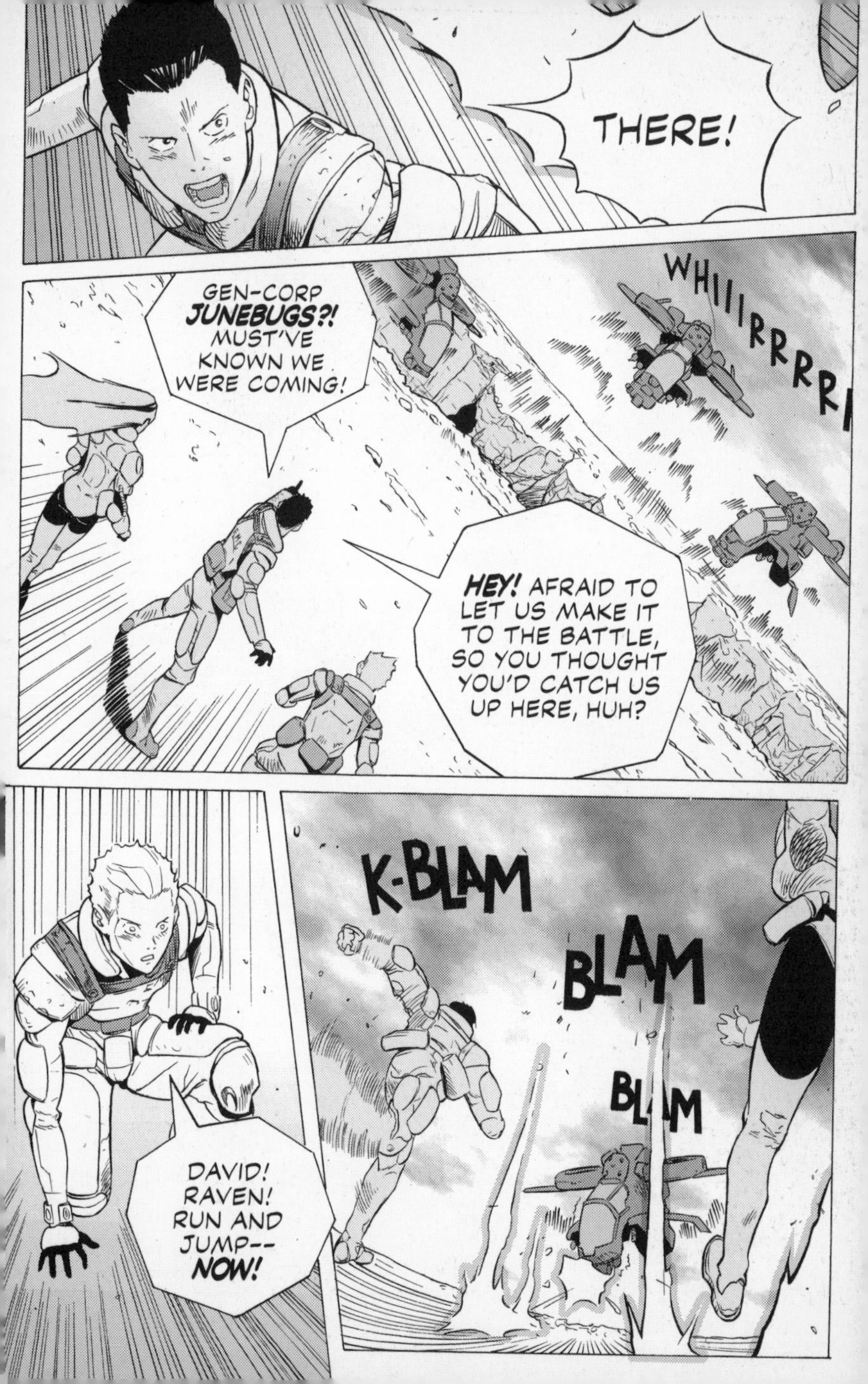
THERE!
GEN-CORP **JUNEBUGS?!** MUST'VE KNOWN WE WERE COMING!
WHIIIRRRRR
HEY! AFRAID TO LET US MAKE IT TO THE BATTLE, SO YOU THOUGHT YOU'D CATCH US UP HERE, HUH?
DAVID! RAVEN! RUN AND JUMP-- **NOW!**
K-BLAM
BLAM
BLAM

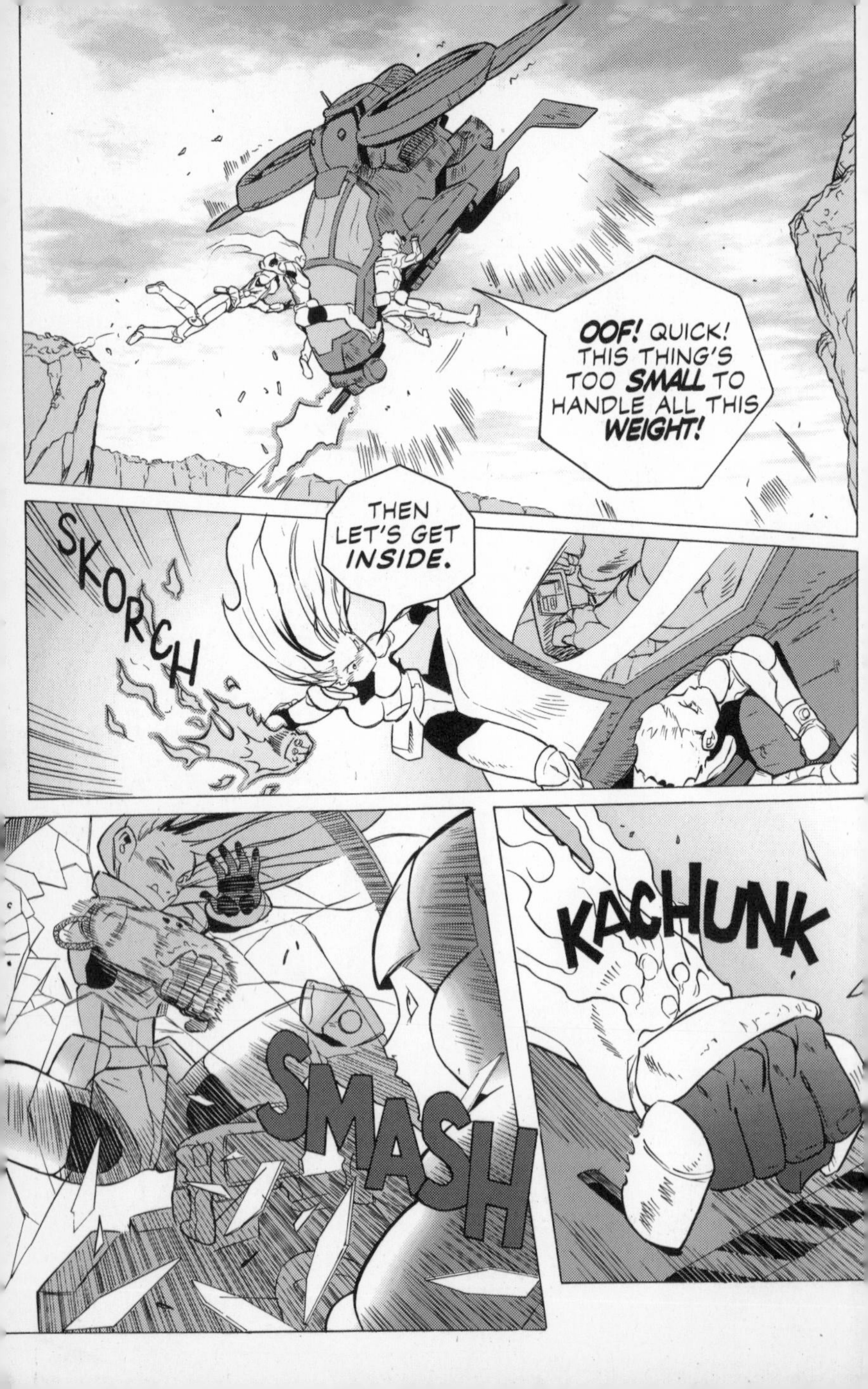
OOF! QUICK! THIS THING'S TOO SMALL TO HANDLE ALL THIS WEIGHT!
SKORCH
THEN LET'S GET INSIDE.
SMASH
KACHUNK

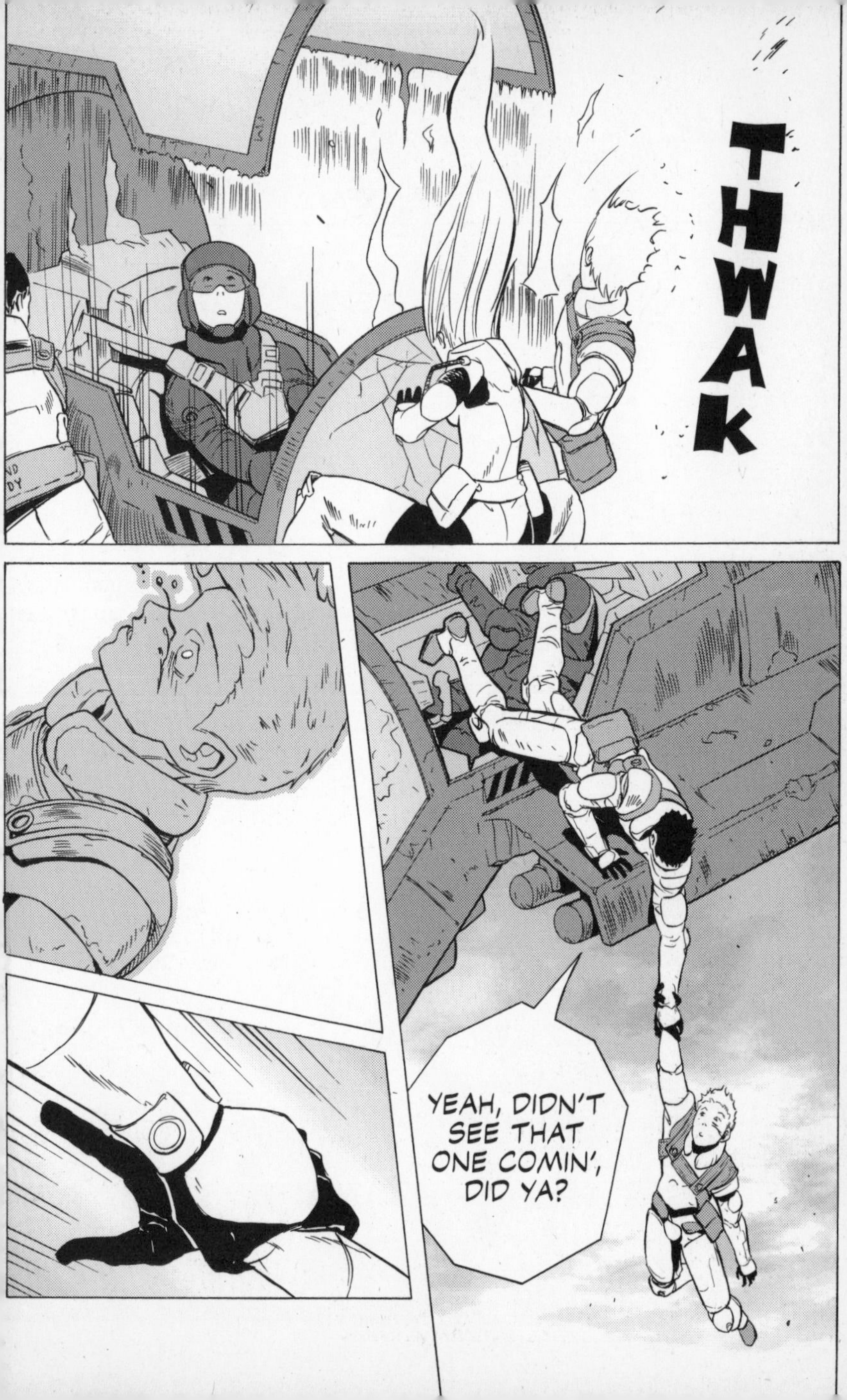
THWAK
YEAH, DIDN'T SEE THAT ONE COMIN', DID YA?

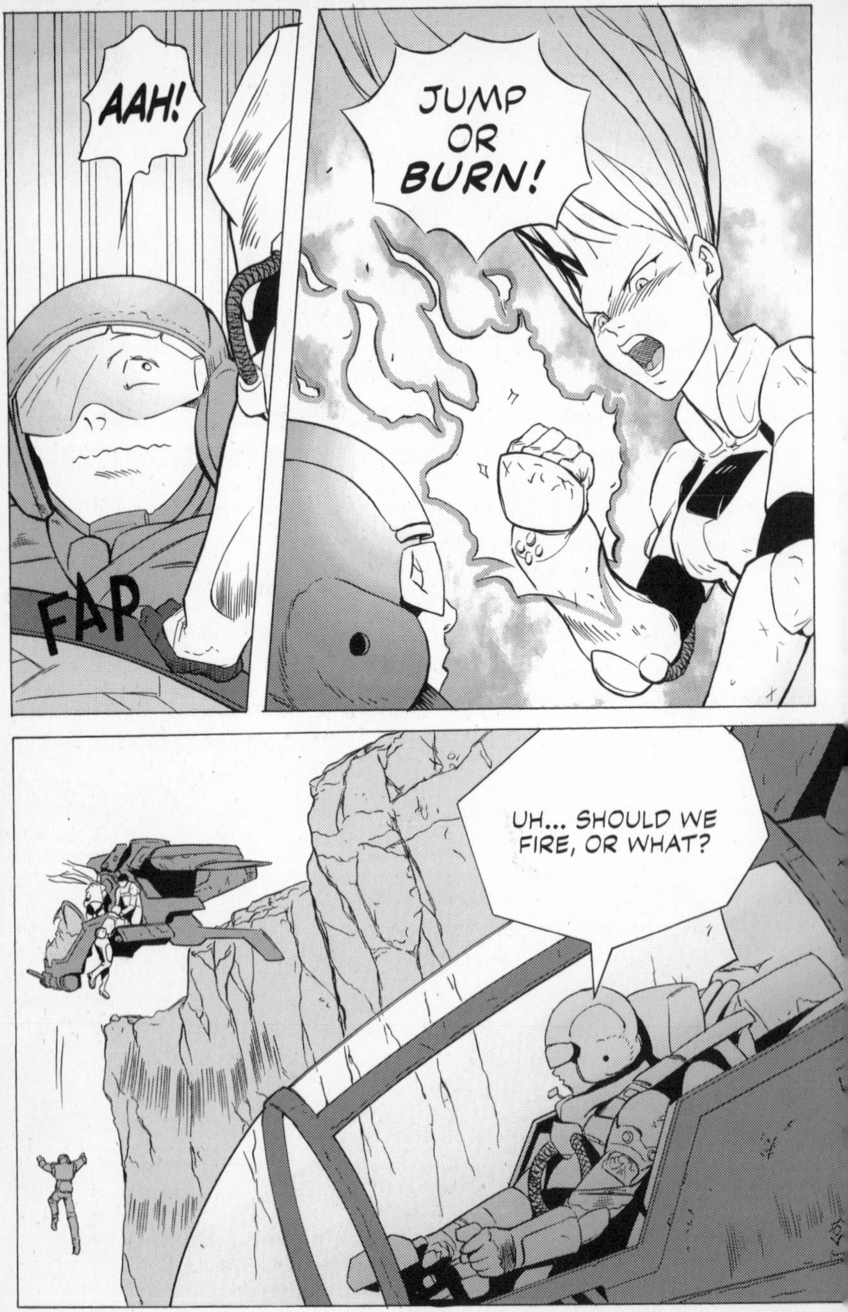
AAH!
JUMP OR BURN!
FAP
UH... SHOULD WE FIRE, OR WHAT?

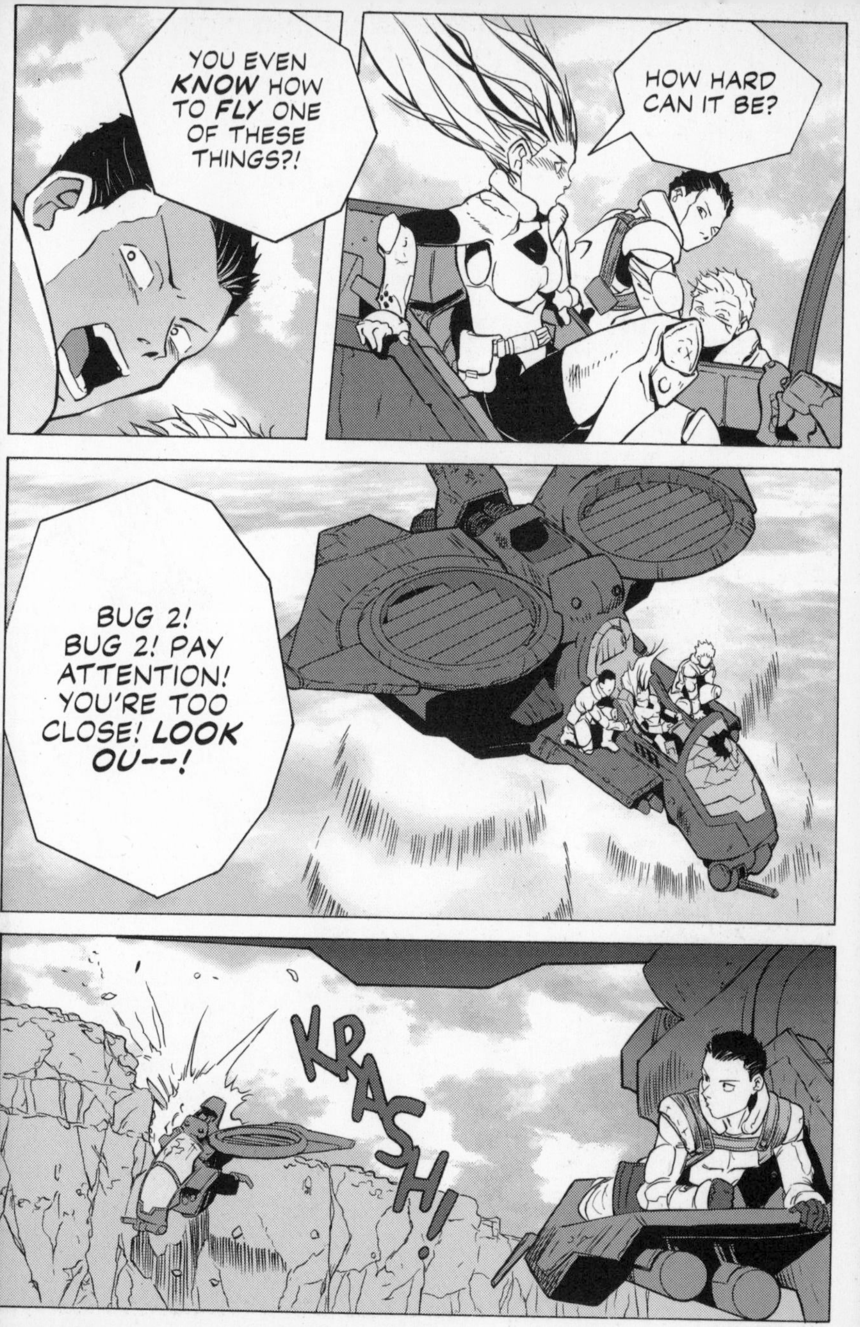
YOU EVEN **KNOW** HOW TO **FLY** ONE OF THESE THINGS?!
HOW HARD CAN IT BE?
BUG 2! BUG 2! PAY ATTENTION! YOU'RE TOO CLOSE! **LOOK OU--!**
KRASH!

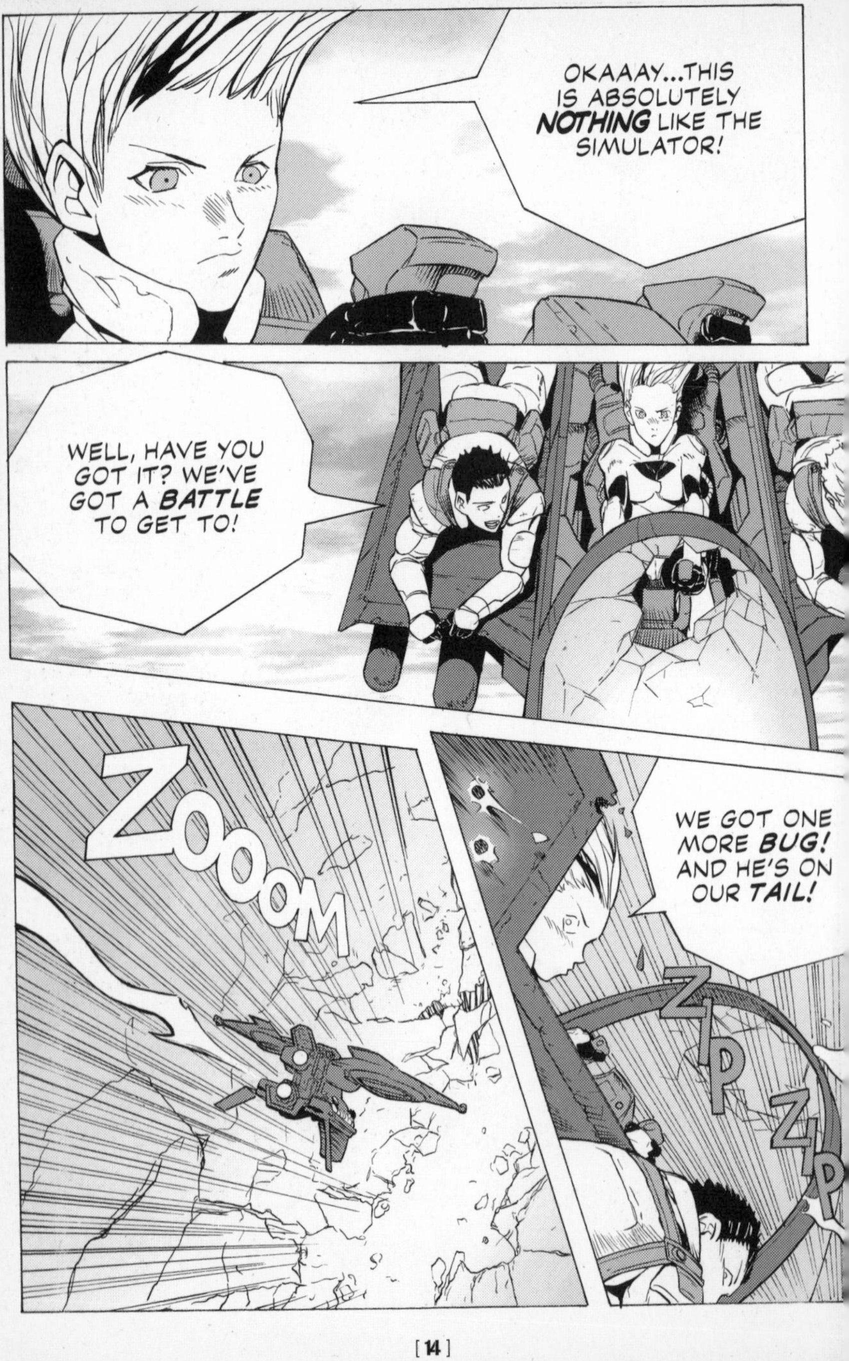

OKAAAY...THIS IS ABSOLUTELY **NOTHING** LIKE THE SIMULATOR!
WELL, HAVE YOU GOT IT? WE'VE GOT A **BATTLE** TO GET TO!
ZOOOOM
WE GOT ONE MORE **BUG!** AND HE'S ON OUR **TAIL!**
ZIP
ZIP
ZIP

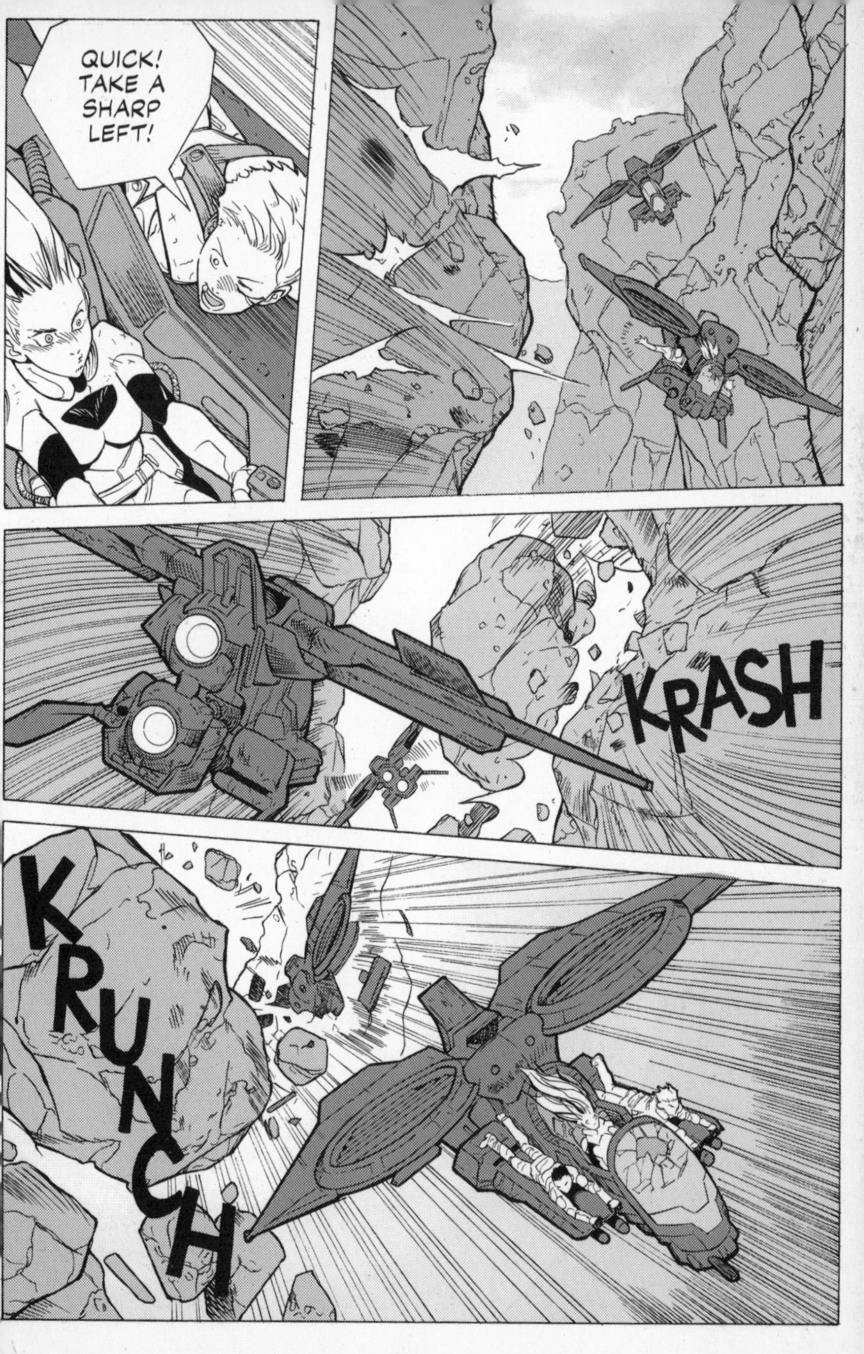
QUICK! TAKE A SHARP LEFT!
KRASH
KRUNCH

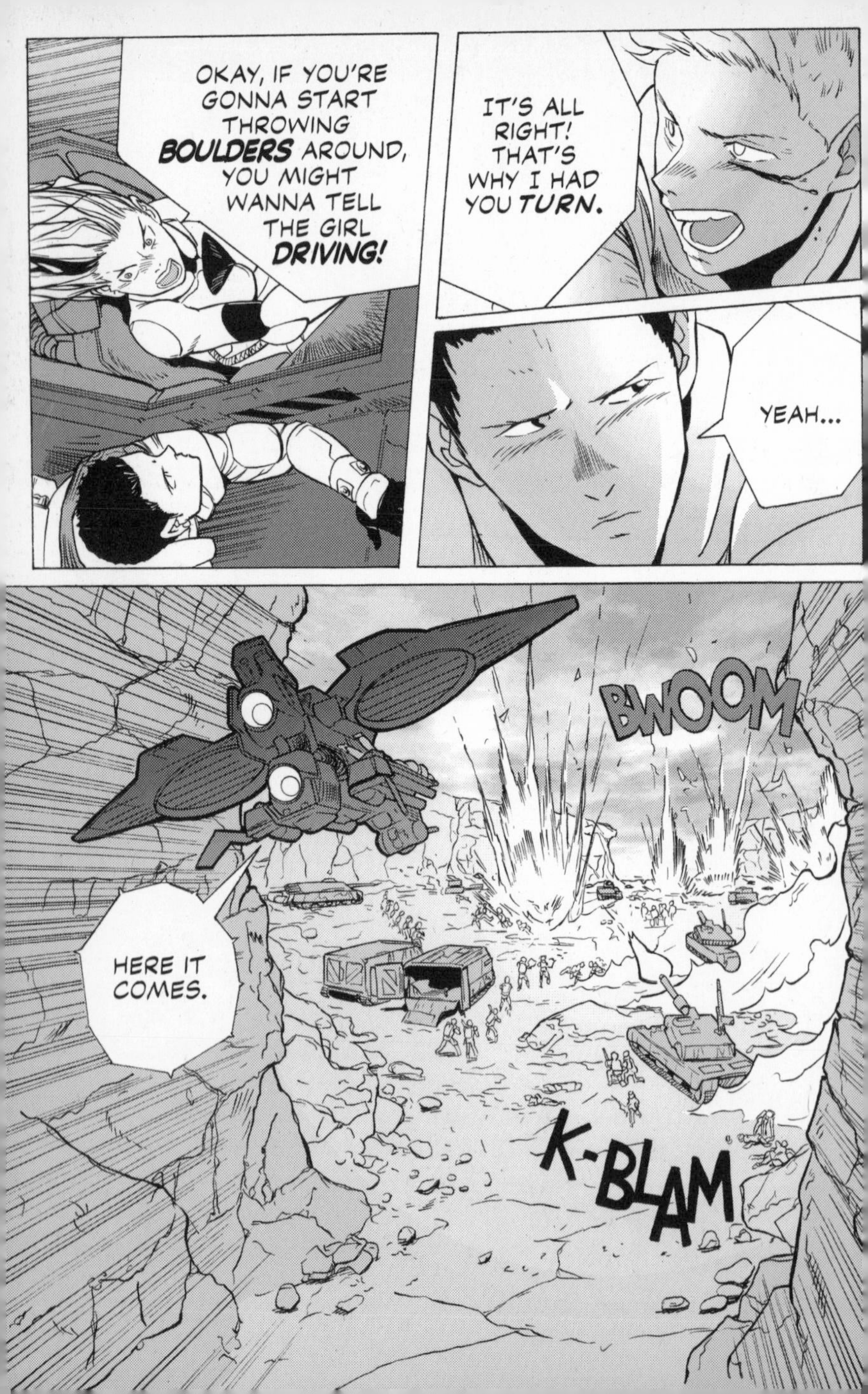
OKAY, IF YOU'RE GONNA START THROWING **BOULDERS** AROUND, YOU MIGHT WANNA TELL THE GIRL **DRIVING!**
IT'S ALL RIGHT! THAT'S WHY I HAD YOU **TURN.**
YEAH...
HERE IT COMES.
BWOOM
K-BLAM

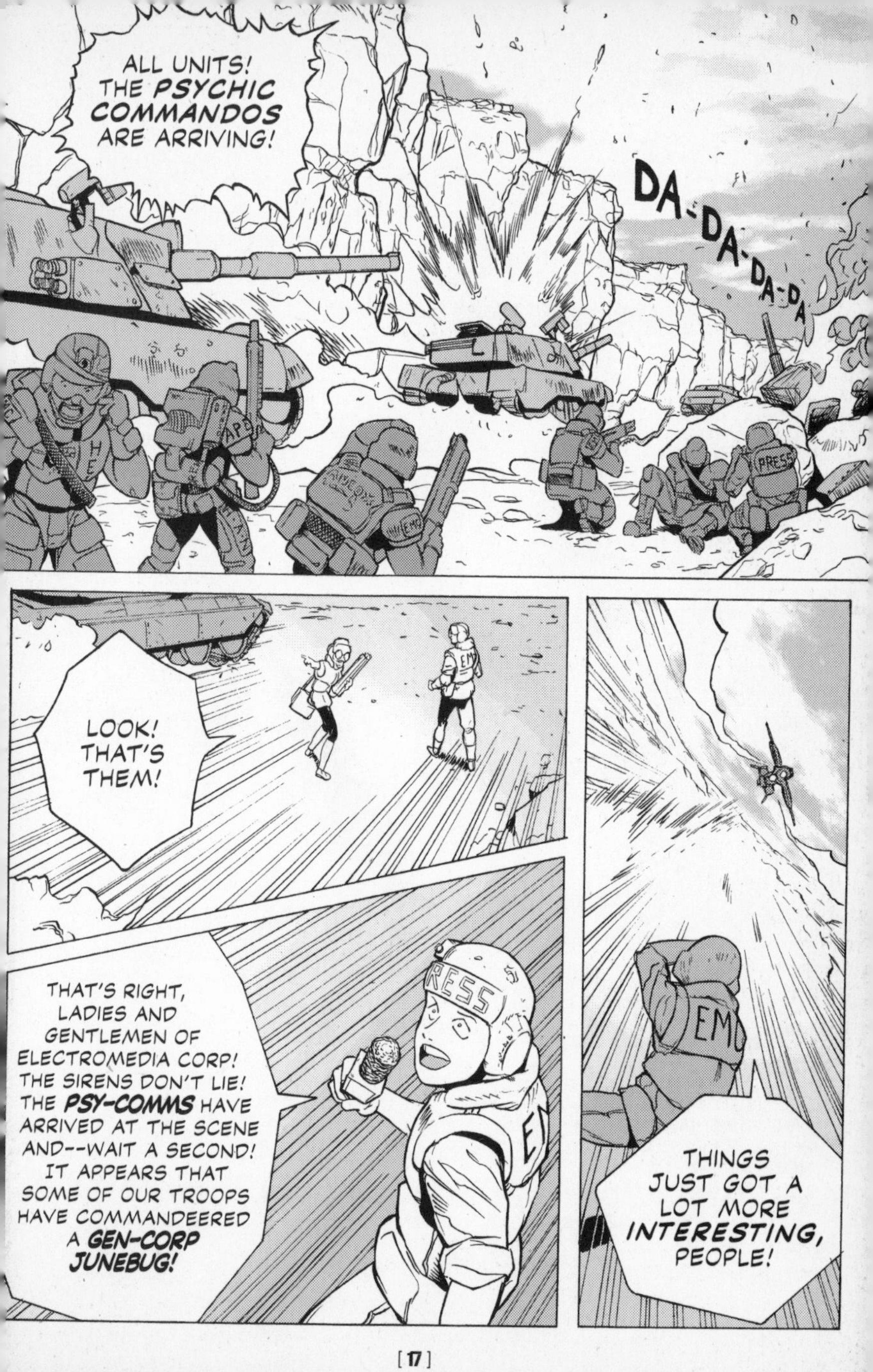
ALL UNITS! THE PSYCHIC COMMANDOS ARE ARRIVING!
DA-DA-DA-DA-DA
LOOK! THAT'S THEM!
THAT'S RIGHT, LADIES AND GENTLEMEN OF ELECTROMEDIA CORP! THE SIRENS DON'T LIE! THE PSY-COMMS HAVE ARRIVED AT THE SCENE AND--WAIT A SECOND! IT APPEARS THAT SOME OF OUR TROOPS HAVE COMMANDEERED A GEN-CORP JUNEBUG!
THINGS JUST GOT A LOT MORE INTERESTING, PEOPLE!

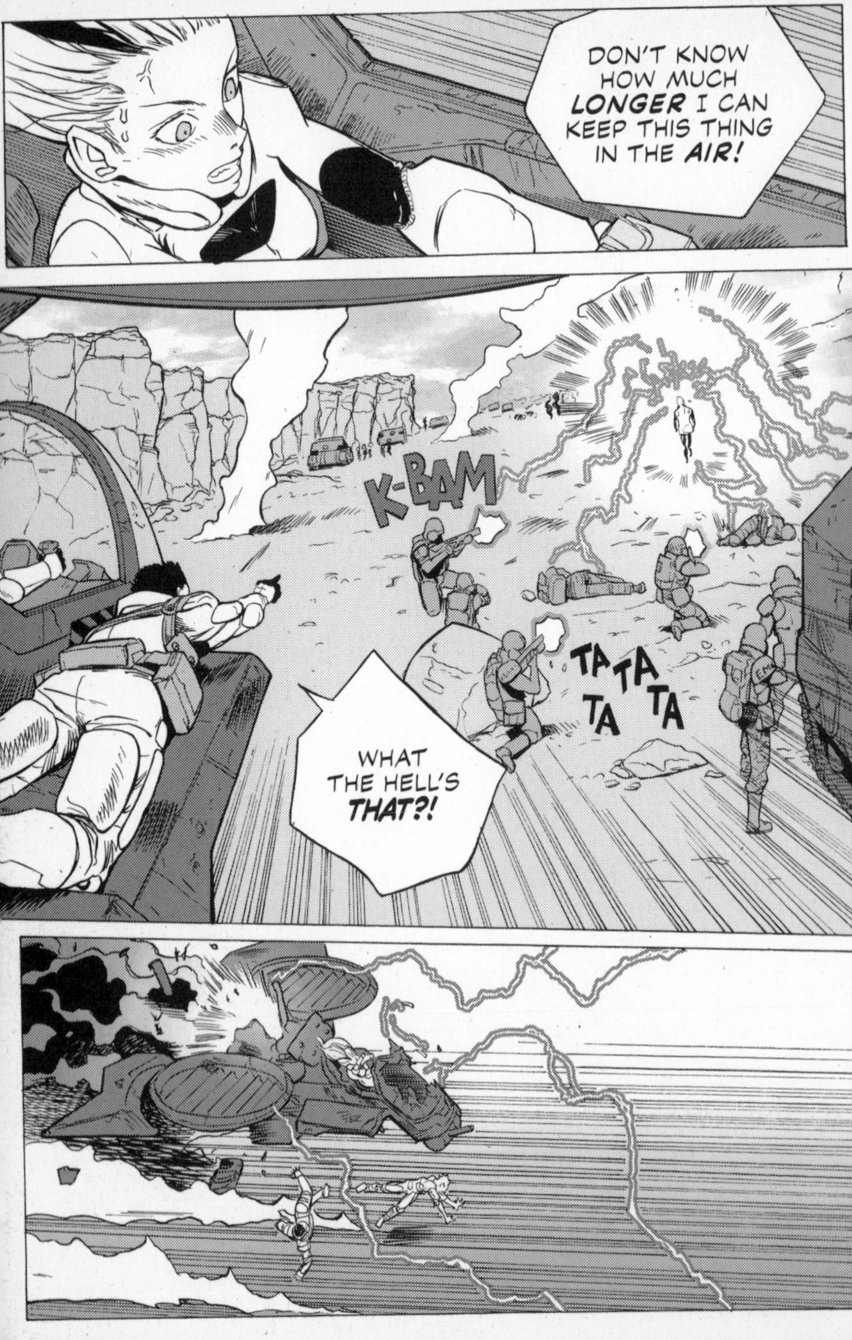
DON'T KNOW HOW MUCH LONGER I CAN KEEP THIS THING IN THE AIR!
K-BAM
TA TA TA TA TA
WHAT THE HELL'S THAT?!

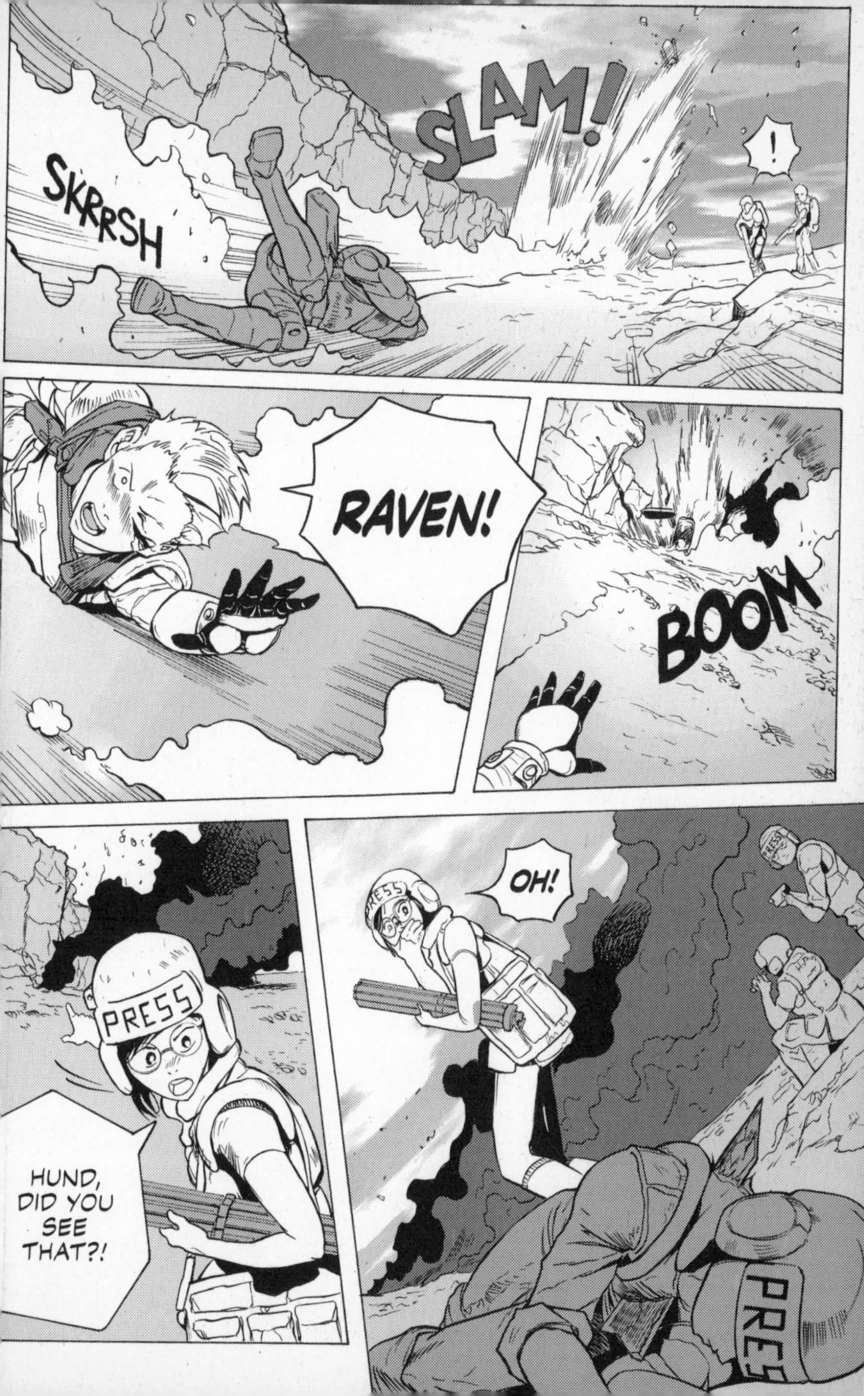
SKRRSH
SLAM!
!
RAVEN!
BOOM
PRESS
HUND, DID YOU SEE THAT?!
PRESS
OH!
PRESS
PRES

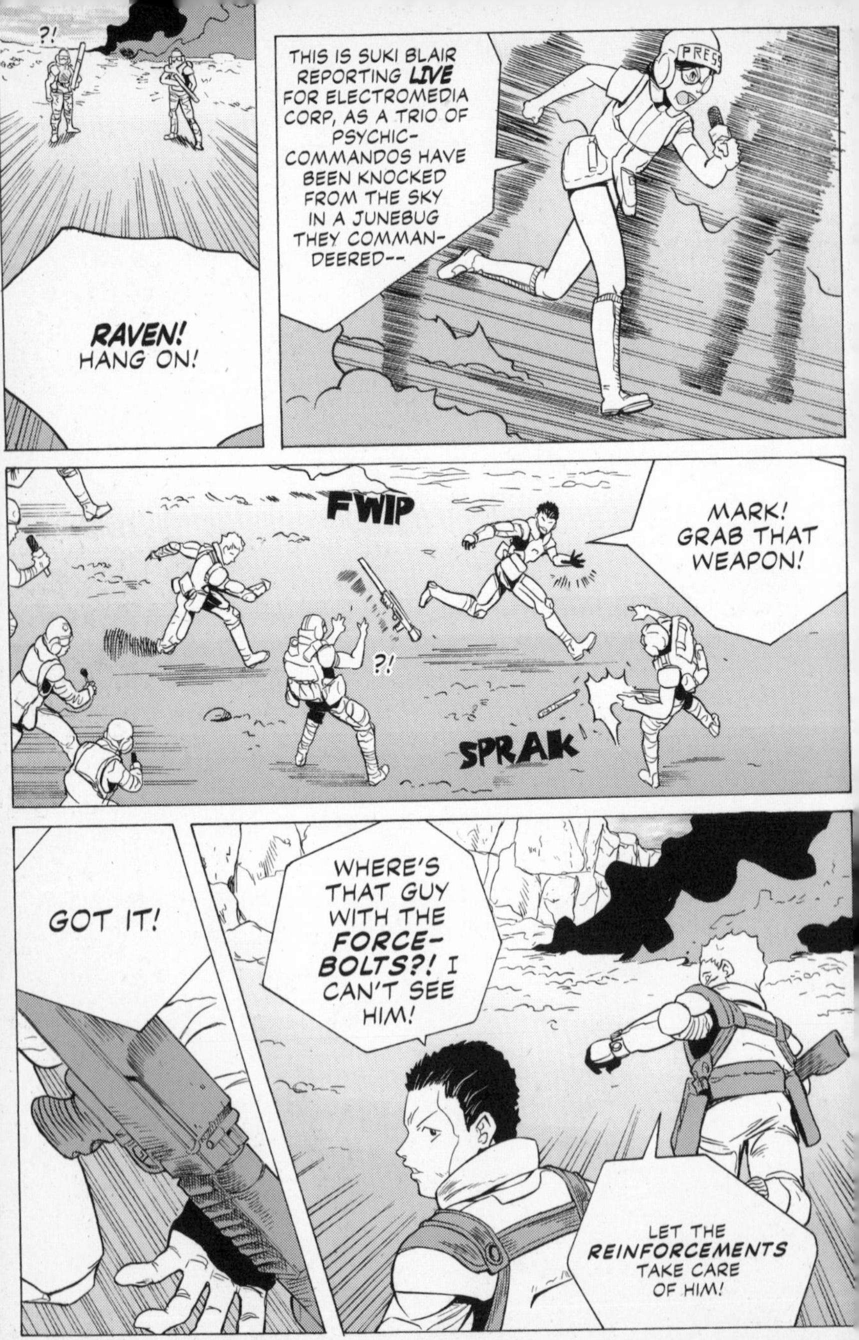
?!
RAVEN! HANG ON!
THIS IS SUKI BLAIR REPORTING LIVE FOR ELECTROMEDIA CORP, AS A TRIO OF PSYCHIC-COMMANDOS HAVE BEEN KNOCKED FROM THE SKY IN A JUNEBUG THEY COMMAN-DEERED--
PRESS
FWIP
?!
SPRAK
MARK! GRAB THAT WEAPON!
GOT IT!
WHERE'S THAT GUY WITH THE FORCE-BOLTS?! I CAN'T SEE HIM!
LET THE REINFORCEMENTS TAKE CARE OF HIM!

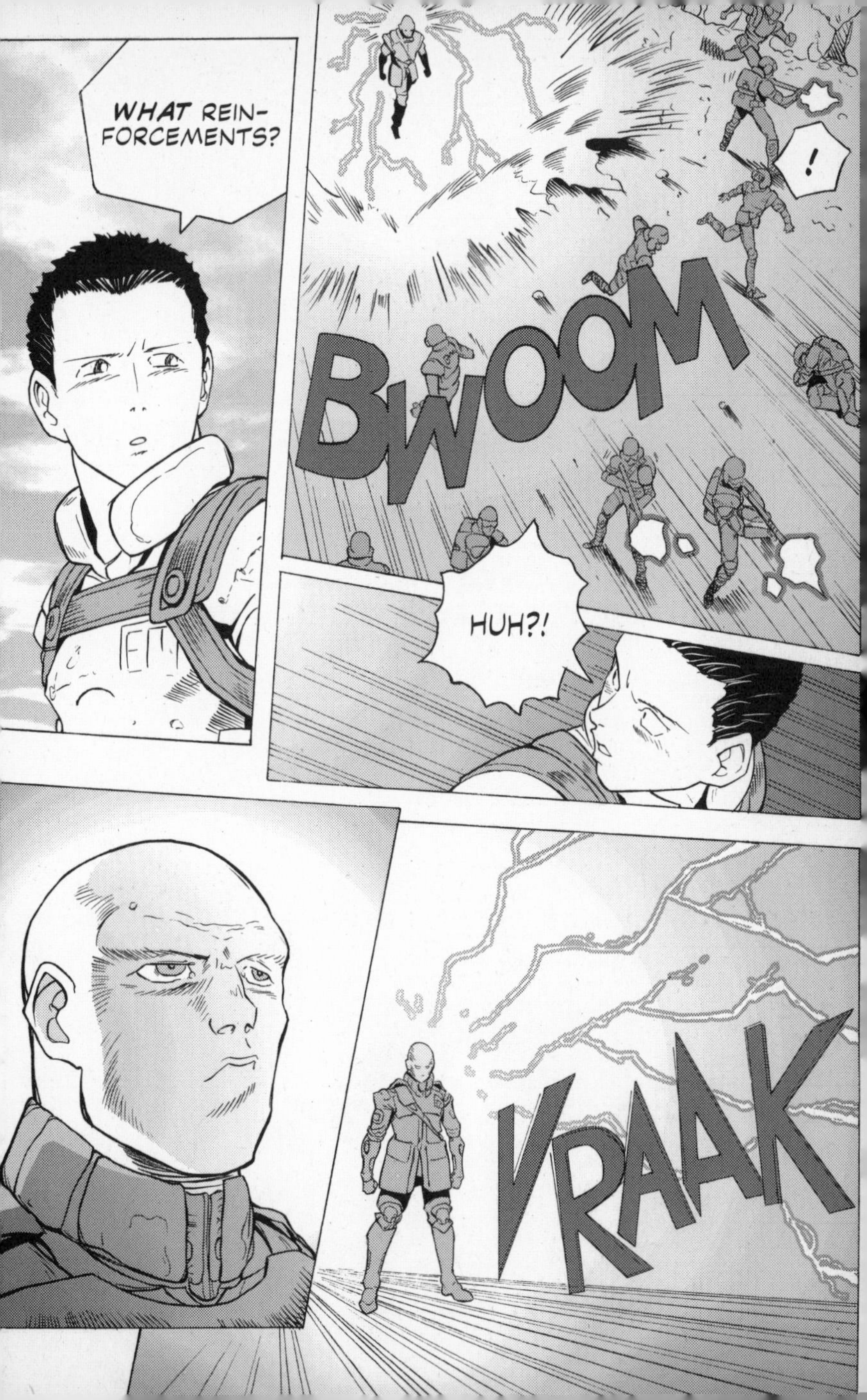
WHAT REIN-FORCEMENTS?
!
BWOOM
HUH?!
VRAAK

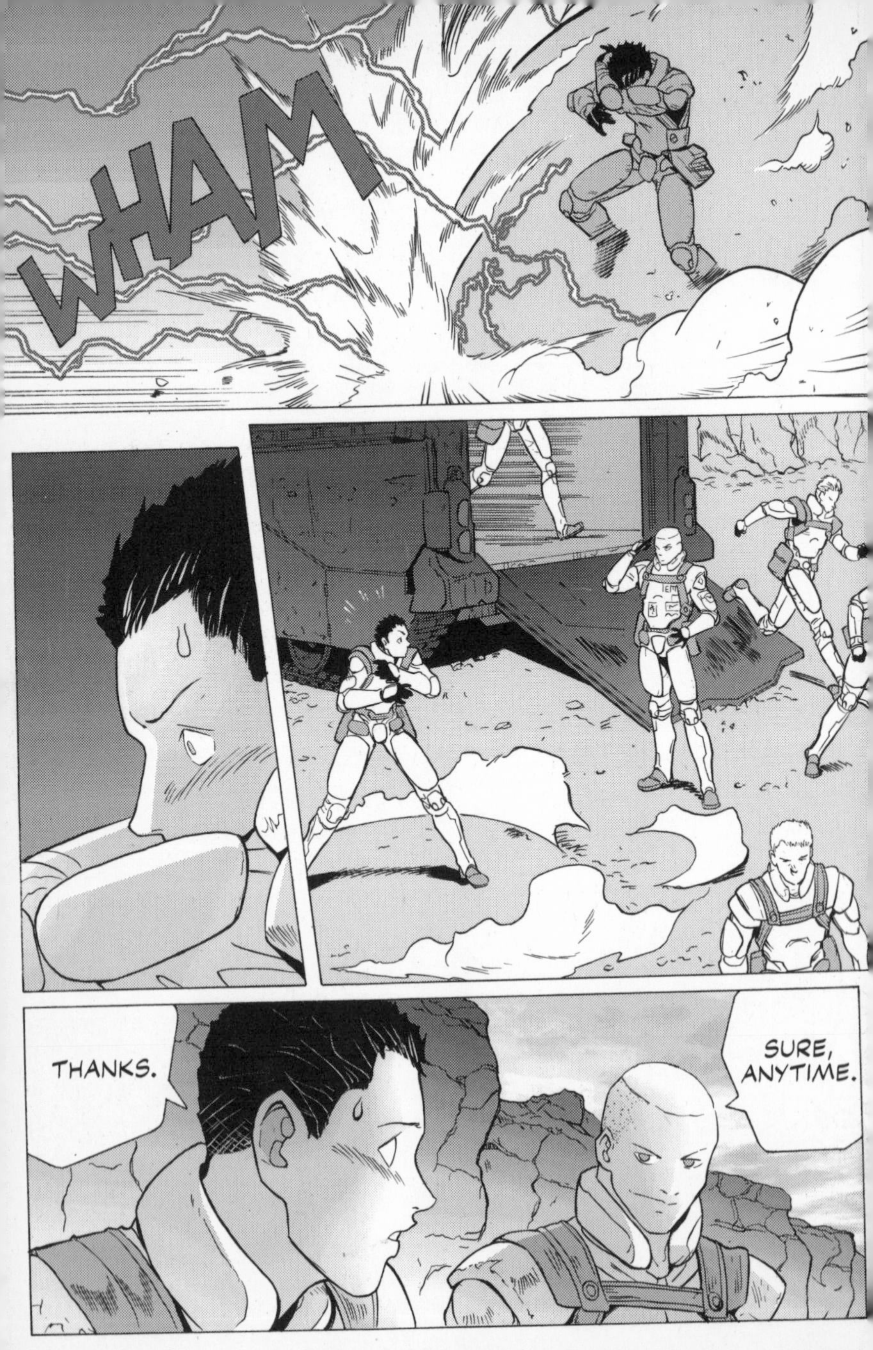
WHAM
THANKS.
SURE, ANYTIME.

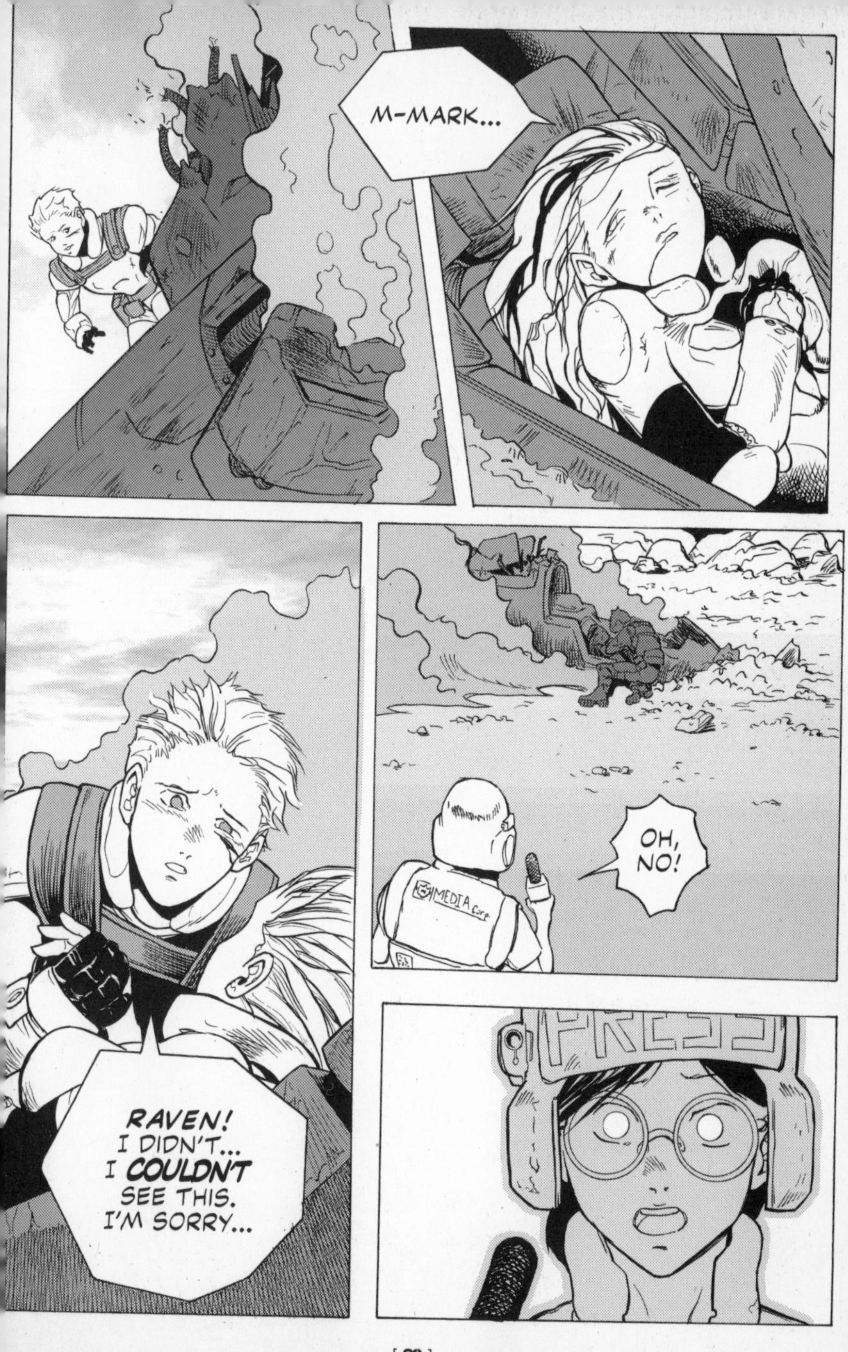
M-MARK...
RAVEN! I DIDN'T... I **COULDN'T** SEE THIS. I'M SORRY...
MEDIA Corp.
OH, NO!
PRESS

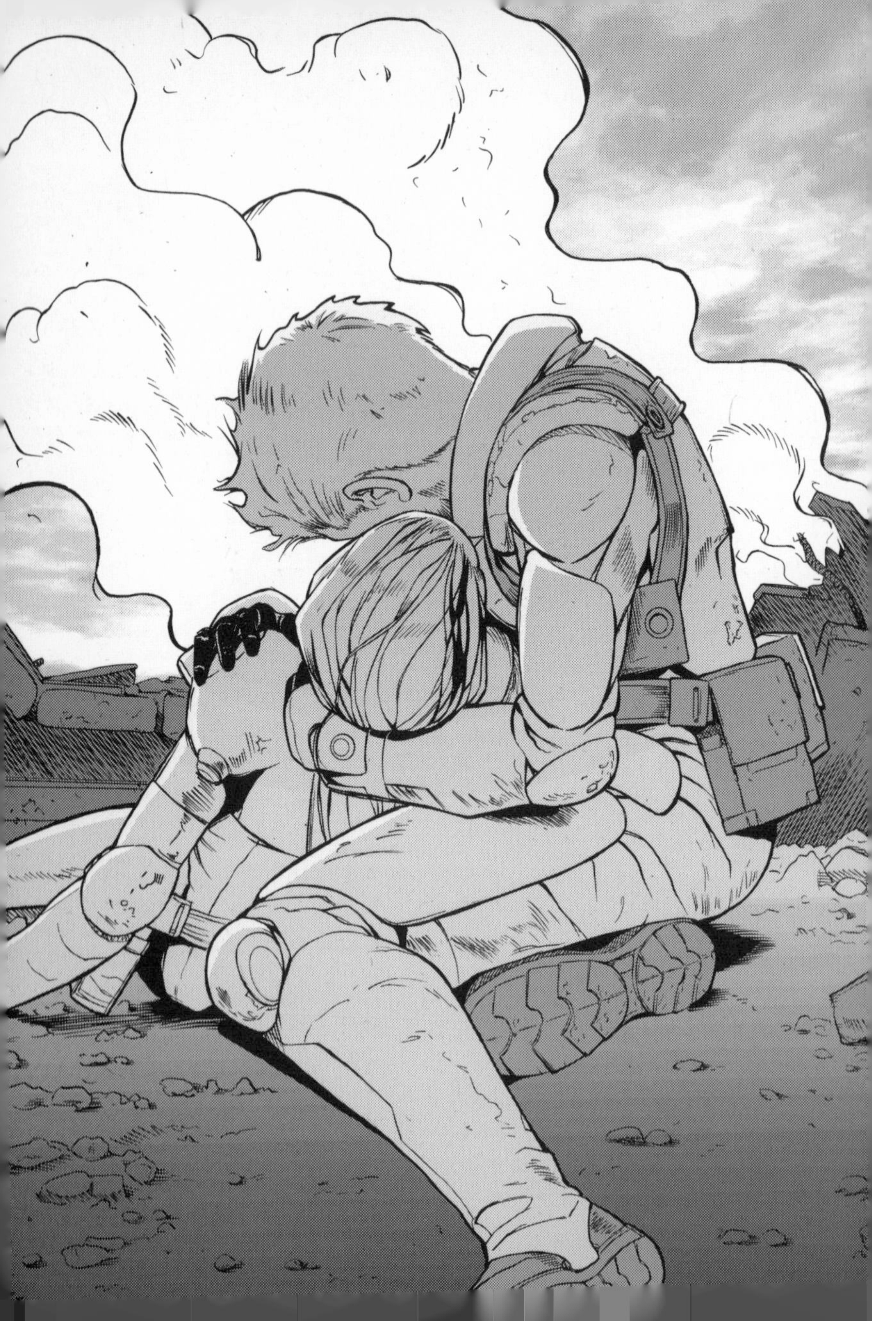

PSY★COMM

CHAPTER [2]

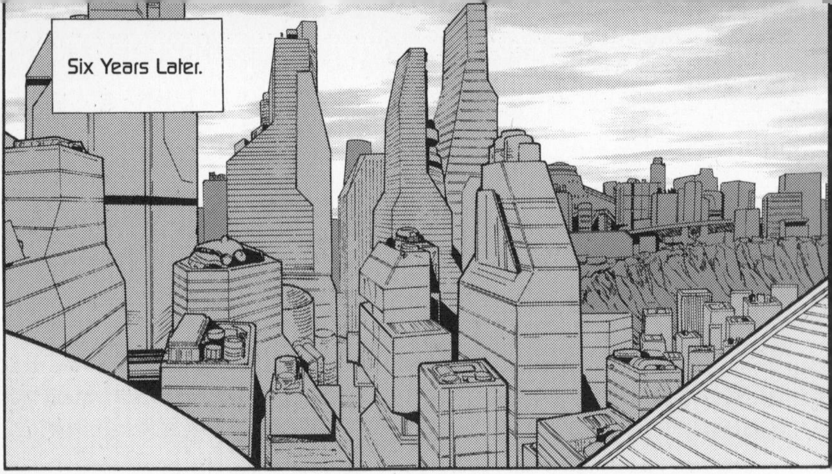
Six Years Later.
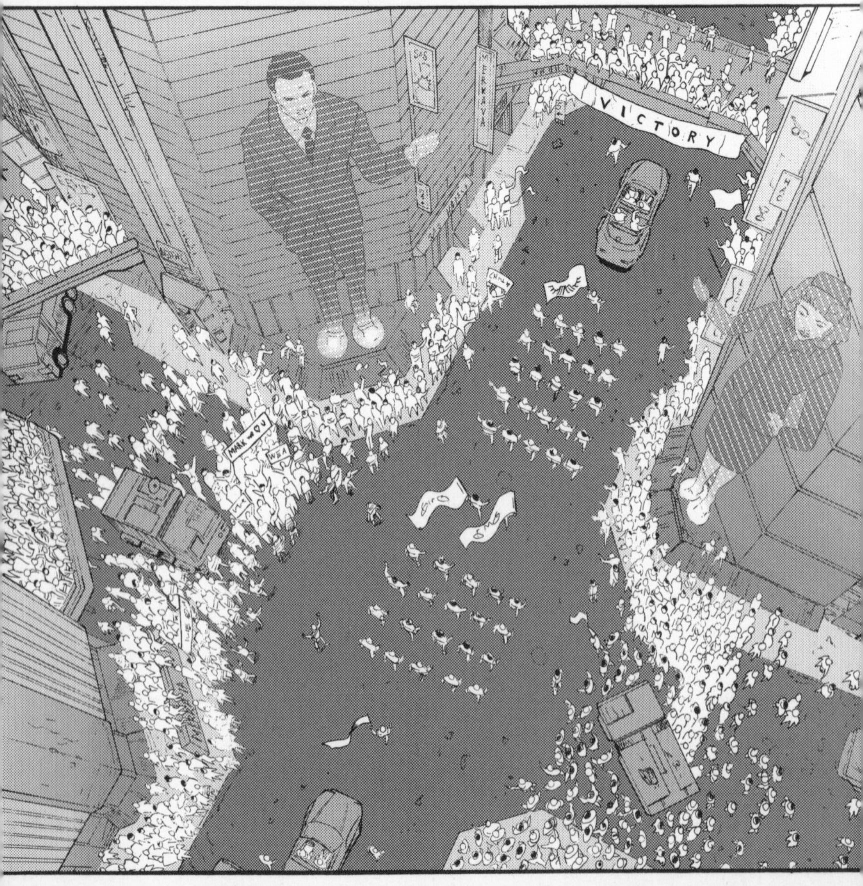
VICTORY

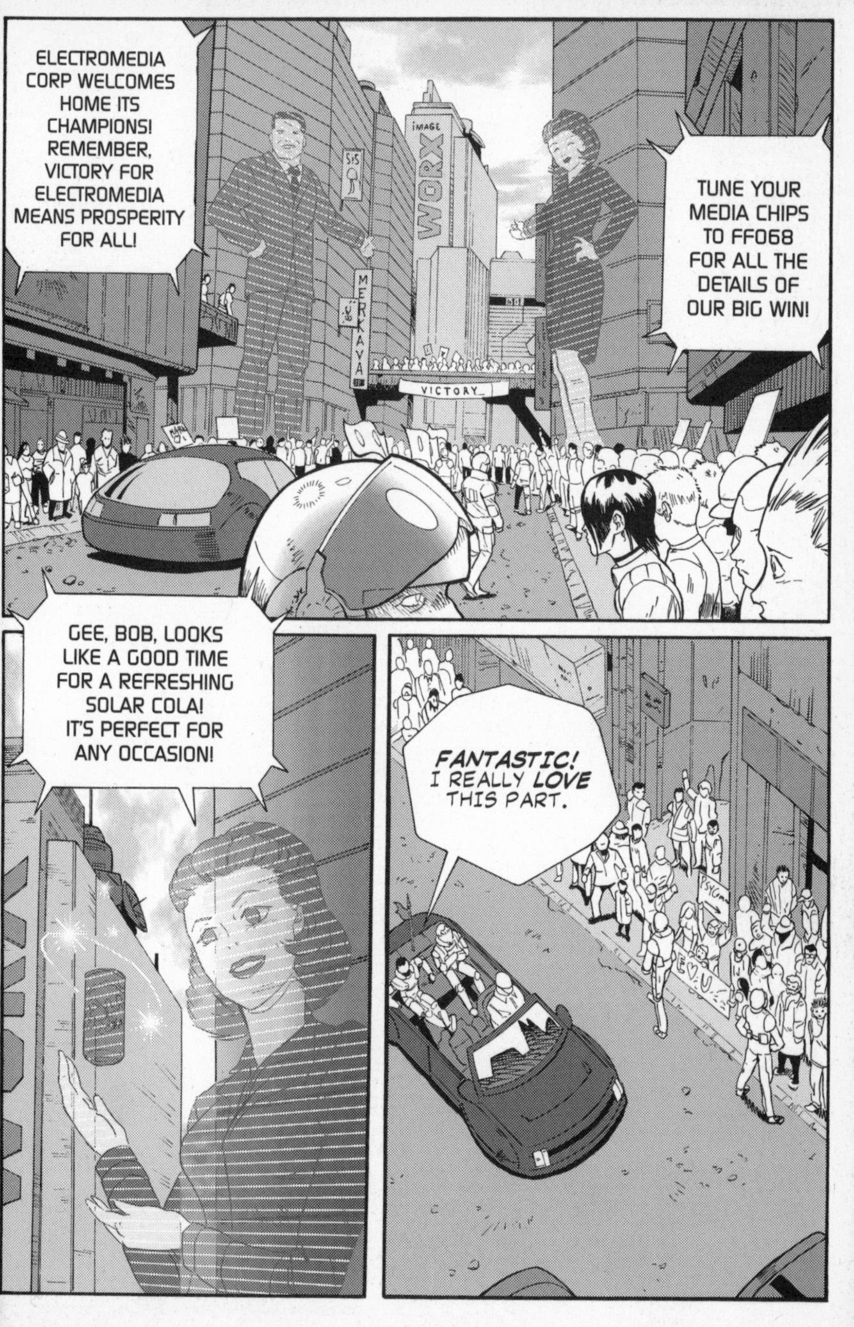
ELECTROMEDIA CORP WELCOMES HOME ITS CHAMPIONS! REMEMBER, VICTORY FOR ELECTROMEDIA MEANS PROSPERITY FOR ALL!
TUNE YOUR MEDIA CHIPS TO FF068 FOR ALL THE DETAILS OF OUR BIG WIN!
IMAGE
WORX
MERKAYA
VICTORY
GEE, BOB, LOOKS LIKE A GOOD TIME FOR A REFRESHING SOLAR COLA! IT'S PERFECT FOR ANY OCCASION!
FANTASTIC! I REALLY *LOVE* THIS PART.

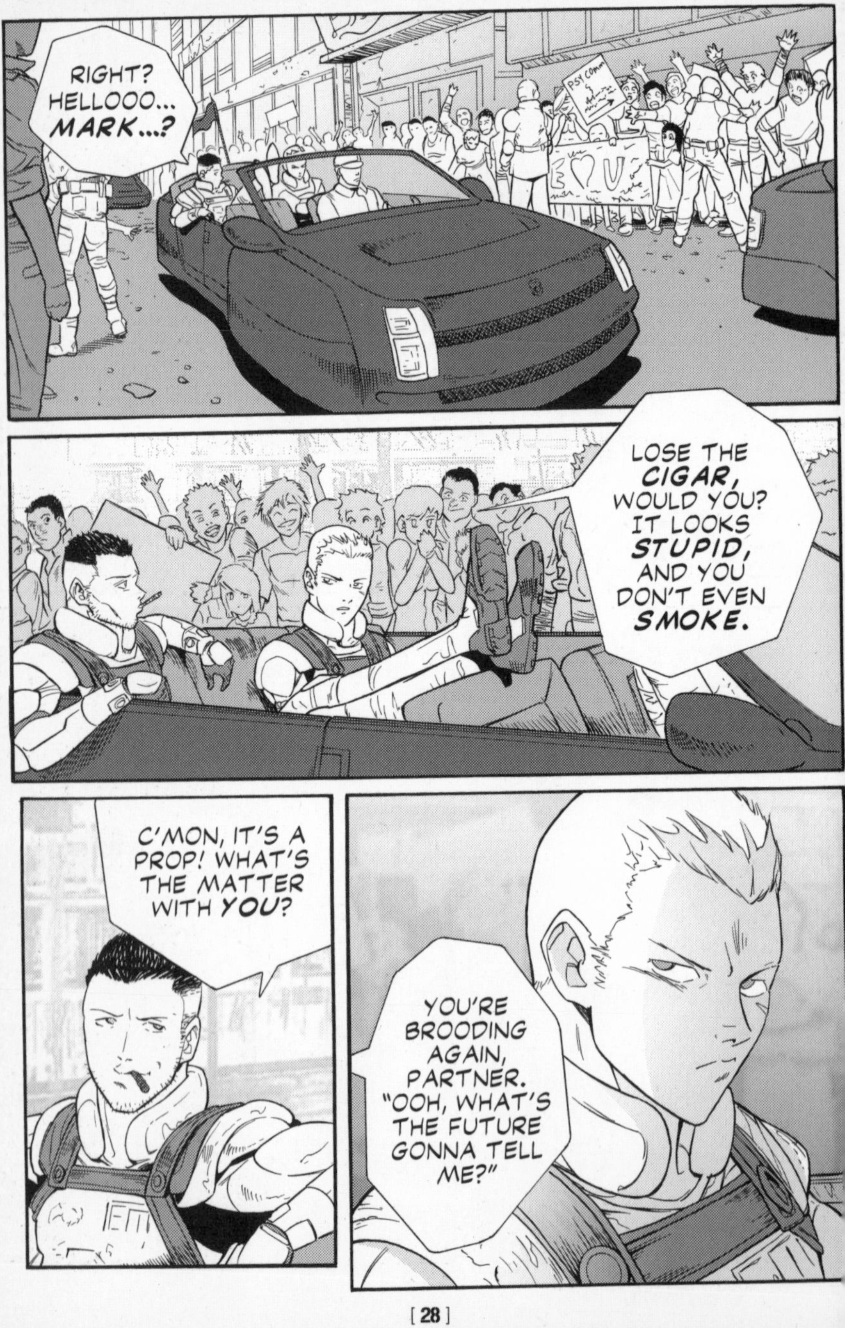
RIGHT? HELLOOO... MARK...?
LOSE THE CIGAR, WOULD YOU? IT LOOKS STUPID, AND YOU DON'T EVEN SMOKE.
C'MON, IT'S A PROP! WHAT'S THE MATTER WITH YOU?
YOU'RE BROODING AGAIN, PARTNER. "OOH, WHAT'S THE FUTURE GONNA TELL ME?"

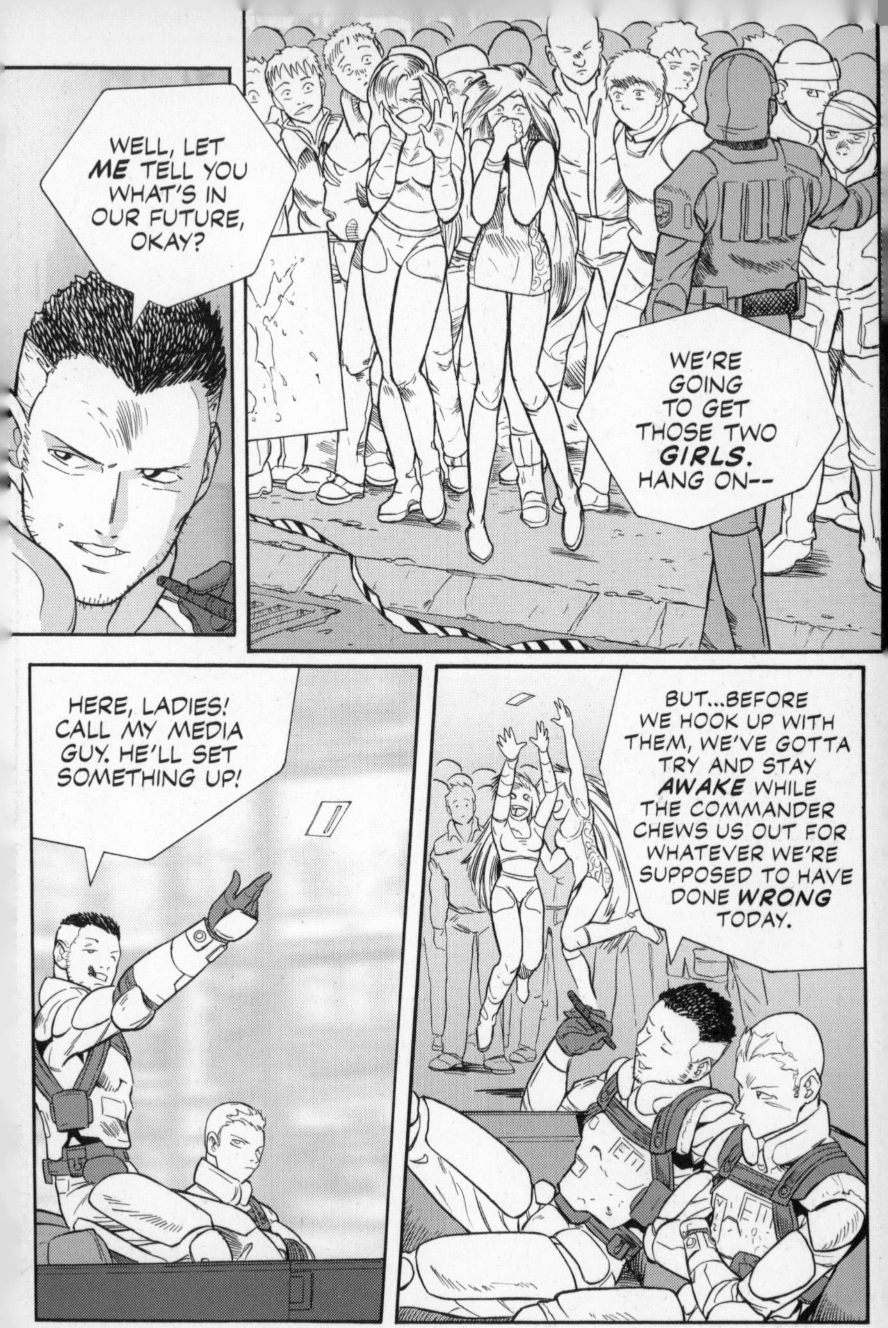
WELL, LET ME TELL YOU WHAT'S IN OUR FUTURE, OKAY?
WE'RE GOING TO GET THOSE TWO GIRLS. HANG ON--
HERE, LADIES! CALL MY MEDIA GUY. HE'LL SET SOMETHING UP!
BUT...BEFORE WE HOOK UP WITH THEM, WE'VE GOTTA TRY AND STAY AWAKE WHILE THE COMMANDER CHEWS US OUT FOR WHATEVER WE'RE SUPPOSED TO HAVE DONE WRONG TODAY.

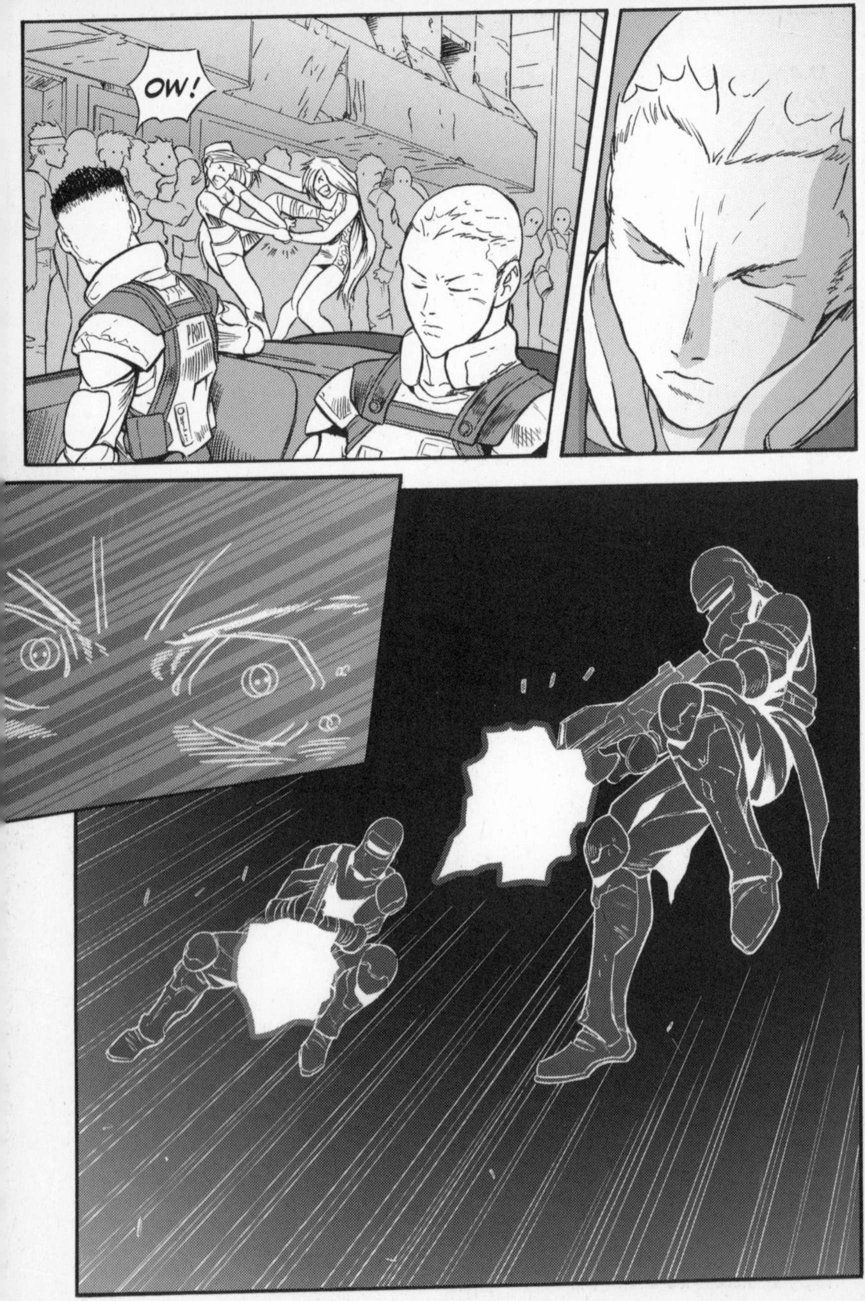
OW!

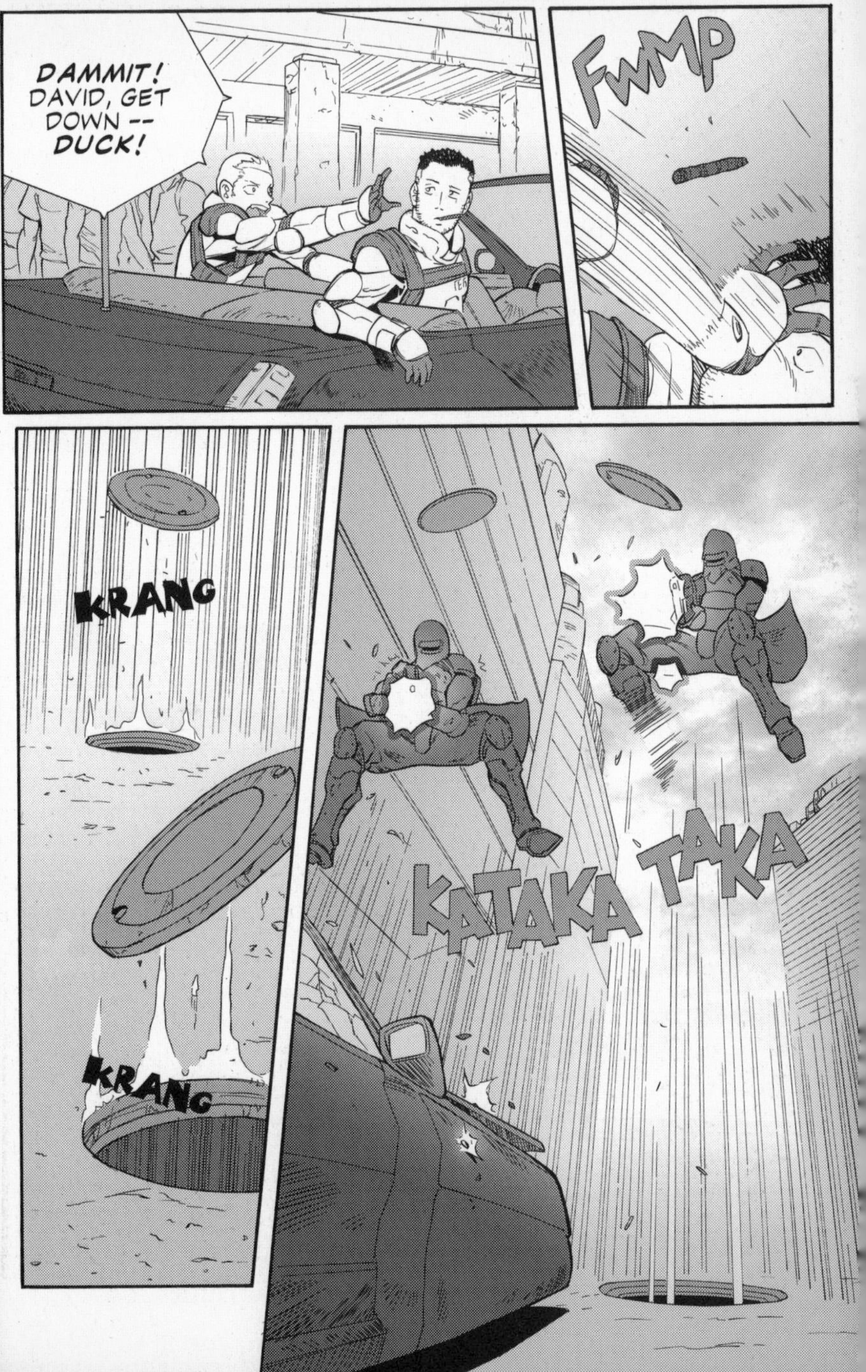
DAMMIT! DAVID, GET DOWN -- DUCK!
FWMP
KRANG
KRANG
KATAKA TAKA

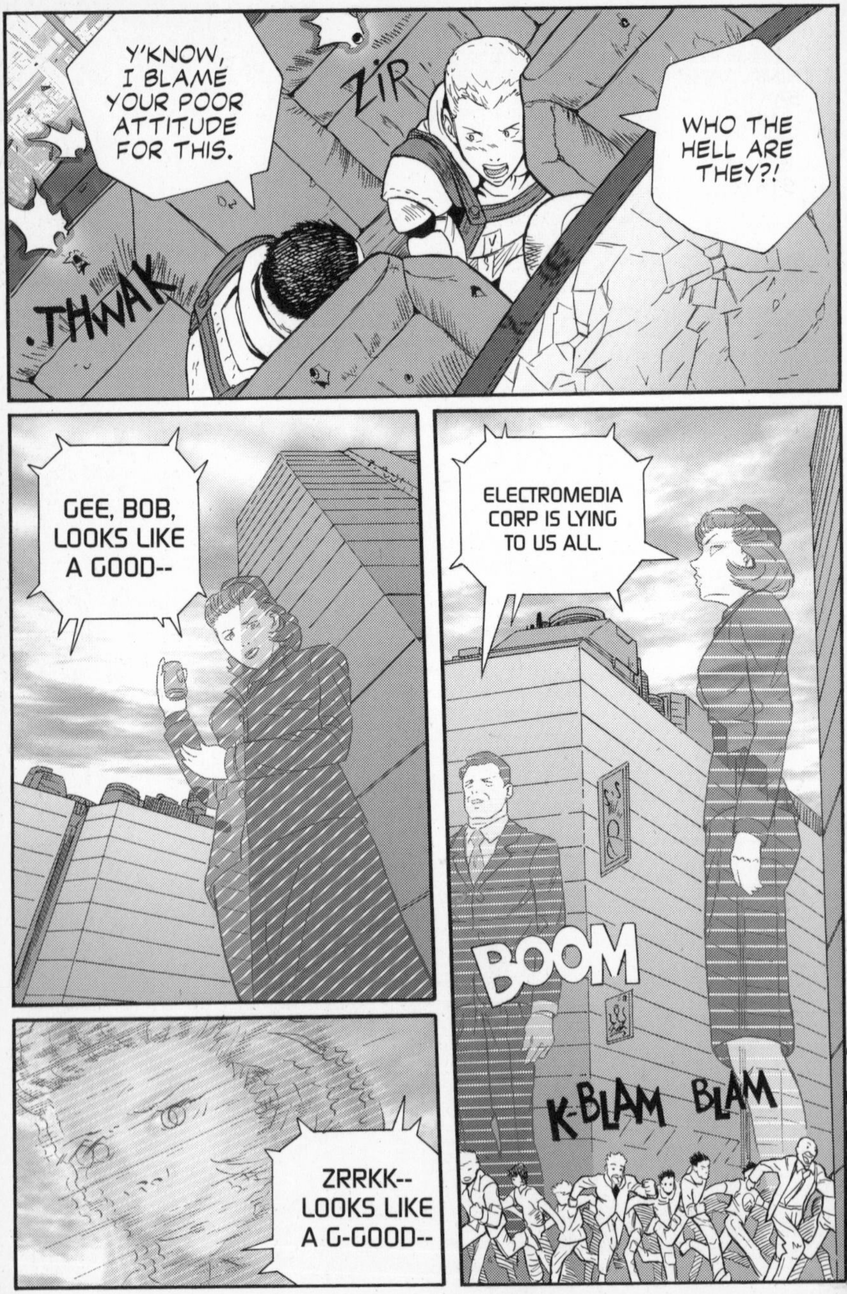

Y'KNOW, I BLAME YOUR POOR ATTITUDE FOR THIS.
ZIP
WHO THE HELL ARE THEY?!
THWAK
GEE, BOB, LOOKS LIKE A GOOD--
ELECTROMEDIA CORP IS LYING TO US ALL.
BOOM
K-BLAM
BLAM
ZRRKK-- LOOKS LIKE A G-GOOD--

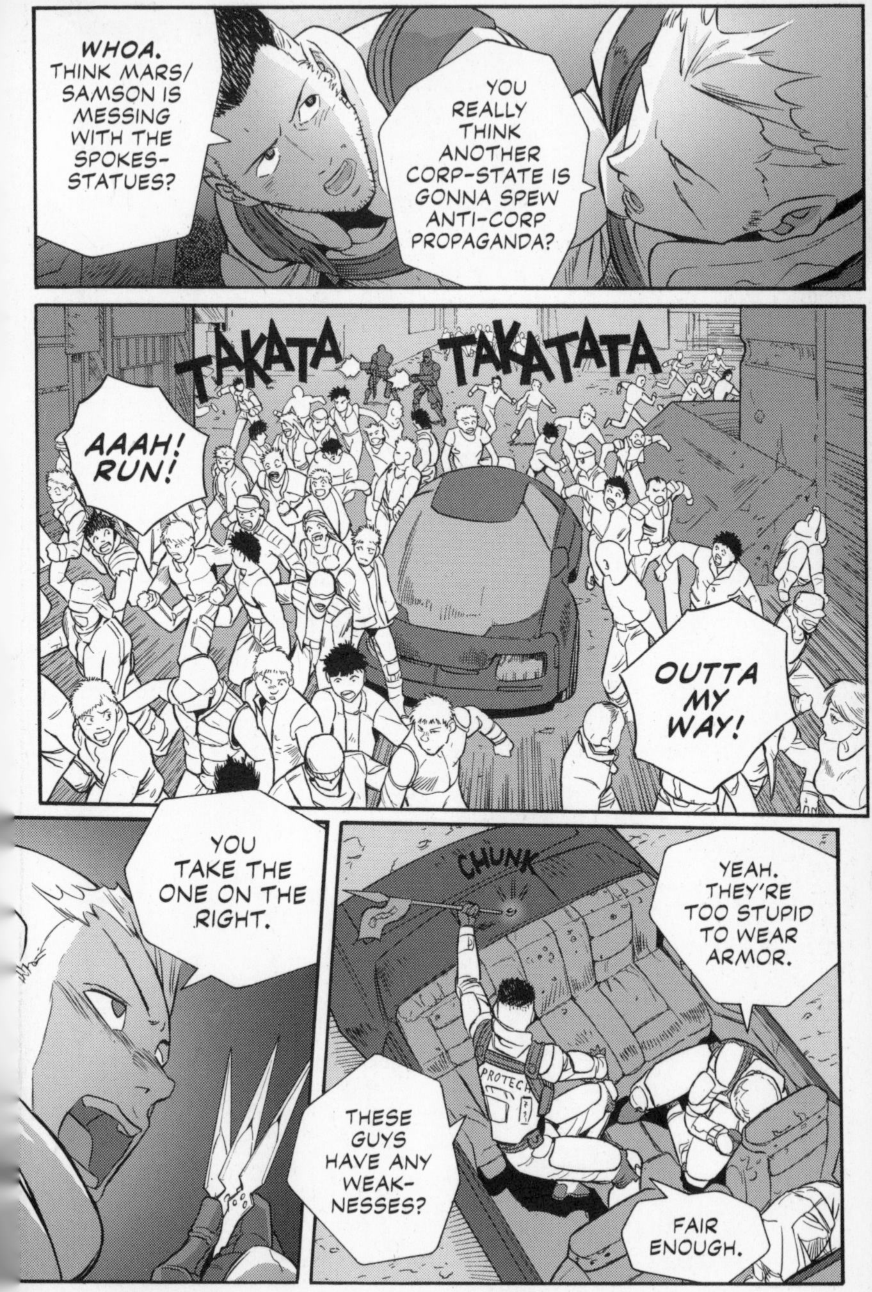
WHOA. THINK MARS/SAMSON IS MESSING WITH THE SPOKES-STATUES?
YOU REALLY THINK ANOTHER CORP-STATE IS GONNA SPEW ANTI-CORP PROPAGANDA?
TAKATA
TAKATATA
AAAH! RUN!
OUTTA MY WAY!
YOU TAKE THE ONE ON THE RIGHT.
CHUNK
YEAH. THEY'RE TOO STUPID TO WEAR ARMOR.
PROTECH
THESE GUYS HAVE ANY WEAK-NESSES?
FAIR ENOUGH.

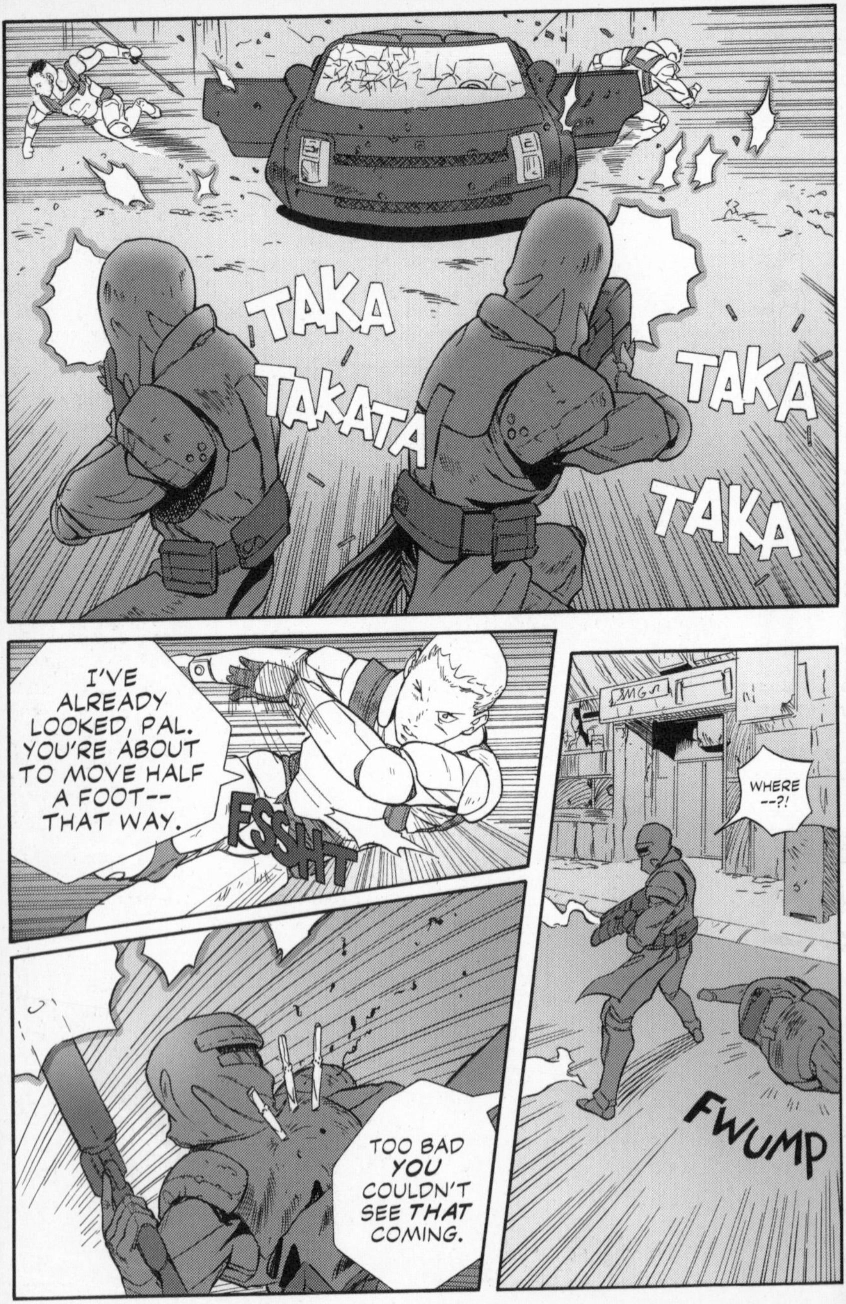
TAKA
TAKATA
TAKA
TAKA
I'VE ALREADY LOOKED, PAL. YOU'RE ABOUT TO MOVE HALF A FOOT-- THAT WAY.
FSSHT
TOO BAD *YOU* COULDN'T SEE *THAT* COMING.
WHERE --?!
FWUMP

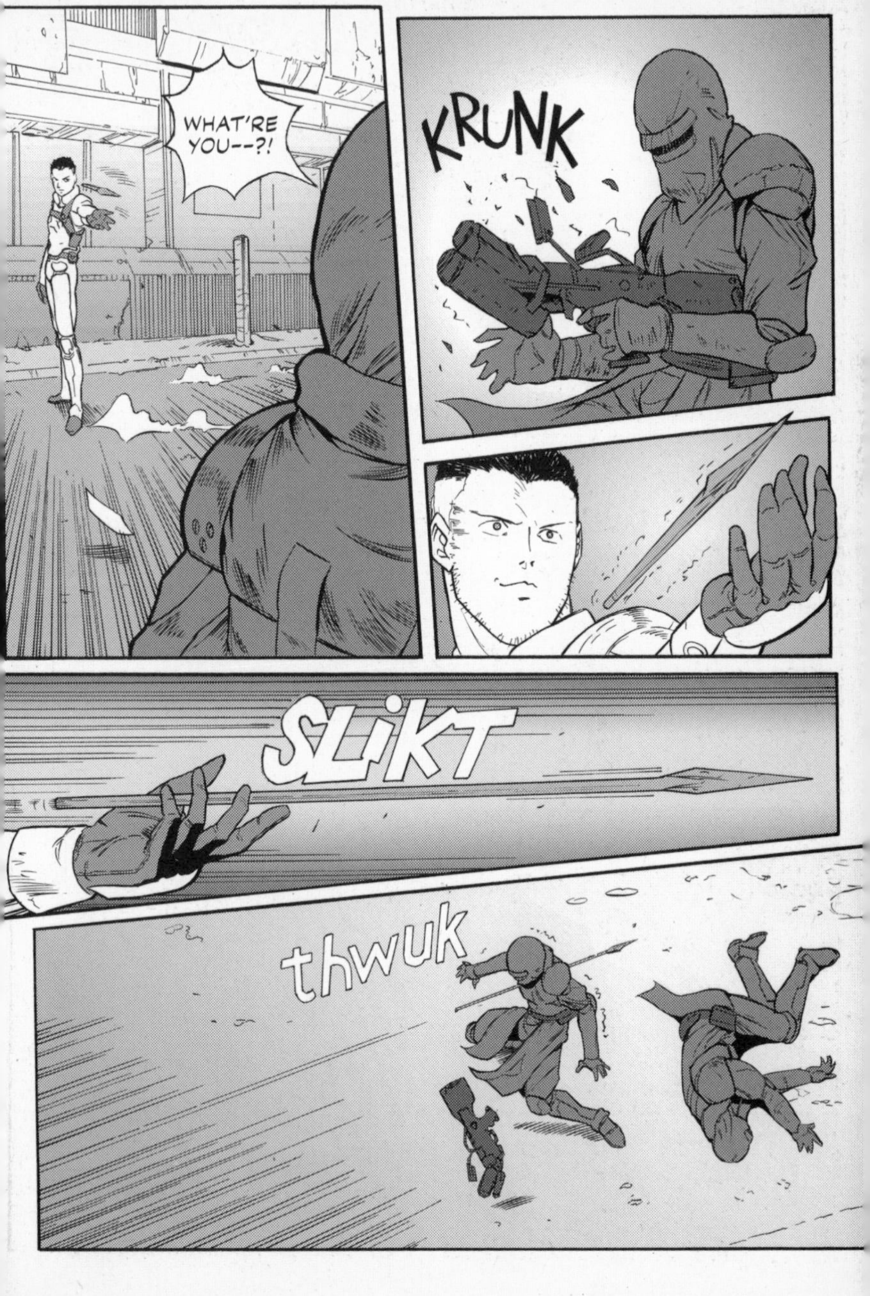
WHAT'RE YOU--?!
KRUNK
SLIKT
thwuk

ELECTROMEDIA CORP IS LYING TO US ALL.

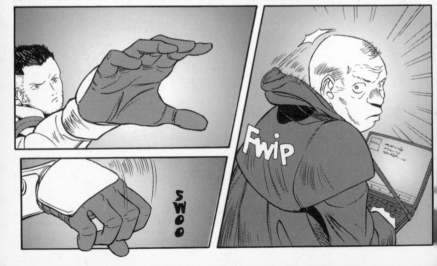

FWIP

SWOO

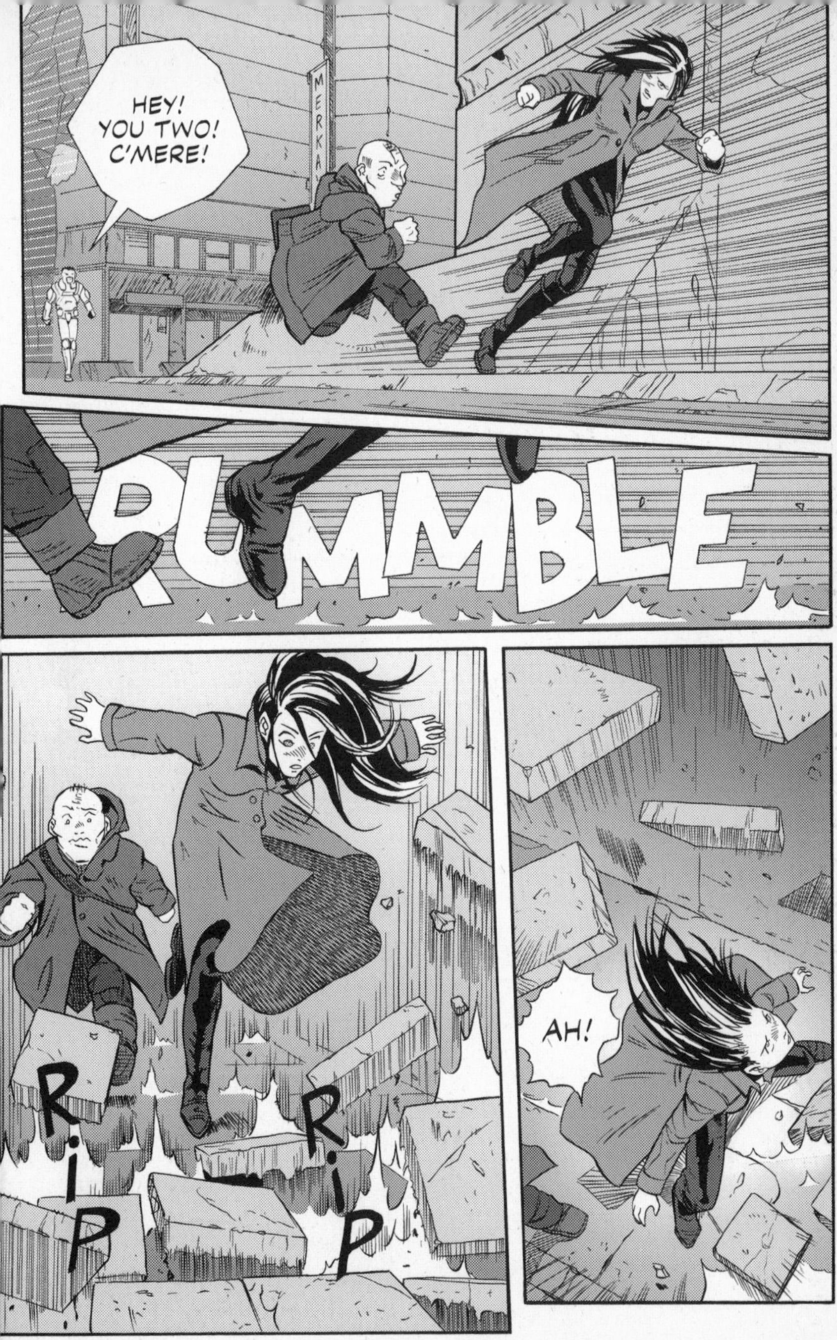
HEY! YOU TWO! C'MERE!
RUMMBLE
RIP
RIP
AH!

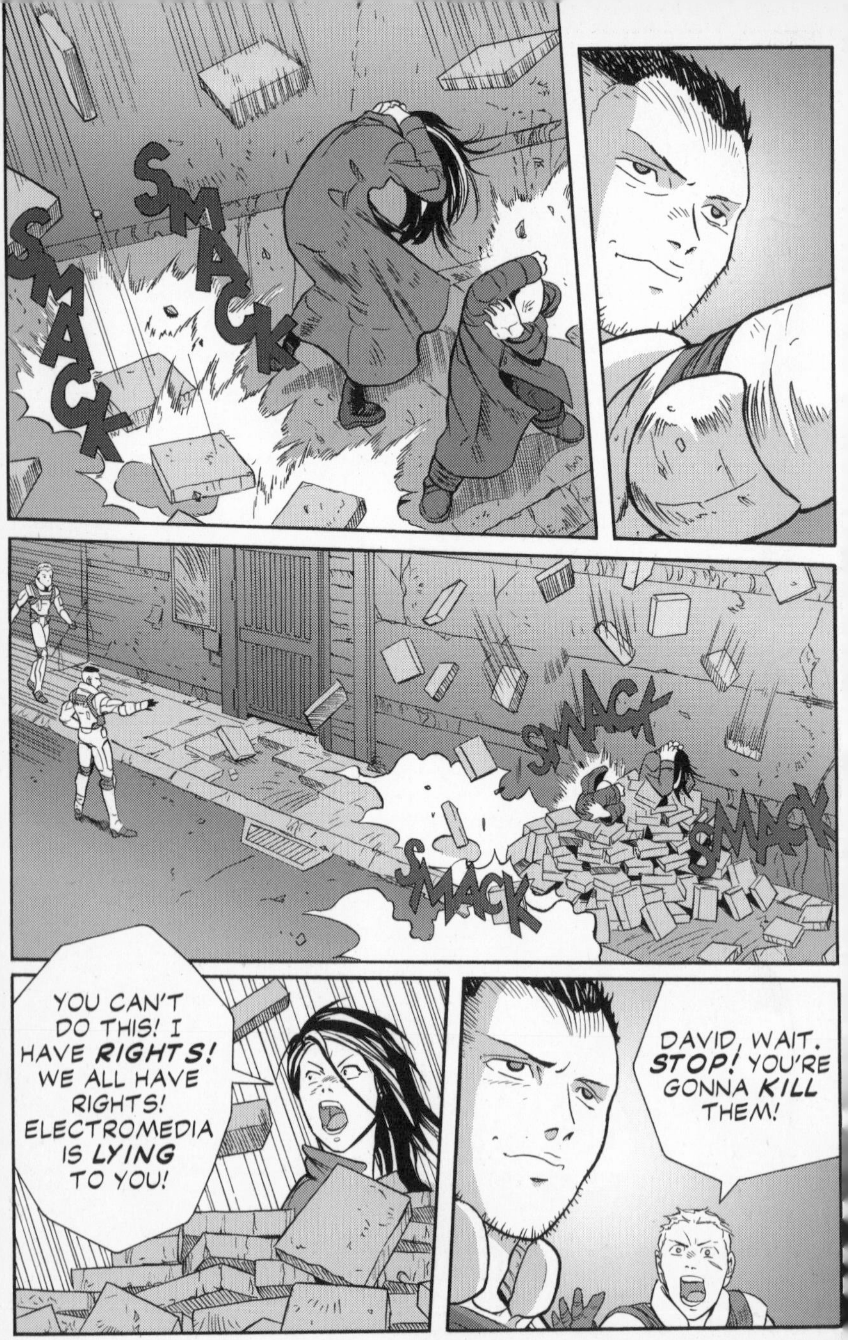
SMACK
SMACK
SMACK
SMACK
SMACK
YOU CAN'T DO THIS! I HAVE RIGHTS! WE ALL HAVE RIGHTS! ELECTROMEDIA IS LYING TO YOU!
DAVID, WAIT. STOP! YOU'RE GONNA KILL THEM!

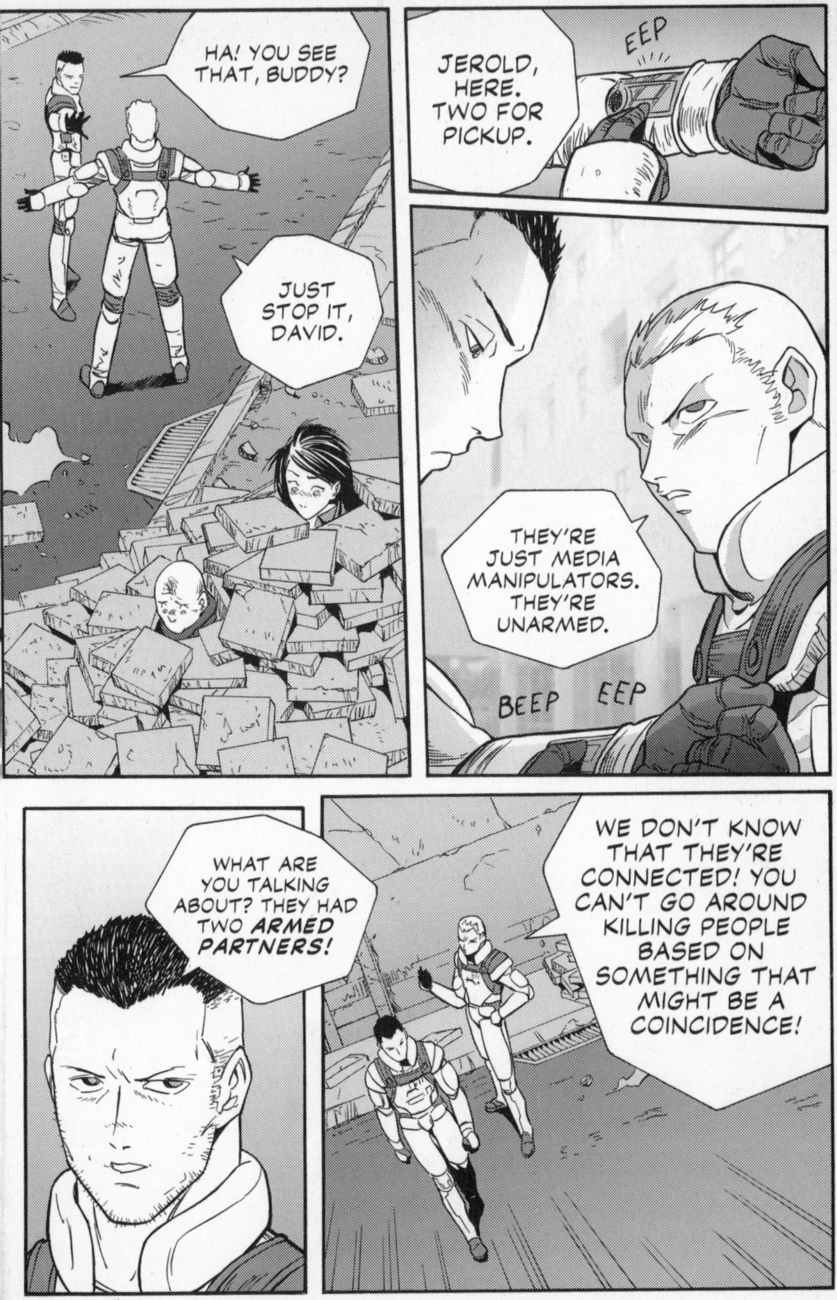
HA! YOU SEE THAT, BUDDY?
JUST STOP IT, DAVID.
JEROLD, HERE. TWO FOR PICKUP.
EEP
THEY'RE JUST MEDIA MANIPULATORS. THEY'RE UNARMED.
BEEP EEP
WHAT ARE YOU TALKING ABOUT? THEY HAD TWO **ARMED PARTNERS!**
WE DON'T KNOW THAT THEY'RE CONNECTED! YOU CAN'T GO AROUND KILLING PEOPLE BASED ON SOMETHING THAT MIGHT BE A COINCIDENCE!

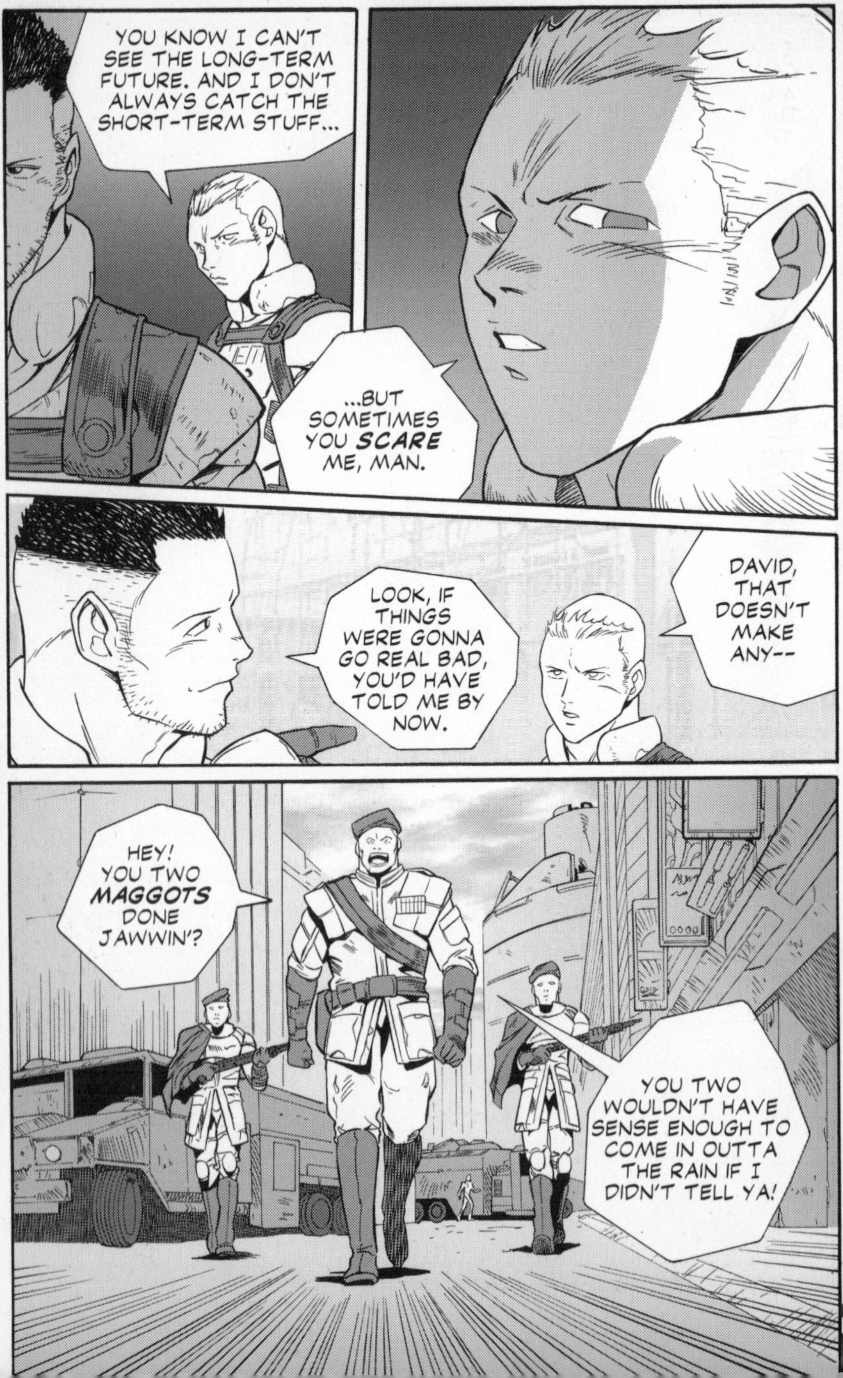
YOU KNOW I CAN'T SEE THE LONG-TERM FUTURE. AND I DON'T ALWAYS CATCH THE SHORT-TERM STUFF...
...BUT SOMETIMES YOU **SCARE** ME, MAN.
LOOK, IF THINGS WERE GONNA GO REAL BAD, YOU'D HAVE TOLD ME BY NOW.
DAVID, THAT DOESN'T MAKE ANY--
HEY! YOU TWO **MAGGOTS** DONE JAWWIN'?
YOU TWO WOULDN'T HAVE SENSE ENOUGH TO COME IN OUTTA THE RAIN IF I DIDN'T TELL YA!

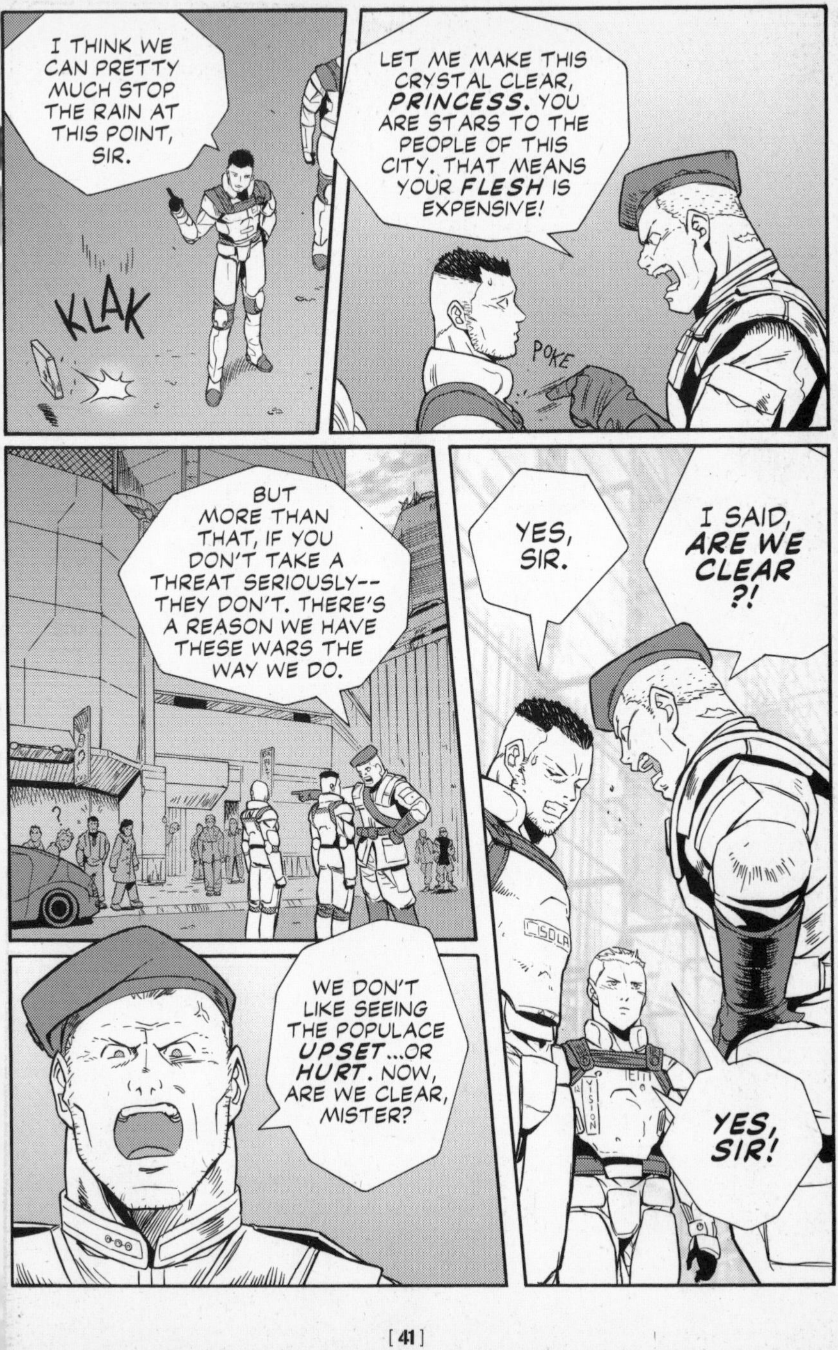
I THINK WE CAN PRETTY MUCH STOP THE RAIN AT THIS POINT, SIR.
KLAK
LET ME MAKE THIS CRYSTAL CLEAR, **PRINCESS.** YOU ARE STARS TO THE PEOPLE OF THIS CITY. THAT MEANS YOUR **FLESH** IS EXPENSIVE!
POKE
BUT MORE THAN THAT, IF YOU DON'T TAKE A THREAT SERIOUSLY-- THEY DON'T. THERE'S A REASON WE HAVE THESE WARS THE WAY WE DO.
WE DON'T LIKE SEEING THE POPULACE **UPSET**...OR **HURT**. NOW, ARE WE CLEAR, MISTER?
YES, SIR.
I SAID, **ARE WE CLEAR?!**
YES, SIR!

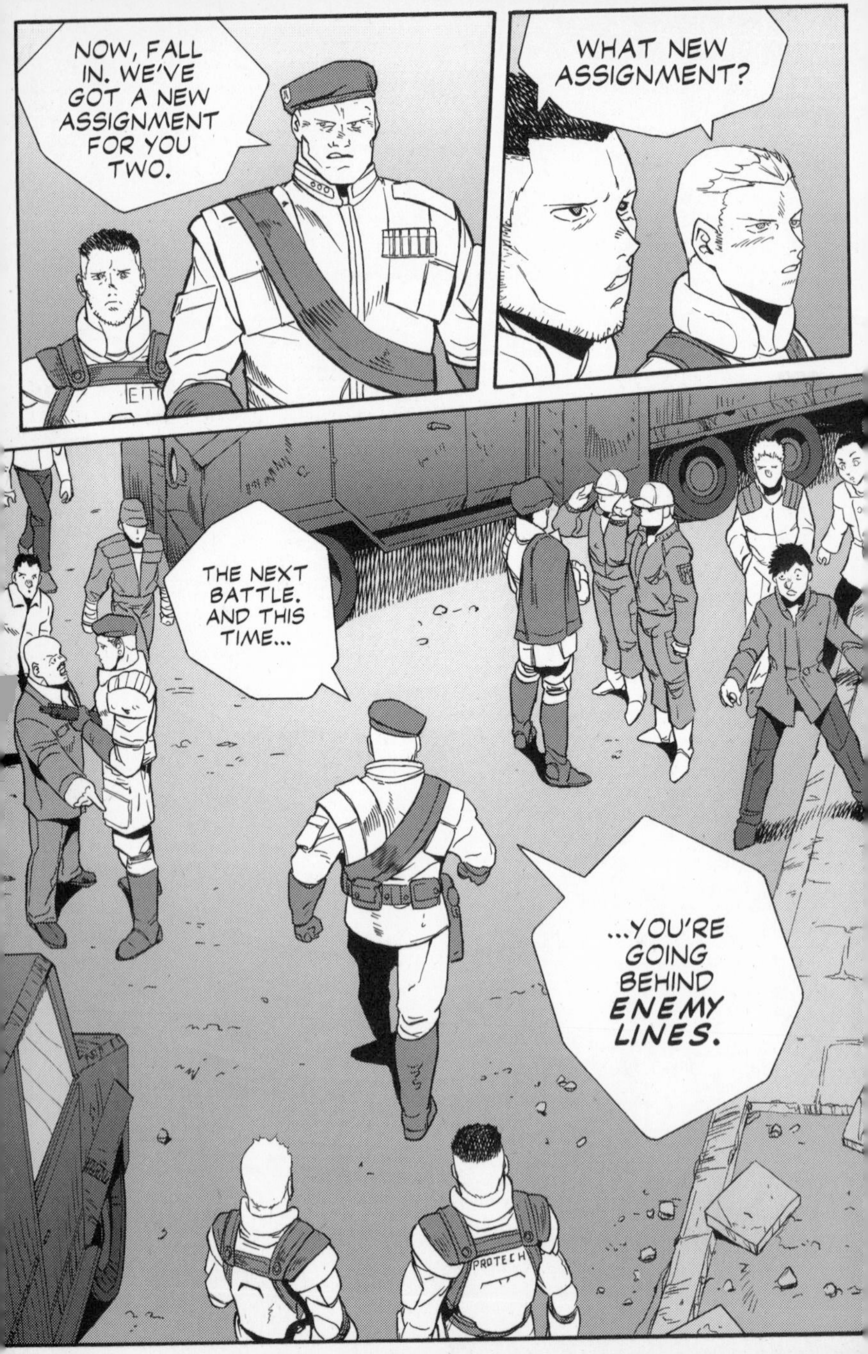
NOW, FALL IN. WE'VE GOT A NEW ASSIGNMENT FOR YOU TWO.
WHAT NEW ASSIGNMENT?
THE NEXT BATTLE. AND THIS TIME...
...YOU'RE GOING BEHIND ENEMY LINES.
PROTECH

PSY★COMM

CHAPTER [3]

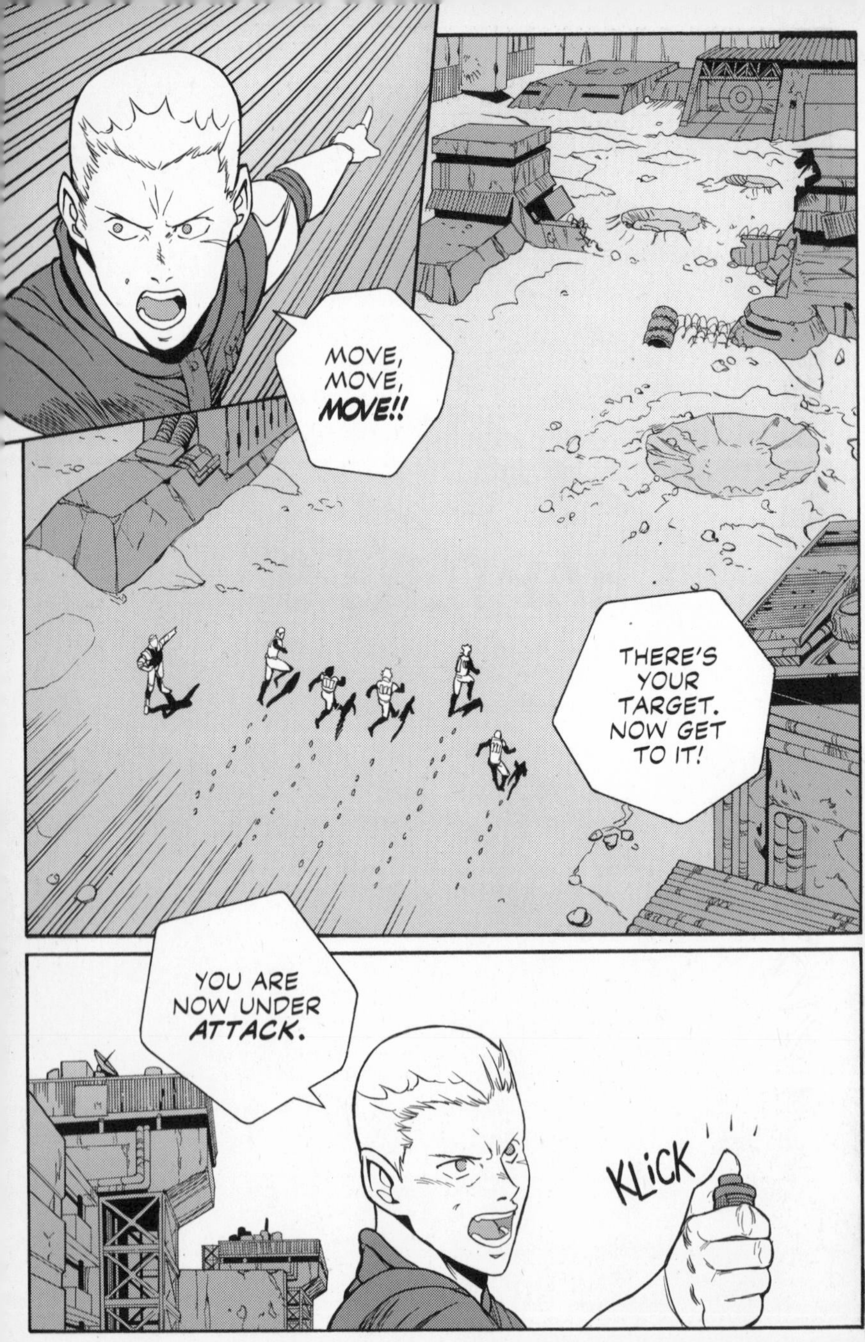
MOVE, MOVE, MOVE!!
THERE'S YOUR TARGET. NOW GET TO IT!
YOU ARE NOW UNDER ATTACK.
KLICK

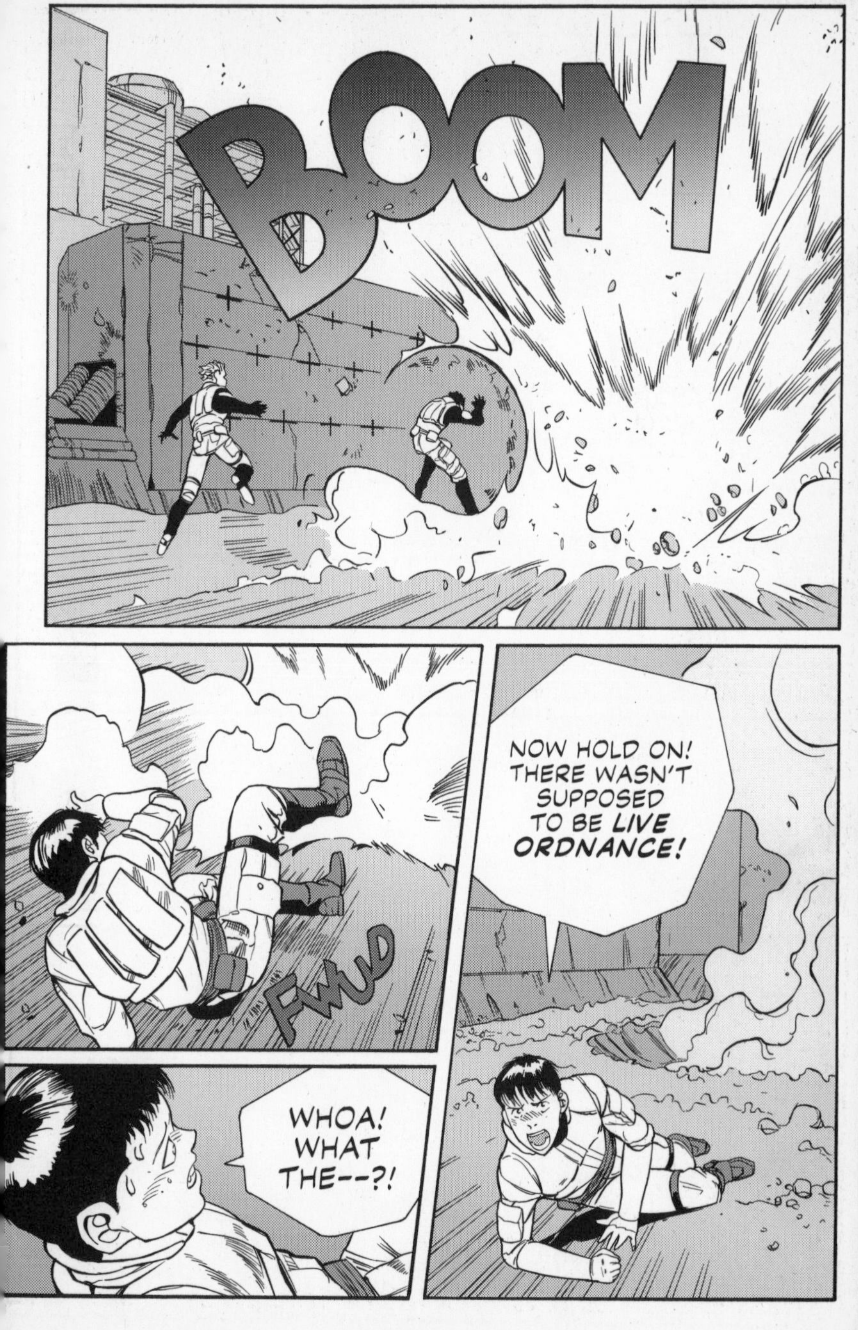
BOOM
FWUD
NOW HOLD ON! THERE WASN'T SUPPOSED TO BE LIVE ORDNANCE!
WHOA! WHAT THE--?!

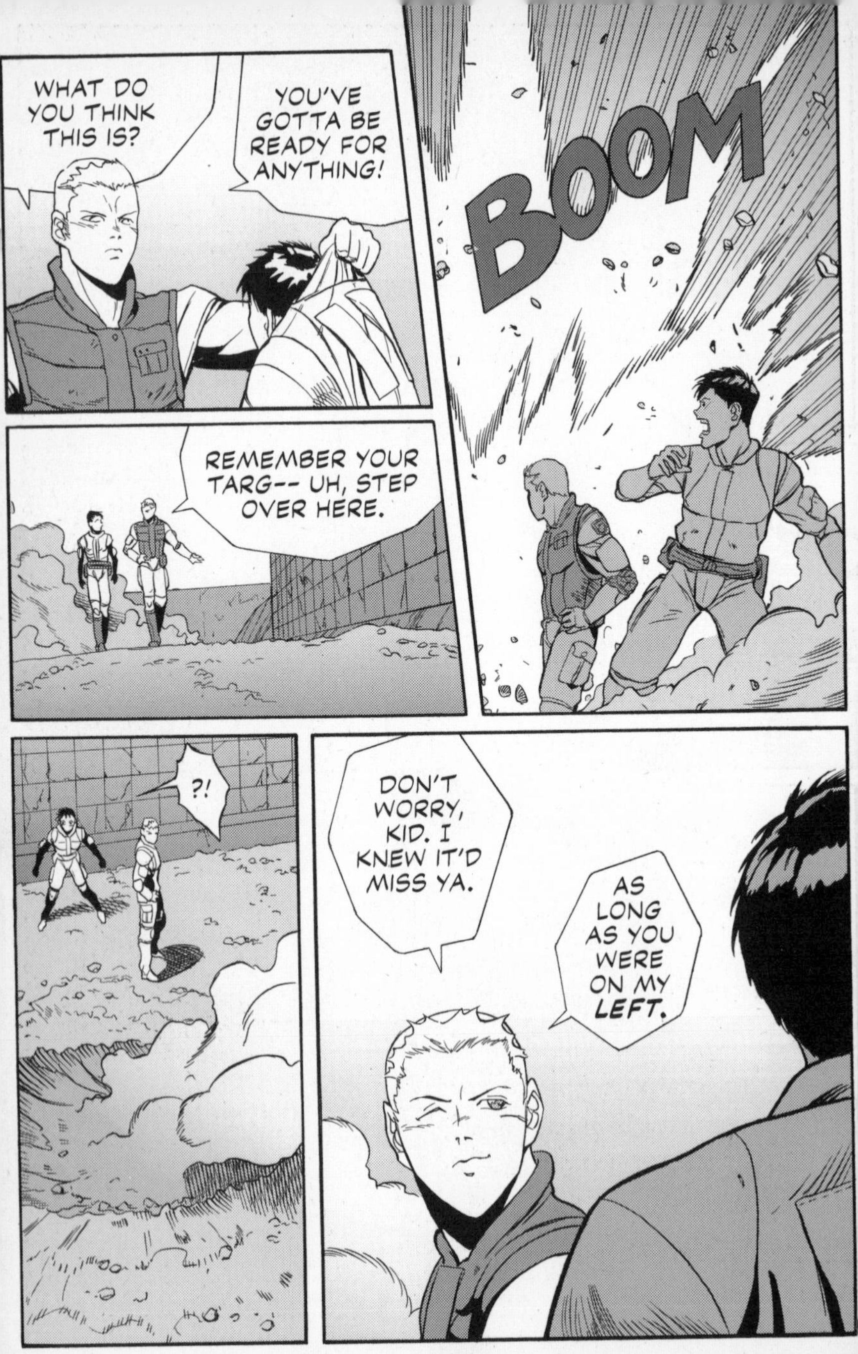
WHAT DO YOU THINK THIS IS?
YOU'VE GOTTA BE READY FOR ANYTHING!
BOOM
REMEMBER YOUR TARG-- UH, STEP OVER HERE.
?!
DON'T WORRY, KID. I KNEW IT'D MISS YA.
AS LONG AS YOU WERE ON MY LEFT.

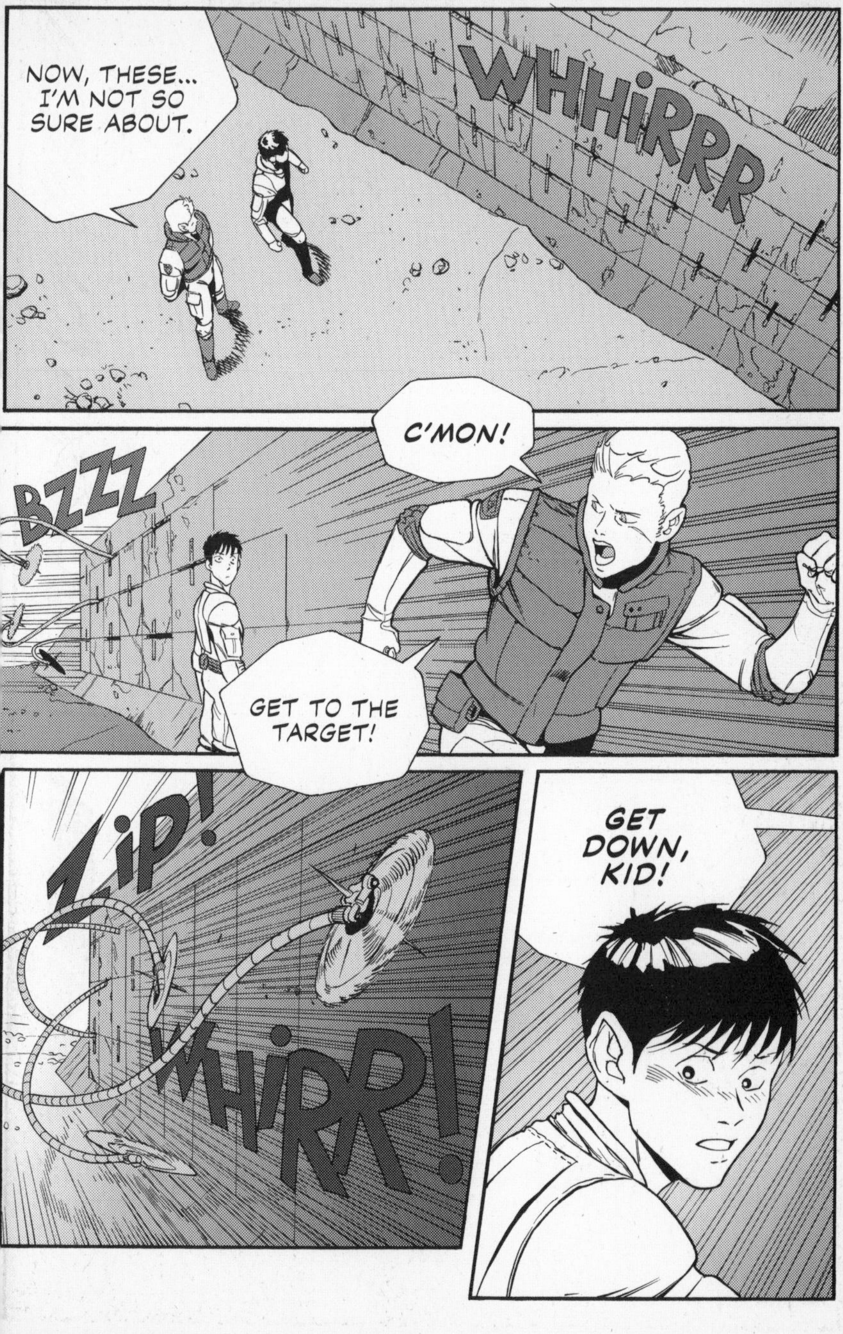
NOW, THESE... I'M NOT SO SURE ABOUT.
WHHiRRR
BZZZ
C'MON!
GET TO THE TARGET!
ZiP!
WHiRR!
GET DOWN, KID!

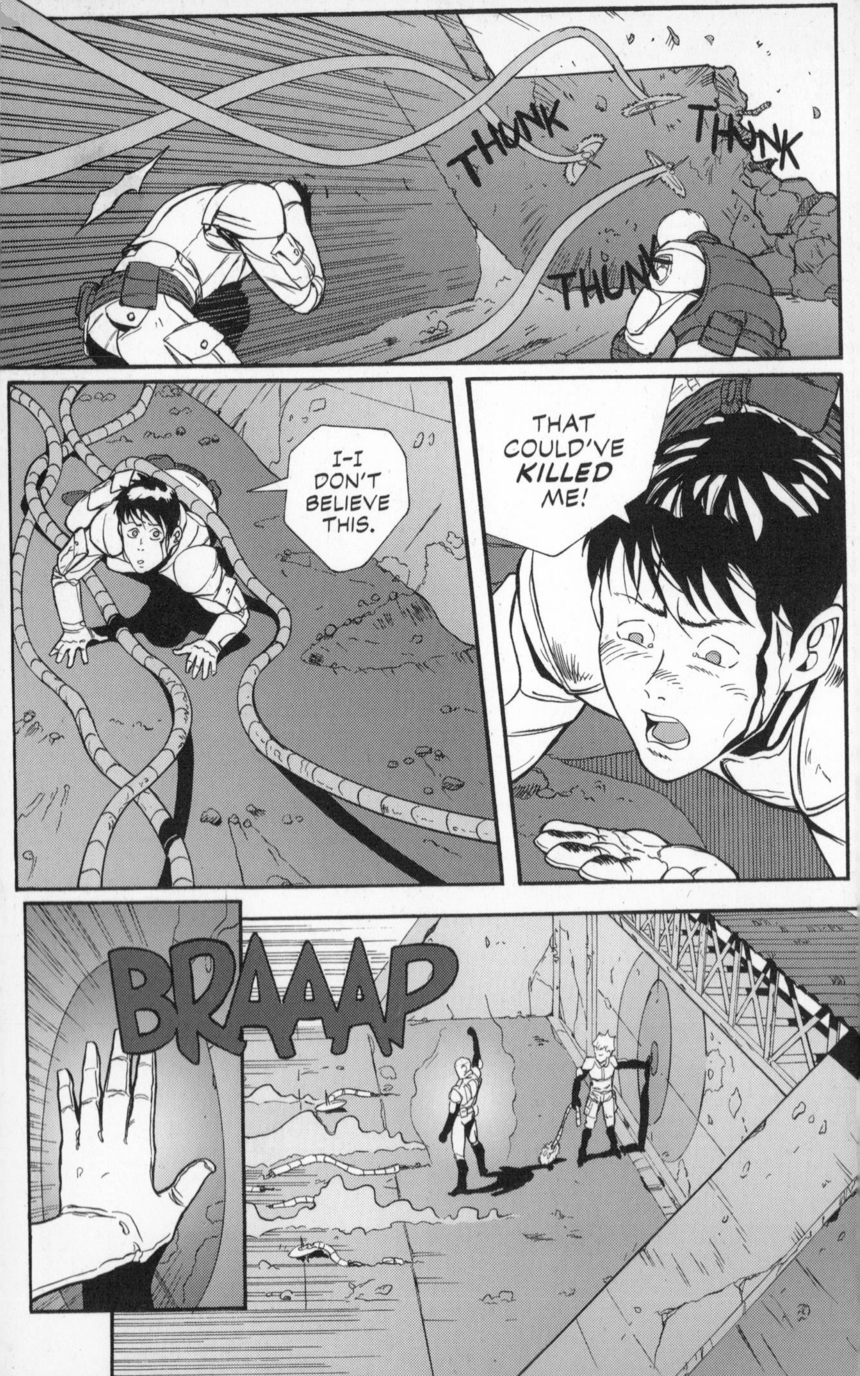
THUNK
THUNK
THUNK
I-I DON'T BELIEVE THIS.
THAT COULD'VE KILLED ME!
BRAAAP

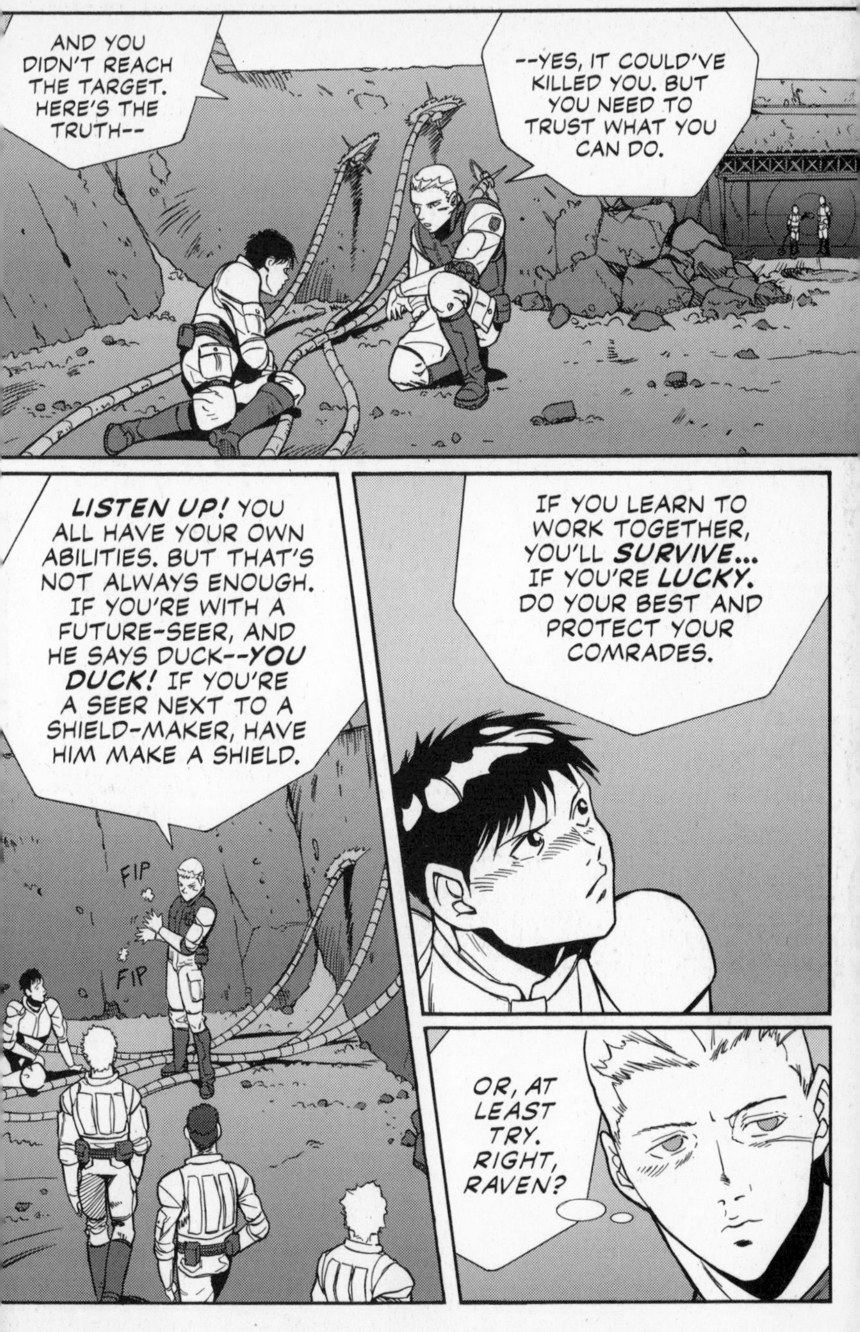
AND YOU DIDN'T REACH THE TARGET. HERE'S THE TRUTH--
--YES, IT COULD'VE KILLED YOU. BUT YOU NEED TO TRUST WHAT YOU CAN DO.
LISTEN UP! YOU ALL HAVE YOUR OWN ABILITIES. BUT THAT'S NOT ALWAYS ENOUGH. IF YOU'RE WITH A FUTURE-SEER, AND HE SAYS DUCK--YOU DUCK! IF YOU'RE A SEER NEXT TO A SHIELD-MAKER, HAVE HIM MAKE A SHIELD.
FIP
FIP
IF YOU LEARN TO WORK TOGETHER, YOU'LL SURVIVE... IF YOU'RE LUCKY. DO YOUR BEST AND PROTECT YOUR COMRADES.
OR, AT LEAST TRY. RIGHT, RAVEN?

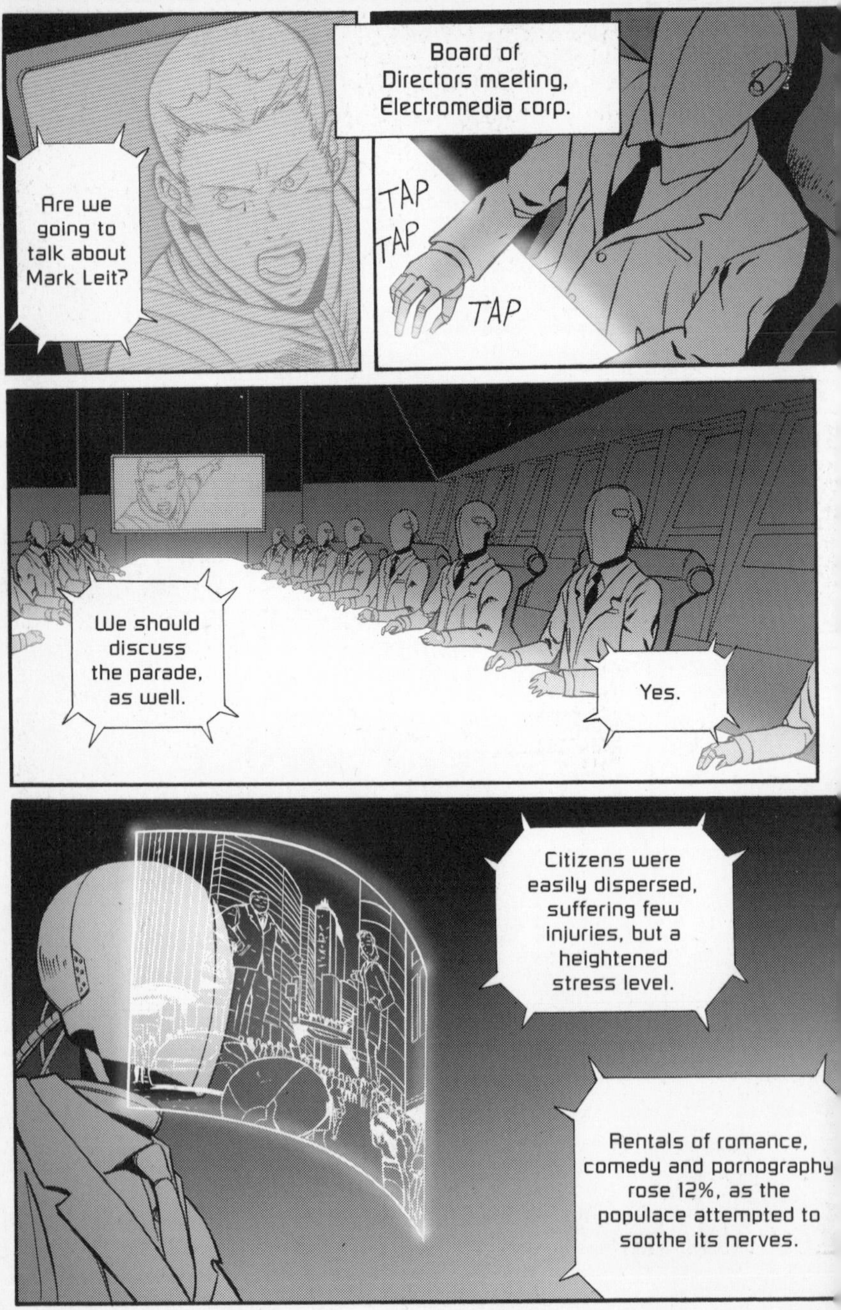
Are we going to talk about Mark Leit?
Board of Directors meeting, Electromedia corp.
TAP
TAP
TAP
We should discuss the parade, as well.
Yes.
Citizens were easily dispersed, suffering few injuries, but a heightened stress level.
Rentals of romance, comedy and pornography rose 12%, as the populace attempted to soothe its nerves.

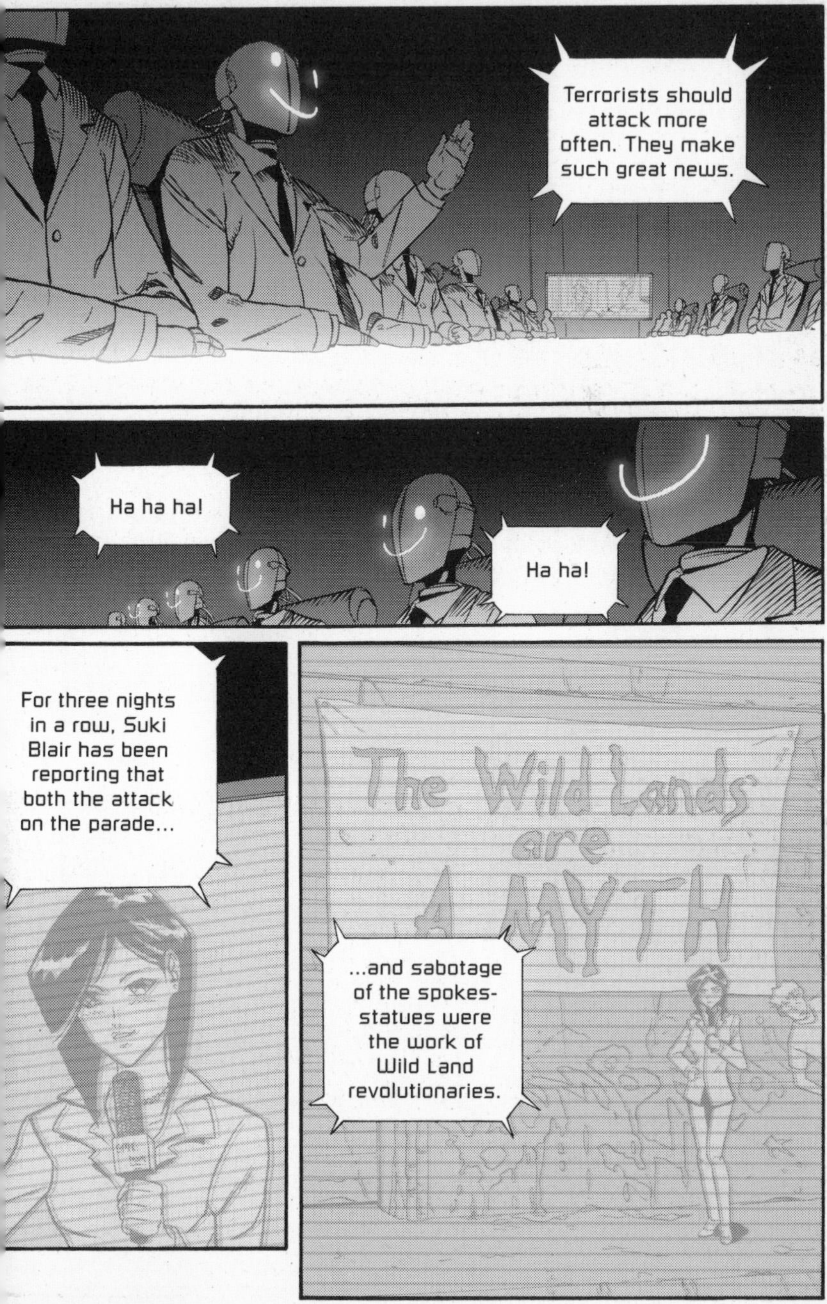
Terrorists should attack more often. They make such great news.
Ha ha ha!
Ha ha!
For three nights in a row, Suki Blair has been reporting that both the attack on the parade...
The Wild Lands are A MYTH
...and sabotage of the spokes-statues were the work of Wild Land revolutionaries.

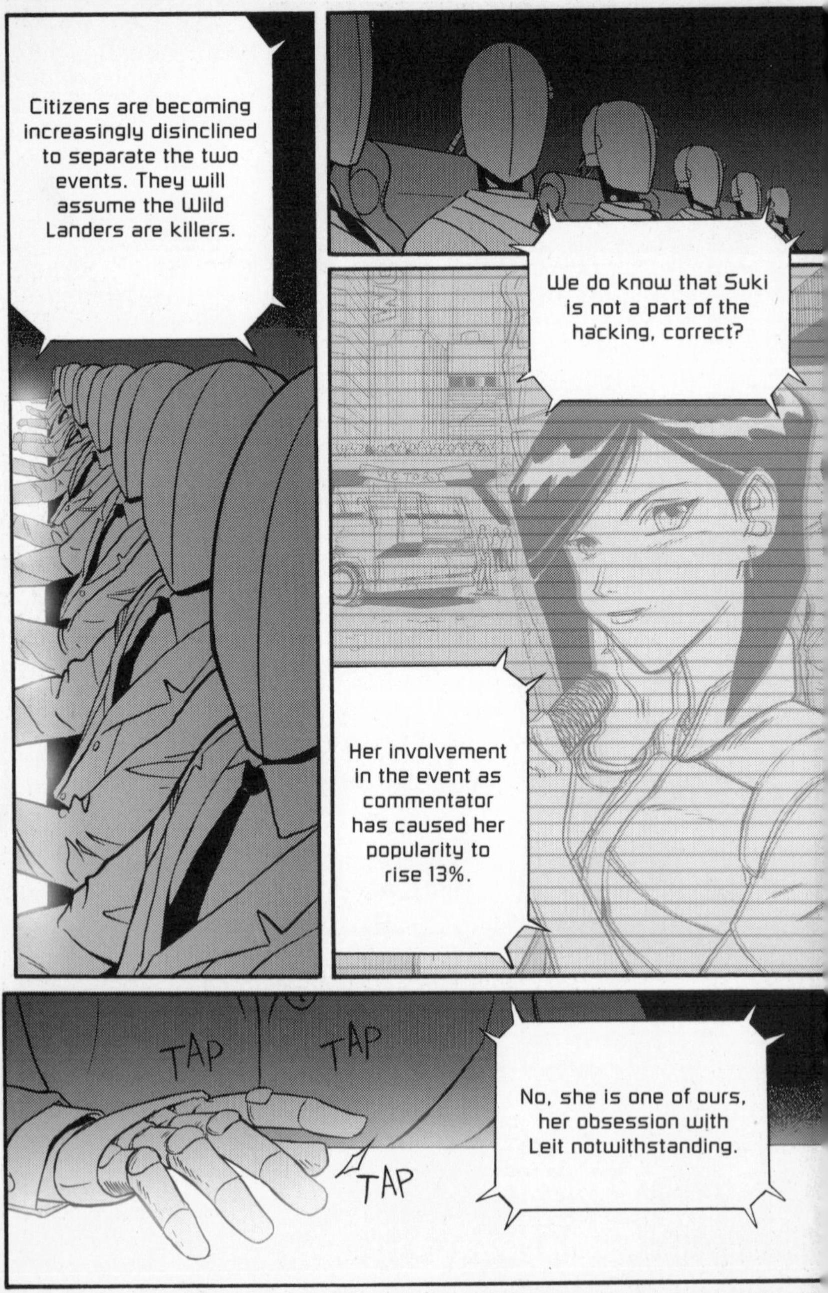
Citizens are becoming increasingly disinclined to separate the two events. They will assume the Wild Landers are killers.
We do know that Suki is not a part of the hacking, correct?
Her involvement in the event as commentator has caused her popularity to rise 13%.
TAP
TAP
TAP
No, she is one of ours, her obsession with Leit notwithstanding.

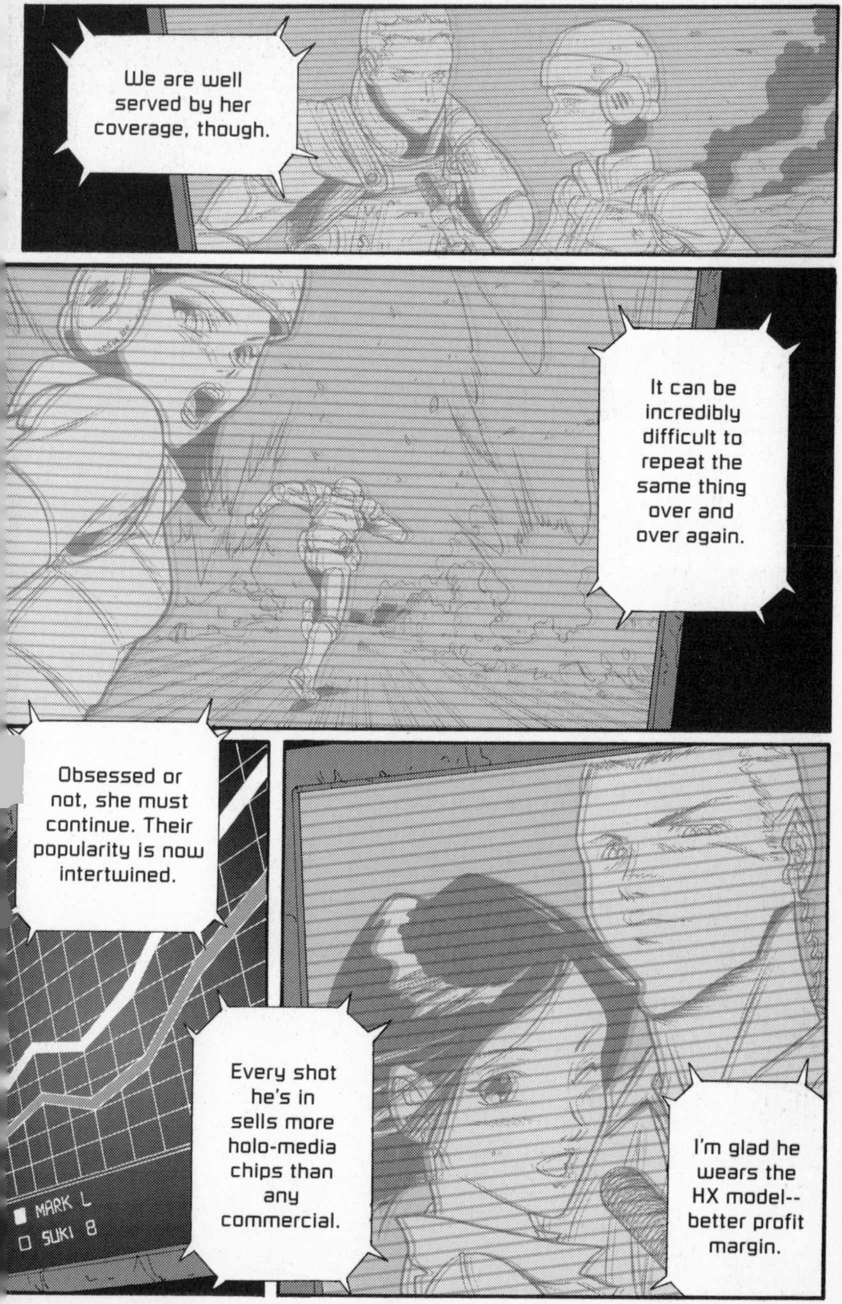
We are well served by her coverage, though.
It can be incredibly difficult to repeat the same thing over and over again.
Obsessed or not, she must continue. Their popularity is now intertwined.
MARK L
SUKI B
Every shot he's in sells more holo-media chips than any commercial.
I'm glad he wears the HX model--better profit margin.

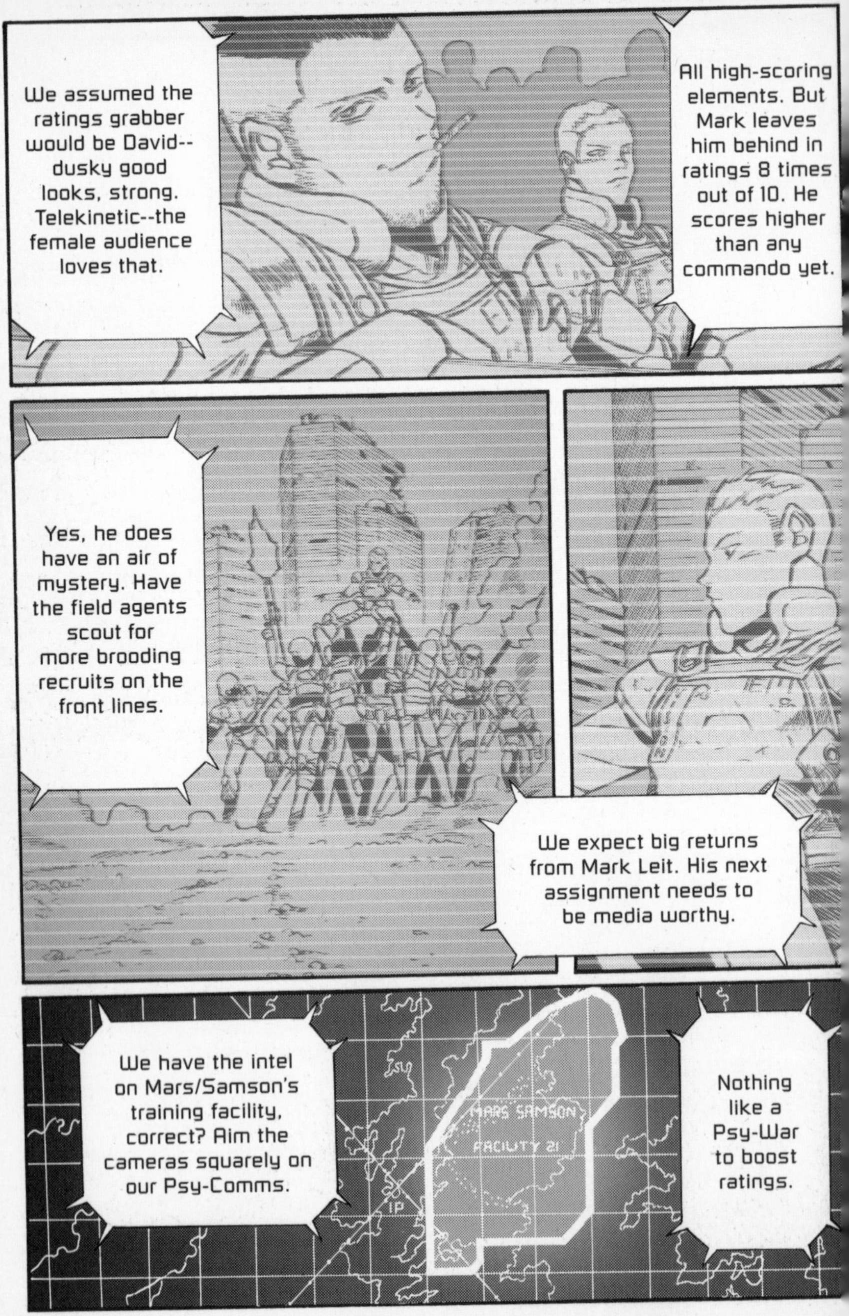
We assumed the ratings grabber would be David--dusky good looks, strong. Telekinetic--the female audience loves that.
All high-scoring elements. But Mark leaves him behind in ratings 8 times out of 10. He scores higher than any commando yet.
Yes, he does have an air of mystery. Have the field agents scout for more brooding recruits on the front lines.
We expect big returns from Mark Leit. His next assignment needs to be media worthy.
We have the intel on Mars/Samson's training facility, correct? Aim the cameras squarely on our Psy-Comms.
MARS SAMSON
FACILITY 21
IP
Nothing like a Psy-War to boost ratings.

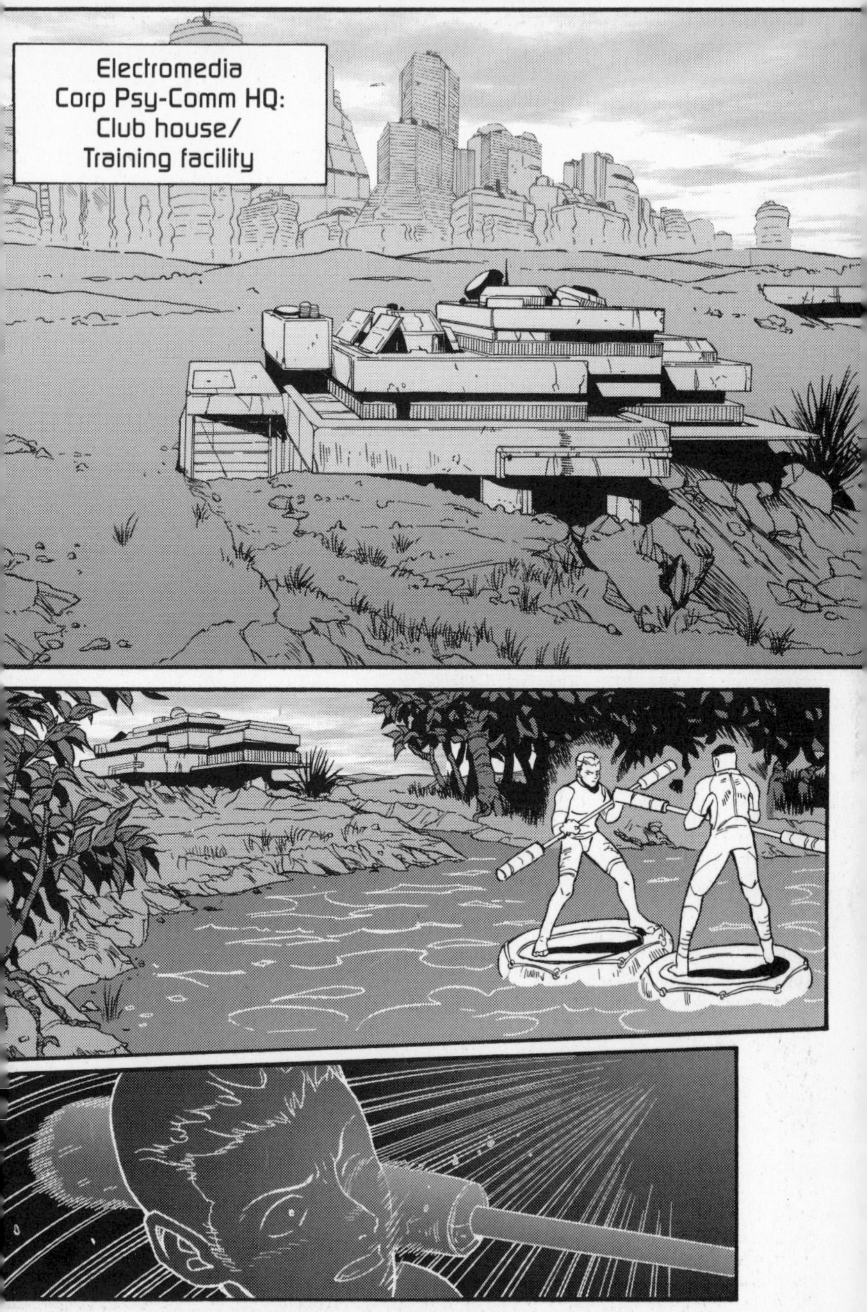
Electromedia Corp Psy-Comm HQ: Club house/ Training facility

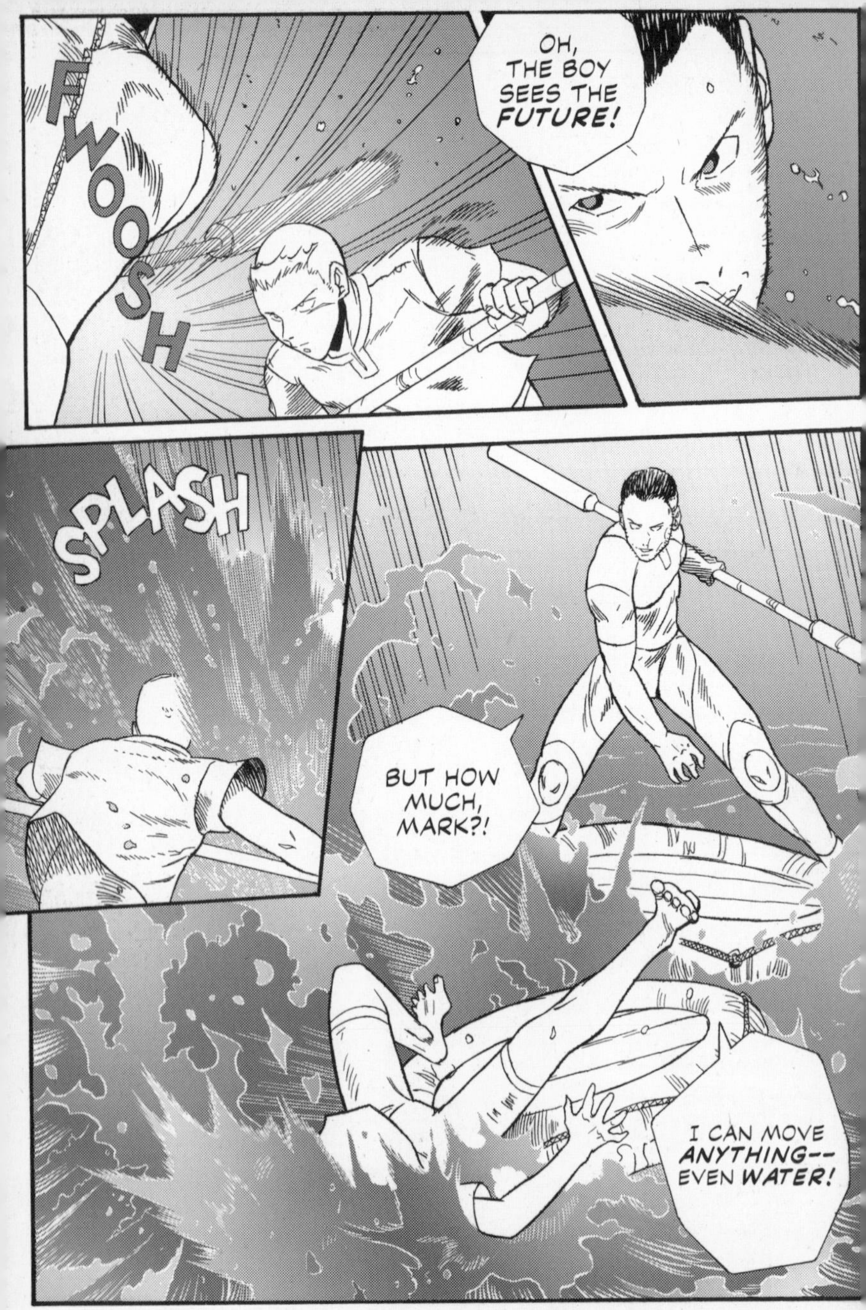
FWOOSH
OH, THE BOY SEES THE FUTURE!
SPLASH
BUT HOW MUCH, MARK?!
I CAN MOVE ANYTHING-- EVEN WATER!

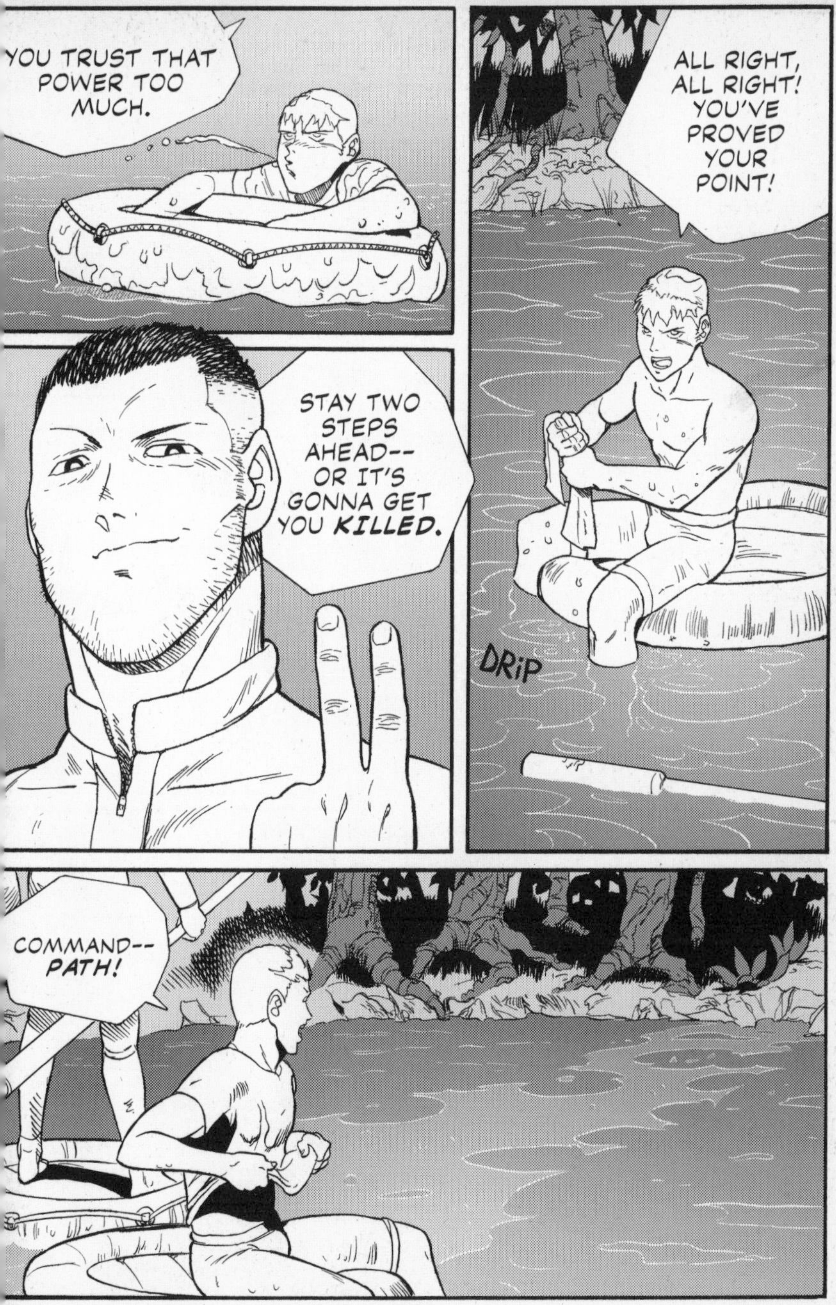
YOU TRUST THAT POWER TOO MUCH.
STAY TWO STEPS AHEAD-- OR IT'S GONNA GET YOU **KILLED**.
ALL RIGHT, ALL RIGHT! YOU'VE PROVED YOUR POINT!
DRiP
COMMAND-- *PATH!*

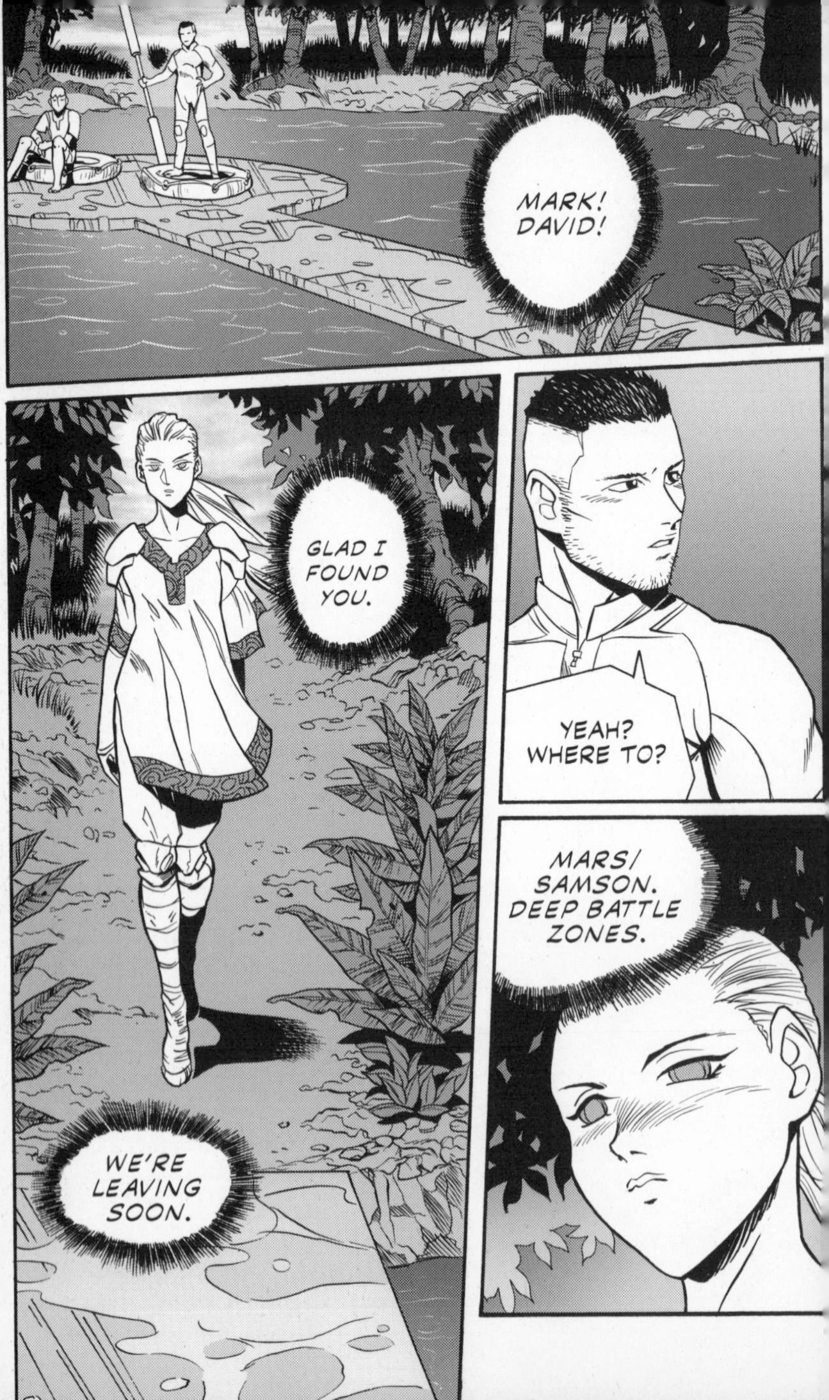
MARK! DAVID!
GLAD I FOUND YOU.
WE'RE LEAVING SOON.
YEAH? WHERE TO?
MARS/ SAMSON. DEEP BATTLE ZONES.

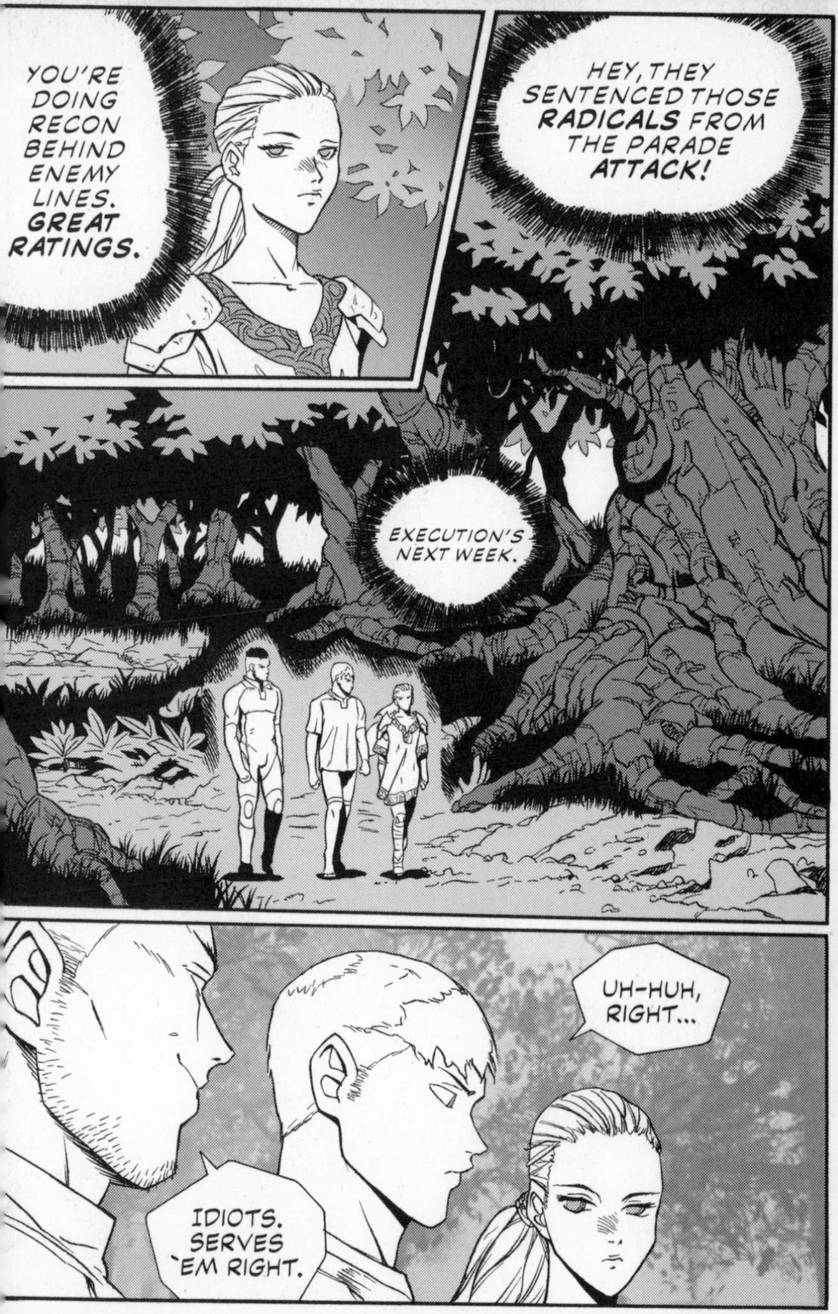
YOU'RE DOING RECON BEHIND ENEMY LINES. GREAT RATINGS.
HEY, THEY SENTENCED THOSE RADICALS FROM THE PARADE ATTACK!
EXECUTION'S NEXT WEEK.
UH-HUH, RIGHT...
IDIOTS. SERVES 'EM RIGHT.

MARK--THIS **GIRL** IN YOUR HEAD. DO YOU **ALWAYS** THINK OF HER BEFORE BATTLE?

IT'S NONE OF YOUR--

I'VE SEEN THE FILE. IT WASN'T YOUR FAULT.

RELAX, THE CORP WILL TAKE CARE OF YOU, MARK.

YOU CAN HAVE ANYONE.

SHUT UP!

STAY OUT OF MY MIND!

NOTHING... IT'S NOTHING.

WHAT'S YOUR **PROBLEM?**

WELL, GET IT TOGETHER. WE'VE GOT A BATTLE.

LIKE, SOON.

YEAH.

I KNOW.

PSY★COMM

CHAPTER [4]

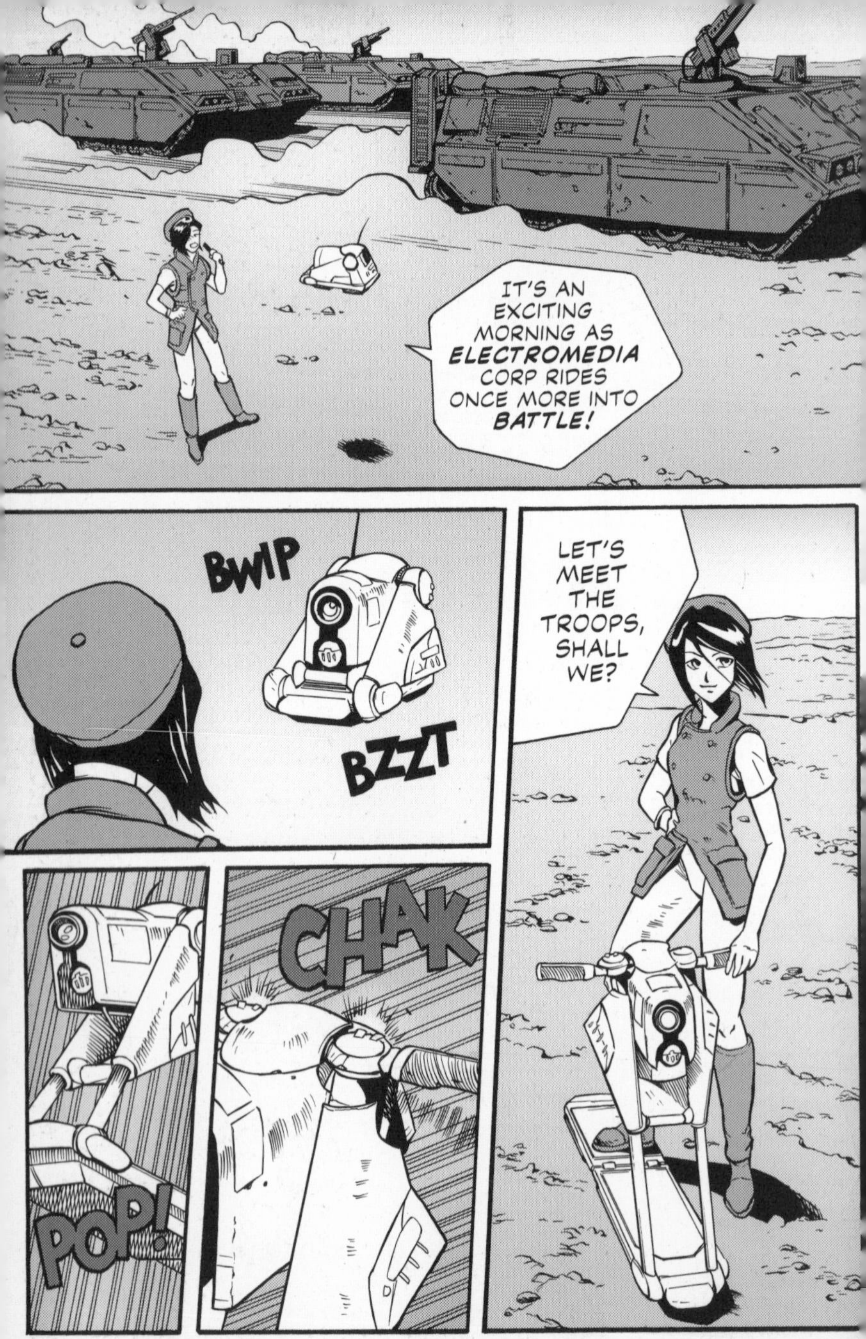
IT'S AN EXCITING MORNING AS *ELECTROMEDIA* CORP RIDES ONCE MORE INTO *BATTLE!*
BWIP
BZZT
POP!
CHAK
LET'S MEET THE TROOPS, SHALL WE?

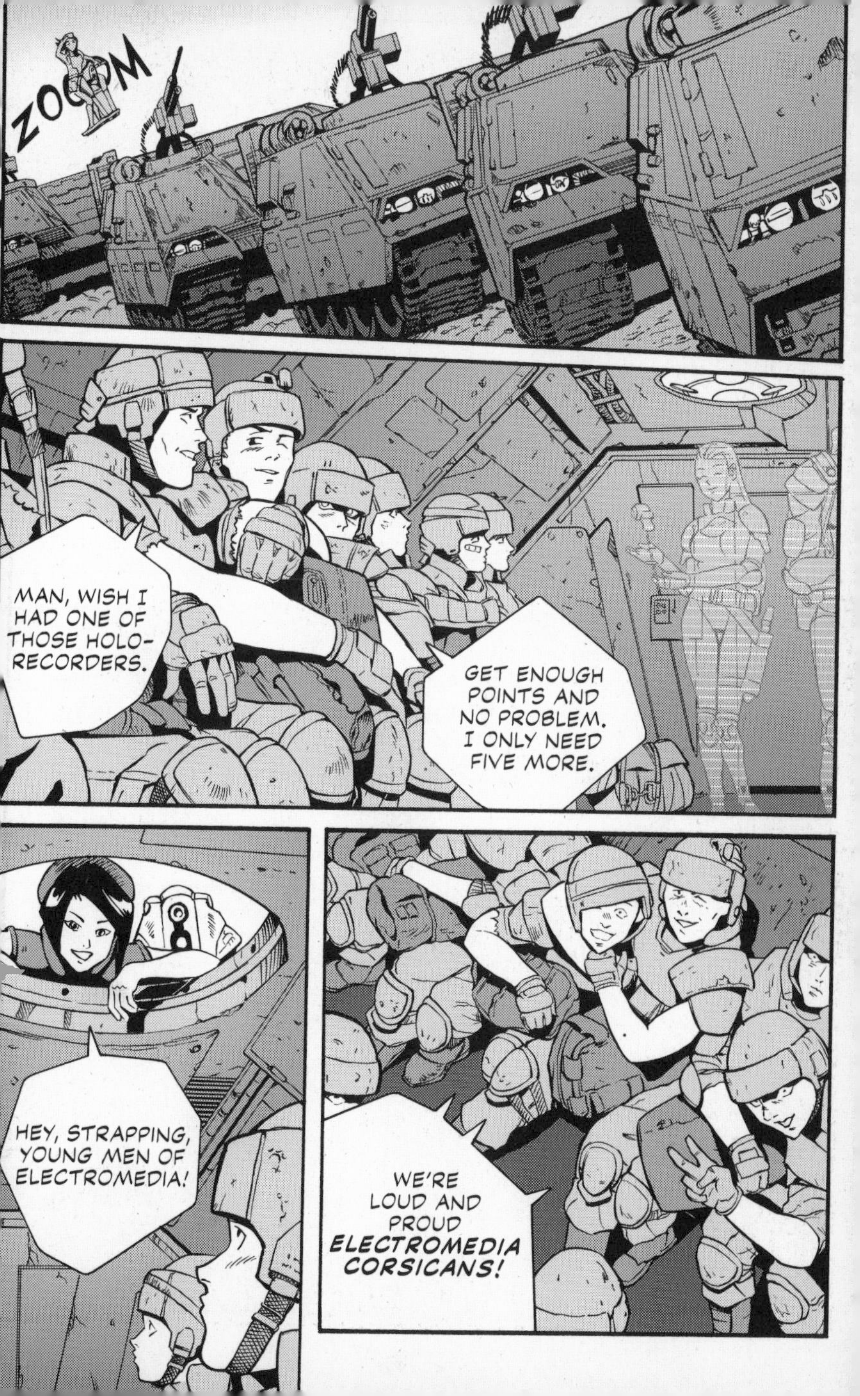
ZOOOM
MAN, WISH I HAD ONE OF THOSE HOLO-RECORDERS.
GET ENOUGH POINTS AND NO PROBLEM. I ONLY NEED FIVE MORE.
HEY, STRAPPING, YOUNG MEN OF ELECTROMEDIA!
WE'RE LOUD AND PROUD *ELECTROMEDIA CORSICANS!*

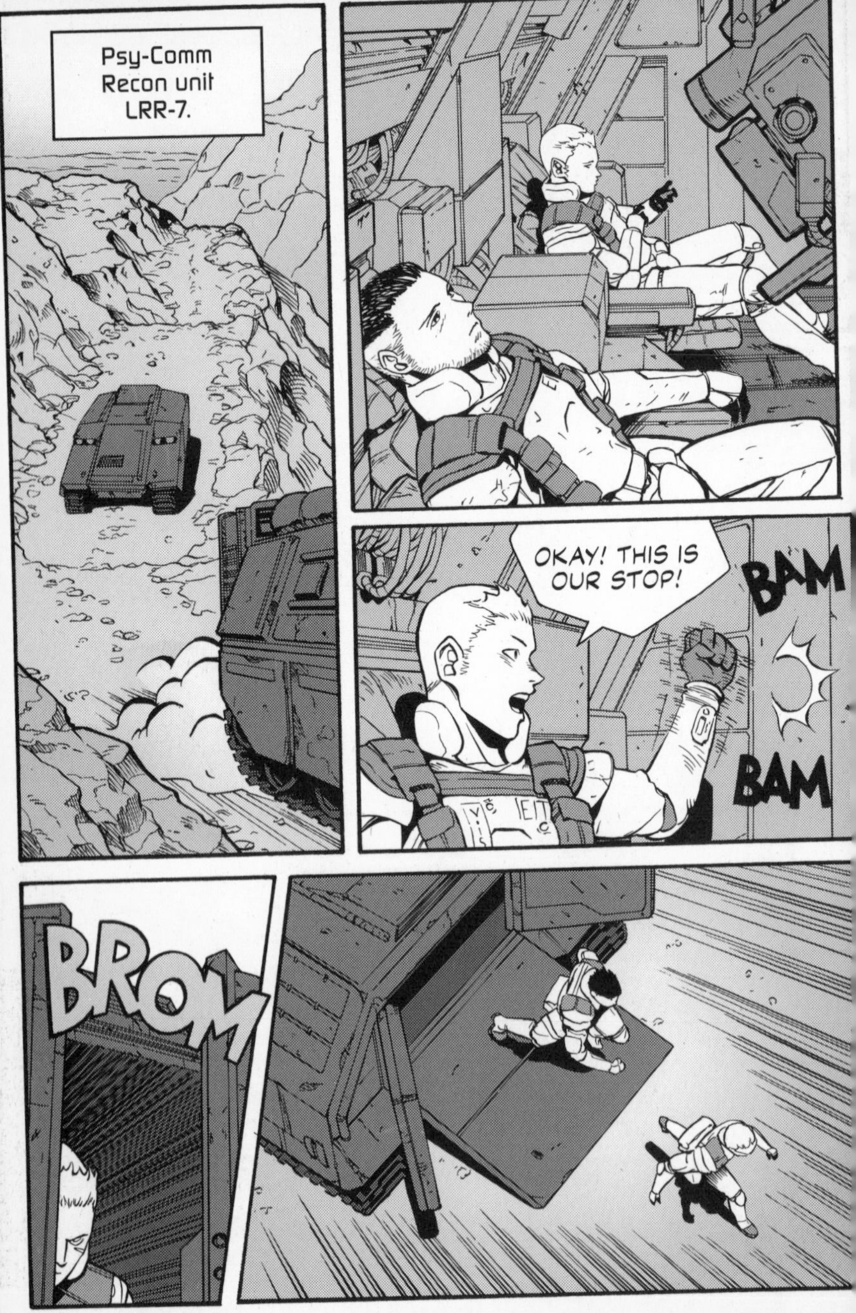
Psy-Comm
Recon unit
LRR-7.
OKAY! THIS IS OUR STOP!
BAM
BAM
BROM

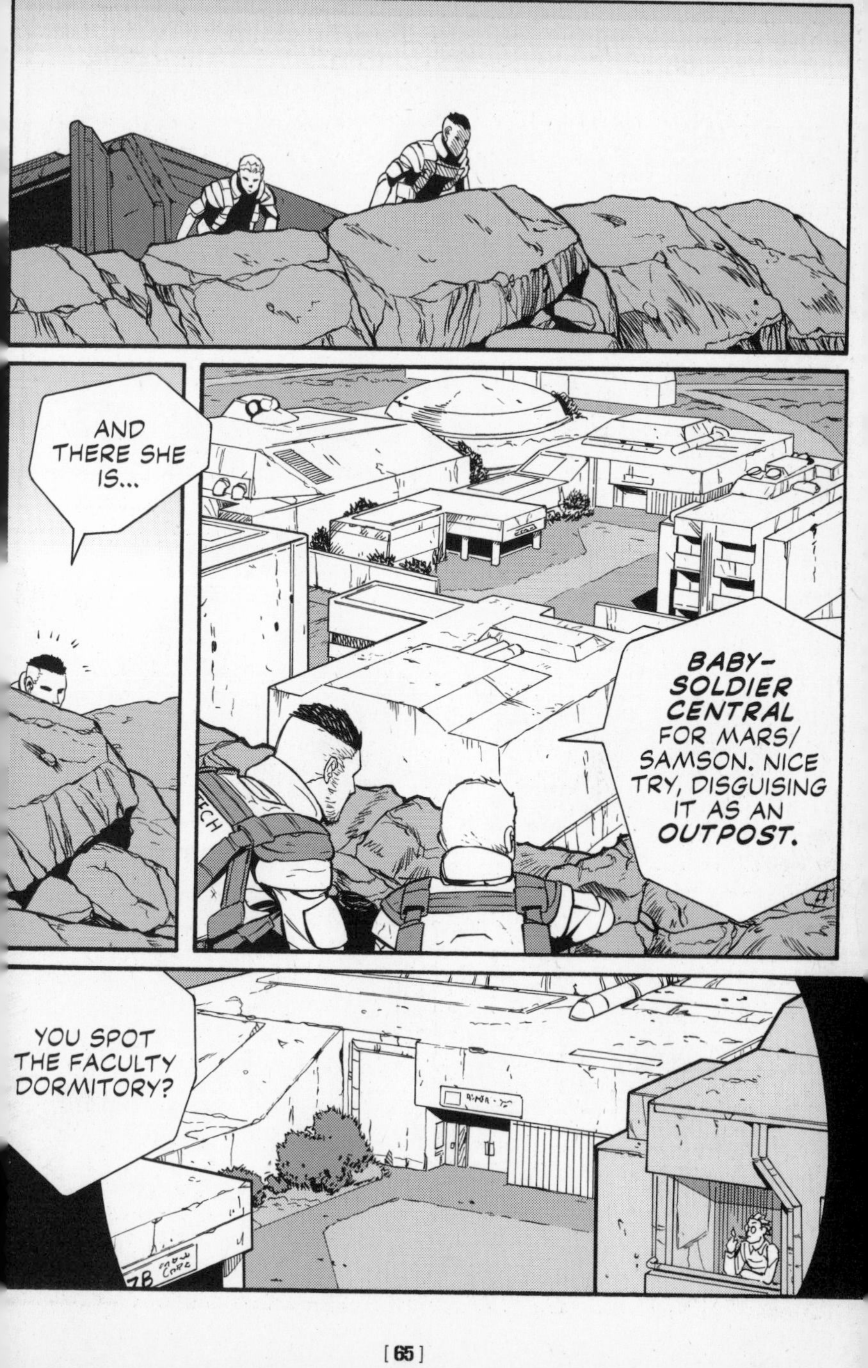
AND THERE SHE IS...
BABY-SOLDIER CENTRAL FOR MARS/SAMSON. NICE TRY, DISGUISING IT AS AN OUTPOST.
YOU SPOT THE FACULTY DORMITORY?

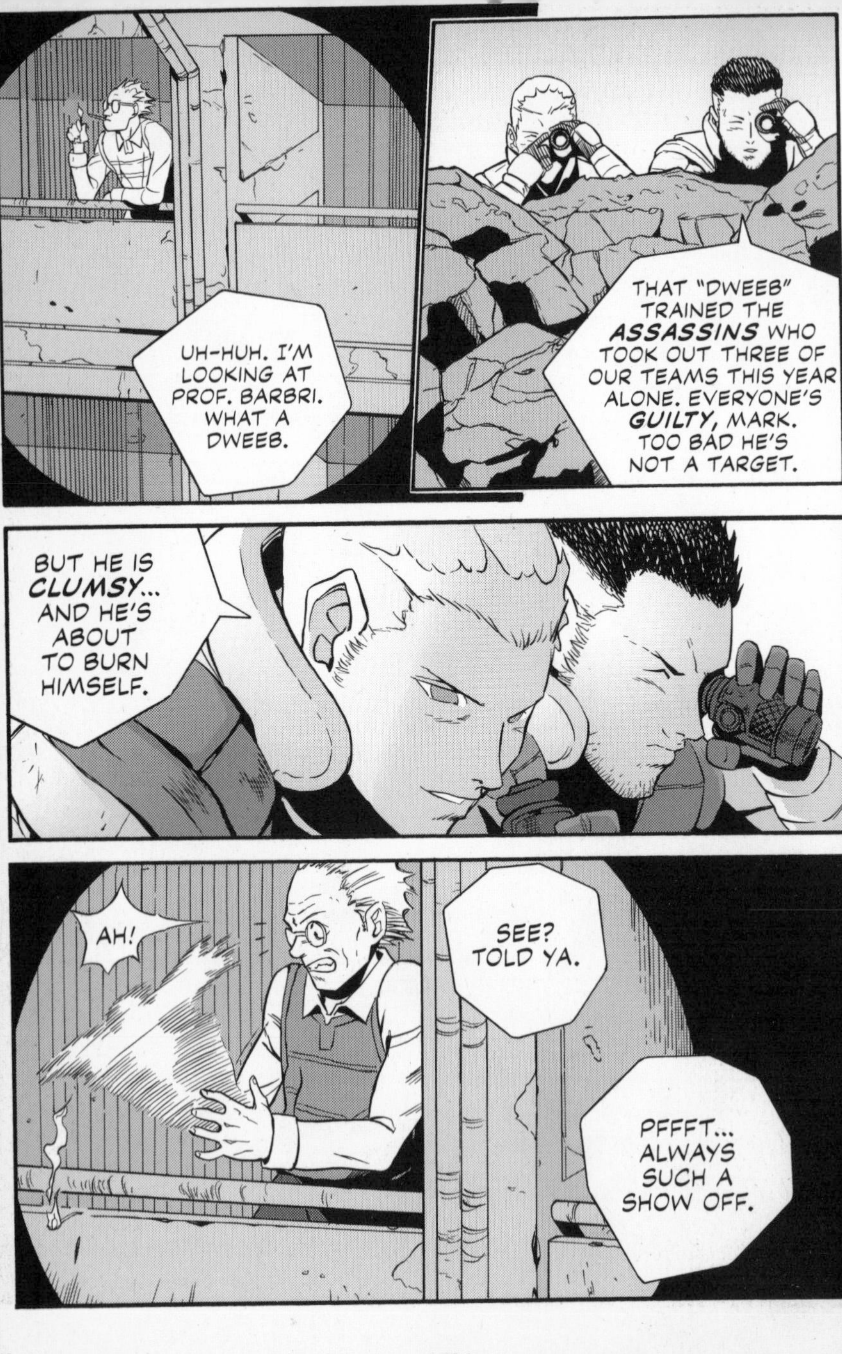
UH-HUH. I'M LOOKING AT PROF. BARBRI. WHAT A DWEEB.
THAT "DWEEB" TRAINED THE ***ASSASSINS*** WHO TOOK OUT THREE OF OUR TEAMS THIS YEAR ALONE. EVERYONE'S ***GUILTY,*** MARK. TOO BAD HE'S NOT A TARGET.
BUT HE IS ***CLUMSY***... AND HE'S ABOUT TO BURN HIMSELF.
AH!
SEE? TOLD YA.
PFFFT... ALWAYS SUCH A SHOW OFF.

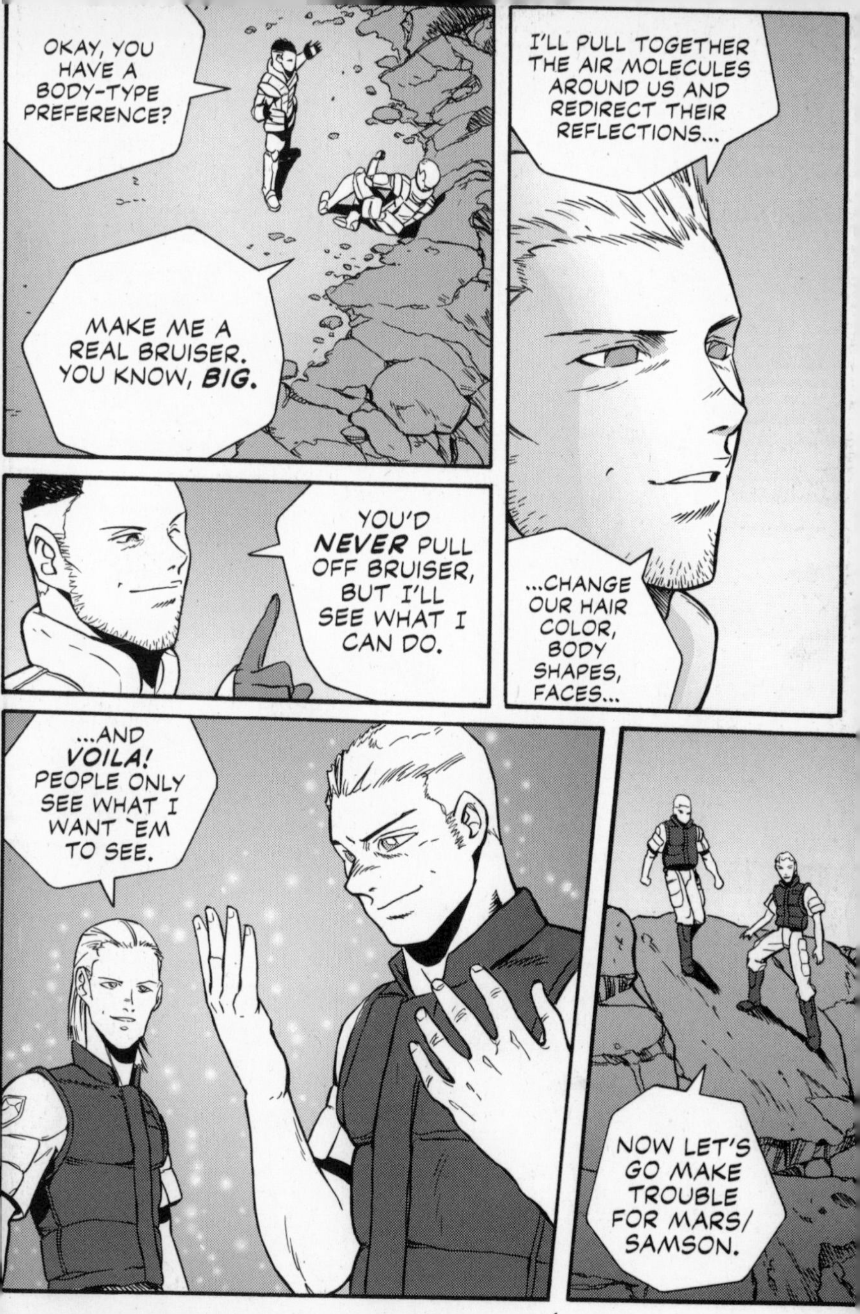
OKAY, YOU HAVE A BODY-TYPE PREFERENCE?
MAKE ME A REAL BRUISER. YOU KNOW, ***BIG.***
I'LL PULL TOGETHER THE AIR MOLECULES AROUND US AND REDIRECT THEIR REFLECTIONS...
...CHANGE OUR HAIR COLOR, BODY SHAPES, FACES...
YOU'D ***NEVER*** PULL OFF BRUISER, BUT I'LL SEE WHAT I CAN DO.
...AND ***VOILA!*** PEOPLE ONLY SEE WHAT I WANT `EM TO SEE.
NOW LET'S GO MAKE TROUBLE FOR MARS/ SAMSON.

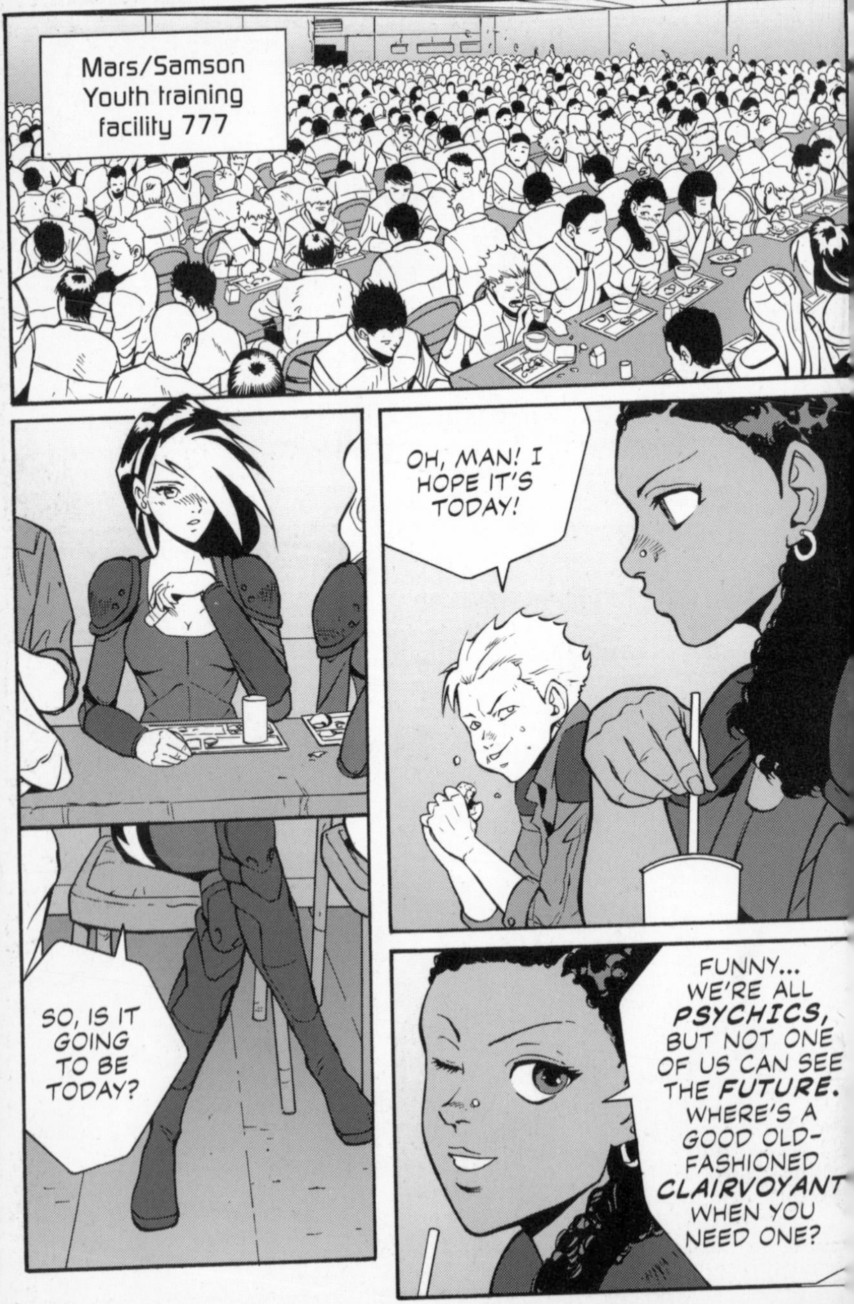
Mars/Samson Youth training facility 777
SO, IS IT GOING TO BE TODAY?
OH, MAN! I HOPE IT'S TODAY!
FUNNY... WE'RE ALL PSYCHICS, BUT NOT ONE OF US CAN SEE THE FUTURE. WHERE'S A GOOD OLD-FASHIONED CLAIRVOYANT WHEN YOU NEED ONE?

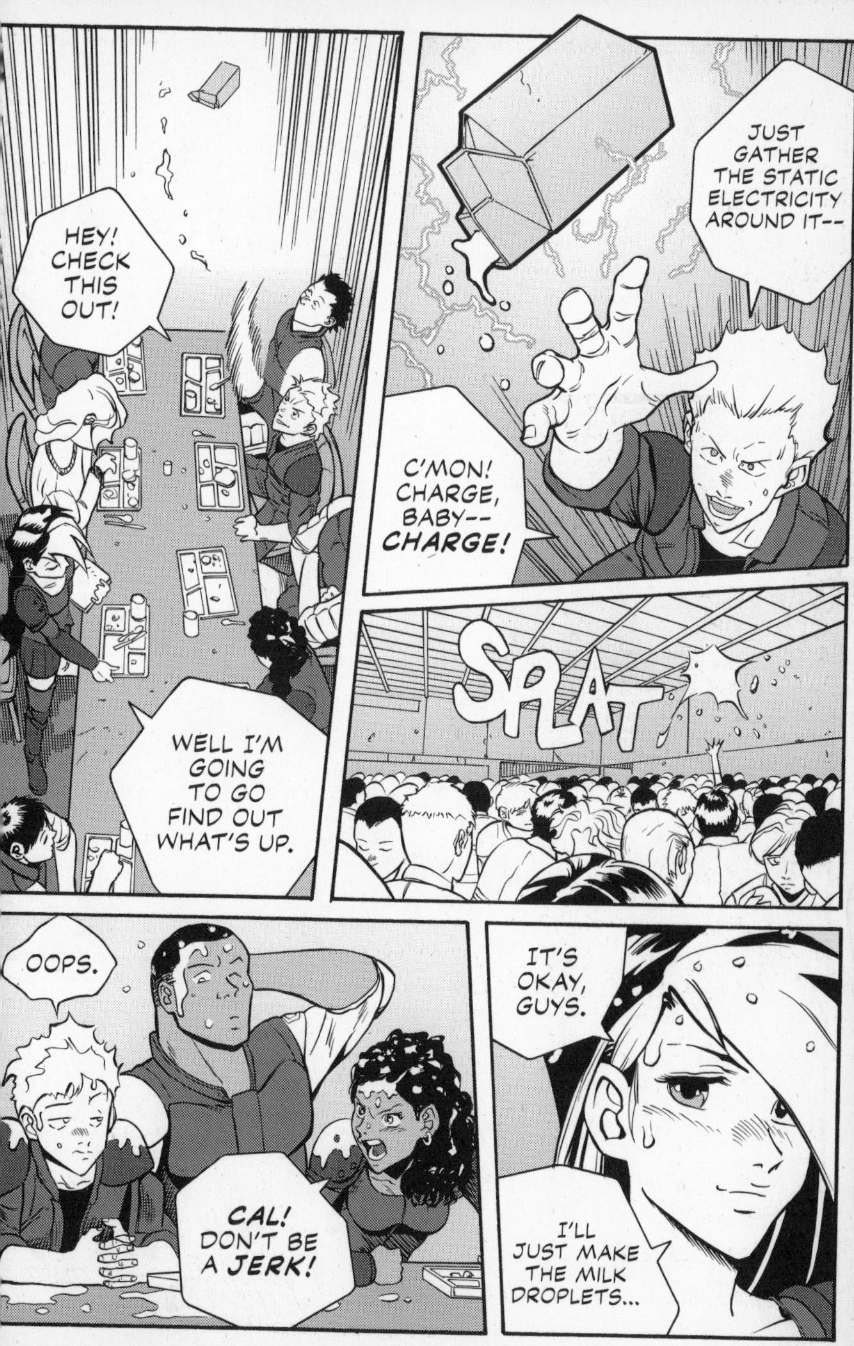
HEY! CHECK THIS OUT!
WELL I'M GOING TO GO FIND OUT WHAT'S UP.
JUST GATHER THE STATIC ELECTRICITY AROUND IT--
C'MON! CHARGE, BABY-- **CHARGE!**
SPLAT
OOPS.
CAL! DON'T BE A **JERK!**
IT'S OKAY, GUYS.
I'LL JUST MAKE THE MILK DROPLETS...

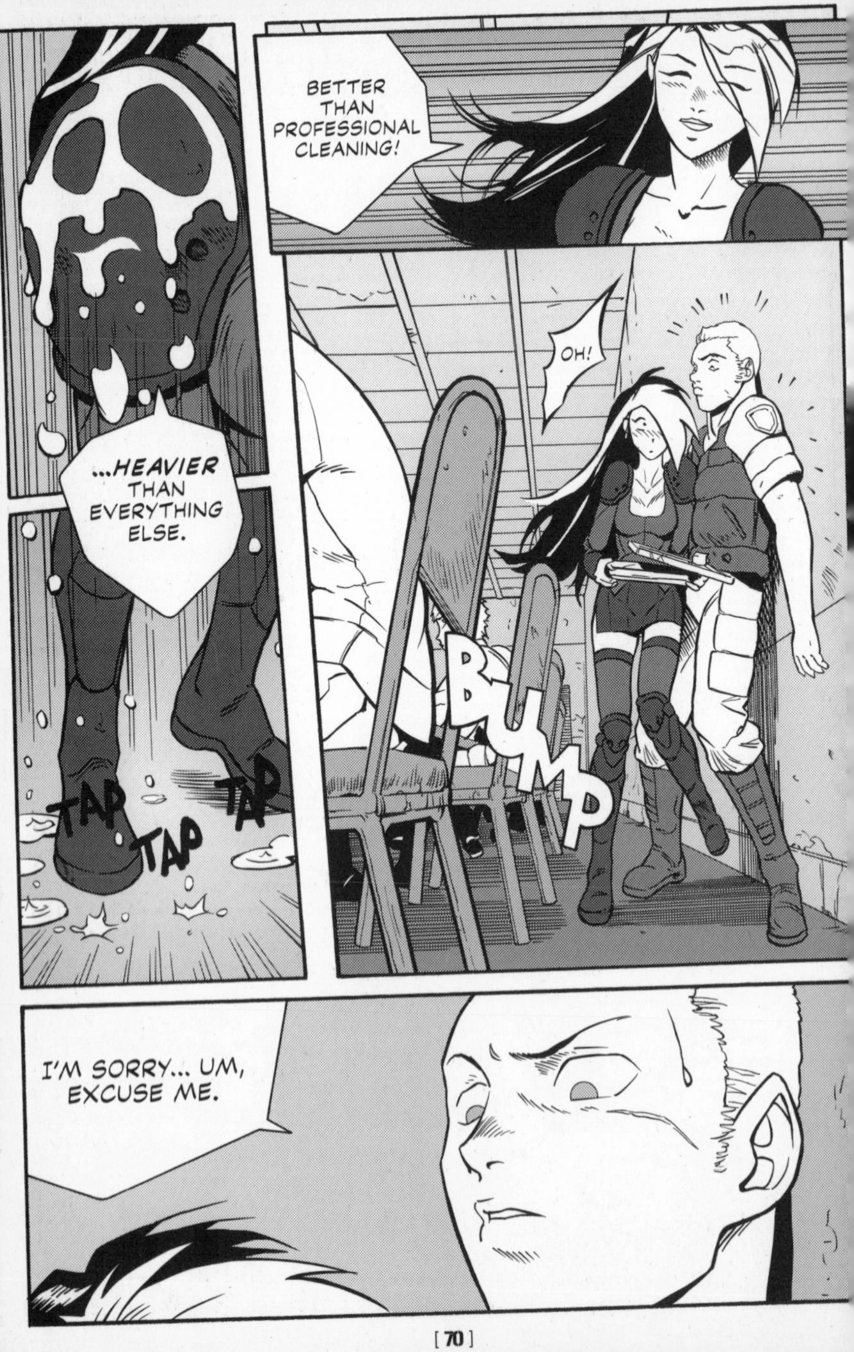
...HEAVIER THAN EVERYTHING ELSE.
TAP TAP TAP
BETTER THAN PROFESSIONAL CLEANING!
OH!
BUMP
I'M SORRY... UM, EXCUSE ME.

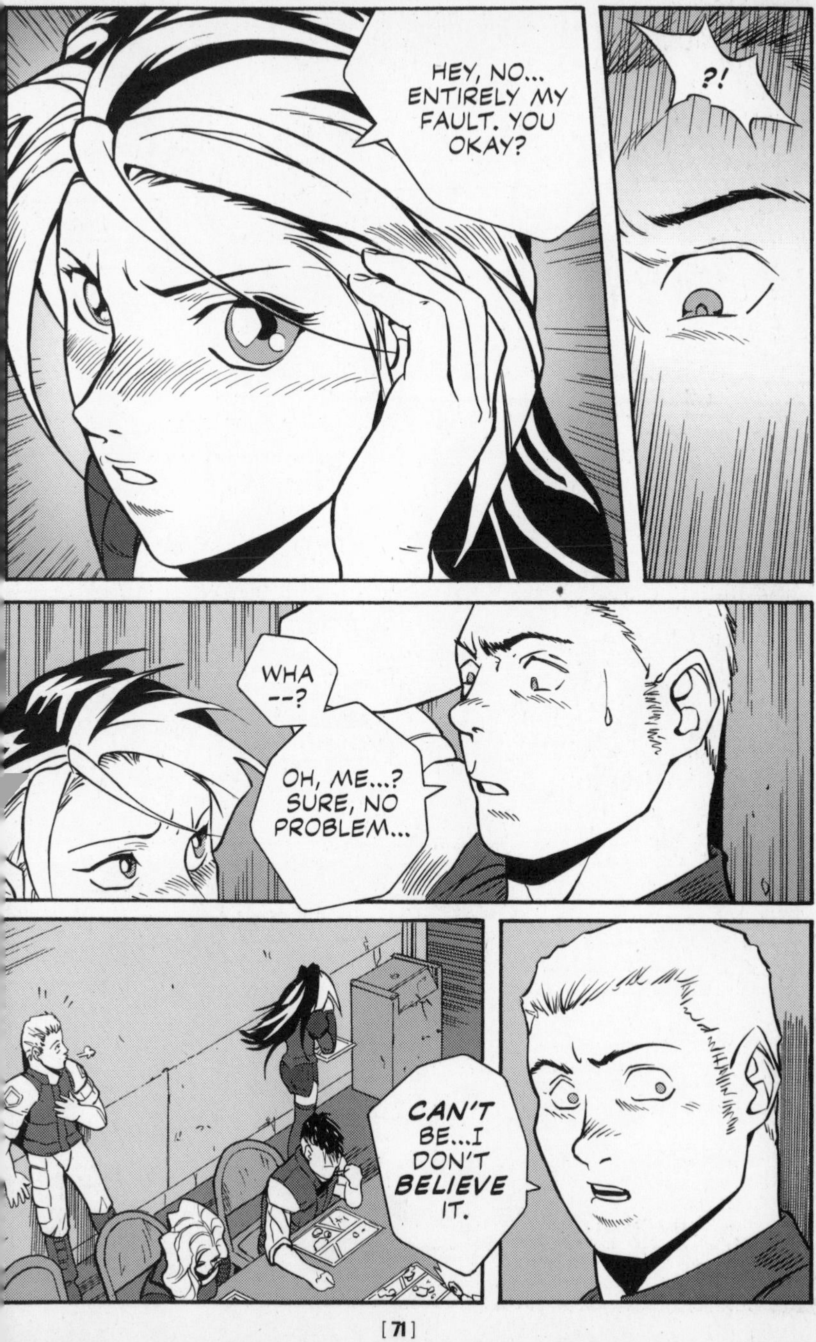
HEY, NO... ENTIRELY MY FAULT. YOU OKAY?
?!
WHA --?
OH, ME...? SURE, NO PROBLEM...
CAN'T BE...I DON'T BELIEVE IT.

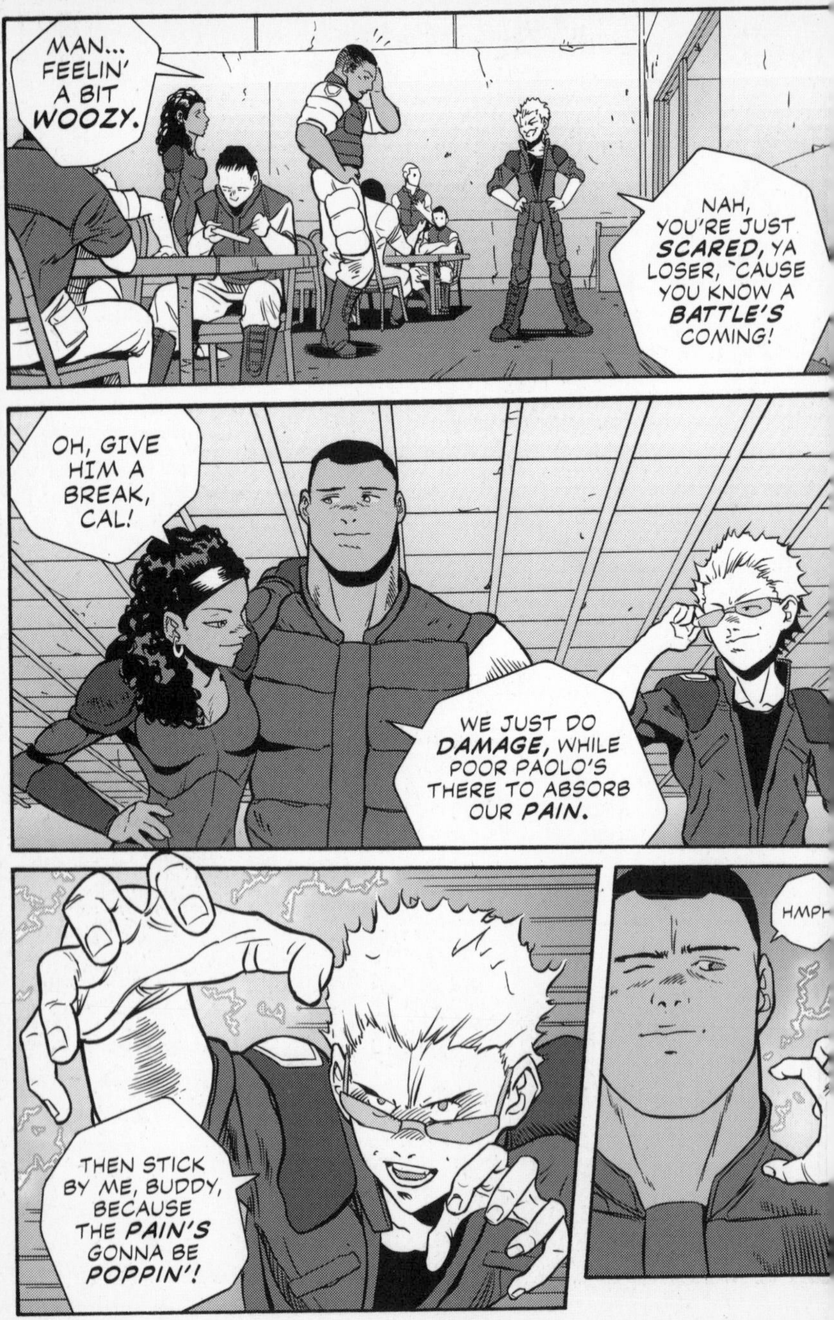
MAN... FEELIN' A BIT WOOZY.
NAH, YOU'RE JUST SCARED, YA LOSER, `CAUSE YOU KNOW A BATTLE'S COMING!
OH, GIVE HIM A BREAK, CAL!
WE JUST DO DAMAGE, WHILE POOR PAOLO'S THERE TO ABSORB OUR PAIN.
THEN STICK BY ME, BUDDY, BECAUSE THE PAIN'S GONNA BE POPPIN'!
HMPH

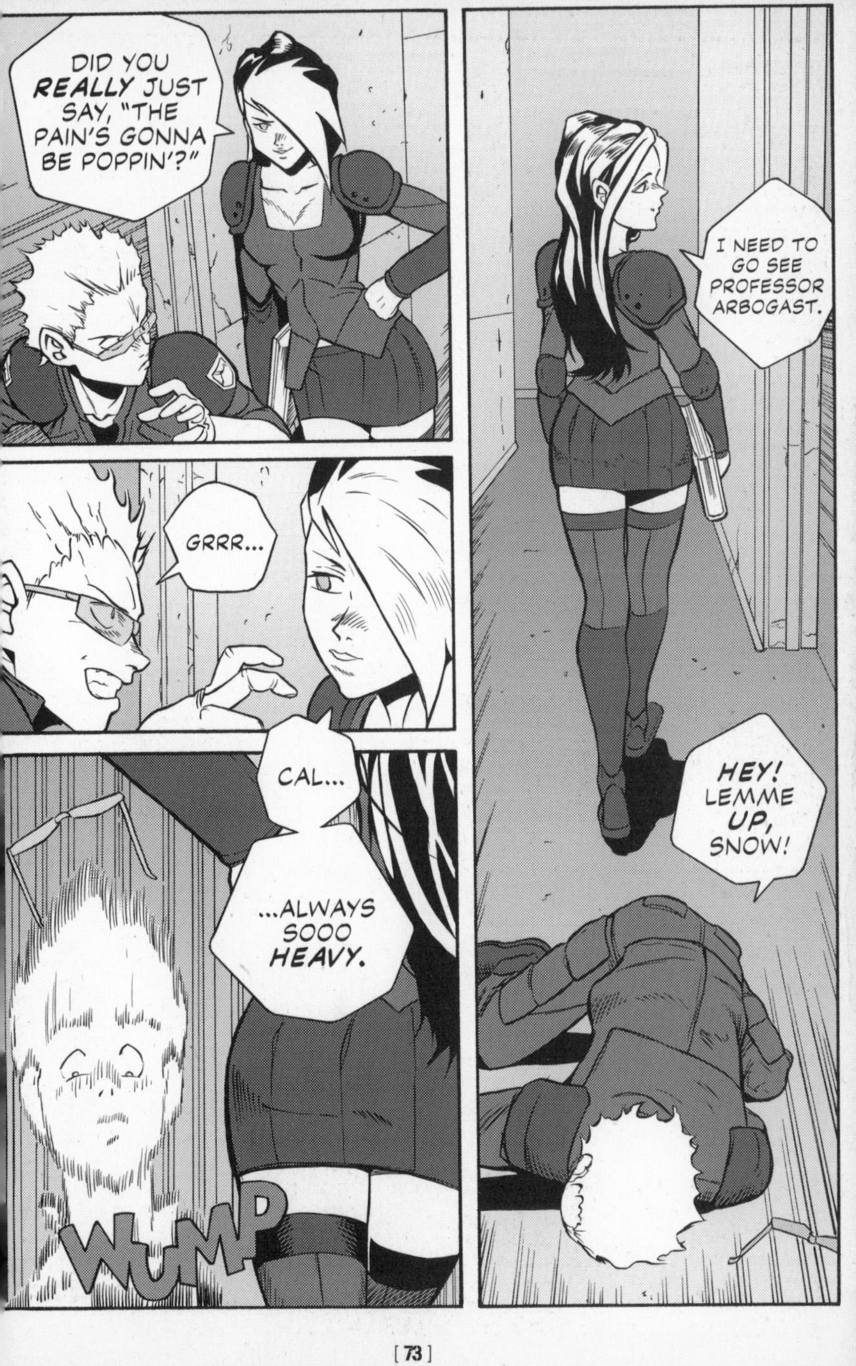
DID YOU **REALLY** JUST SAY, "THE PAIN'S GONNA BE POPPIN'?"
GRRR...
CAL...
...ALWAYS SOOO **HEAVY.**
WUMP
I NEED TO GO SEE PROFESSOR ARBOGAST.
HEY! LEMME **UP,** SNOW!

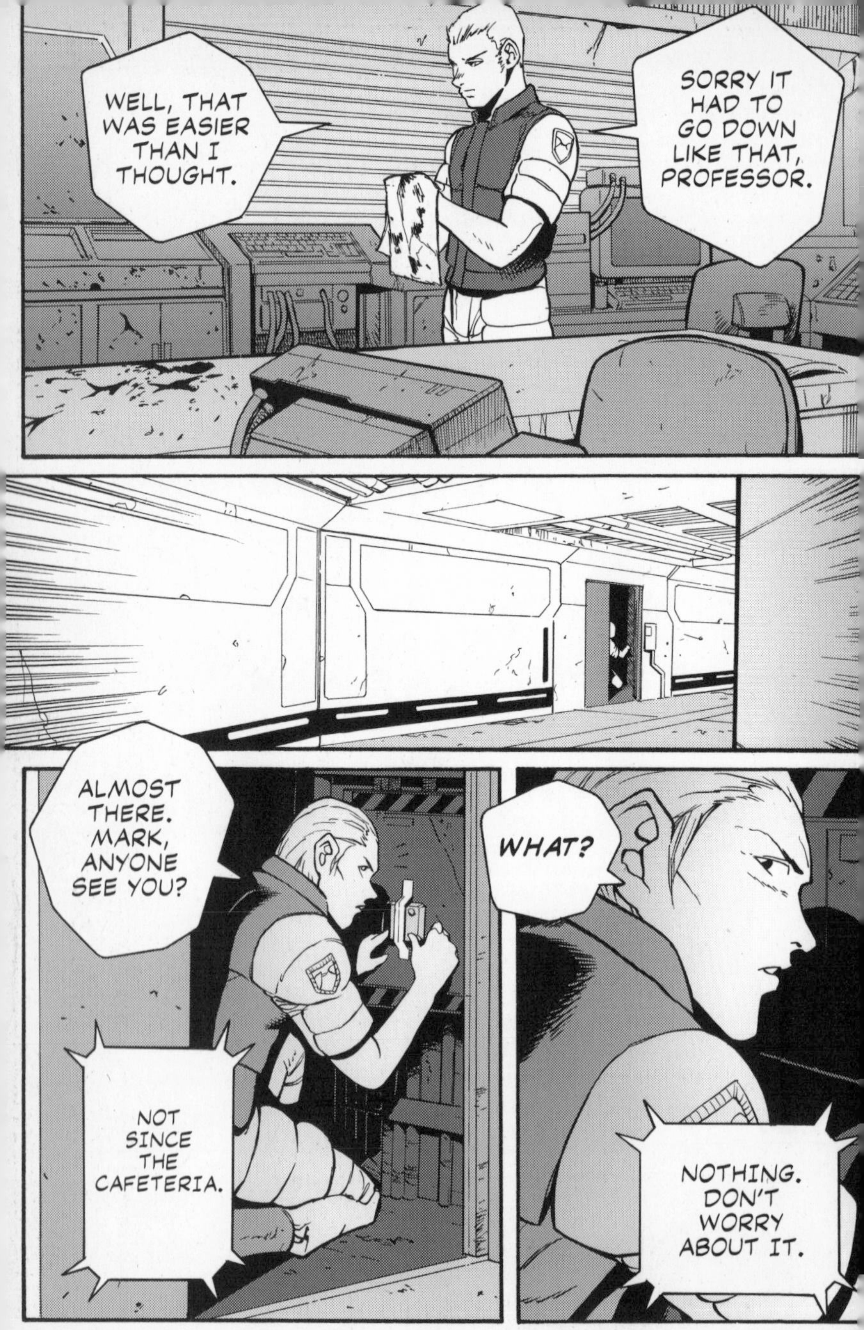
WELL, THAT WAS EASIER THAN I THOUGHT.
SORRY IT HAD TO GO DOWN LIKE THAT, PROFESSOR.
ALMOST THERE. MARK, ANYONE SEE YOU?
NOT SINCE THE CAFETERIA.
WHAT?
NOTHING. DON'T WORRY ABOUT IT.

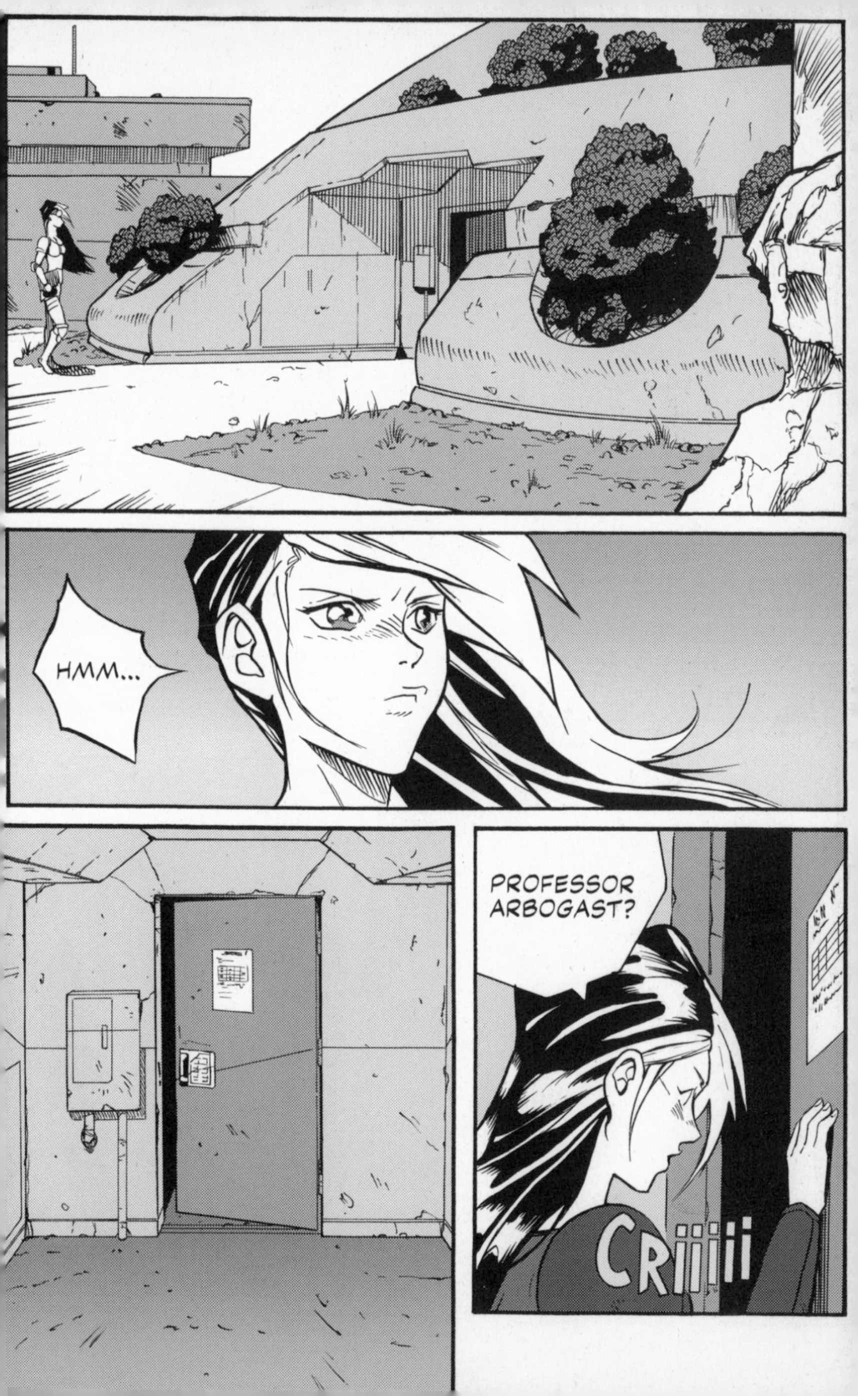
HMM...
PROFESSOR ARBOGAST?
CRiiiii

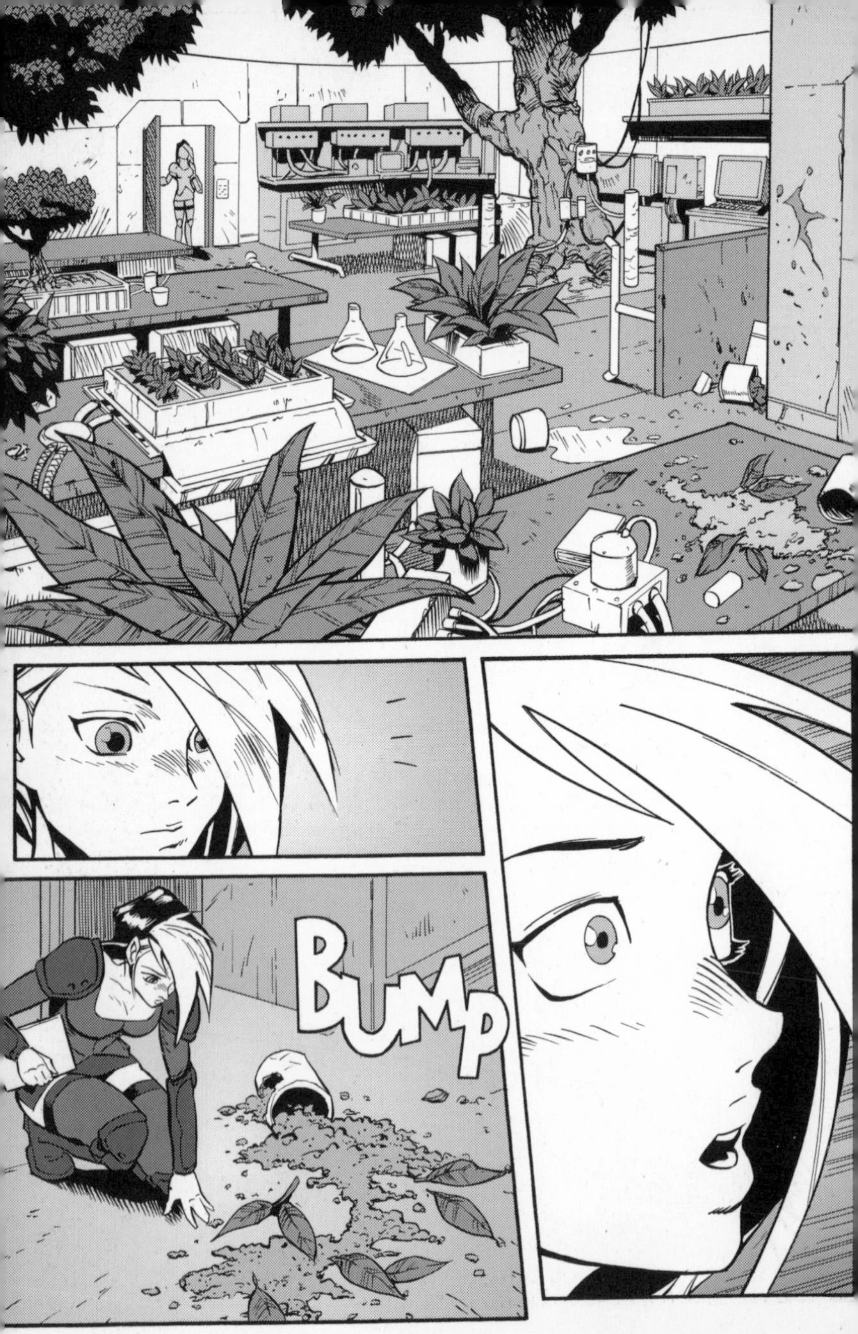
BUMP

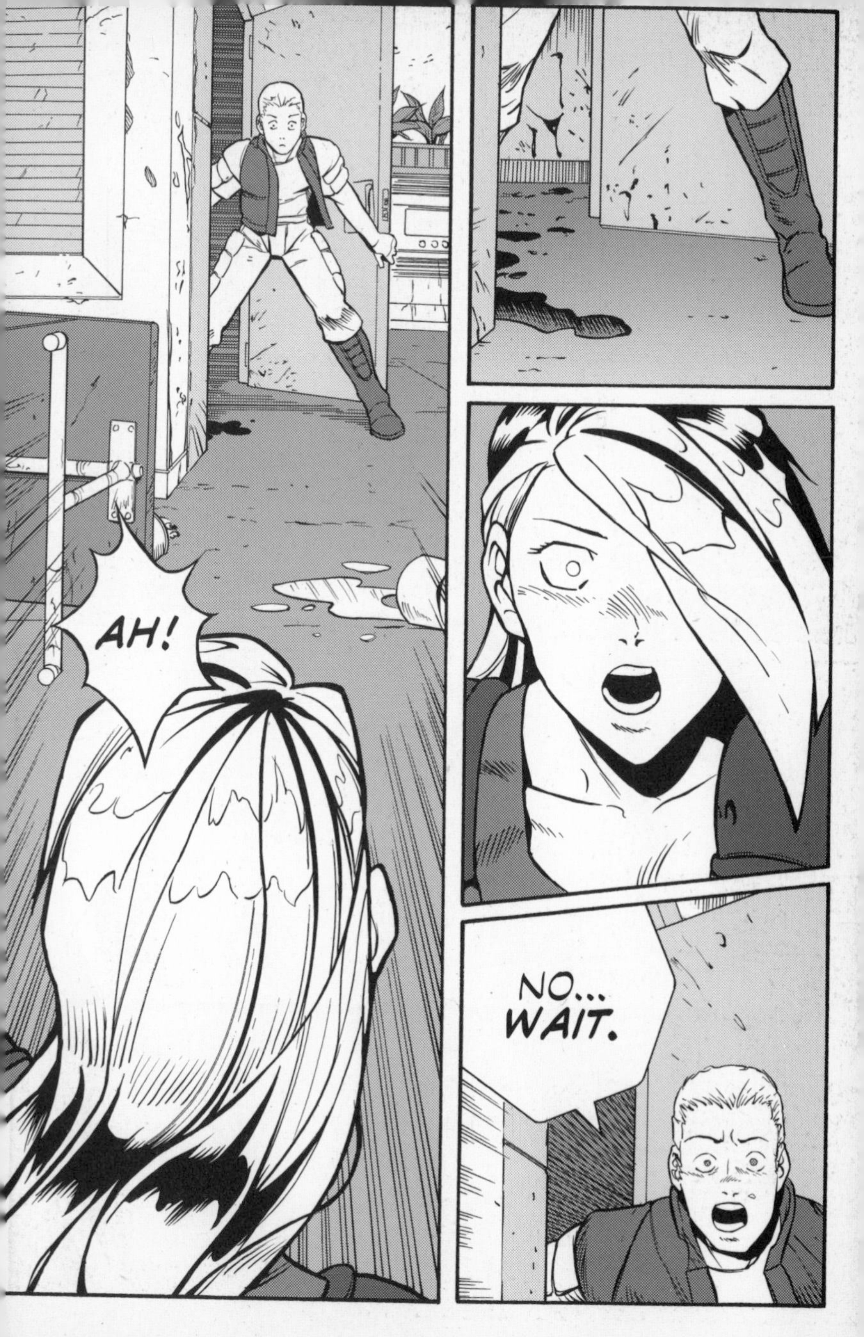
AH!
NO... WAIT.

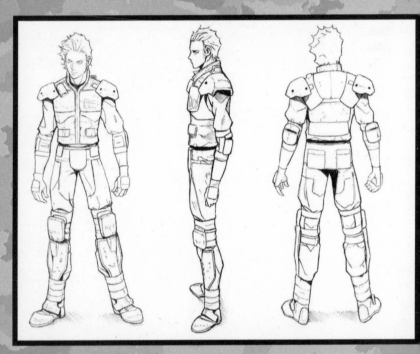

**EARLY DESIGN SKETCH FOR MARK LEIT:
A SHORTER, MORE MILITARY HAIR STYLE
WOULD EVENTUALLY REPLACE THIS LOOK.**

PSY★COMM

CHAPTER [5]

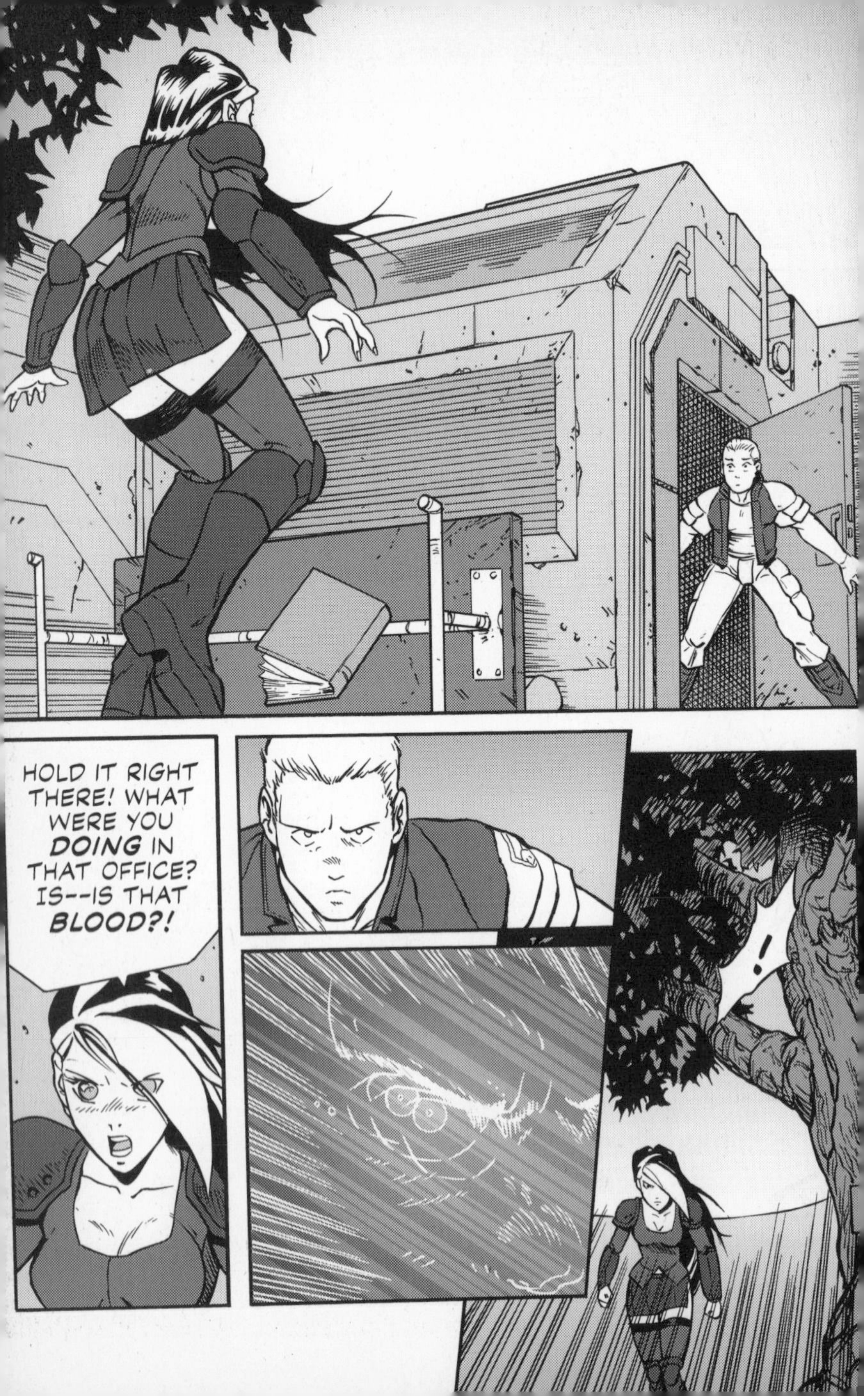
HOLD IT RIGHT THERE! WHAT WERE YOU **DOING** IN THAT OFFICE? IS--IS THAT **BLOOD?!**
!

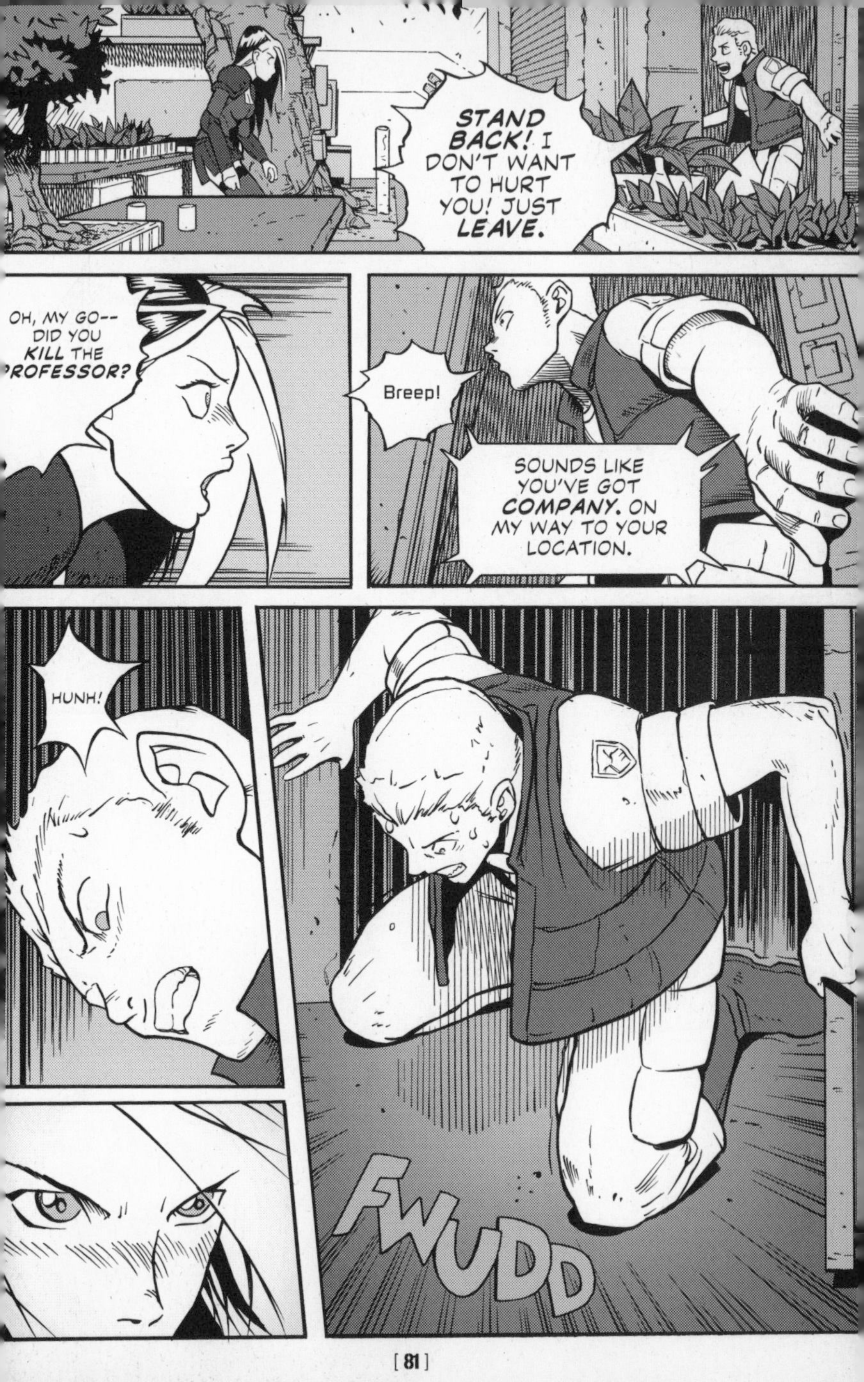
STAND BACK! I DON'T WANT TO HURT YOU! JUST LEAVE.
OH, MY GO-- DID YOU KILL THE PROFESSOR?
Breep!
SOUNDS LIKE YOU'VE GOT COMPANY. ON MY WAY TO YOUR LOCATION.
HUNH!
FWUDD

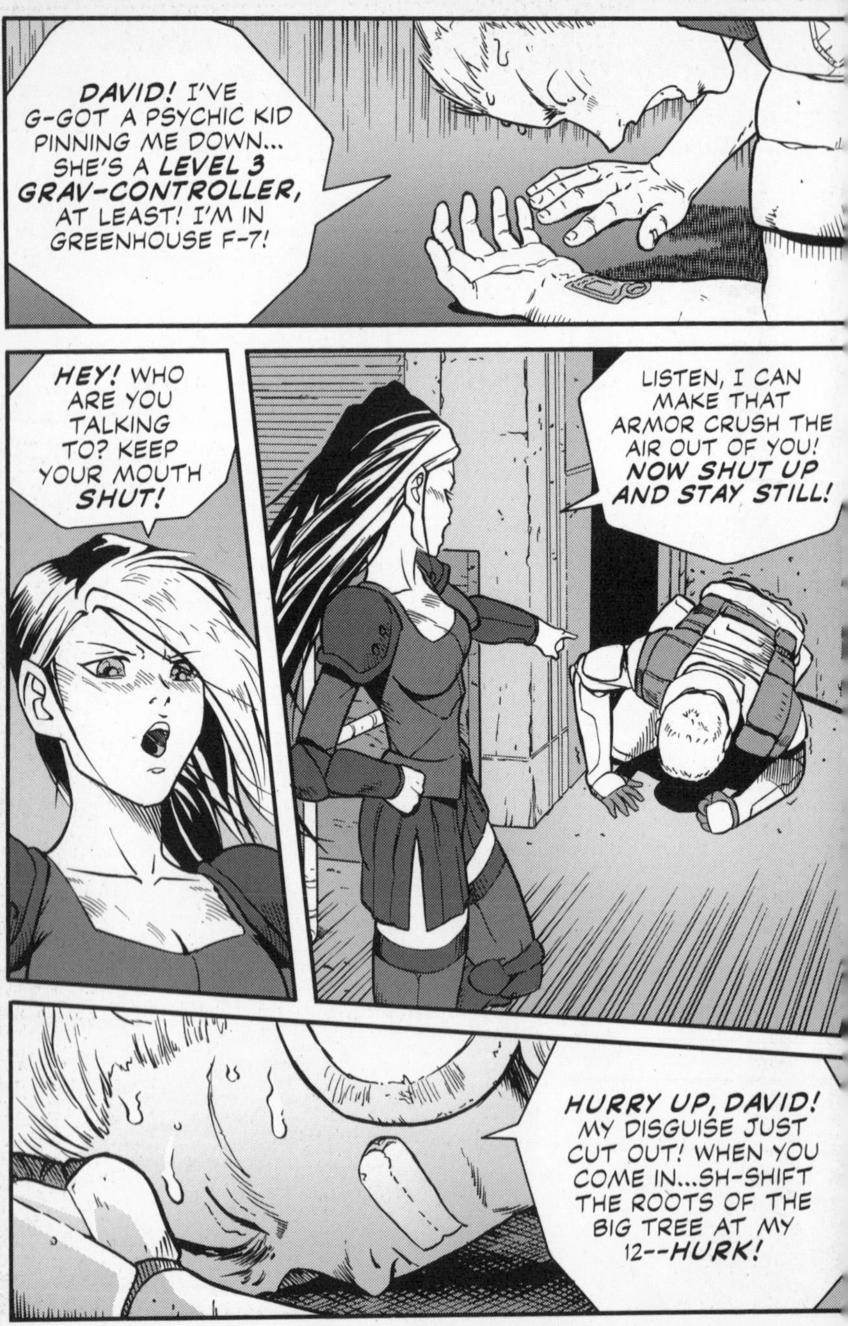
DAVID! I'VE G-GOT A PSYCHIC KID PINNING ME DOWN... SHE'S A LEVEL 3 GRAV-CONTROLLER, AT LEAST! I'M IN GREENHOUSE F-7!
HEY! WHO ARE YOU TALKING TO? KEEP YOUR MOUTH SHUT!
LISTEN, I CAN MAKE THAT ARMOR CRUSH THE AIR OUT OF YOU! NOW SHUT UP AND STAY STILL!
HURRY UP, DAVID! MY DISGUISE JUST CUT OUT! WHEN YOU COME IN...SH-SHIFT THE ROOTS OF THE BIG TREE AT MY 12--HURK!

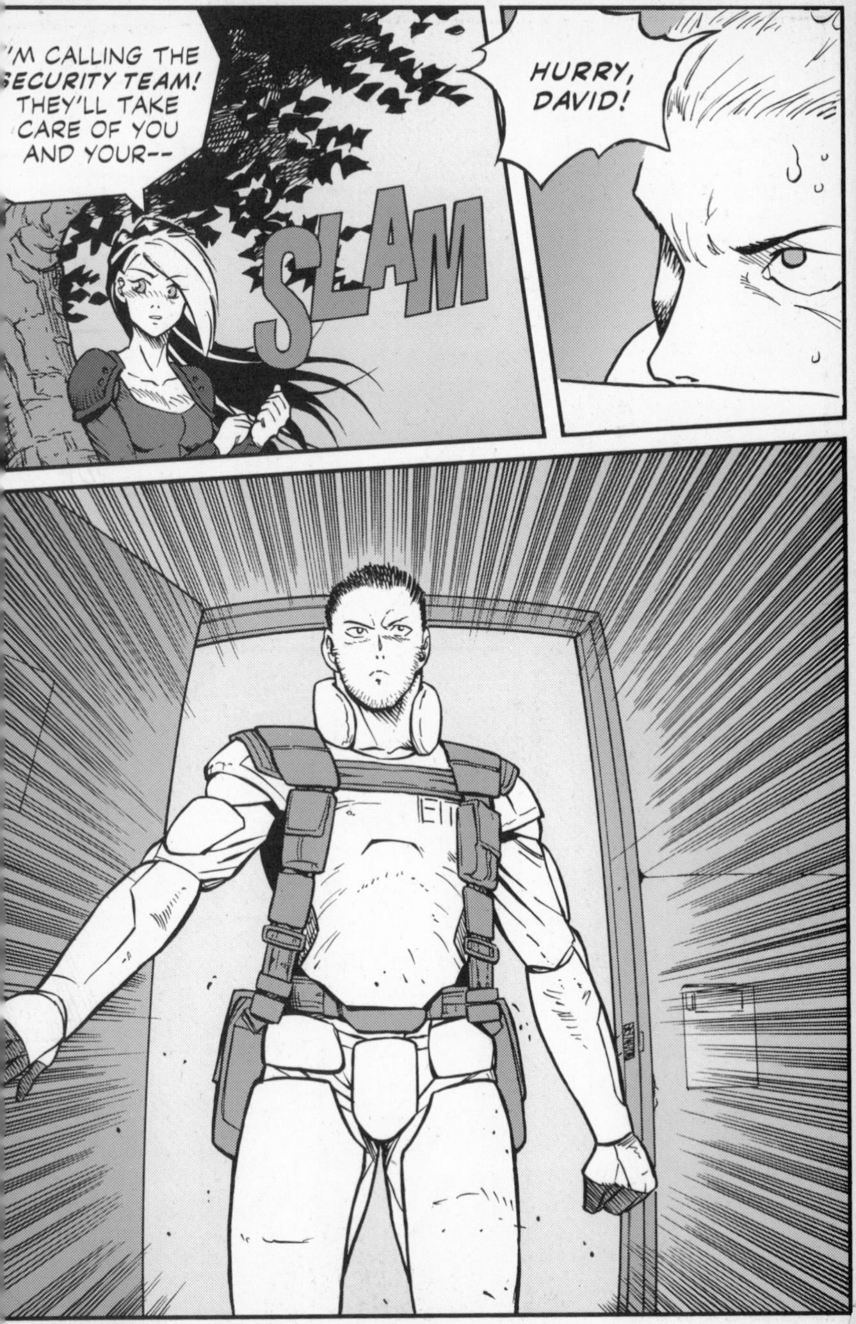
'M CALLING THE
SECURITY TEAM!
THEY'LL TAKE
CARE OF YOU
AND YOUR--
SLAM
HURRY,
DAVID!

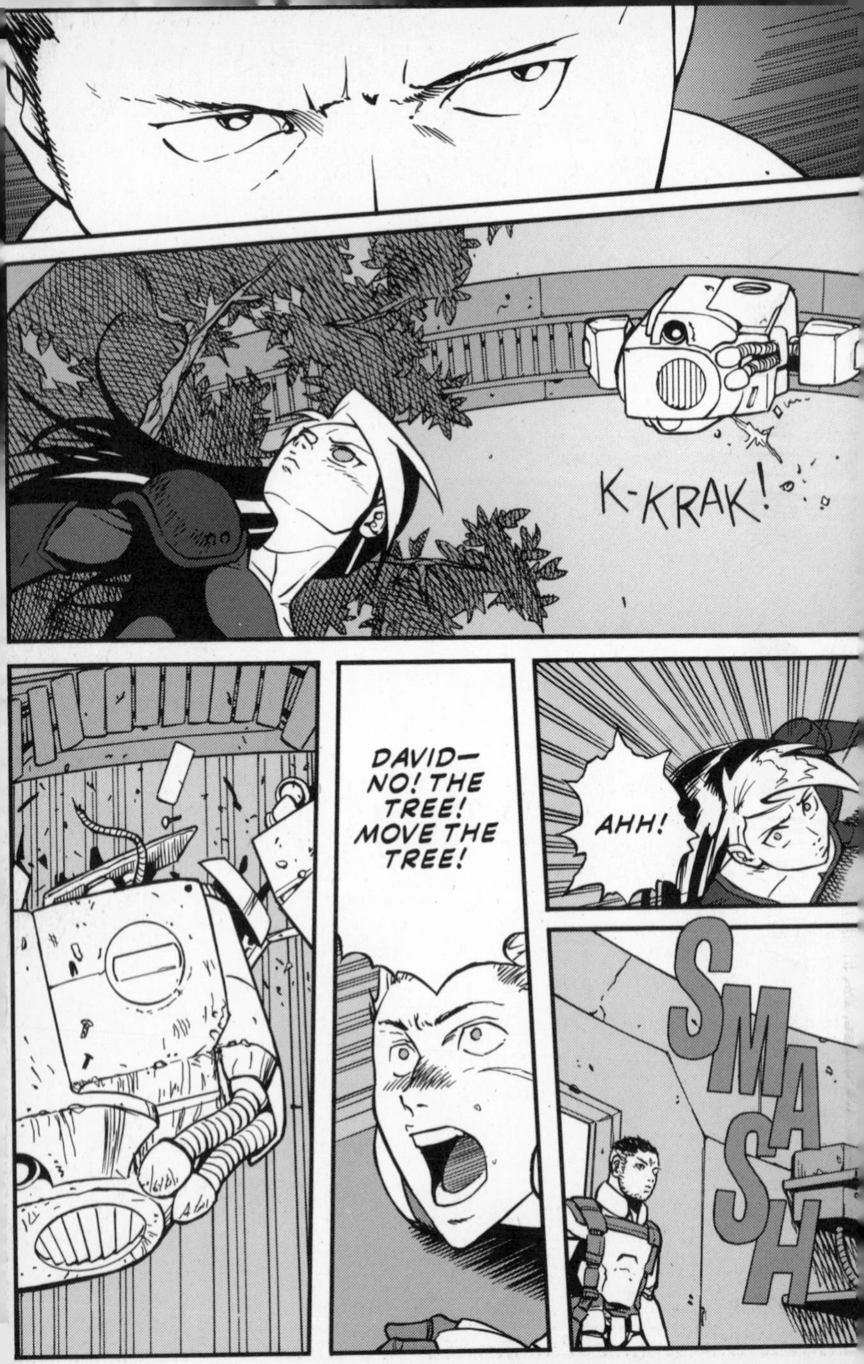
K-KRAK!
DAVID— NO! THE TREE! MOVE THE TREE!
AHH!
SMASH

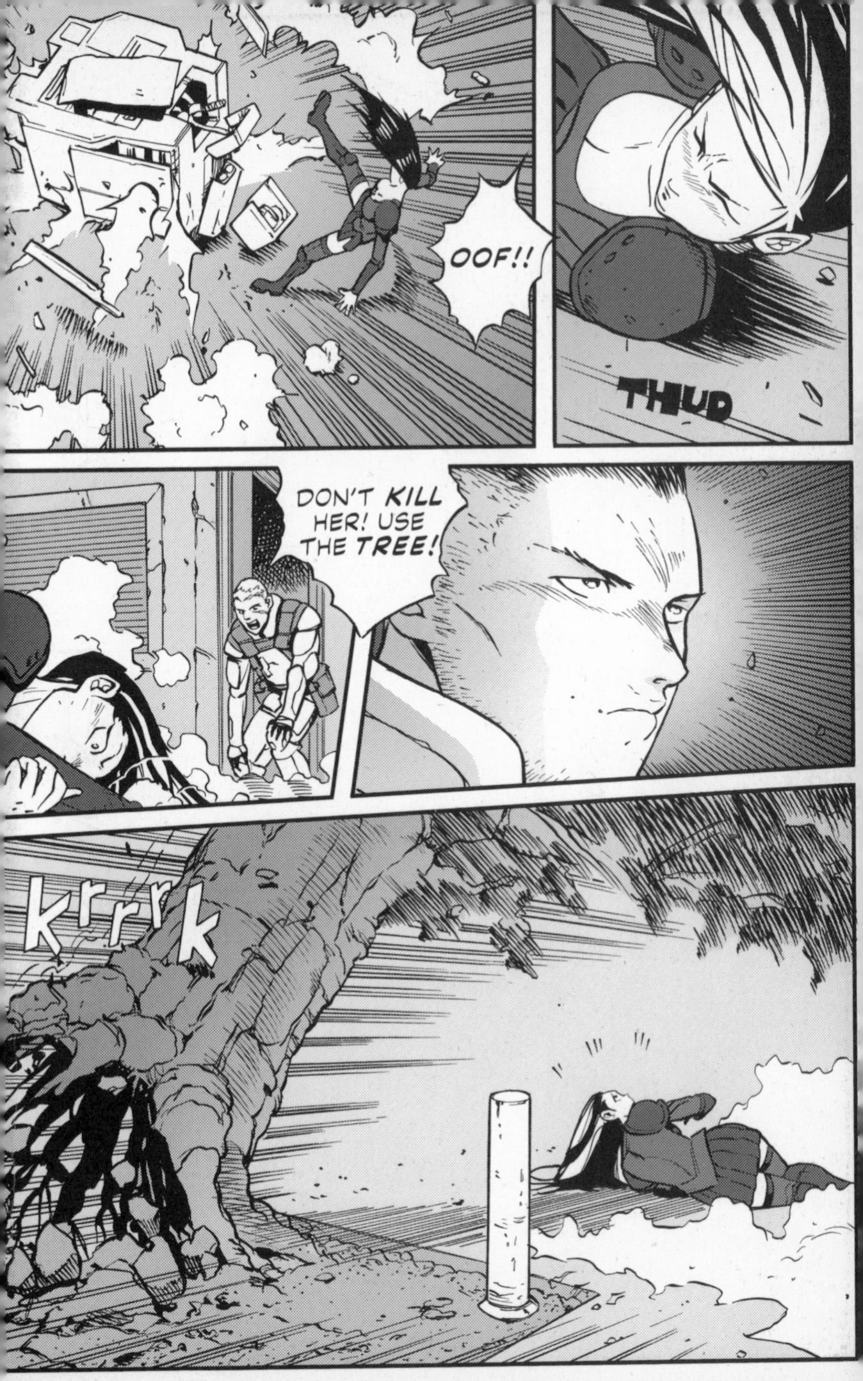
OOF!!
THUD
DON'T KILL HER! USE THE TREE!
krrrk

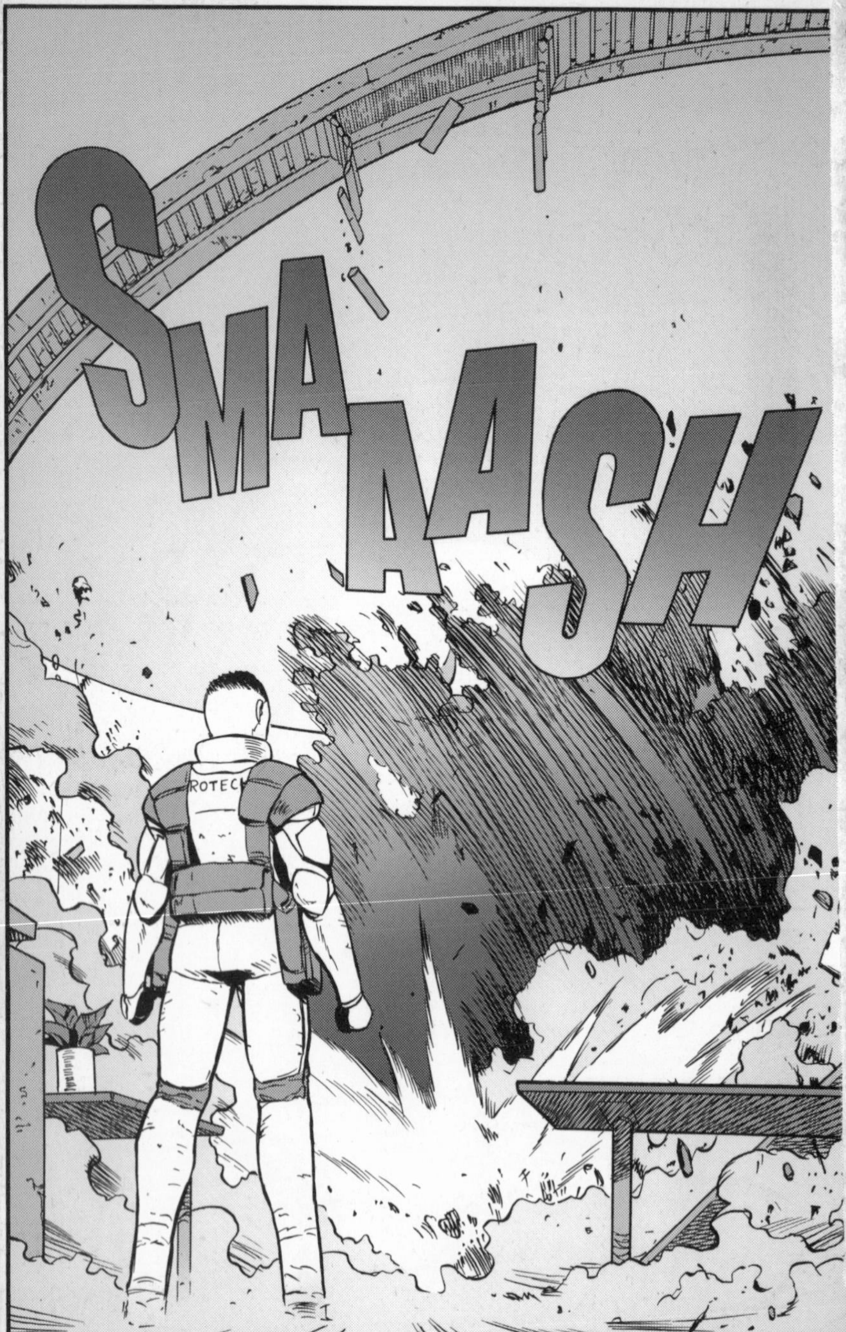
SMAAASH
ROTECH

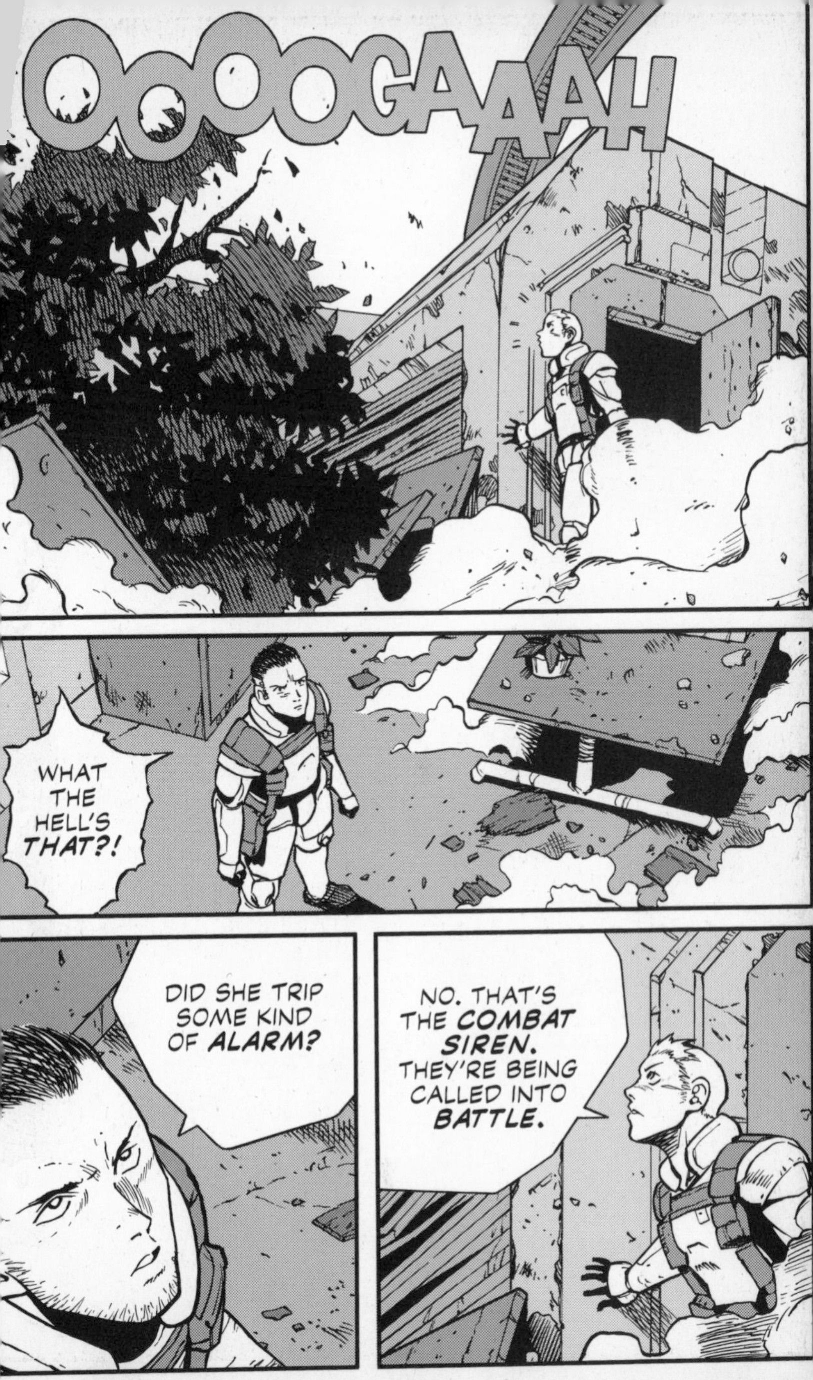
OOOOGAAAAH
WHAT THE HELL'S *THAT?!*
DID SHE TRIP SOME KIND OF *ALARM?*
NO. THAT'S THE *COMBAT SIREN.* THEY'RE BEING CALLED INTO *BATTLE.*

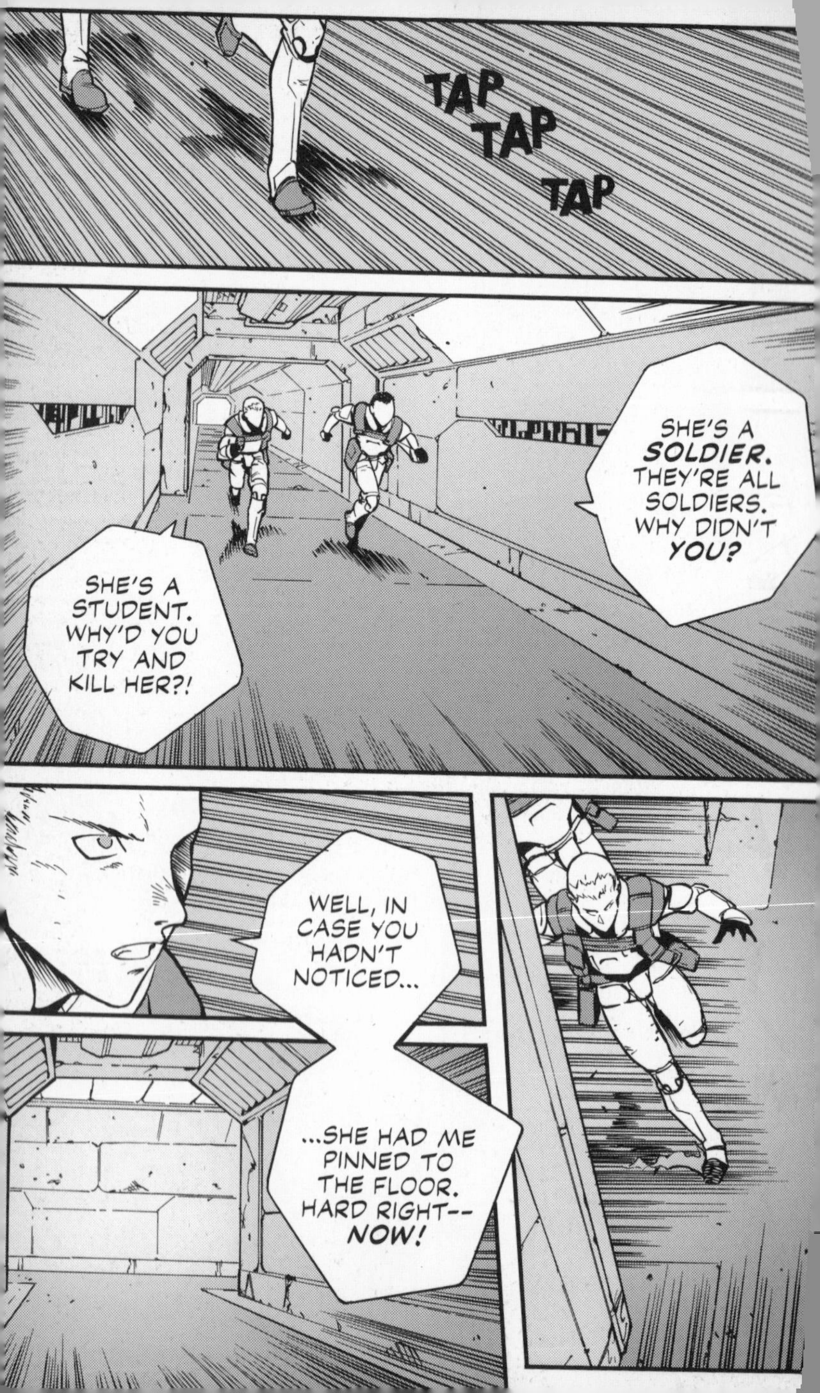
TAP TAP TAP
SHE'S A STUDENT. WHY'D YOU TRY AND KILL HER?!
SHE'S A *SOLDIER.* THEY'RE ALL SOLDIERS. WHY DIDN'T *YOU?*
WELL, IN CASE YOU HADN'T NOTICED...
...SHE HAD ME PINNED TO THE FLOOR. HARD RIGHT-- *NOW!*

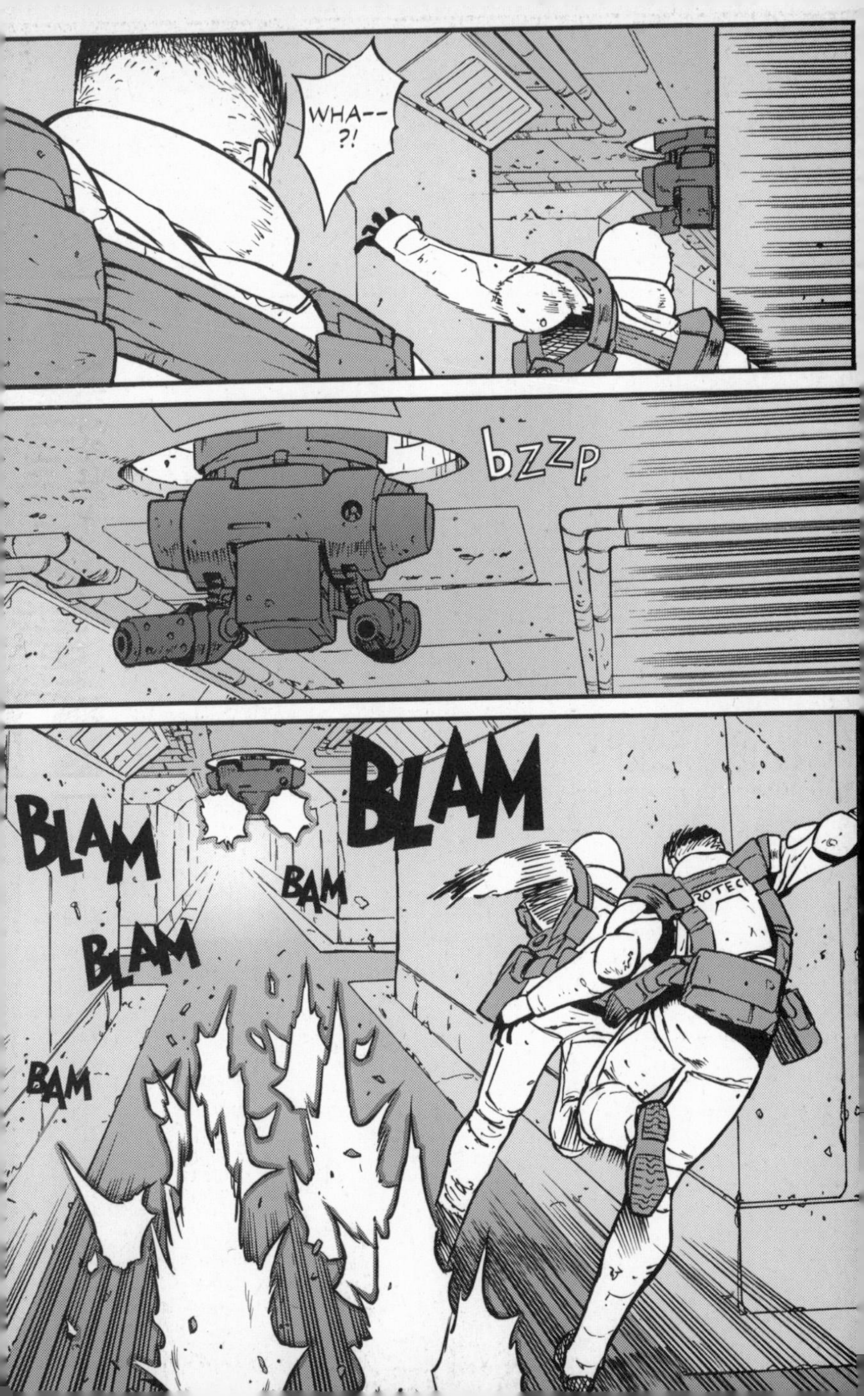

WHA-- ?!
bzzp
BLAM
BLAM
BAM
BLAM
BAM
ROTEC

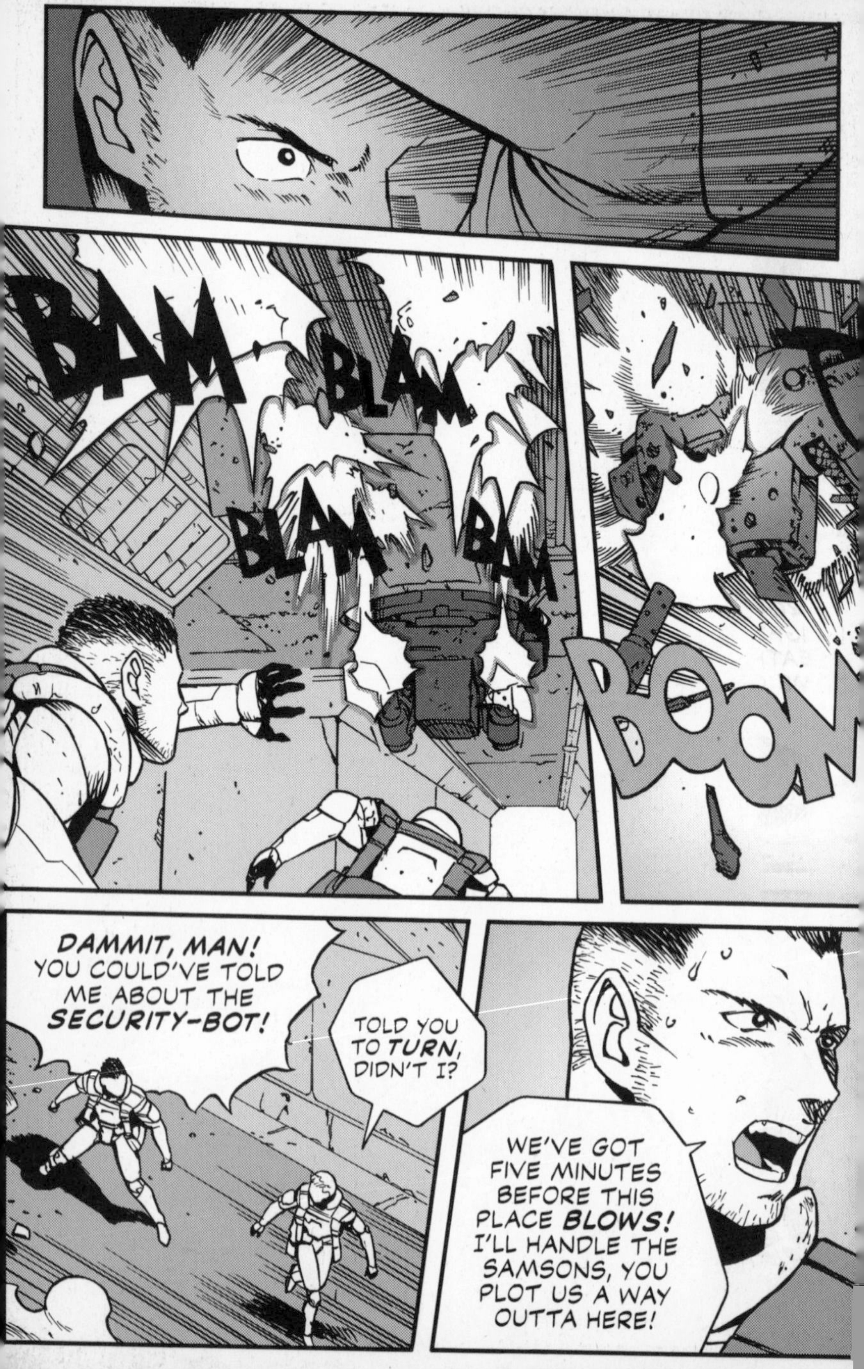
BAM
BLAM
BLAM
BAM
BOOM
DAMMIT, MAN! YOU COULD'VE TOLD ME ABOUT THE SECURITY-BOT!
TOLD YOU TO TURN, DIDN'T I?
WE'VE GOT FIVE MINUTES BEFORE THIS PLACE BLOWS! I'LL HANDLE THE SAMSONS, YOU PLOT US A WAY OUTTA HERE!

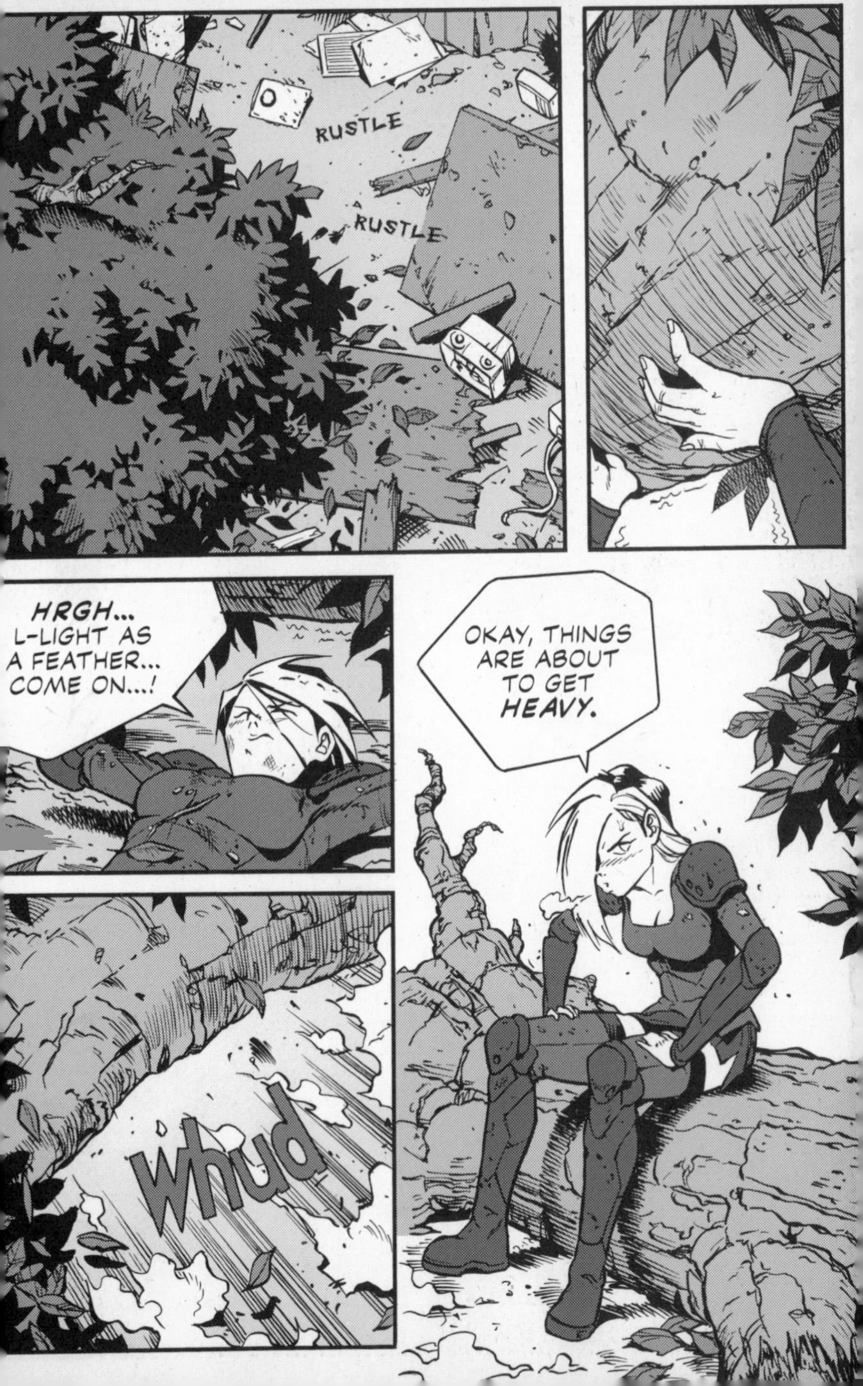
RUSTLE
RUSTLE
HRGH... L-LIGHT AS A FEATHER... COME ON...!
OKAY, THINGS ARE ABOUT TO GET HEAVY.
whud

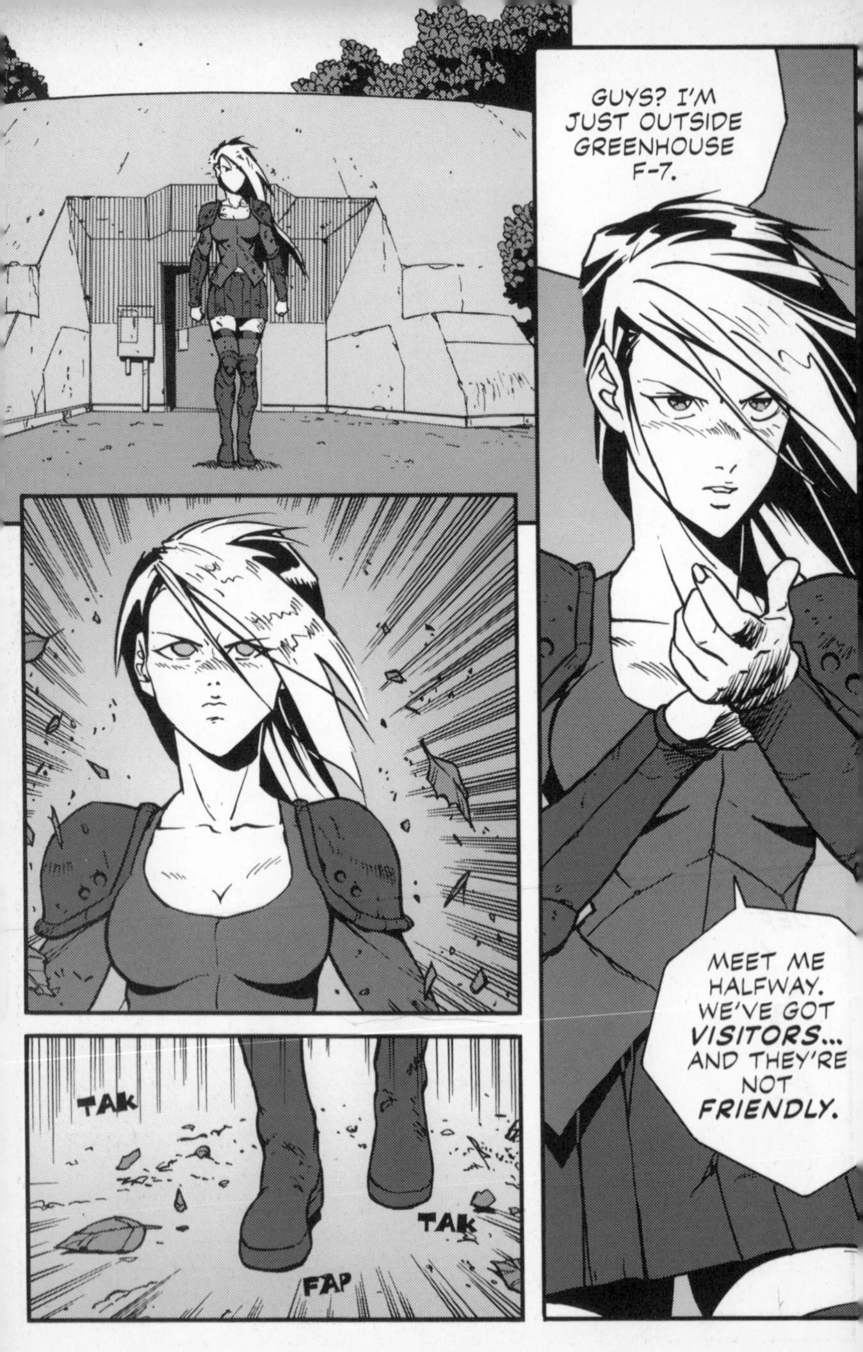
GUYS? I'M JUST OUTSIDE GREENHOUSE F-7.
TAK
TAK
FAP
MEET ME HALFWAY. WE'VE GOT *VISITORS*... AND THEY'RE NOT *FRIENDLY*.

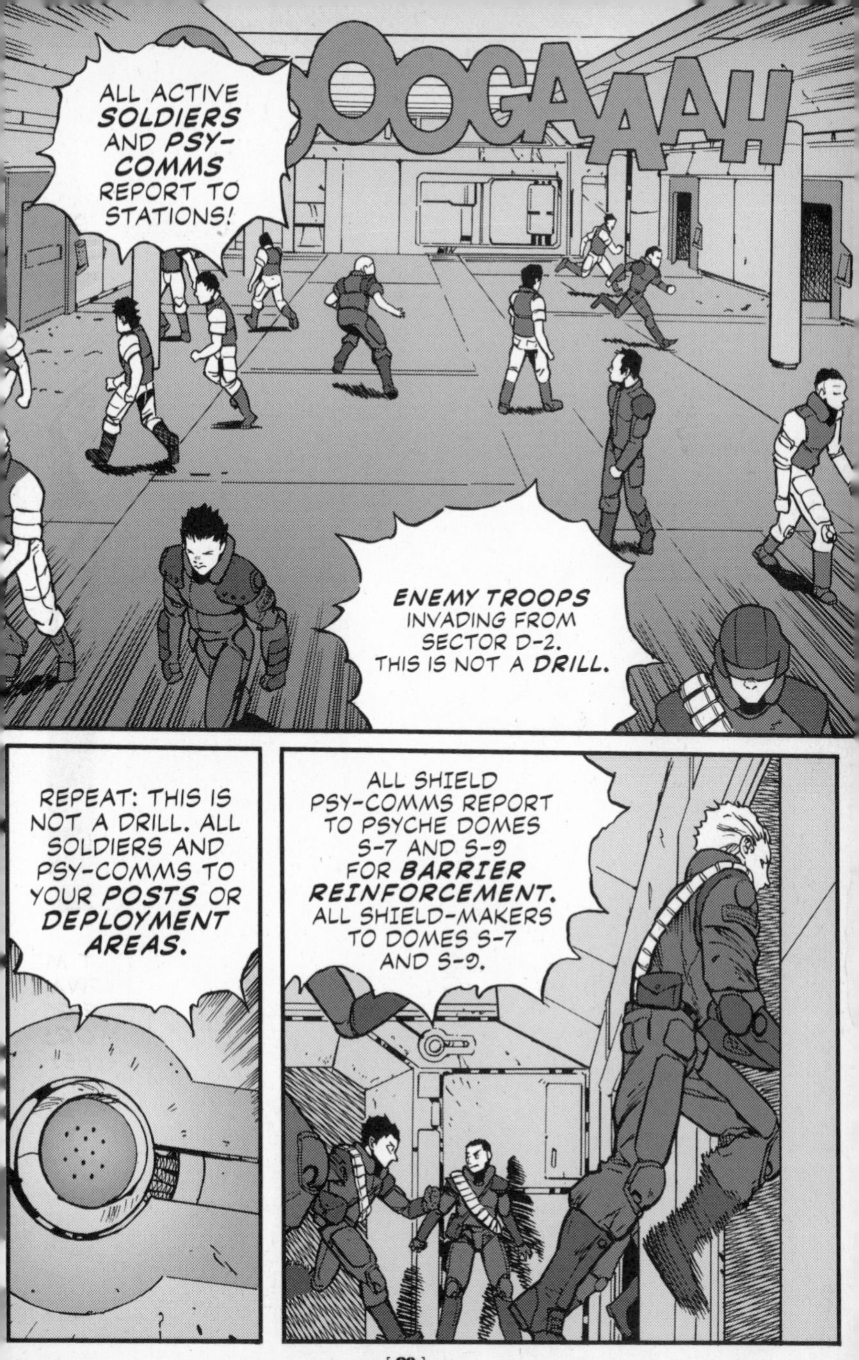
ALL ACTIVE SOLDIERS AND PSY-COMMS REPORT TO STATIONS!
OOGAAAH
ENEMY TROOPS INVADING FROM SECTOR D-2. THIS IS NOT A DRILL.
REPEAT: THIS IS NOT A DRILL. ALL SOLDIERS AND PSY-COMMS TO YOUR POSTS OR DEPLOYMENT AREAS.
ALL SHIELD PSY-COMMS REPORT TO PSYCHE DOMES S-7 AND S-9 FOR BARRIER REINFORCEMENT. ALL SHIELD-MAKERS TO DOMES S-7 AND S-9.

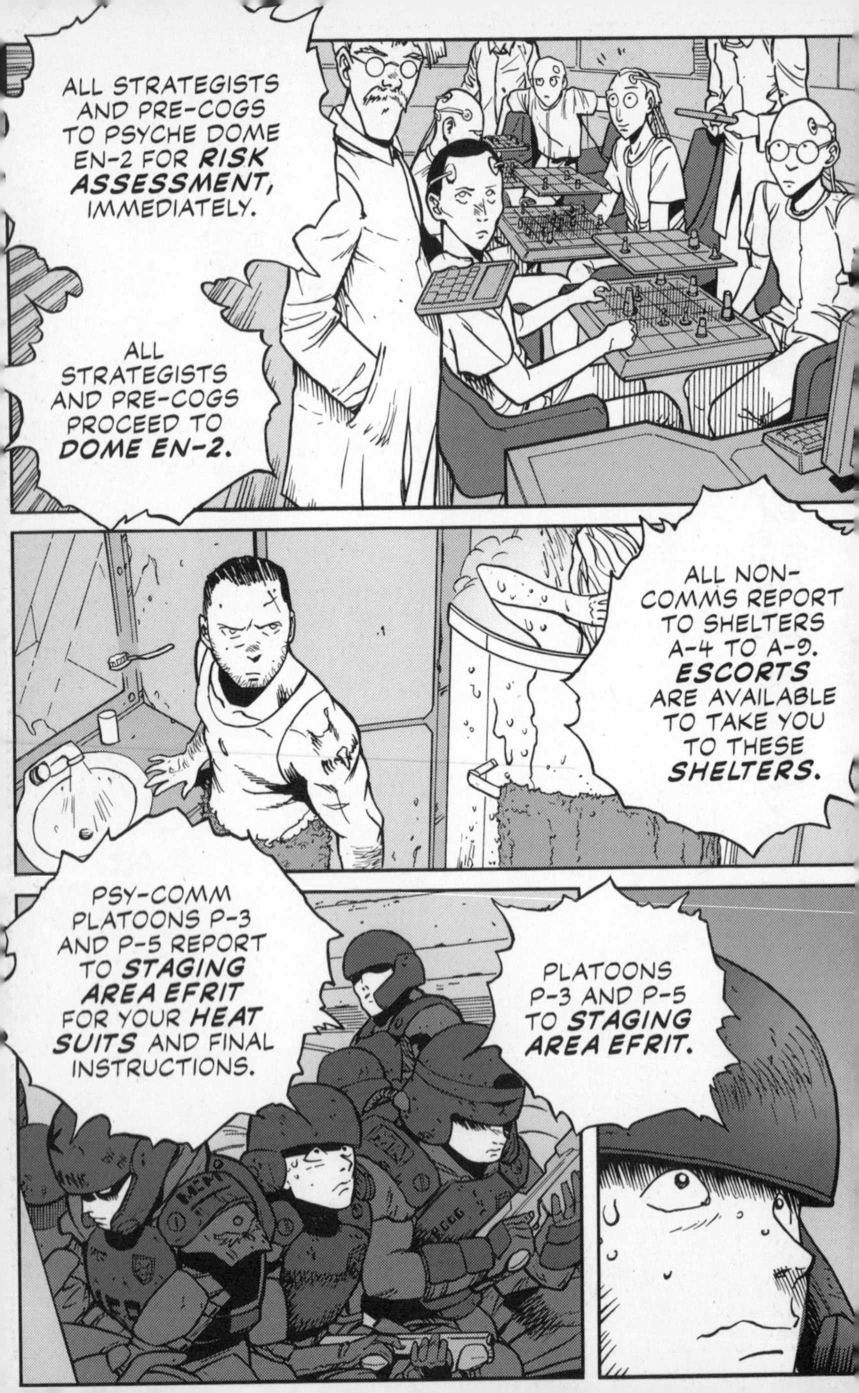
ALL STRATEGISTS AND PRE-COGS TO PSYCHE DOME EN-2 FOR RISK ASSESSMENT, IMMEDIATELY.
ALL STRATEGISTS AND PRE-COGS PROCEED TO DOME EN-2.
ALL NON-COMMS REPORT TO SHELTERS A-4 TO A-9. ESCORTS ARE AVAILABLE TO TAKE YOU TO THESE SHELTERS.
PSY-COMM PLATOONS P-3 AND P-5 REPORT TO STAGING AREA EFRIT FOR YOUR HEAT SUITS AND FINAL INSTRUCTIONS.
PLATOONS P-3 AND P-5 TO STAGING AREA EFRIT.

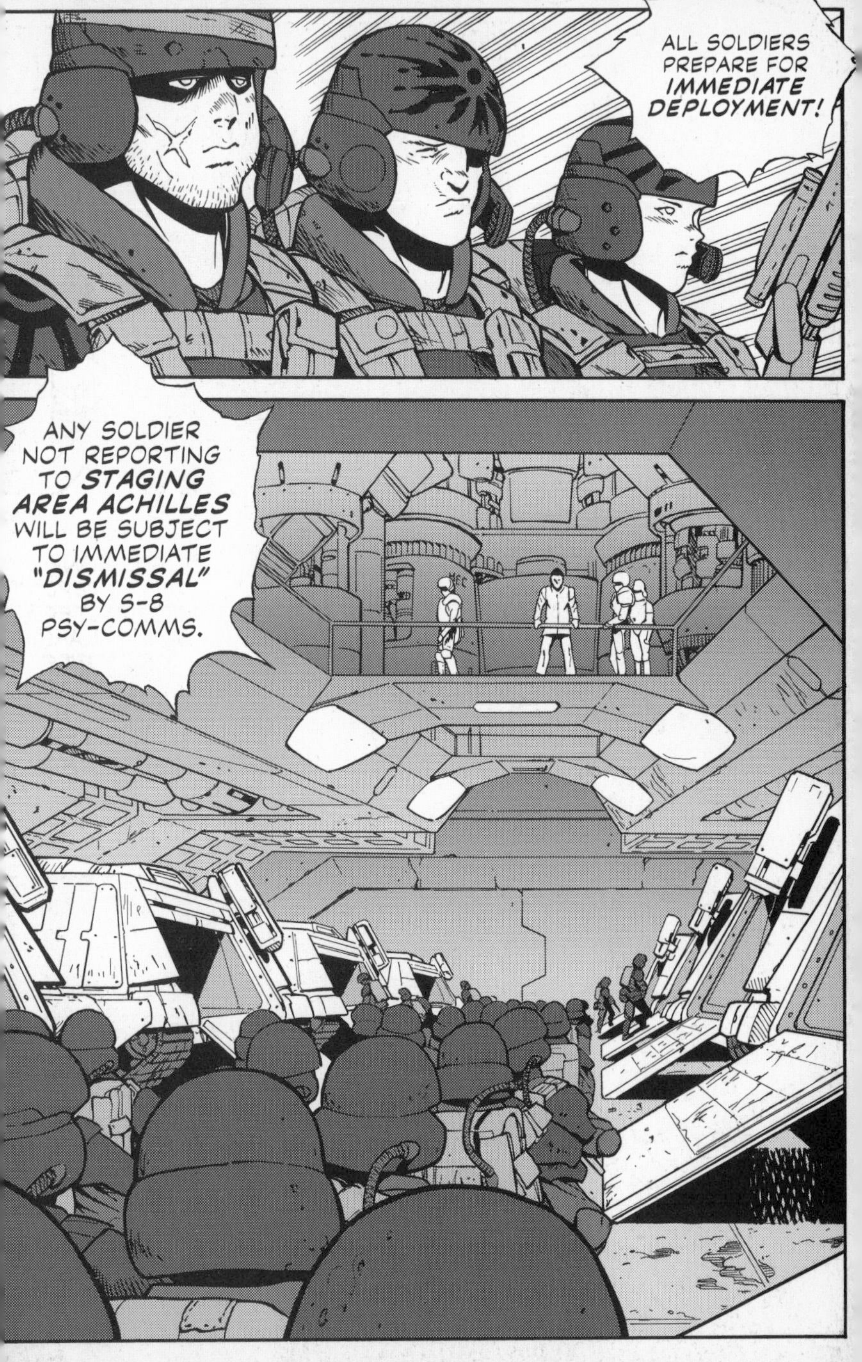

ALL SOLDIERS PREPARE FOR IMMEDIATE DEPLOYMENT!
ANY SOLDIER NOT REPORTING TO STAGING AREA ACHILLES WILL BE SUBJECT TO IMMEDIATE "DISMISSAL" BY S-8 PSY-COMMS.

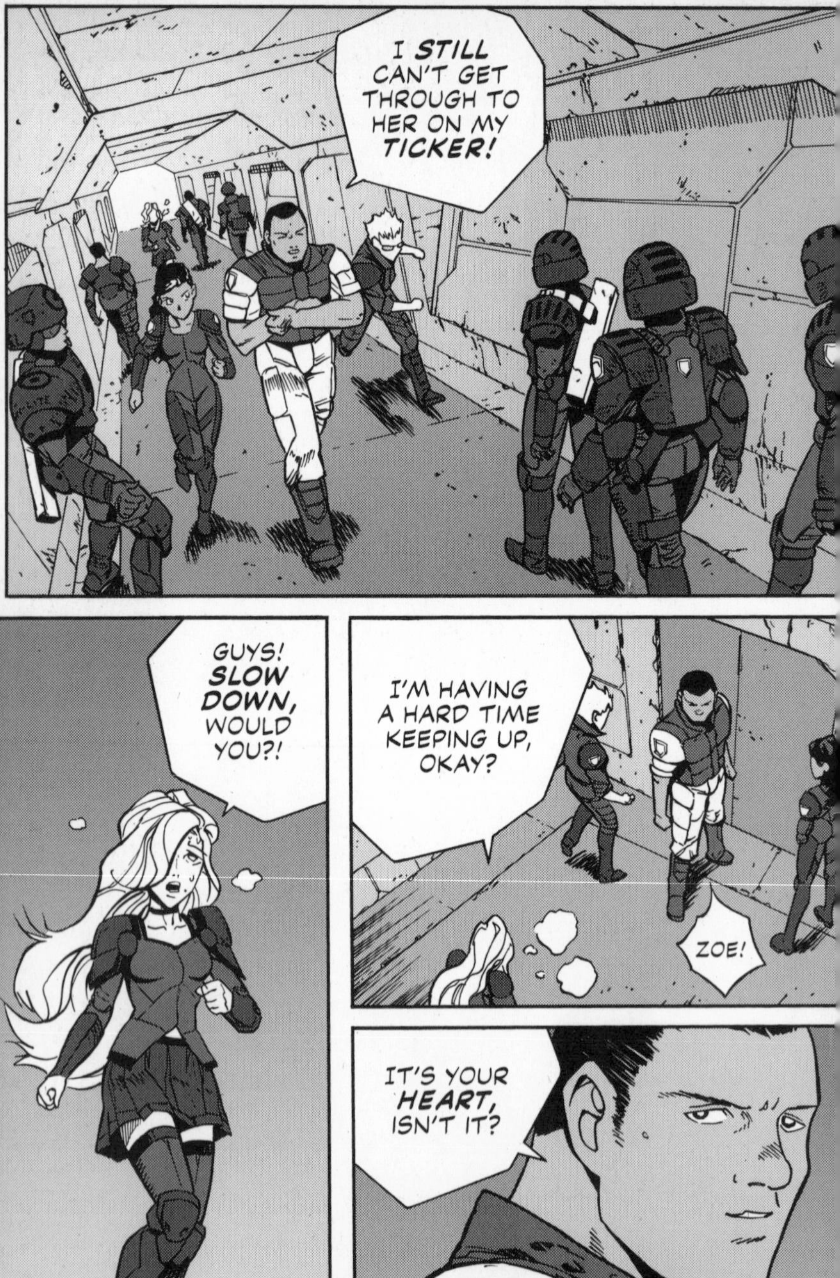
I STILL CAN'T GET THROUGH TO HER ON MY TICKER!
GUYS! SLOW DOWN, WOULD YOU?!
I'M HAVING A HARD TIME KEEPING UP, OKAY?
ZOE!
IT'S YOUR HEART, ISN'T IT?

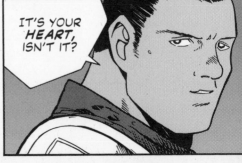

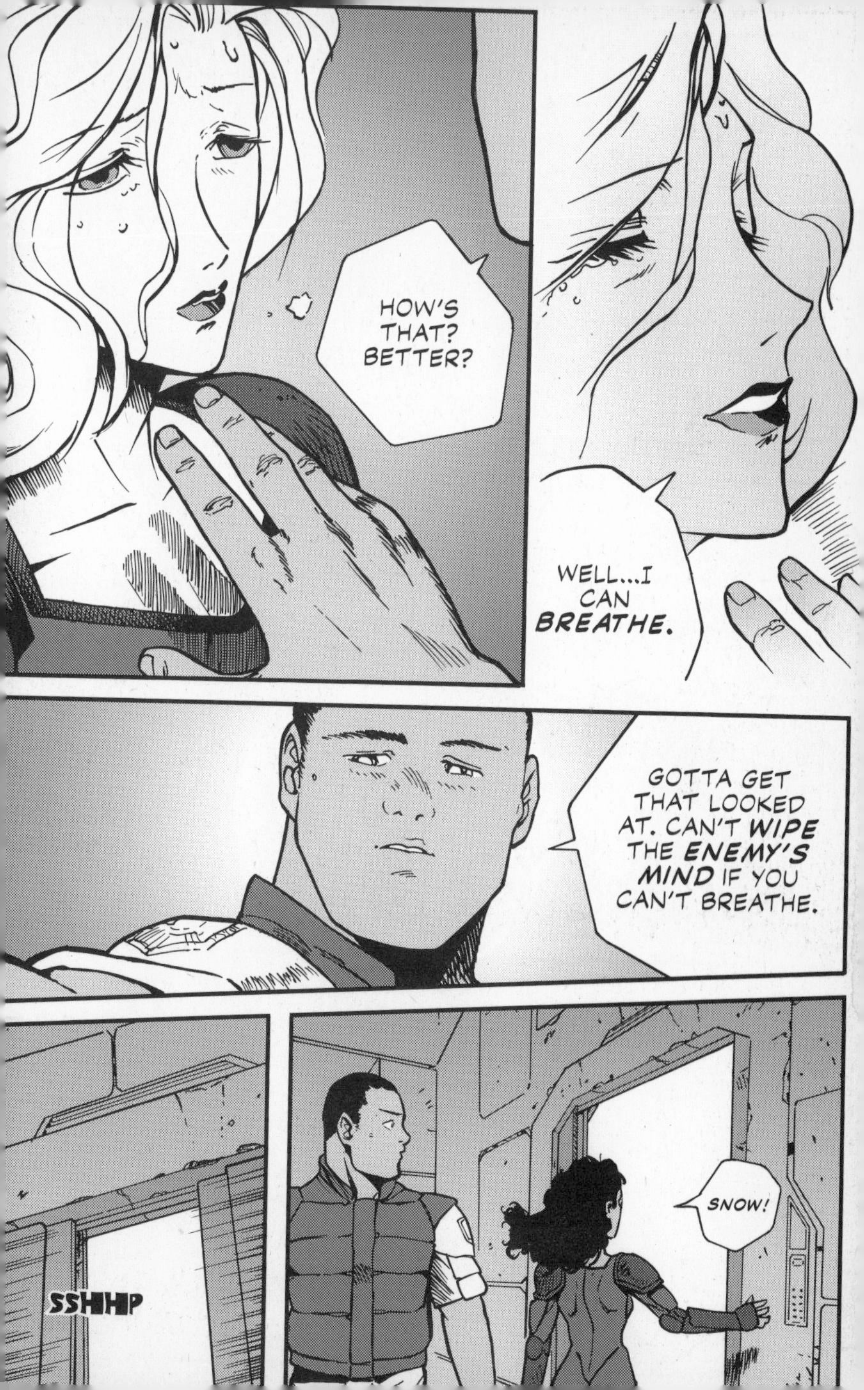
HOW'S THAT? BETTER?
WELL...I CAN BREATHE.
GOTTA GET THAT LOOKED AT. CAN'T WIPE THE ENEMY'S MIND IF YOU CAN'T BREATHE.
SSHHP
SNOW!

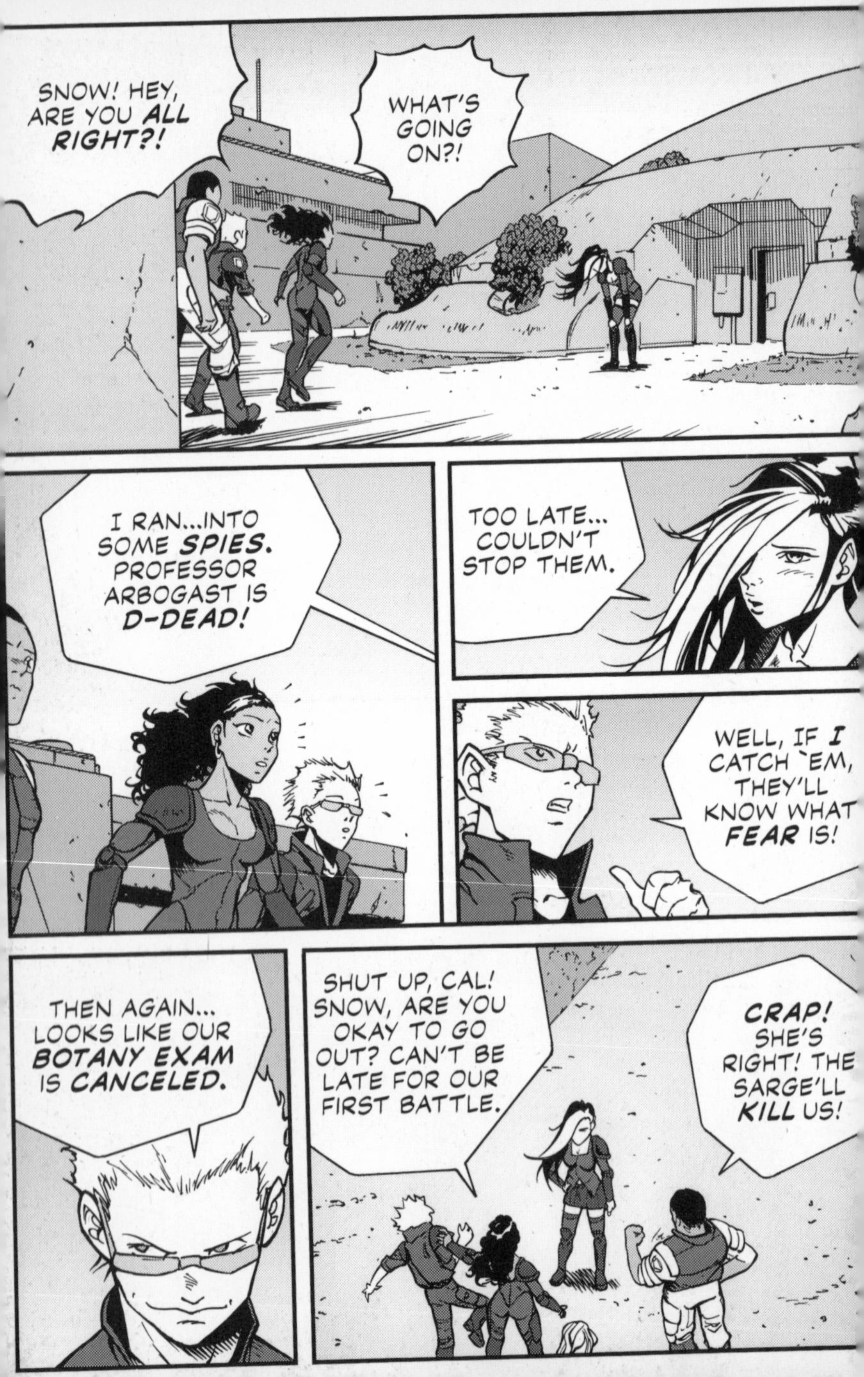
SNOW! HEY, ARE YOU ALL RIGHT?!
WHAT'S GOING ON?!
I RAN...INTO SOME SPIES. PROFESSOR ARBOGAST IS D-DEAD!
TOO LATE... COULDN'T STOP THEM.
WELL, IF I CATCH `EM, THEY'LL KNOW WHAT FEAR IS!
THEN AGAIN... LOOKS LIKE OUR BOTANY EXAM IS CANCELED.
SHUT UP, CAL! SNOW, ARE YOU OKAY TO GO OUT? CAN'T BE LATE FOR OUR FIRST BATTLE.
CRAP! SHE'S RIGHT! THE SARGE'LL KILL US!

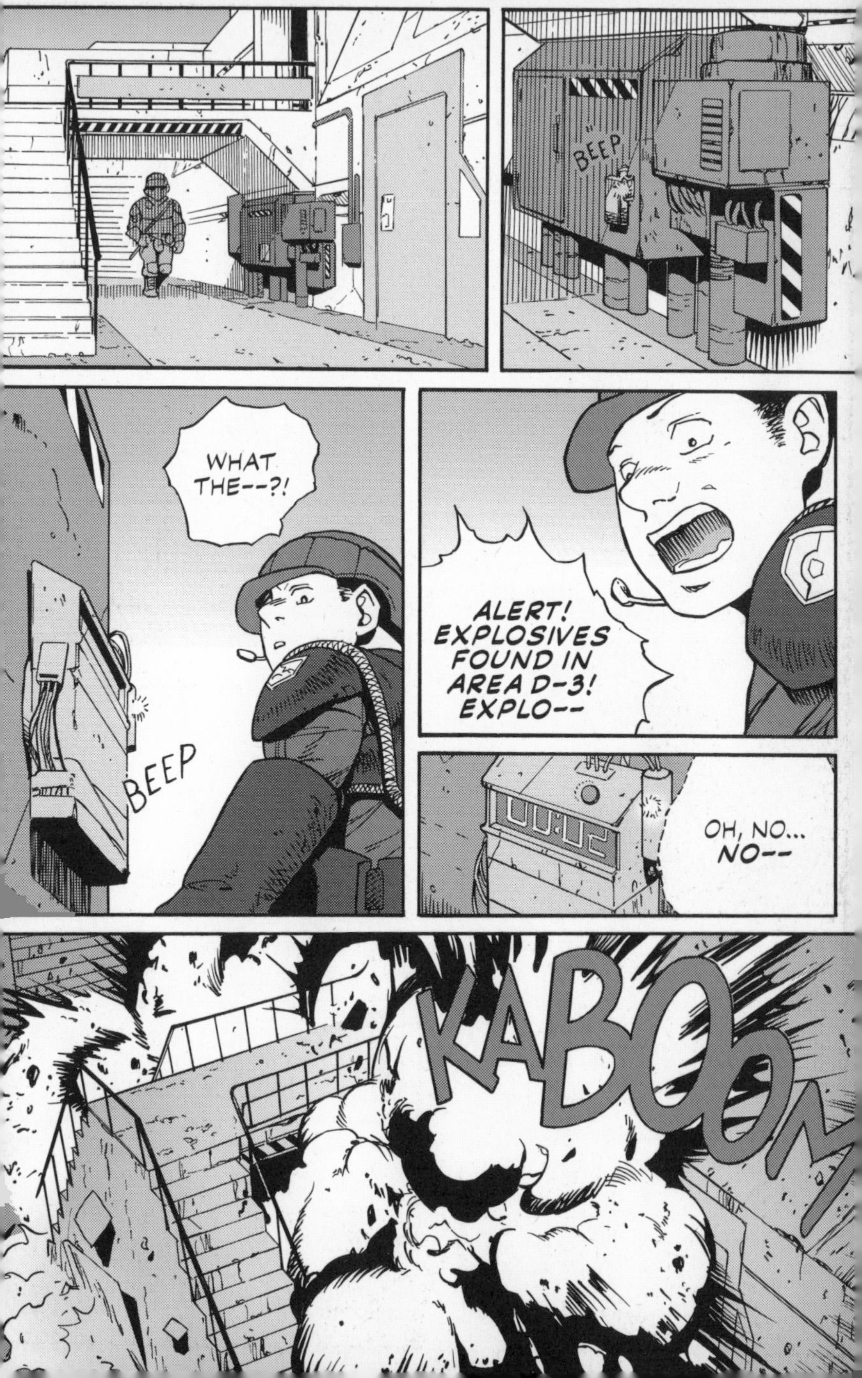
BEEP
WHAT THE--?!
BEEP
ALERT! EXPLOSIVES FOUND IN AREA D-3! EXPLO--
OH, NO... NO--
KABOOM

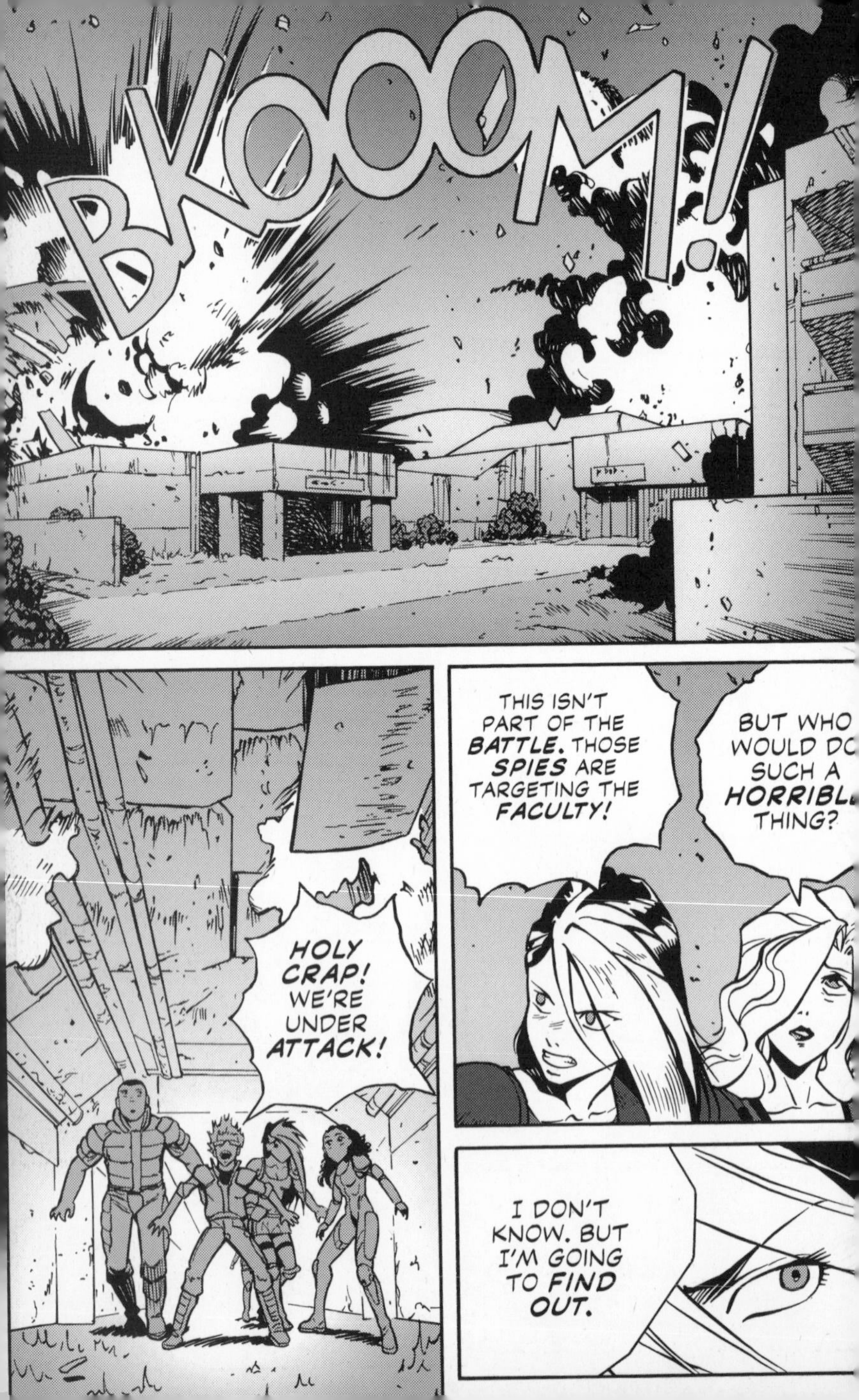
BKOOM!!
HOLY CRAP! WE'RE UNDER ATTACK!
THIS ISN'T PART OF THE BATTLE. THOSE SPIES ARE TARGETING THE FACULTY!
BUT WHO WOULD DO SUCH A HORRIBL THING?
I DON'T KNOW. BUT I'M GOING TO FIND OUT.

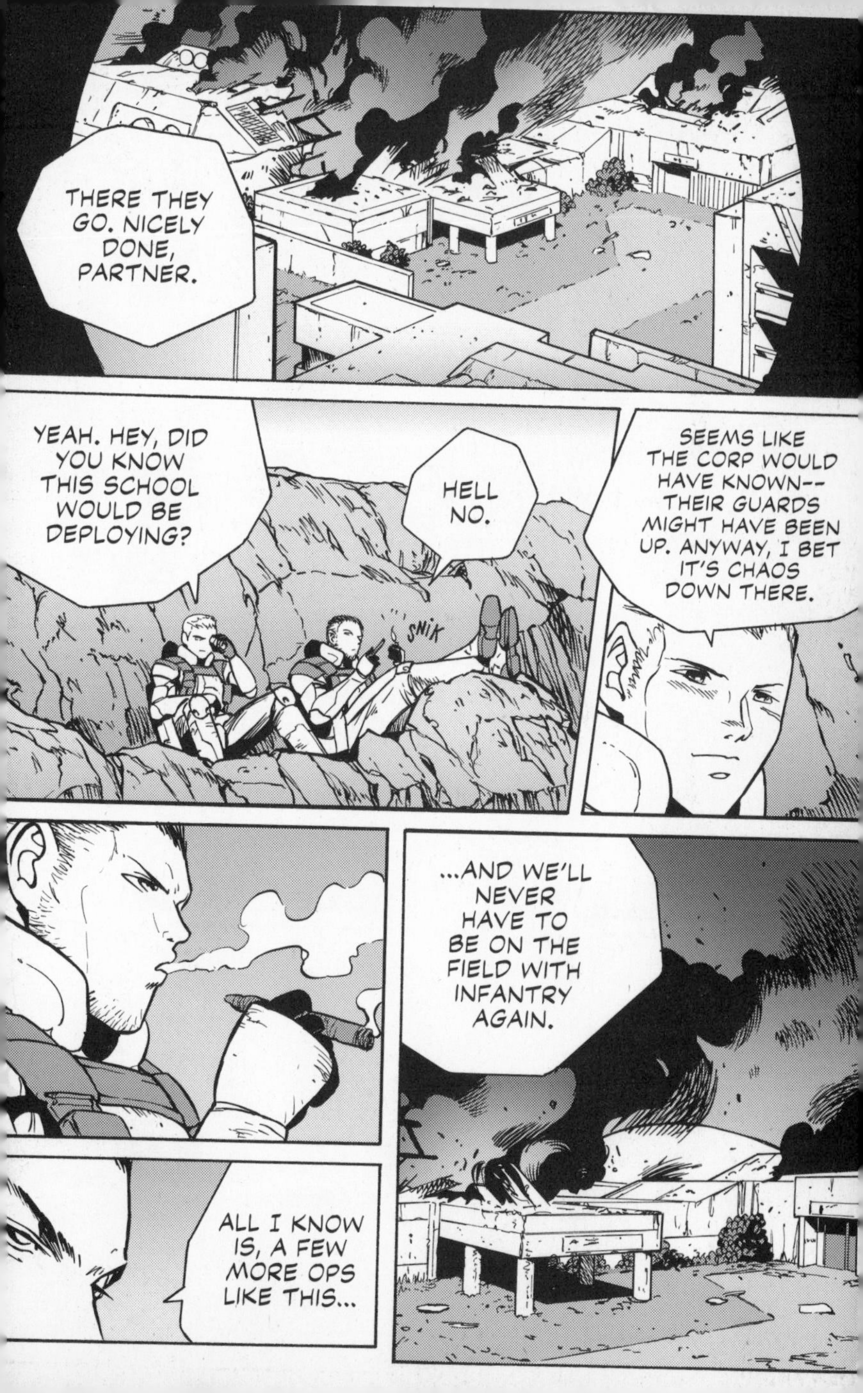
THERE THEY GO. NICELY DONE, PARTNER.
YEAH. HEY, DID YOU KNOW THIS SCHOOL WOULD BE DEPLOYING?
HELL NO.
SNIK
SEEMS LIKE THE CORP WOULD HAVE KNOWN-- THEIR GUARDS MIGHT HAVE BEEN UP. ANYWAY, I BET IT'S CHAOS DOWN THERE.
ALL I KNOW IS, A FEW MORE OPS LIKE THIS...
...AND WE'LL NEVER HAVE TO BE ON THE FIELD WITH INFANTRY AGAIN.

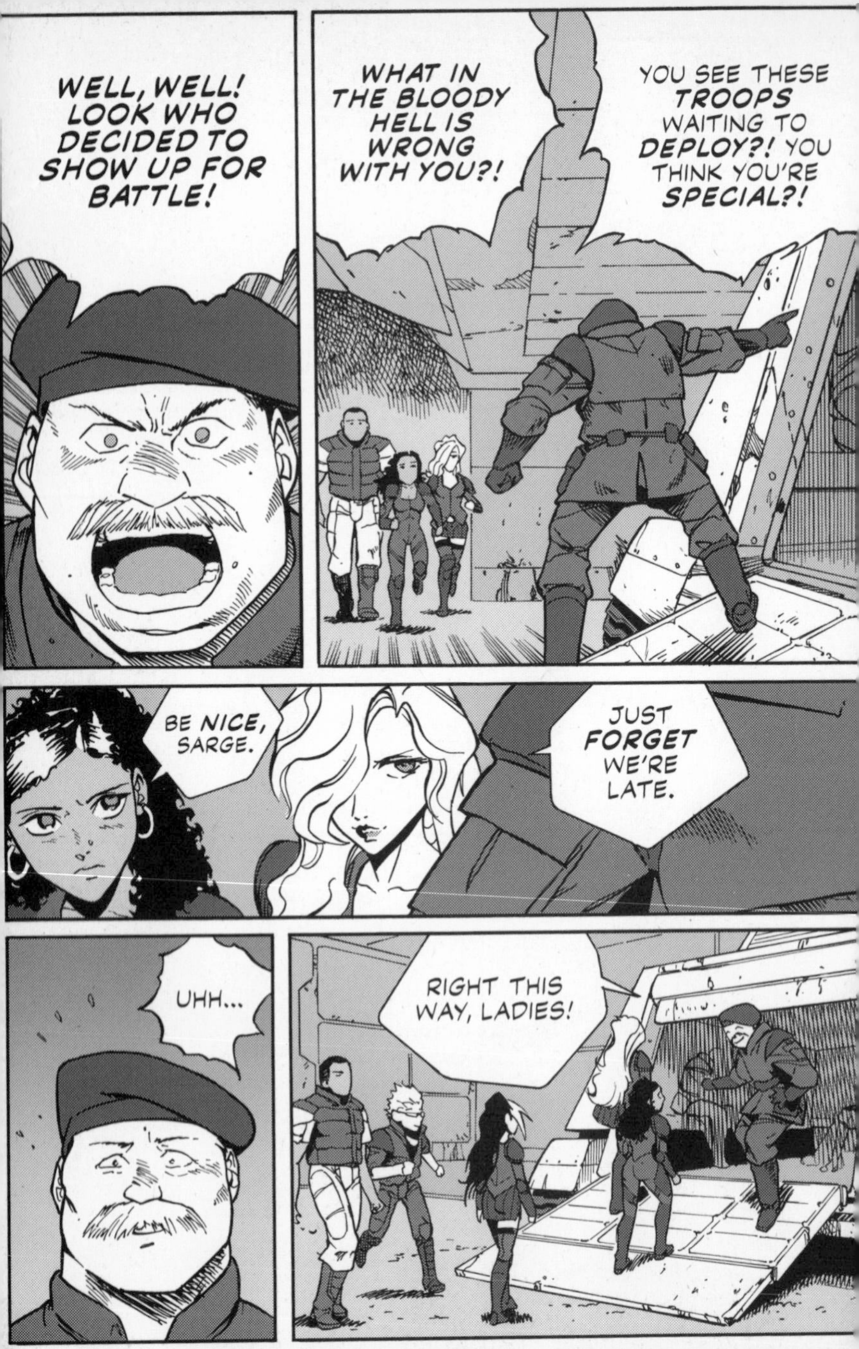
WELL, WELL! LOOK WHO DECIDED TO SHOW UP FOR BATTLE!
WHAT IN THE BLOODY HELL IS WRONG WITH YOU?!
YOU SEE THESE TROOPS WAITING TO DEPLOY?! YOU THINK YOU'RE SPECIAL?!
BE NICE, SARGE.
JUST FORGET WE'RE LATE.
UHH...
RIGHT THIS WAY, LADIES!

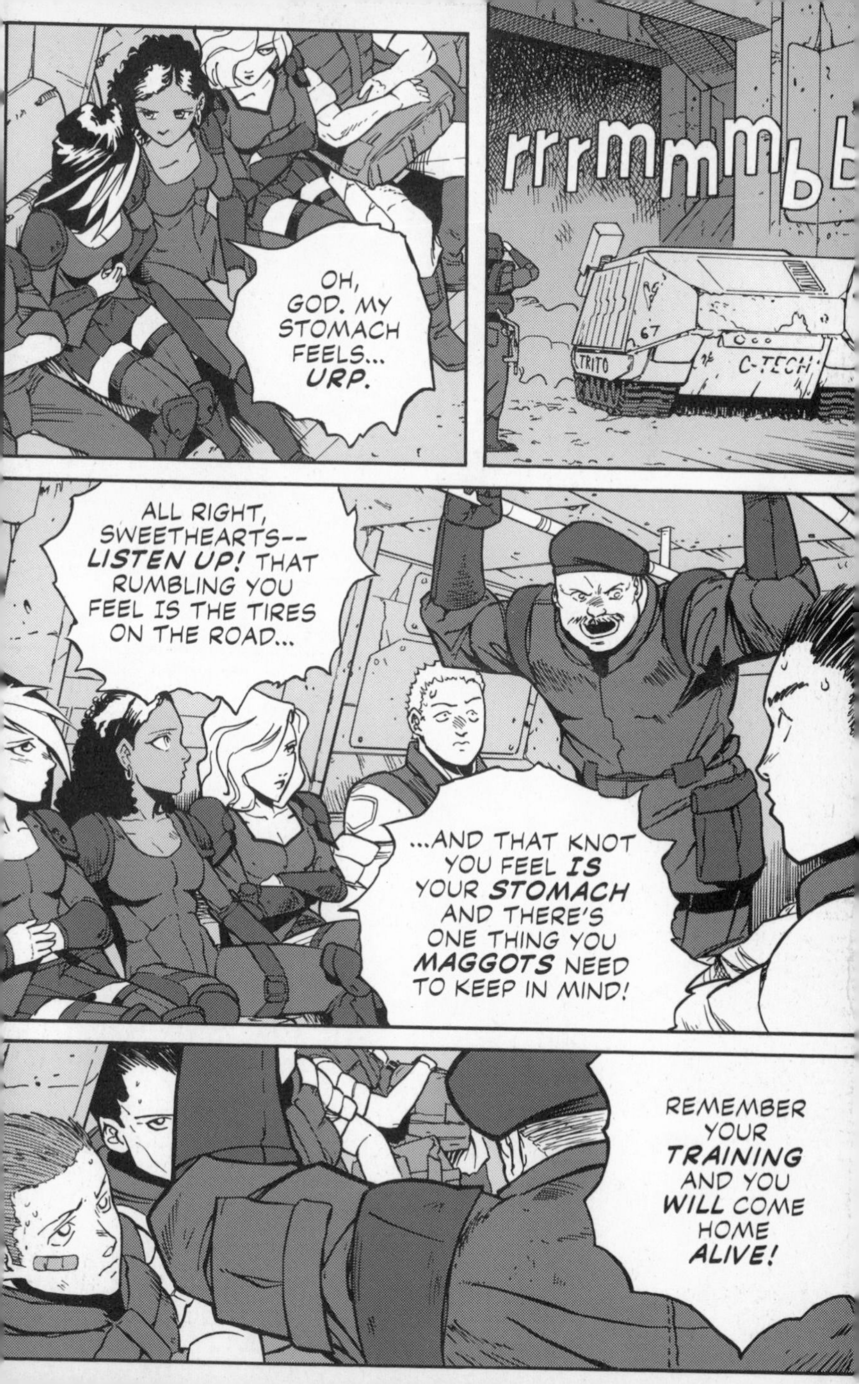
OH, GOD. MY STOMACH FEELS... **URP.**
rrrmmmbb
TRITO
67
C-TECH
ALL RIGHT, SWEETHEARTS-- ***LISTEN UP!*** THAT RUMBLING YOU FEEL IS THE TIRES ON THE ROAD...
...AND THAT KNOT YOU FEEL ***IS*** YOUR ***STOMACH*** AND THERE'S ONE THING YOU ***MAGGOTS*** NEED TO KEEP IN MIND!
REMEMBER YOUR ***TRAINING*** AND YOU ***WILL*** COME HOME ***ALIVE!***

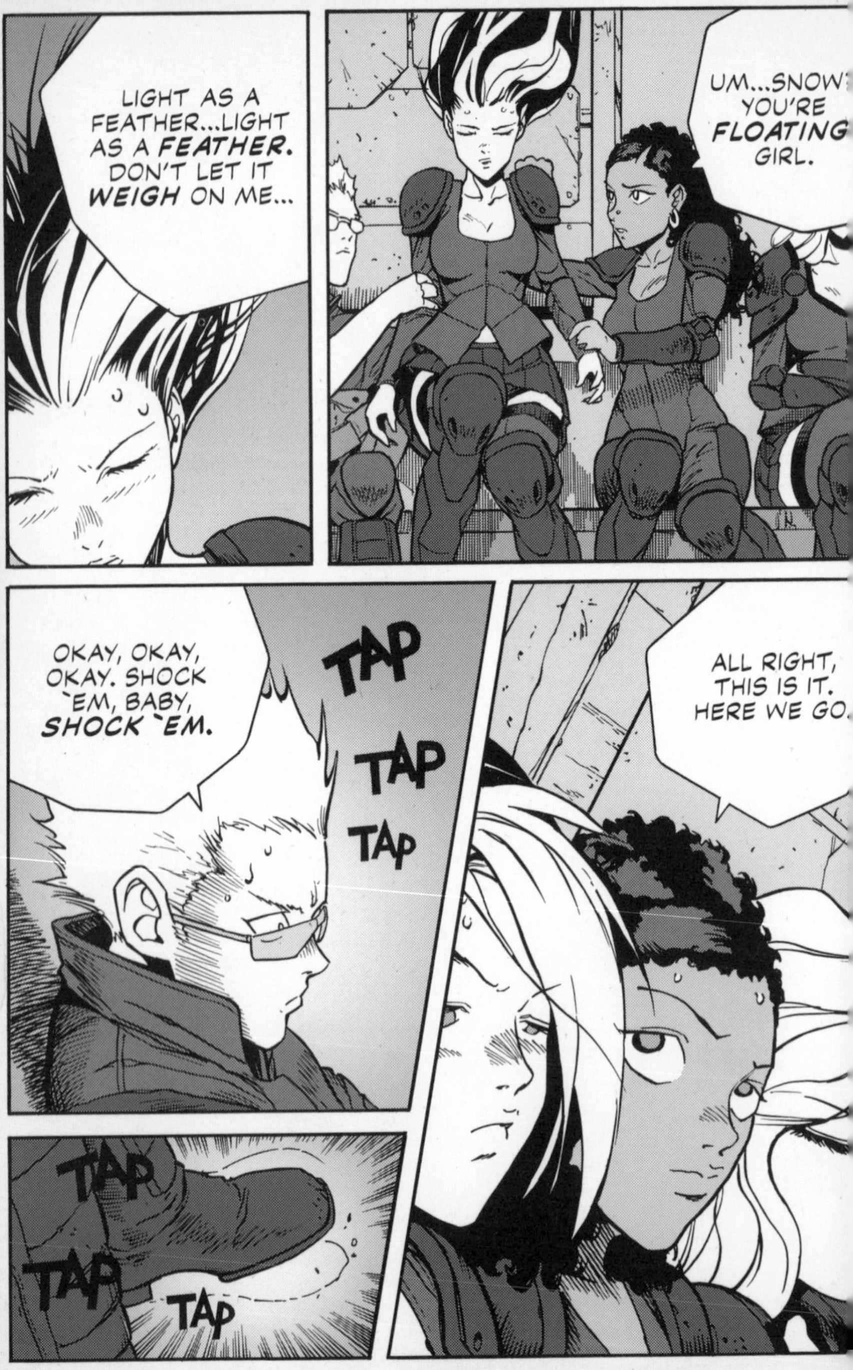
LIGHT AS A FEATHER...LIGHT AS A FEATHER. DON'T LET IT WEIGH ON ME...
UM...SNOW? YOU'RE FLOATING GIRL.
OKAY, OKAY, OKAY. SHOCK `EM, BABY, SHOCK `EM.
TAP
TAP
TAP
ALL RIGHT, THIS IS IT. HERE WE GO.
TAP
TAP
TAP

PSY★COMM

CHAPTER [6]

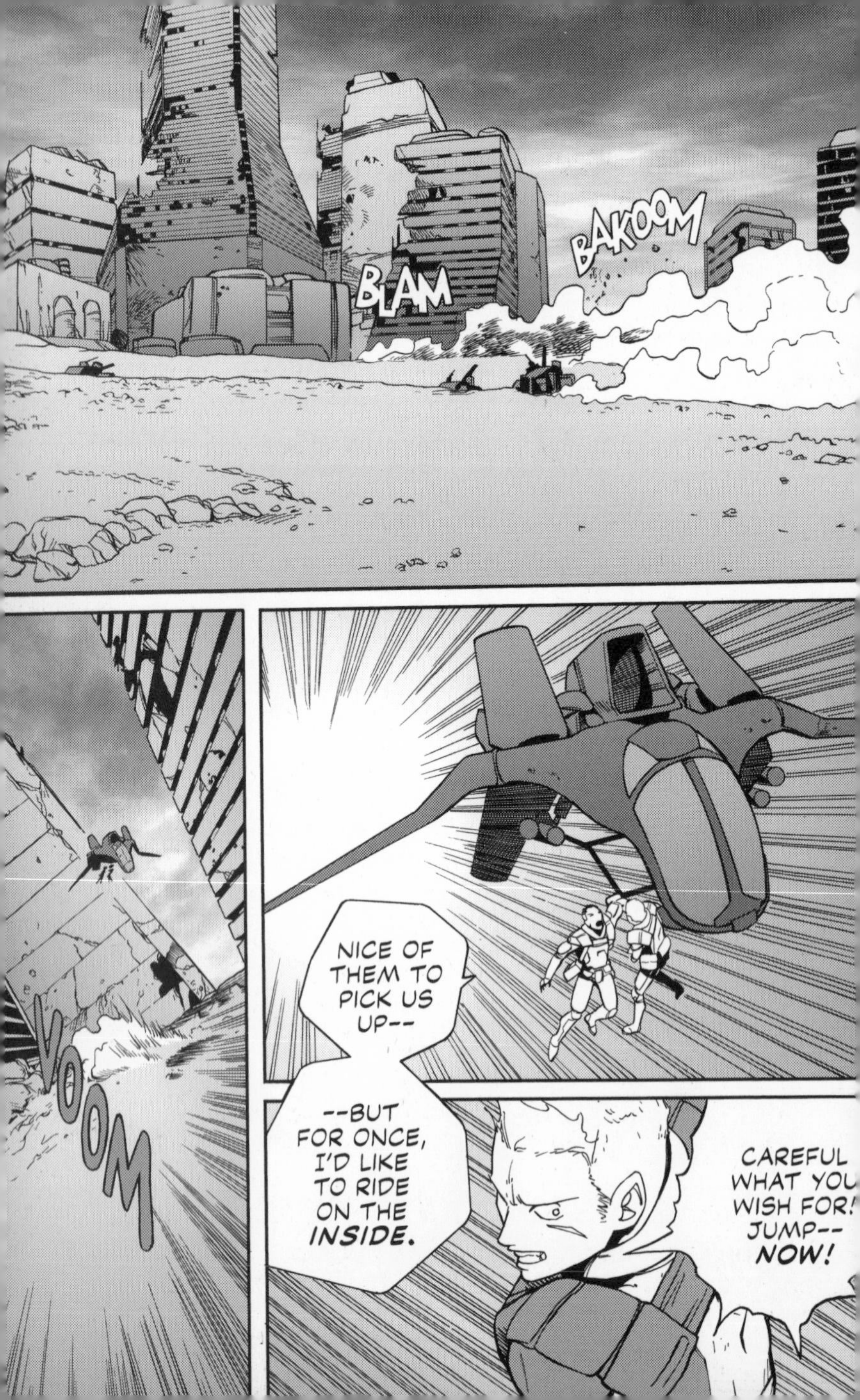

BLAM
BAKOOM
VOOM
NICE OF THEM TO PICK US UP--
--BUT FOR ONCE, I'D LIKE TO RIDE ON THE *INSIDE.*
CAREFUL WHAT YOU WISH FOR! JUMP-- *NOW!*

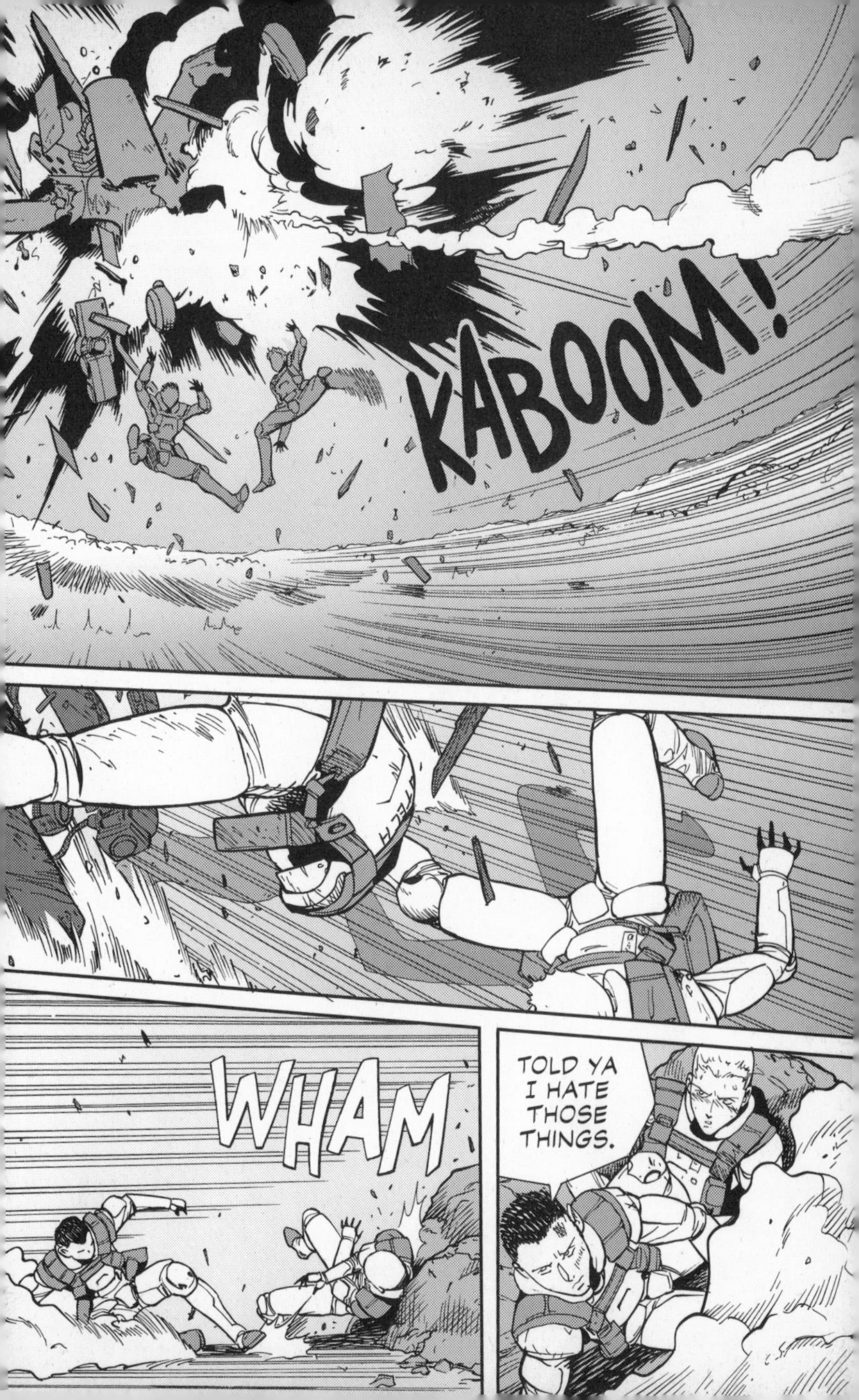
KABOOM!
WHAM
TOLD YA I HATE THOSE THINGS.

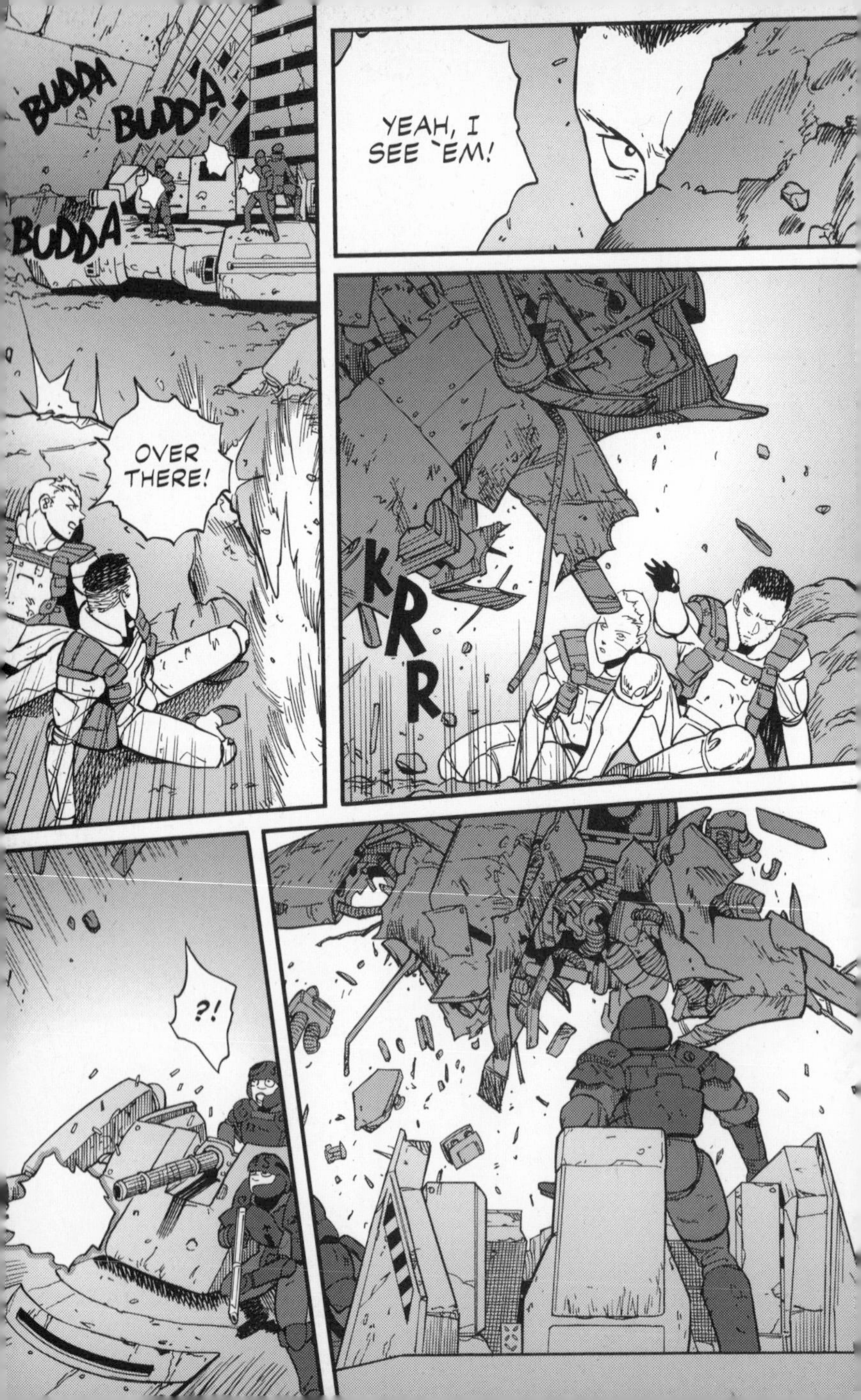
BUDDA
BUDDA
BUDDA
OVER THERE!
YEAH, I SEE `EM!
KRR
?!

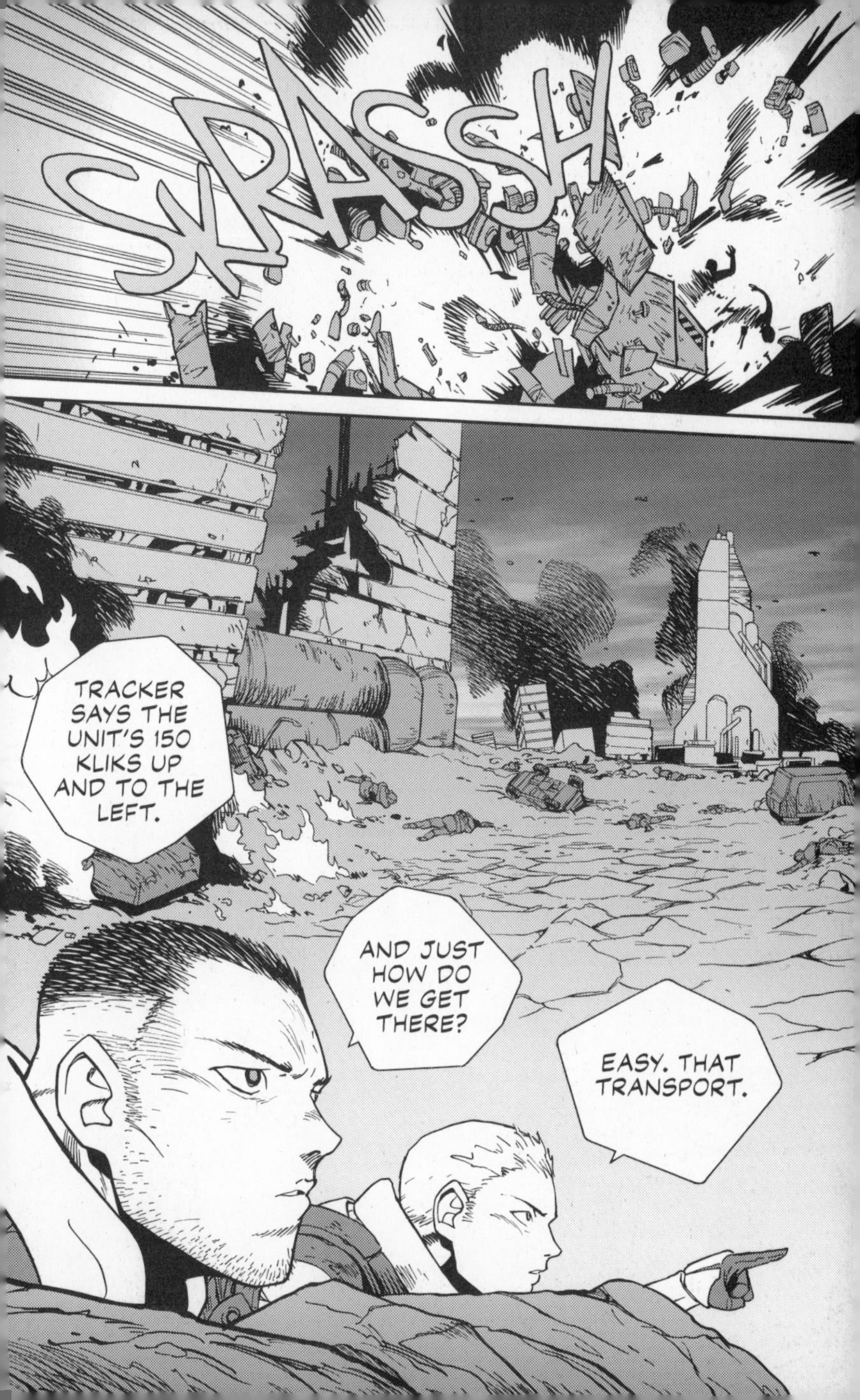
SKRASSH
TRACKER SAYS THE UNIT'S 150 KLIKS UP AND TO THE LEFT.
AND JUST HOW DO WE GET THERE?
EASY. THAT TRANSPORT.

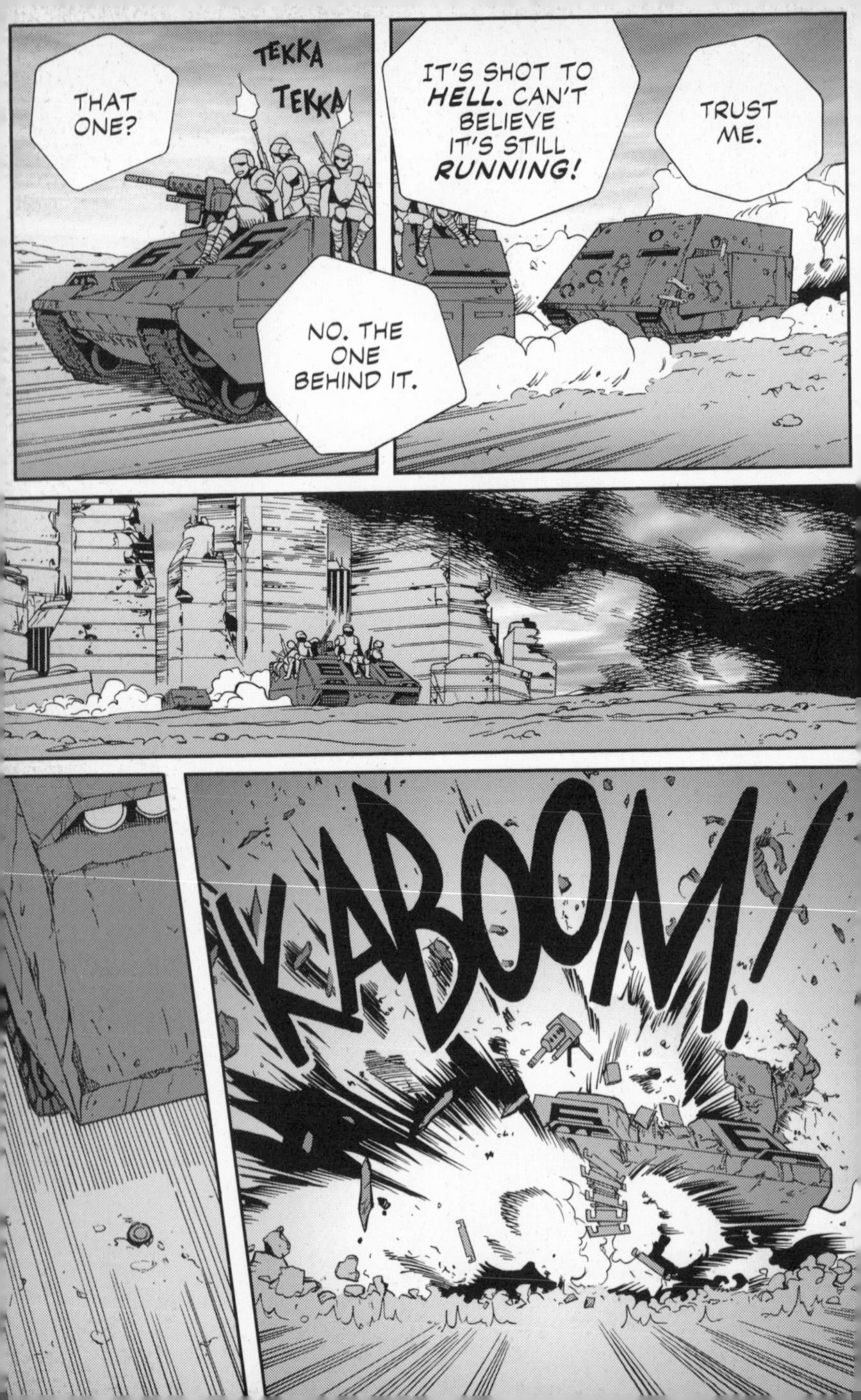

THAT ONE?
TEKKA
TEKKA
NO. THE ONE BEHIND IT.
IT'S SHOT TO HELL. CAN'T BELIEVE IT'S STILL RUNNING!
TRUST ME.
KABOOM!

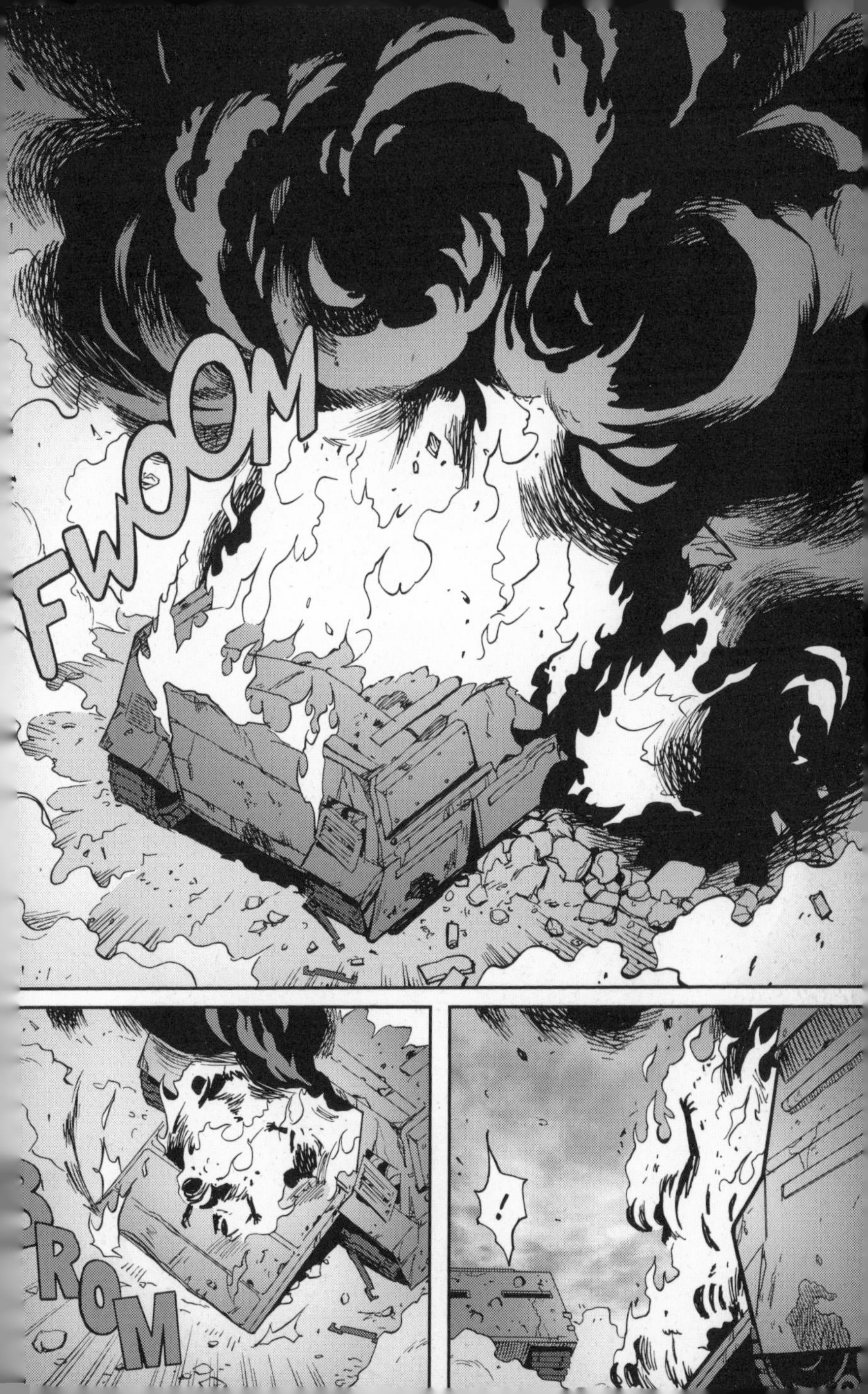
FWOOM
BROM
!

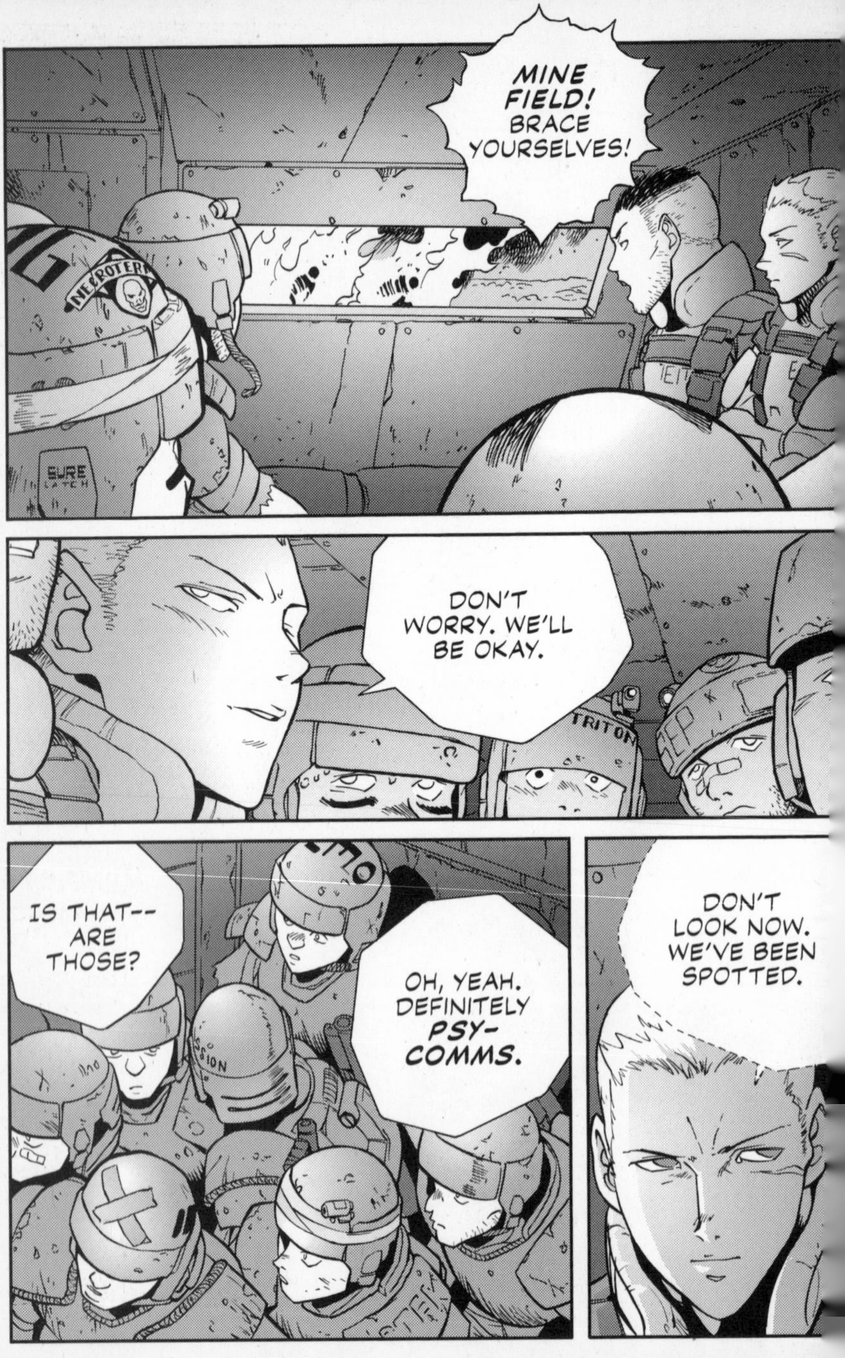
MINE FIELD! BRACE YOURSELVES!
DON'T WORRY. WE'LL BE OKAY.
IS THAT-- ARE THOSE?
OH, YEAH. DEFINITELY PSY-COMMS.
DON'T LOOK NOW. WE'VE BEEN SPOTTED.

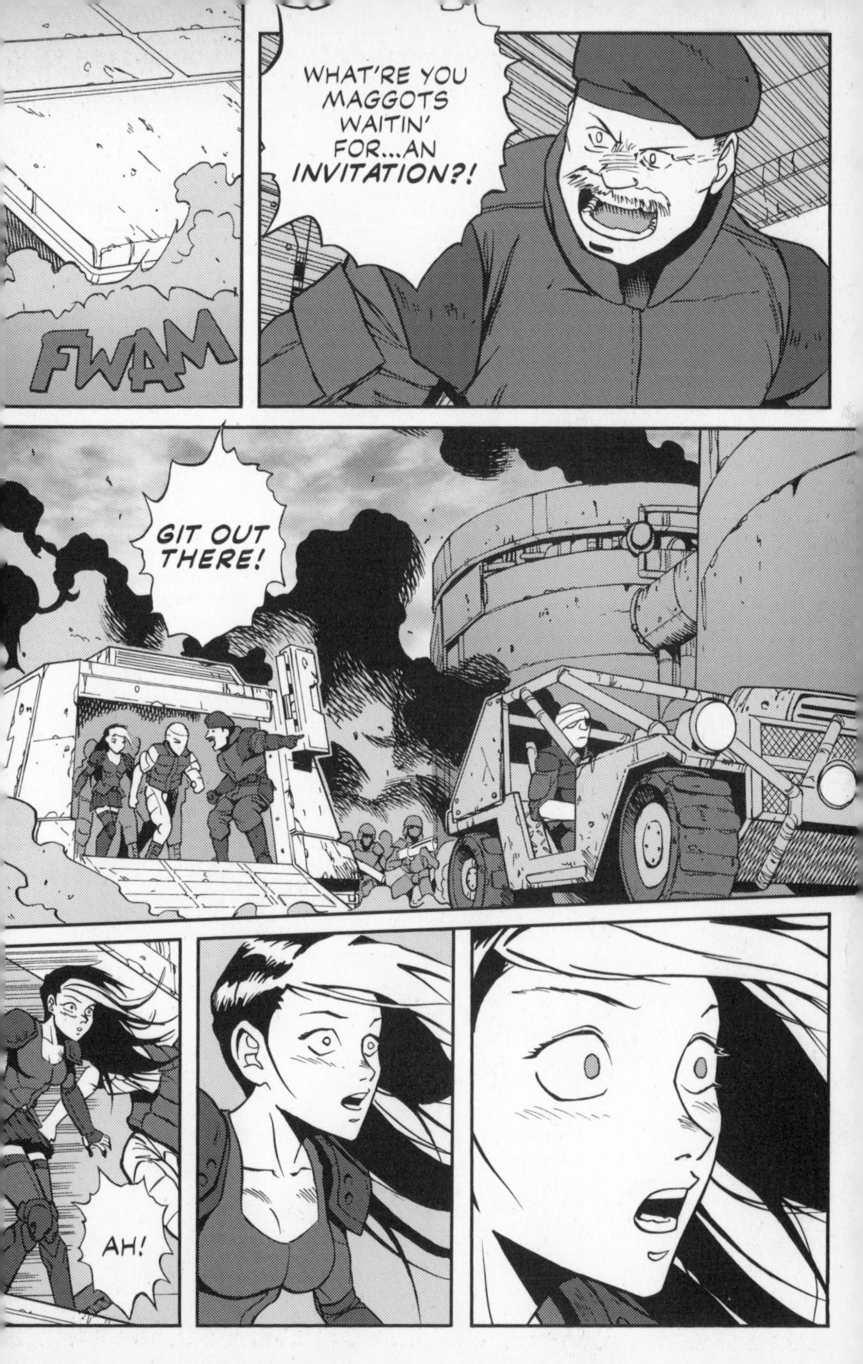
FWAM
WHAT'RE YOU MAGGOTS WAITIN' FOR...AN INVITATION?!
GIT OUT THERE!
AH!

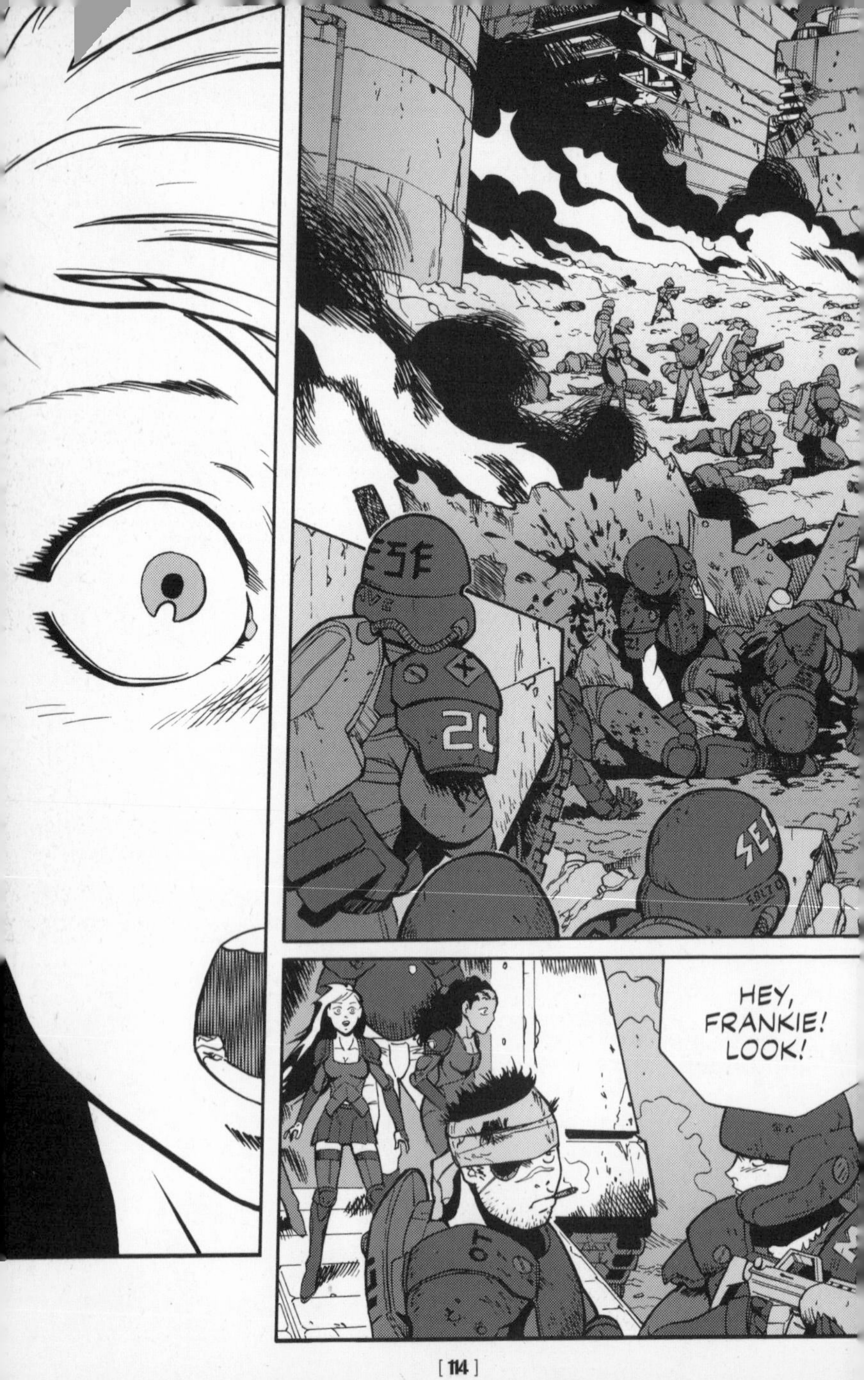
HEY, FRANKIE! LOOK!

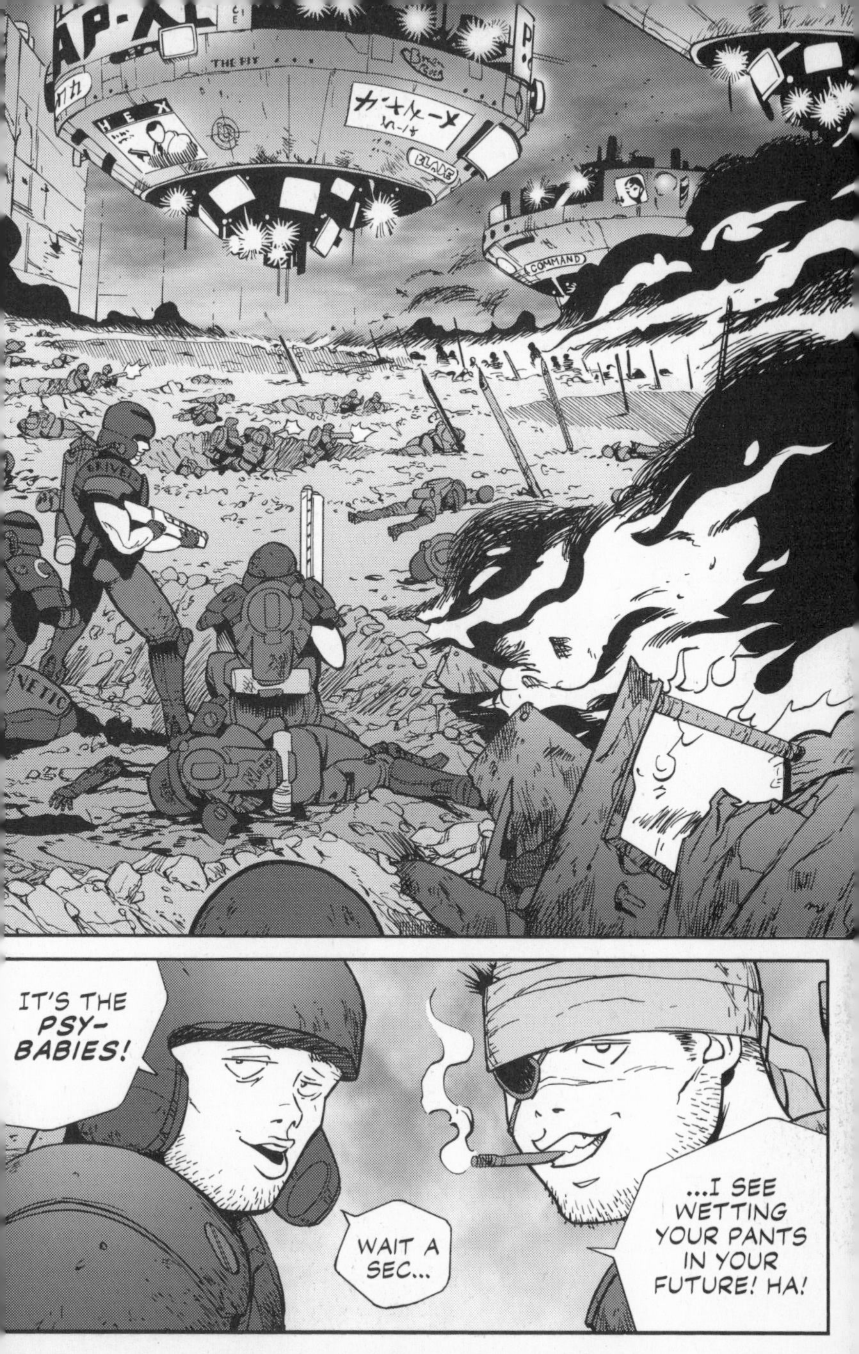
THE PIT
HEX
BLADE
COMMAND
IT'S THE *PSY-BABIES!*
WAIT A SEC...
...I SEE WETTING YOUR PANTS IN YOUR FUTURE! HA!

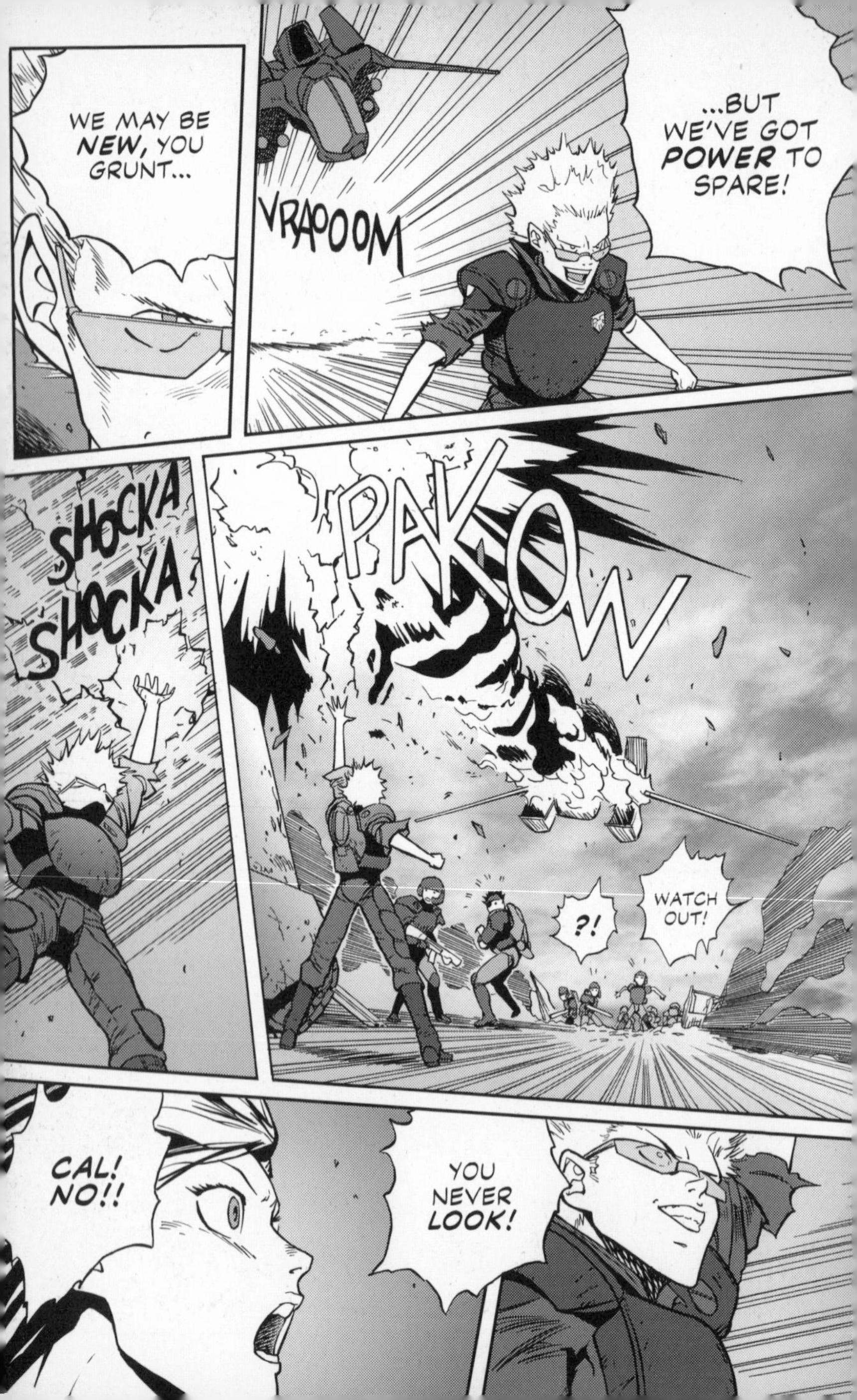
WE MAY BE NEW, YOU GRUNT...
VRAOOOM
...BUT WE'VE GOT POWER TO SPARE!
SHOCKA SHOCKA
PAKOW
?!
WATCH OUT!
CAL! NO!!
YOU NEVER LOOK!

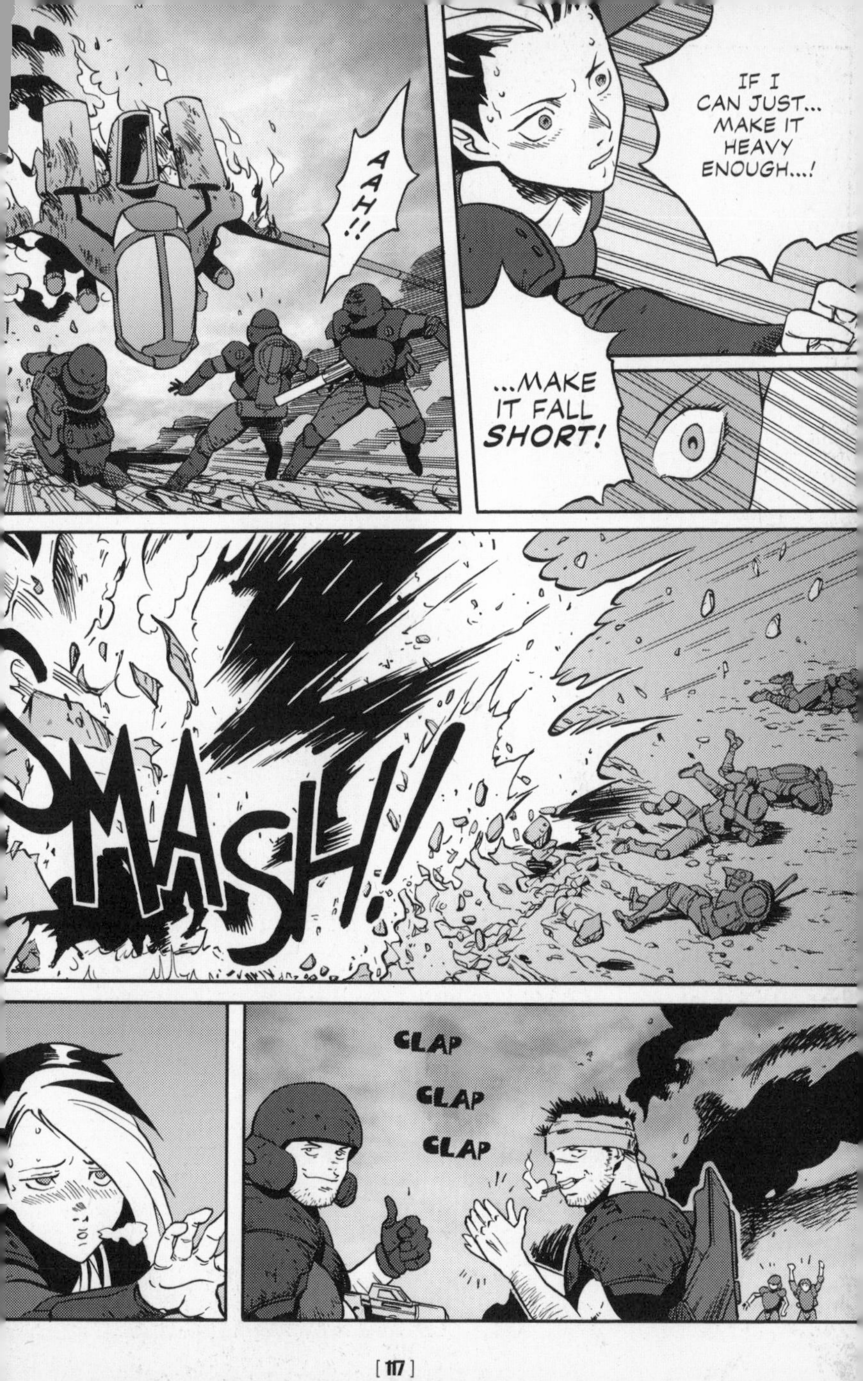
AAH!!
IF I CAN JUST... MAKE IT HEAVY ENOUGH...!
...MAKE IT FALL SHORT!
SMASH!!
CLAP
CLAP
CLAP

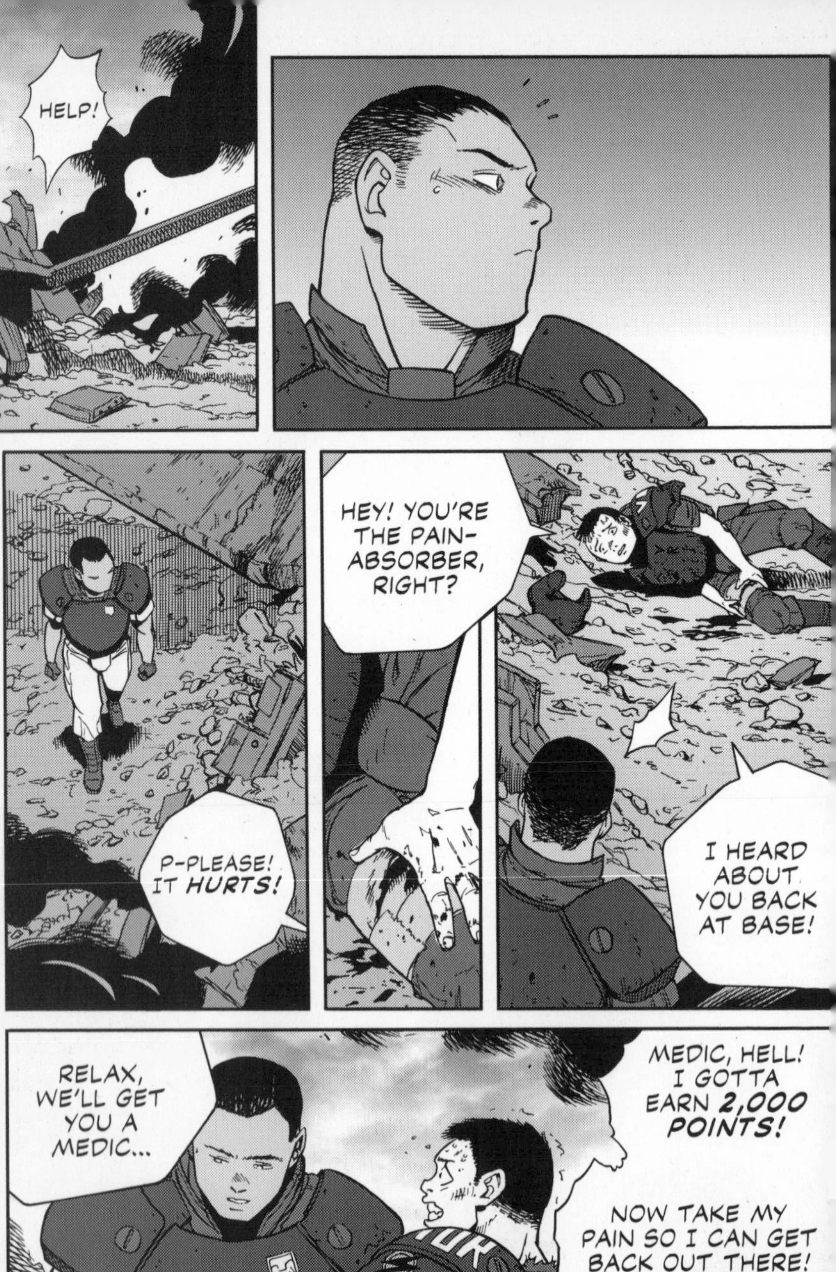
HELP!
P-PLEASE! IT HURTS!
HEY! YOU'RE THE PAIN-ABSORBER, RIGHT?
I HEARD ABOUT YOU BACK AT BASE!
RELAX, WE'LL GET YOU A MEDIC...
MEDIC, HELL! I GOTTA EARN 2,000 POINTS!
NOW TAKE MY PAIN SO I CAN GET BACK OUT THERE! PLEASE!

BUT ALL I DO IS PAIN...

IT WON'T BE FIXED.

BESIDES, YOU **DON'T** WANT ANY MORE POINTS TODAY.

YOU **DON'T** EVEN **CARE** ABOUT POINTS ANYMORE, RIGHT?

JUST **FORGET** IT.

YOU DON'T EVEN **REMEMBER** HOW TO COUNT FIELD POINTS NOW.

WOW...THE PAIN'S ALL GONE!

WHAT WAS I...?

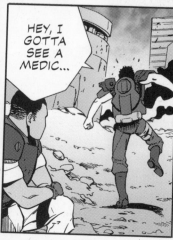

HEY, I GOTTA SEE A MEDIC...

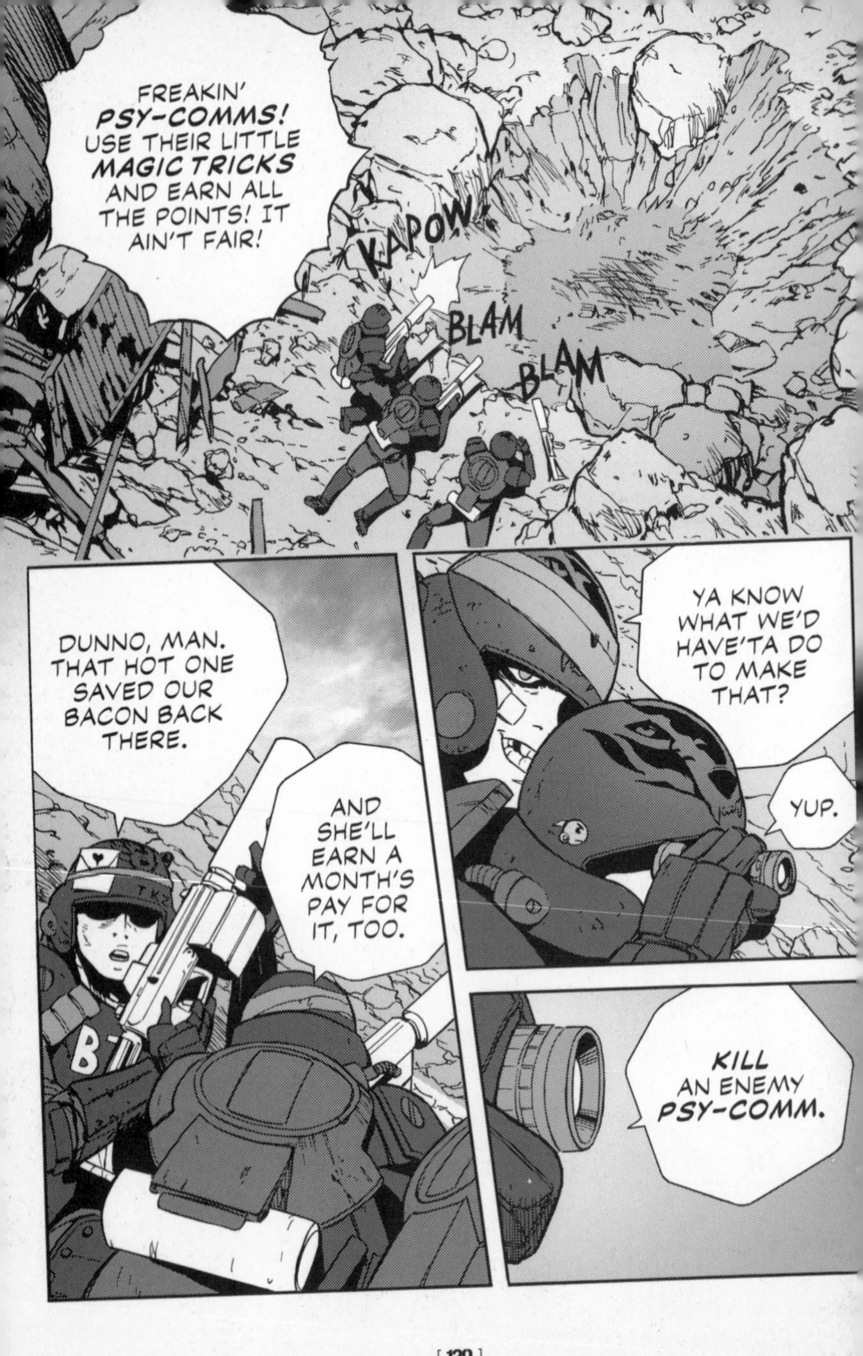
FREAKIN' ***PSY-COMMS!*** USE THEIR LITTLE ***MAGIC TRICKS*** AND EARN ALL THE POINTS! IT AIN'T FAIR!
KAPOW
BLAM
BLAM
DUNNO, MAN. THAT HOT ONE SAVED OUR BACON BACK THERE.
AND SHE'LL EARN A MONTH'S PAY FOR IT, TOO.
YA KNOW WHAT WE'D HAVE'TA DO TO MAKE THAT?
YUP.
KILL AN ENEMY ***PSY-COMM.***

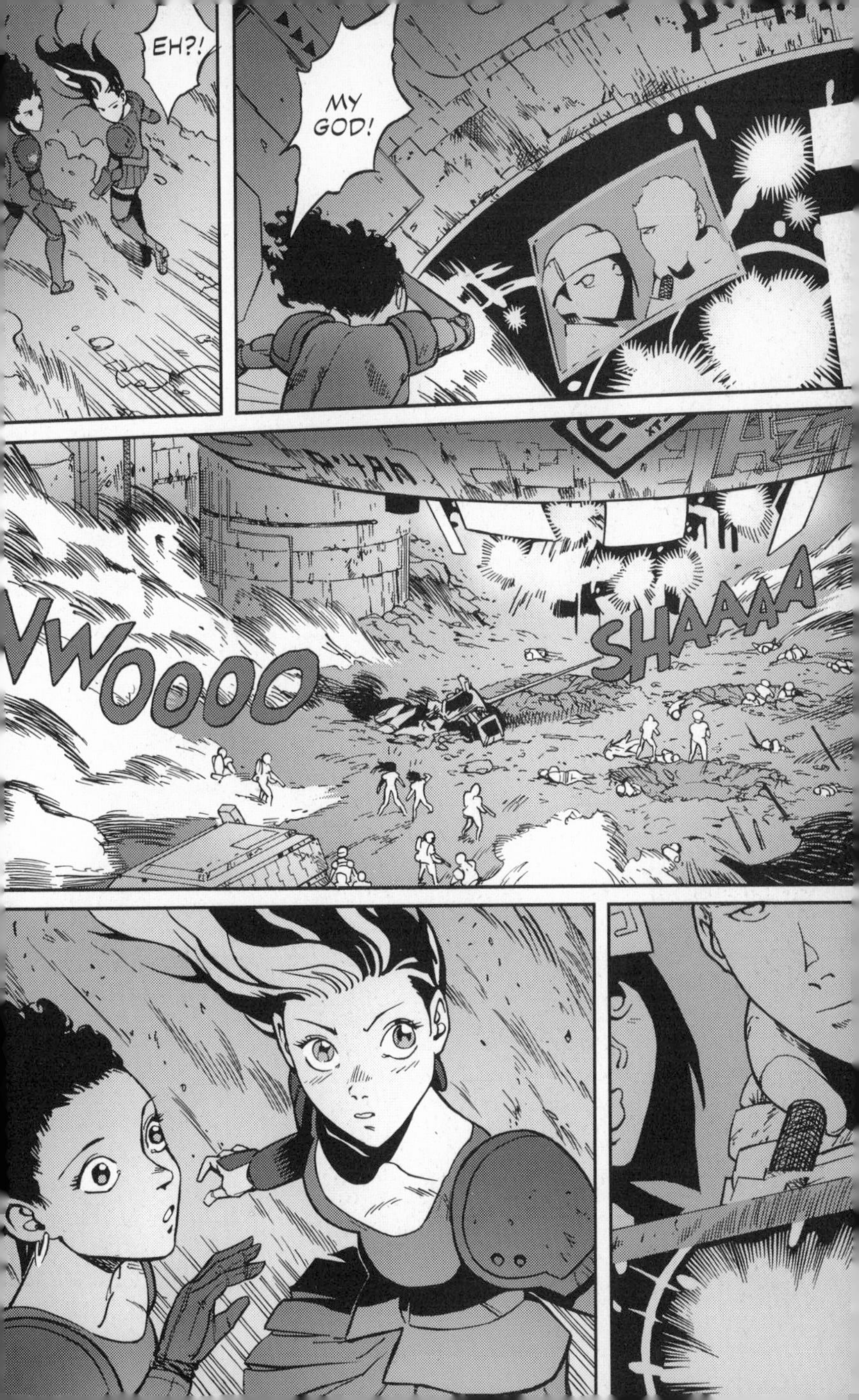
EH?!
MY GOD!
VWOOOO
SHAAAA

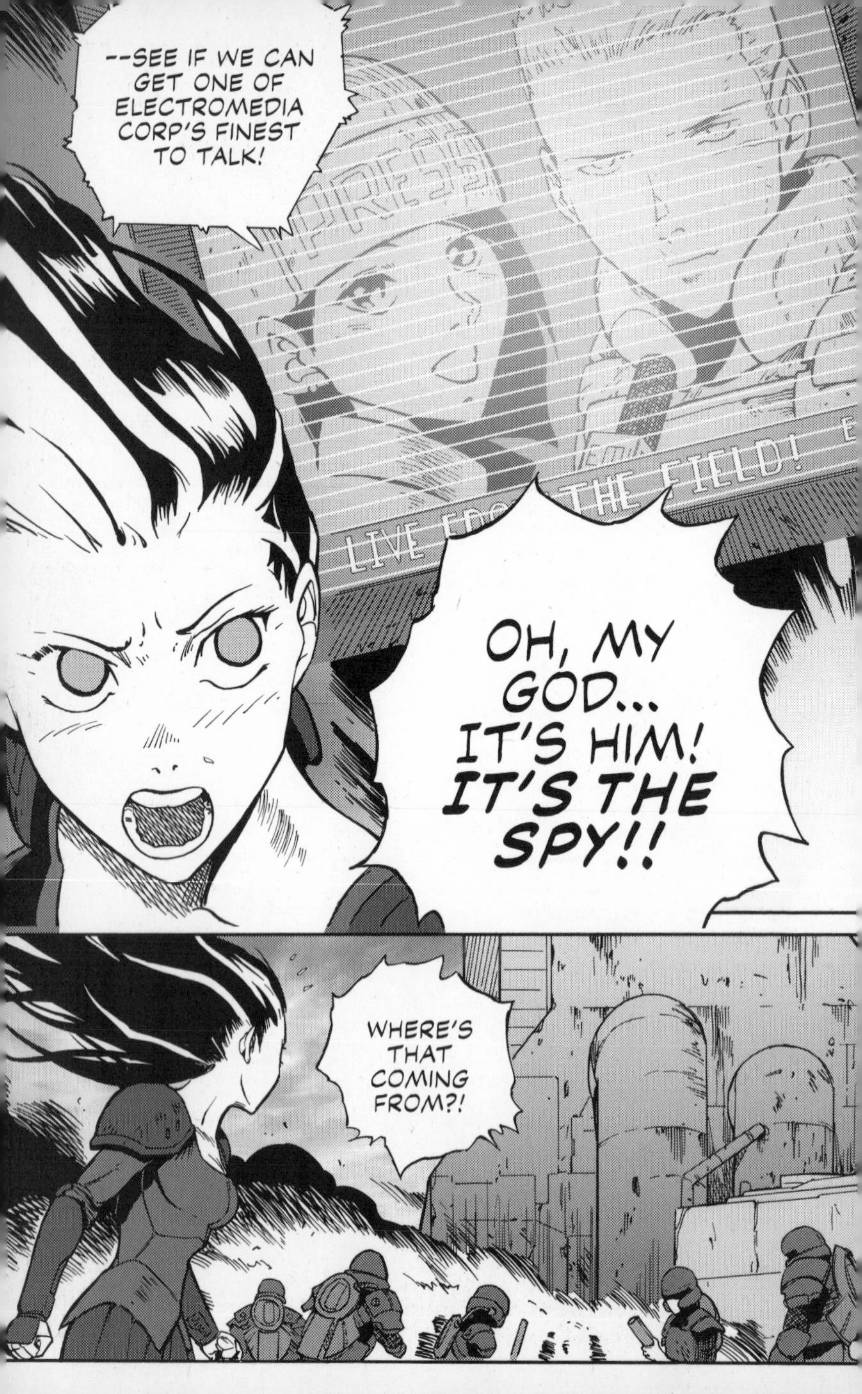
--SEE IF WE CAN GET ONE OF ELECTROMEDIA CORP'S FINEST TO TALK!
THE FIELD!
OH, MY GOD... IT'S HIM! ***IT'S THE SPY!!***
WHERE'S THAT COMING FROM?!

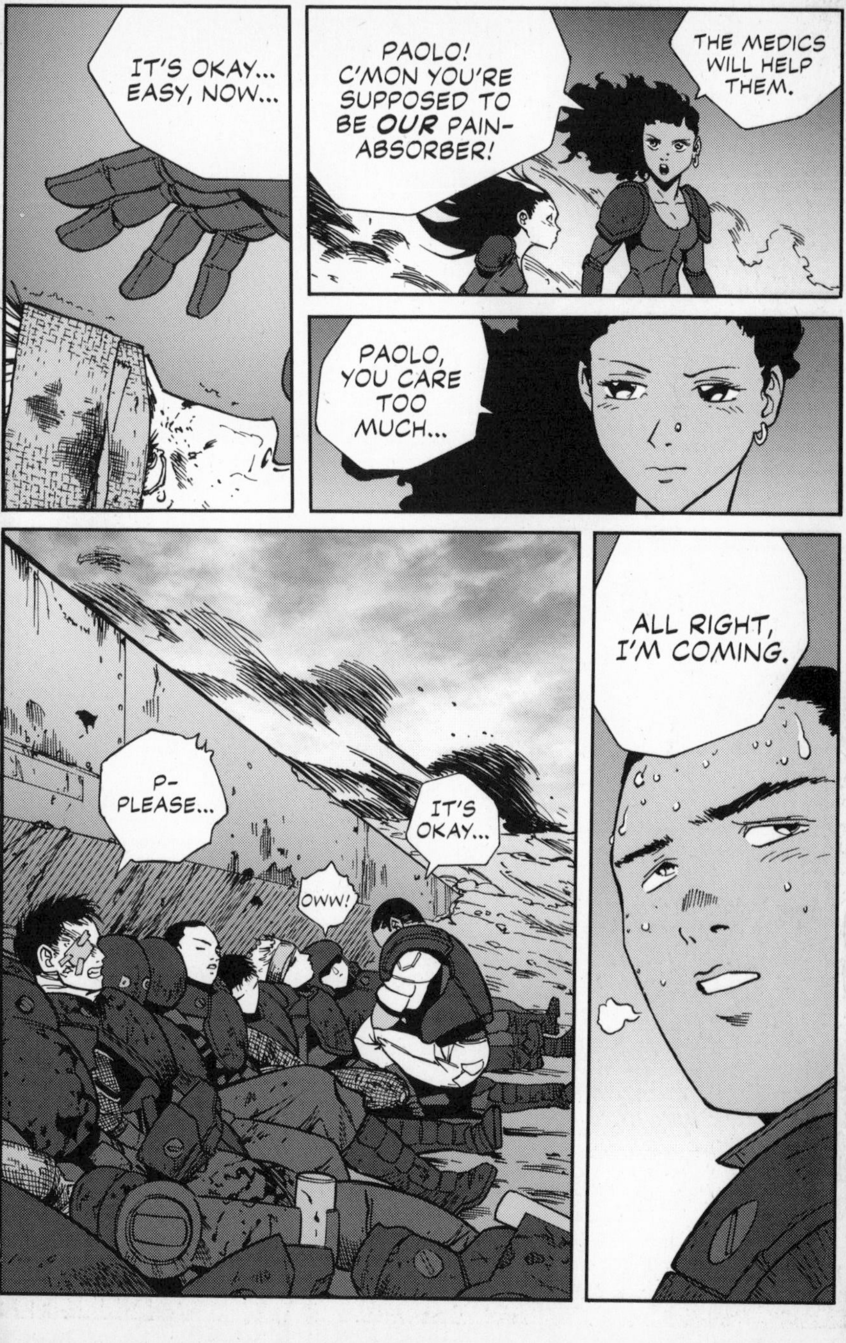
IT'S OKAY... EASY, NOW...
PAOLO! C'MON YOU'RE SUPPOSED TO BE OUR PAIN-ABSORBER!
THE MEDICS WILL HELP THEM.
PAOLO, YOU CARE TOO MUCH...
P-PLEASE...
IT'S OKAY...
OWW!
ALL RIGHT, I'M COMING.

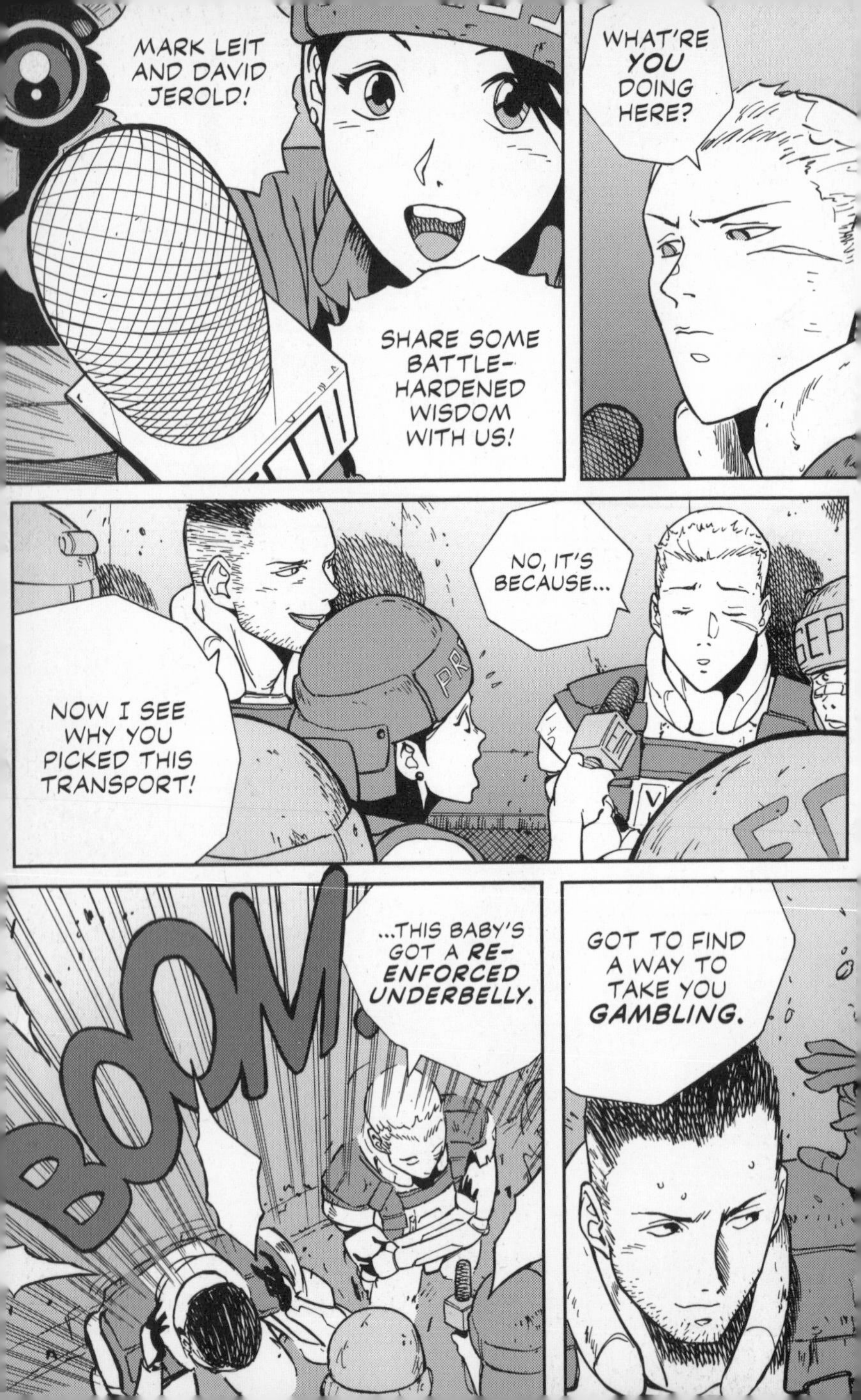
MARK LEIT AND DAVID JEROLD!
SHARE SOME BATTLE-HARDENED WISDOM WITH US!
WHAT'RE **YOU** DOING HERE?
NOW I SEE WHY YOU PICKED THIS TRANSPORT!
NO, IT'S BECAUSE...
BOOOM
...THIS BABY'S GOT A ***RE-ENFORCED UNDERBELLY.***
GOT TO FIND A WAY TO TAKE YOU **GAMBLING.**

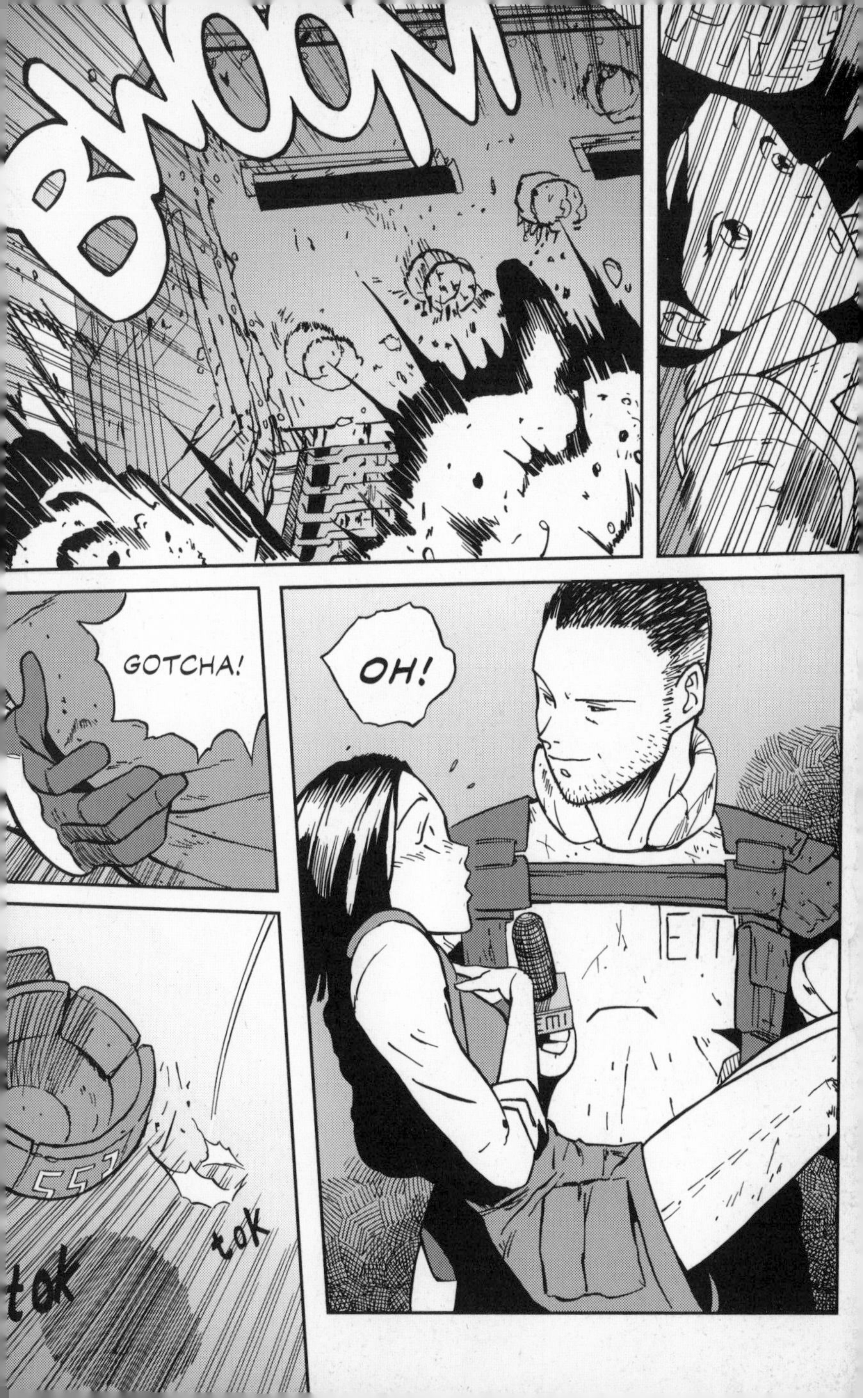
BWOOM
GOTCHA!
tok
tok
OH!

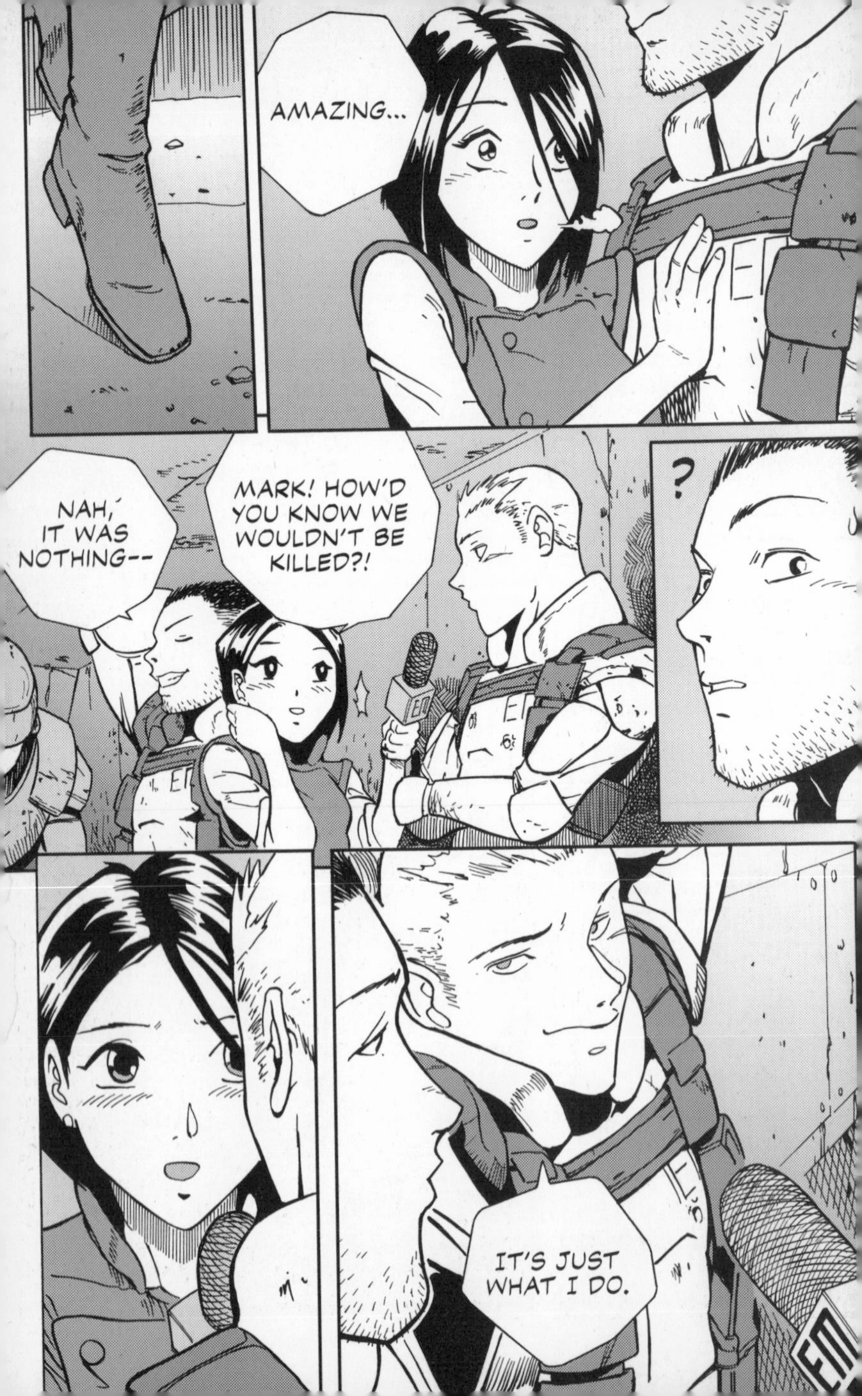
AMAZING...
?
MARK! HOW'D YOU KNOW WE WOULDN'T BE KILLED?!
NAH, IT WAS NOTHING--
IT'S JUST WHAT I DO.

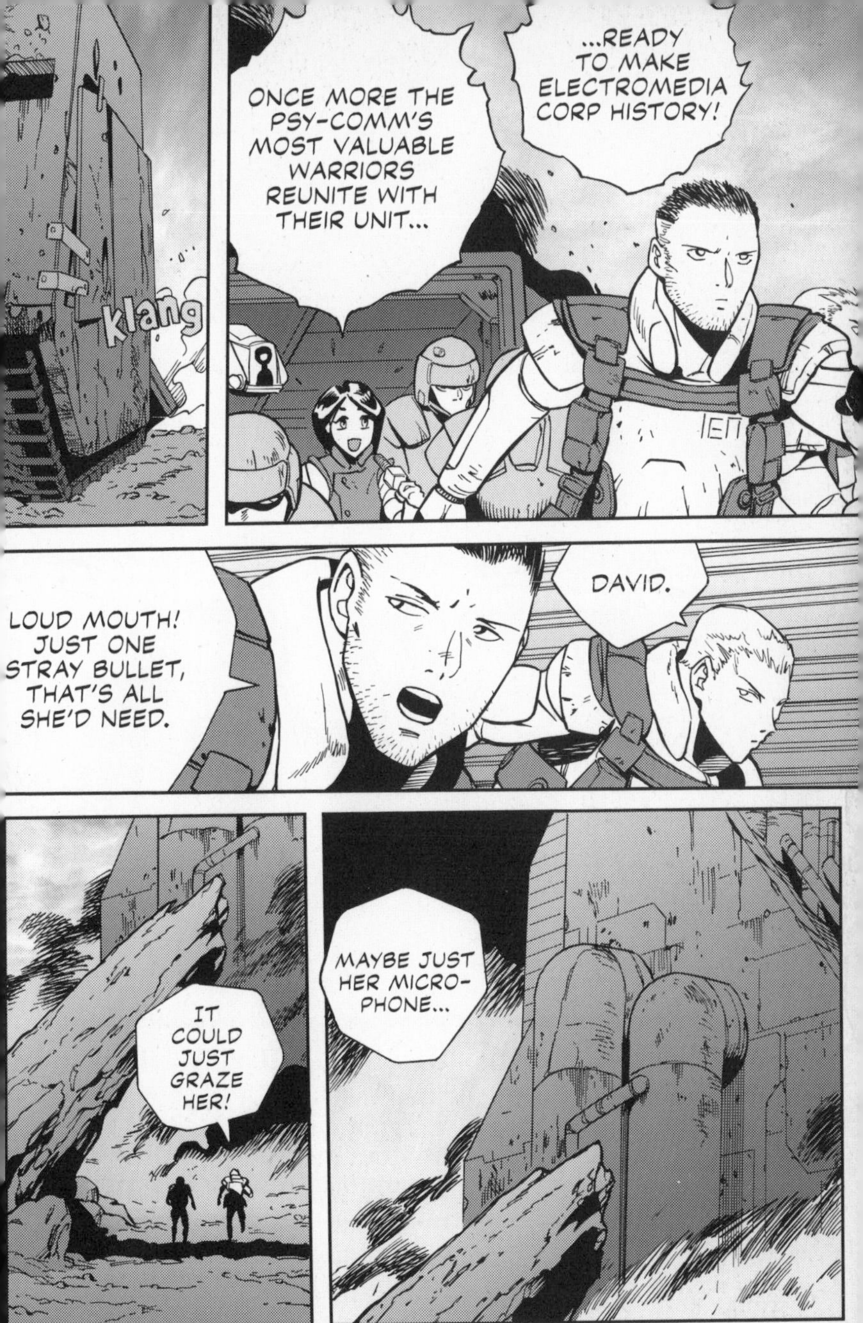
klang
ONCE MORE THE PSY-COMM'S MOST VALUABLE WARRIORS REUNITE WITH THEIR UNIT...
...READY TO MAKE ELECTROMEDIA CORP HISTORY!
LOUD MOUTH! JUST ONE STRAY BULLET, THAT'S ALL SHE'D NEED.
DAVID.
IT COULD JUST GRAZE HER!
MAYBE JUST HER MICRO-PHONE...

PSY★COMM

David
Stealth Gear
integrated shoulder pads
Pistol mags
integrated holster

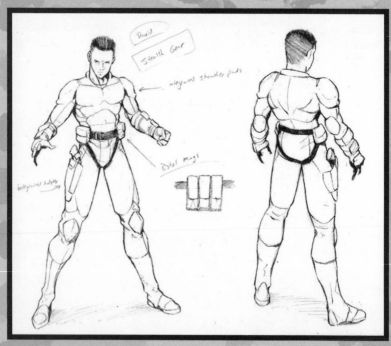

**STEALTH GEAR SUIT FOR DAVID JEROLD:
THIS DESIGN WENT UNUSED IN THE FINAL BOOK.
A SLEEK-LOOKING OUTFIT, NONETHELESS.**

PSY★COMM
CHAPTER [7]

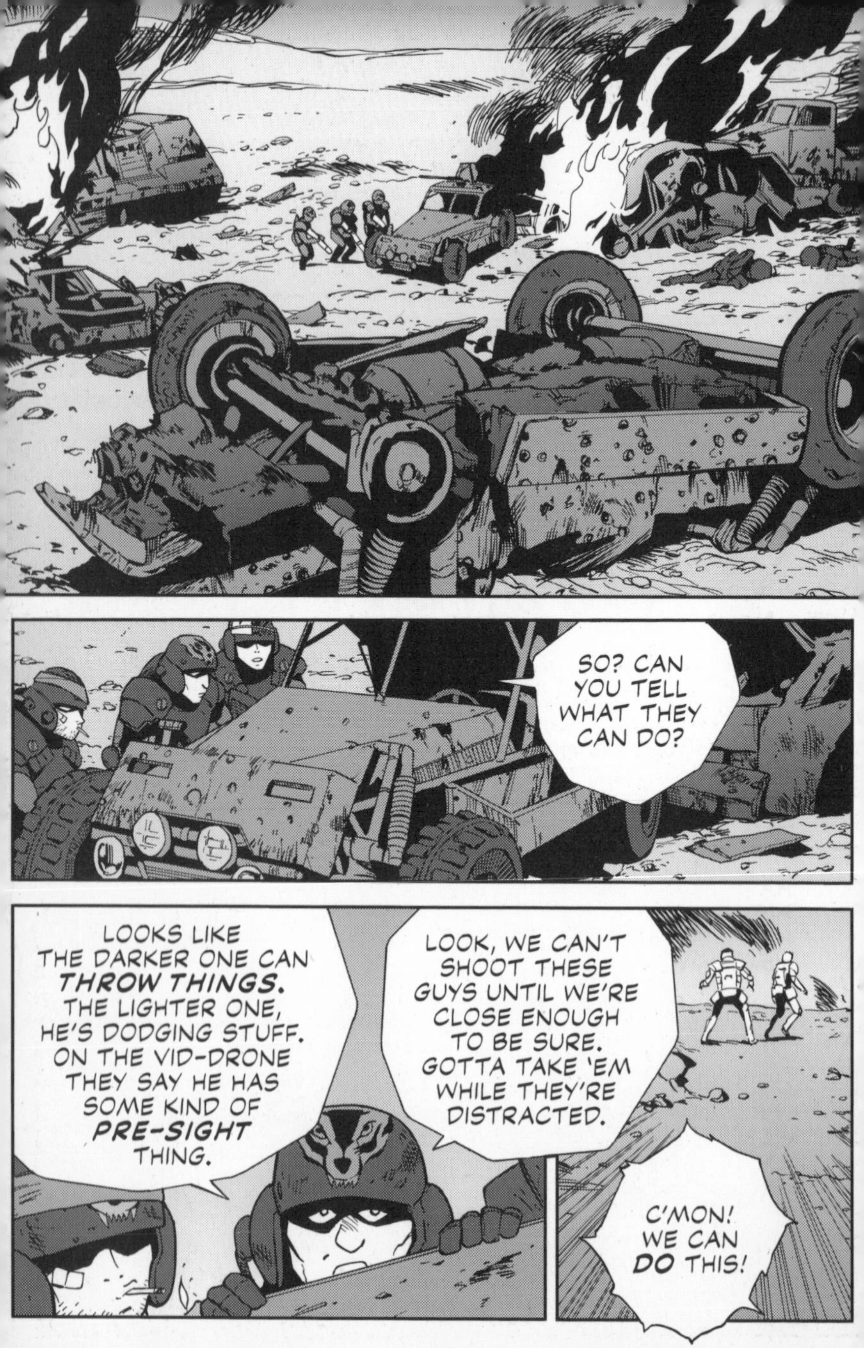
SO? CAN YOU TELL WHAT THEY CAN DO?
LOOKS LIKE THE DARKER ONE CAN **THROW THINGS.** THE LIGHTER ONE, HE'S DODGING STUFF. ON THE VID-DRONE THEY SAY HE HAS SOME KIND OF ***PRE-SIGHT*** THING.
LOOK, WE CAN'T SHOOT THESE GUYS UNTIL WE'RE CLOSE ENOUGH TO BE SURE. GOTTA TAKE 'EM WHILE THEY'RE DISTRACTED.
C'MON! WE CAN ***DO*** THIS!

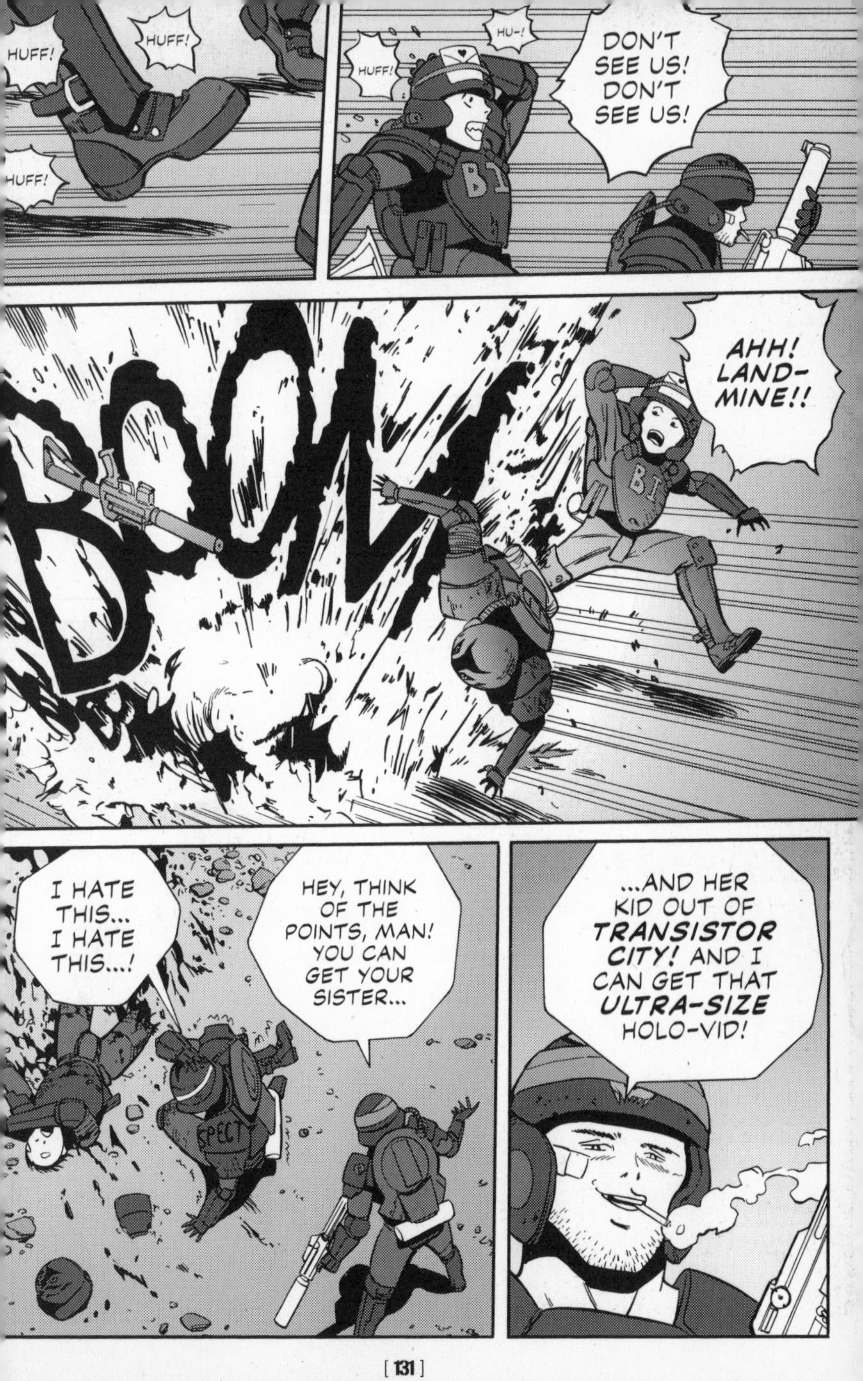
HUFF!
HUFF!
HUFF!
HUFF!
HU-!
DON'T SEE US! DON'T SEE US!
BOOM
AHH! LAND-MINE!!
I HATE THIS... I HATE THIS...!
HEY, THINK OF THE POINTS, MAN! YOU CAN GET YOUR SISTER...
...AND HER KID OUT OF TRANSISTOR CITY! AND I CAN GET THAT ULTRA-SIZE HOLO-VID!

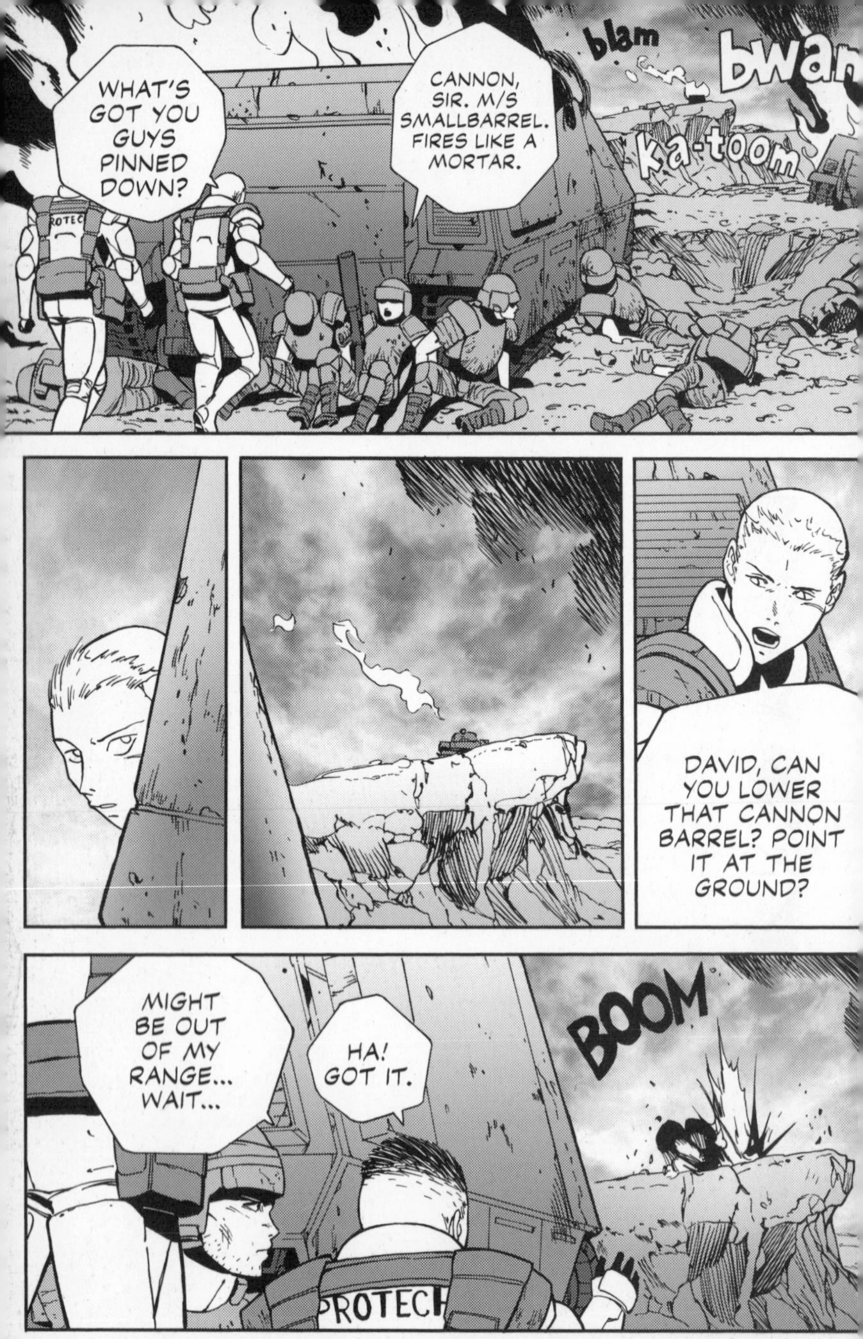
WHAT'S GOT YOU GUYS PINNED DOWN?
CANNON, SIR. M/S SMALLBARREL. FIRES LIKE A MORTAR.
blam
bwam
ka-toom
PROTEC
DAVID, CAN YOU LOWER THAT CANNON BARREL? POINT IT AT THE GROUND?
MIGHT BE OUT OF MY RANGE... WAIT...
HA! GOT IT.
BOOM
PROTECH

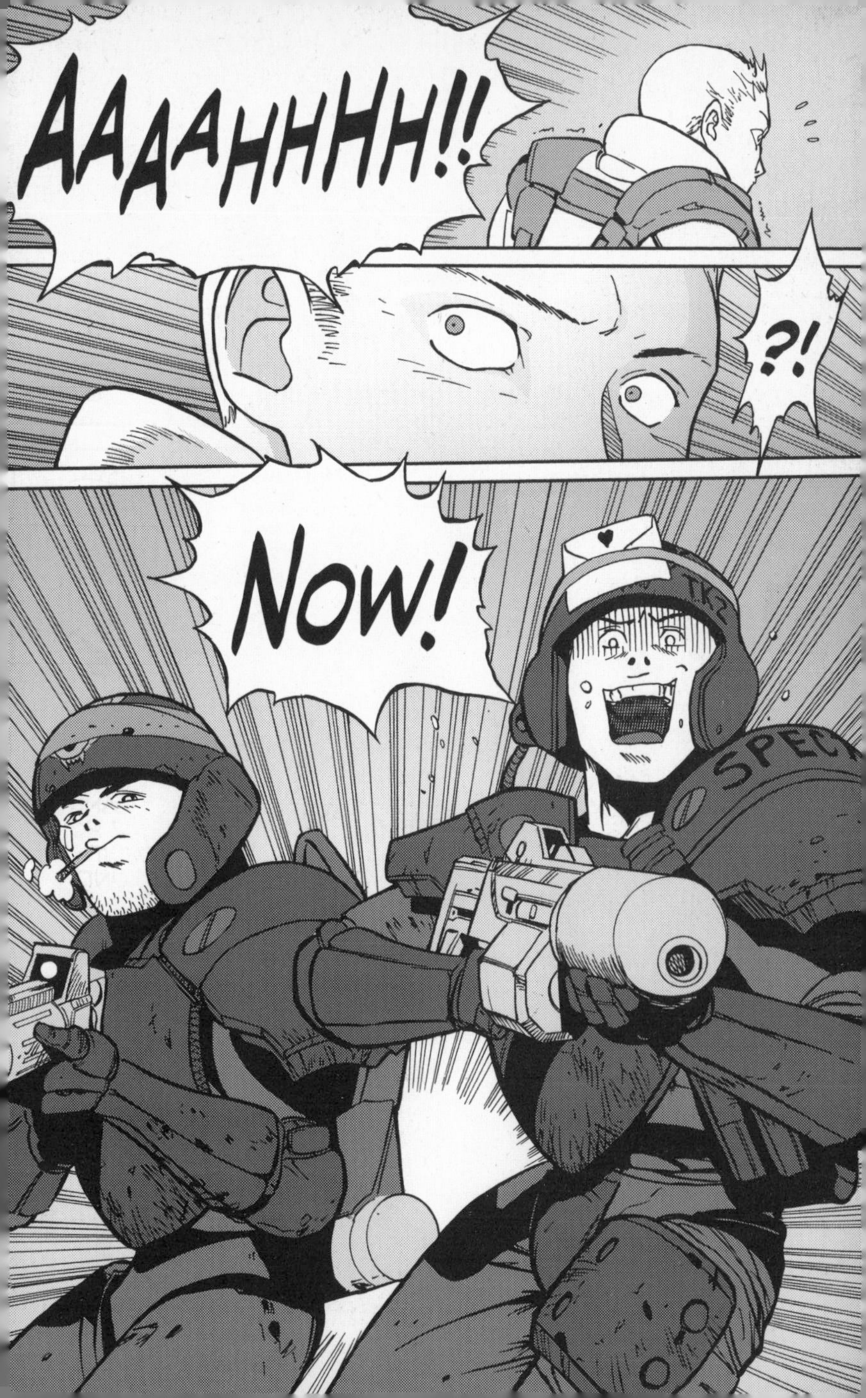
AAAAHHHH!!
?!
Now!
TK2
SPEC

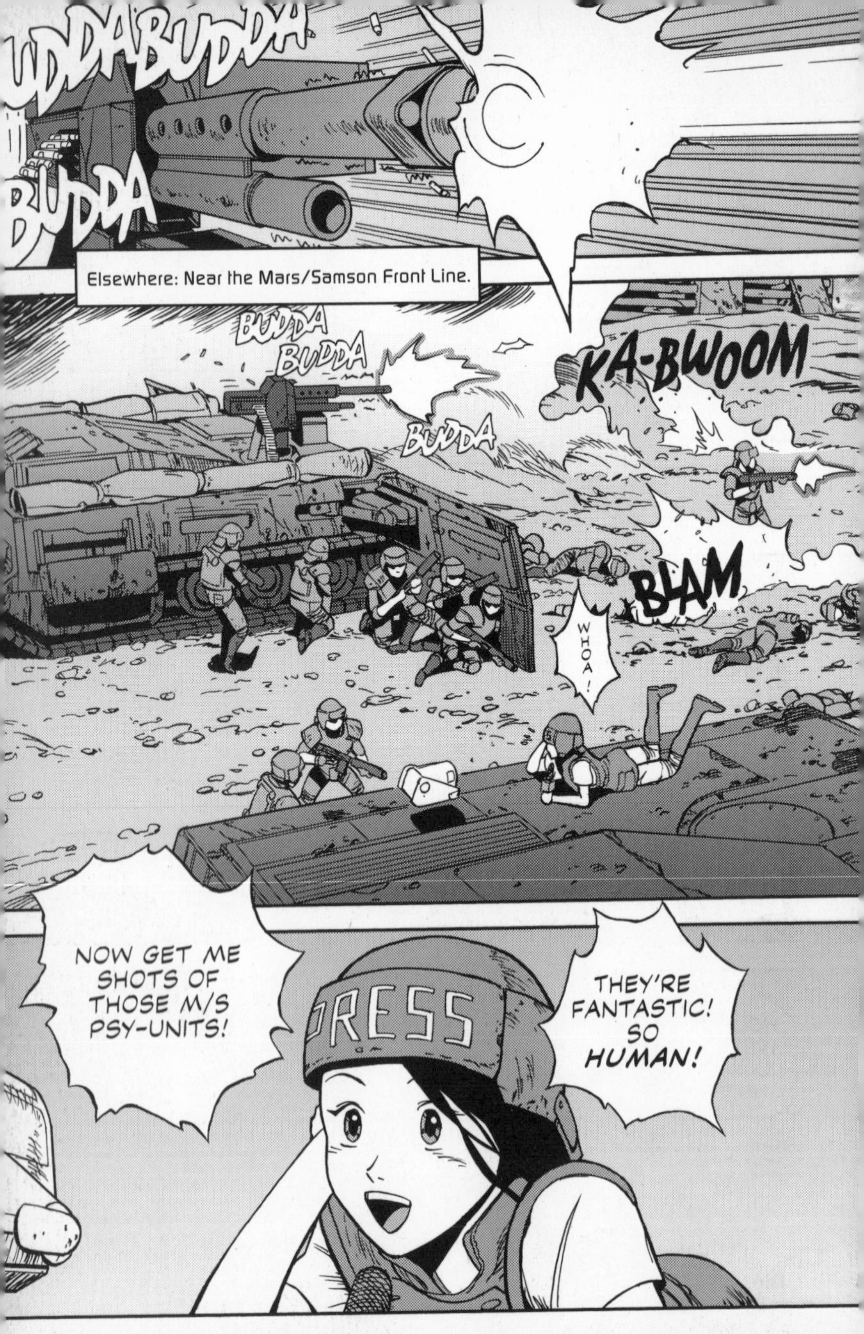

UDDABUDDA
BUDDA
Elsewhere: Near the Mars/Samson Front Line.
BUDDA
BUDDA
BUDDA
KA-BWOOM
BLAM
WHOA!
NOW GET ME SHOTS OF THOSE M/S PSY-UNITS!
THEY'RE FANTASTIC! SO *HUMAN!*
PRESS

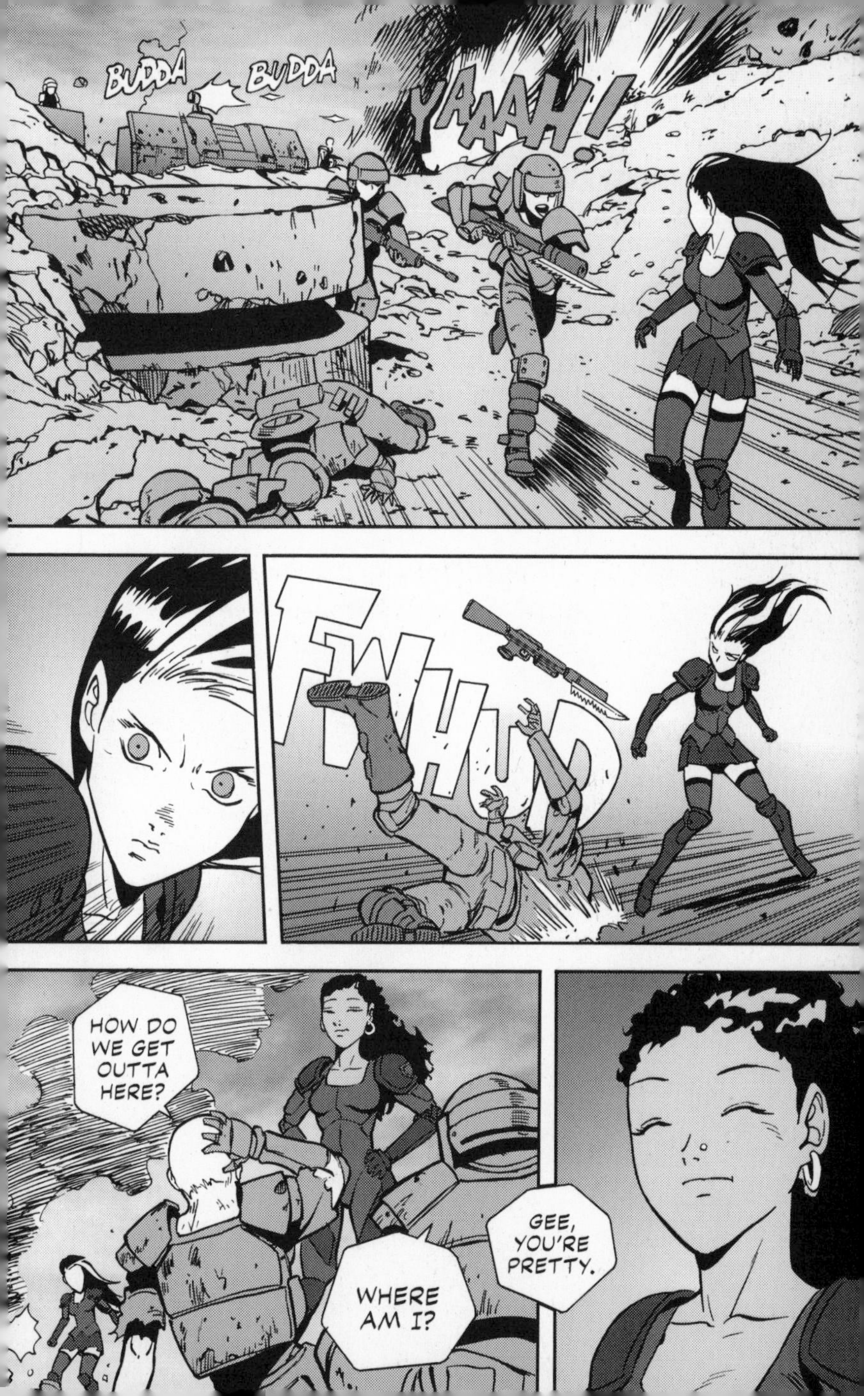
BUDDA
BUDDA
YAAAH!
FWHUD
HOW DO WE GET OUTTA HERE?
WHERE AM I?
GEE, YOU'RE PRETTY.

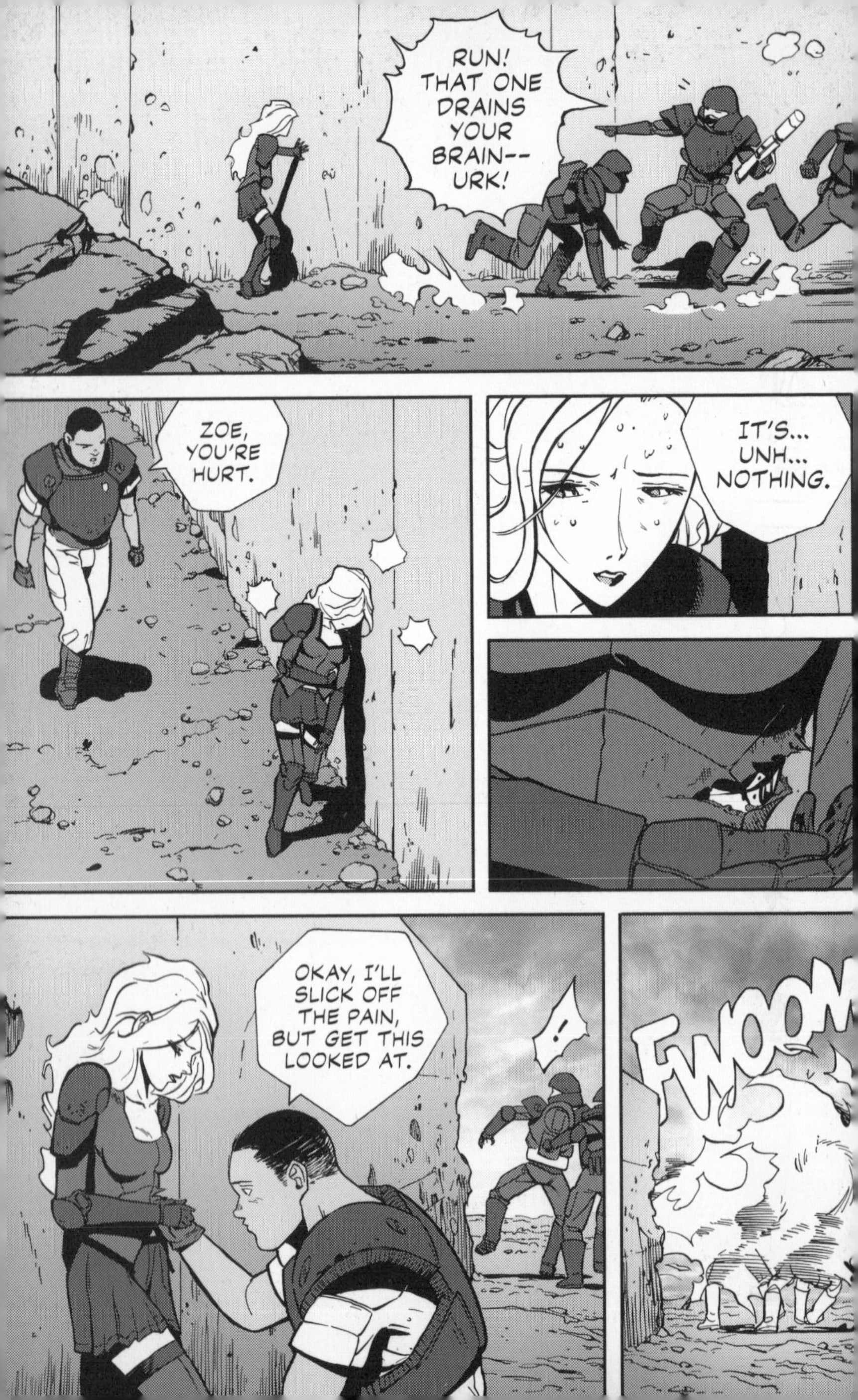
RUN! THAT ONE DRAINS YOUR BRAIN-- URK!
ZOE, YOU'RE HURT.
IT'S... UNH... NOTHING.
OKAY, I'LL SLICK OFF THE PAIN, BUT GET THIS LOOKED AT.
!
FWOOM

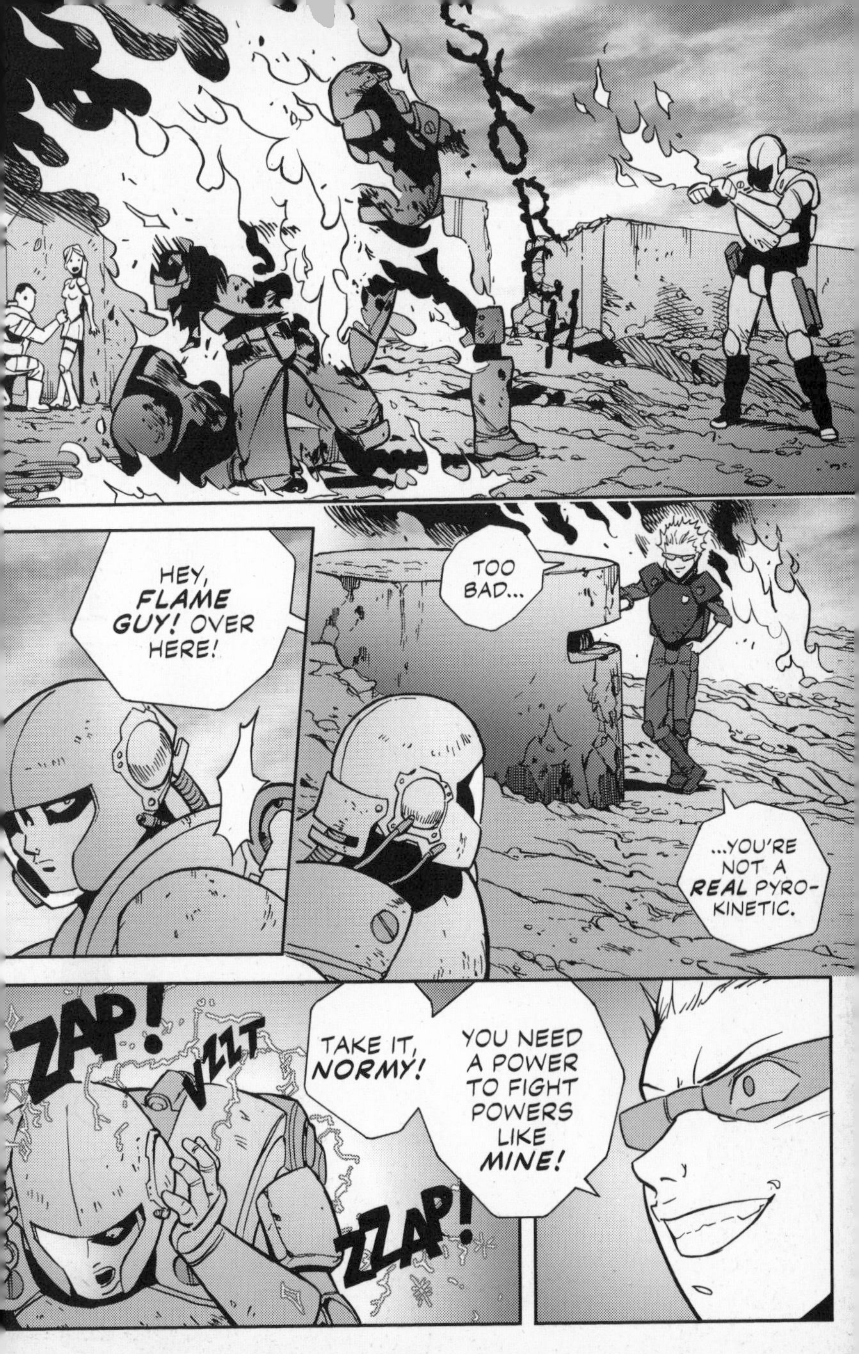
SKORCH
HEY, FLAME GUY! OVER HERE!
TOO BAD...
...YOU'RE NOT A REAL PYRO-KINETIC.
ZAP!
VZZT
TAKE IT, NORMY!
YOU NEED A POWER TO FIGHT POWERS LIKE MINE!
ZZAP!

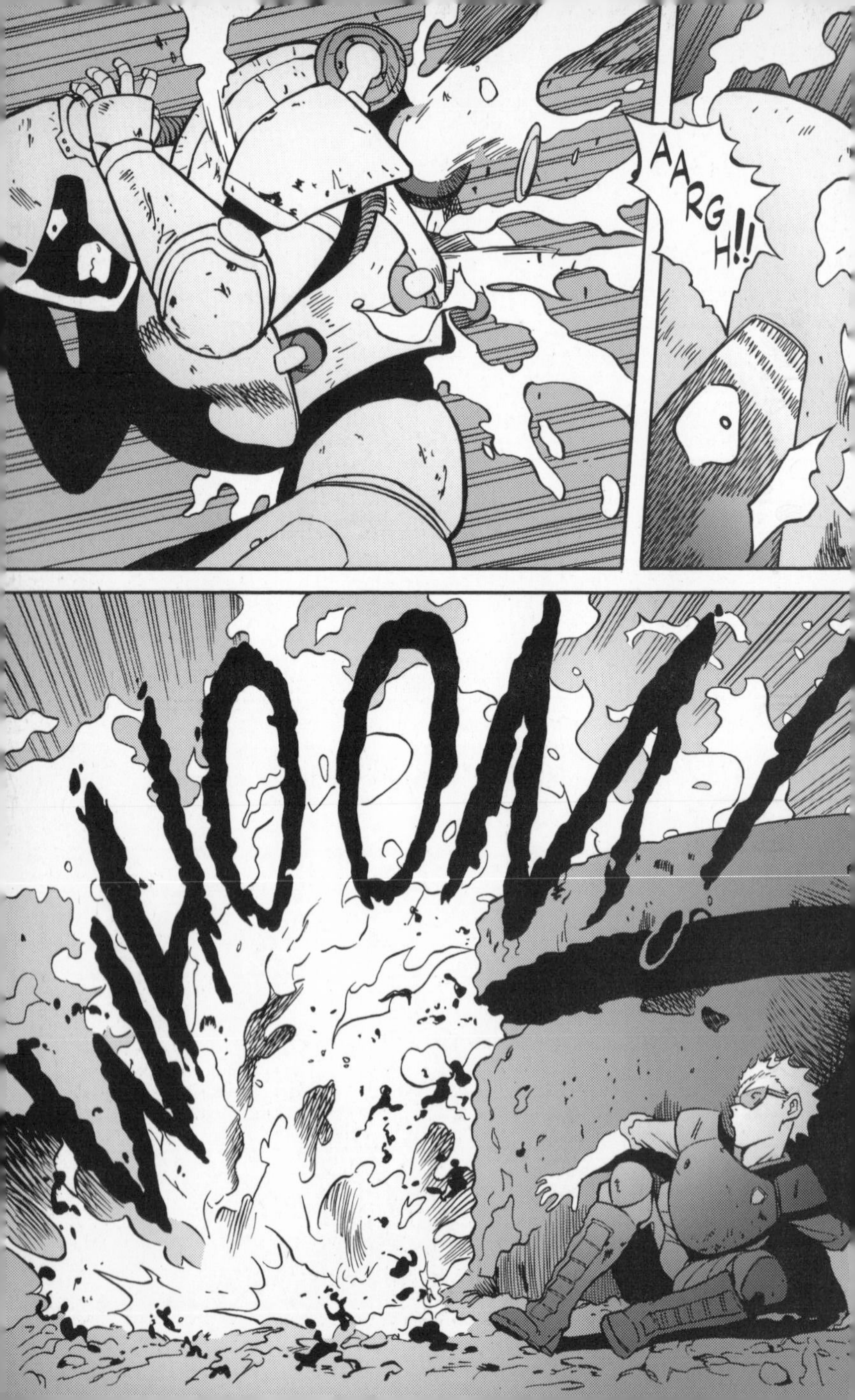
AARGH!!
WHOOM

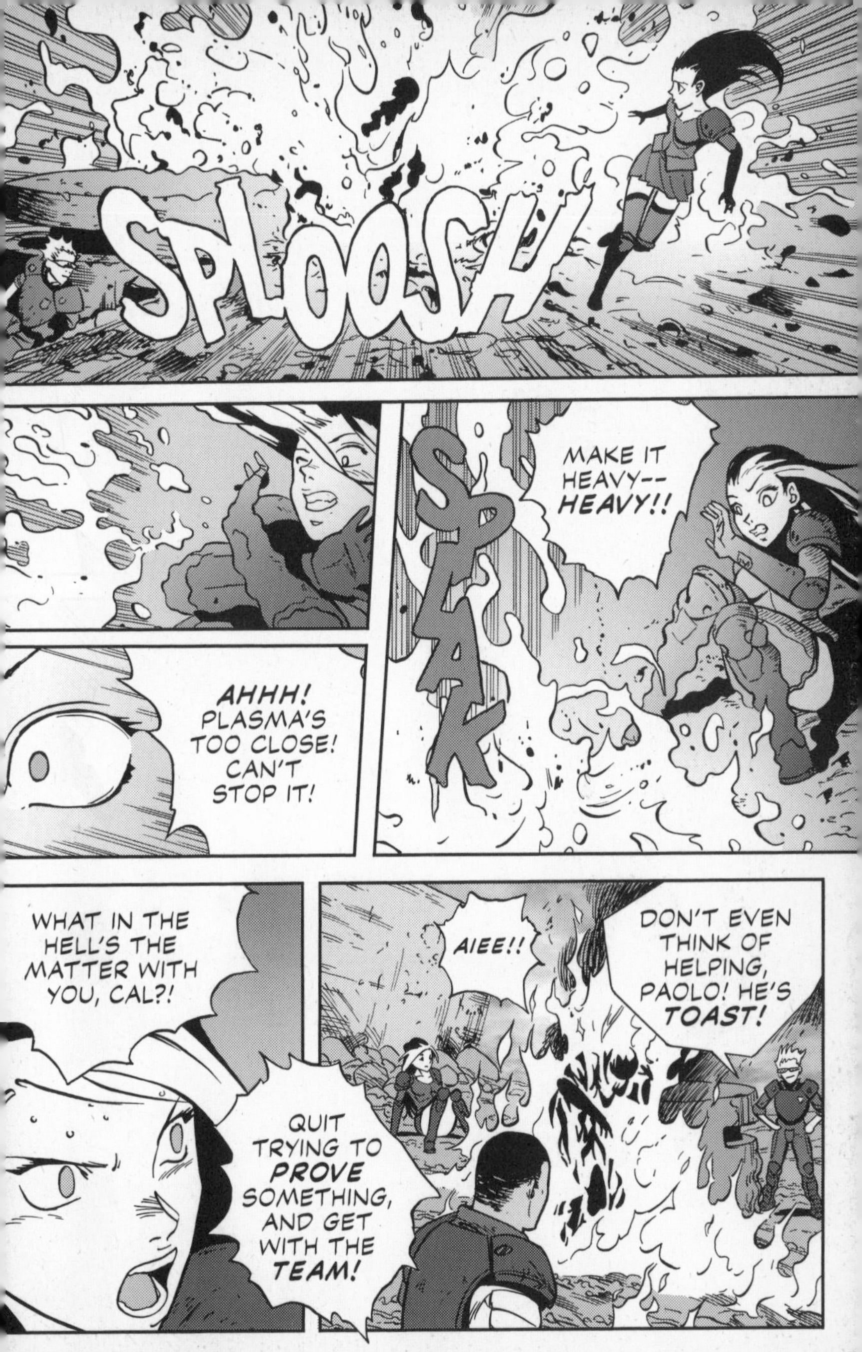
SPLOOSH
AHHH! PLASMA'S TOO CLOSE! CAN'T STOP IT!
SPAK
MAKE IT HEAVY-- HEAVY!!
WHAT IN THE HELL'S THE MATTER WITH YOU, CAL?!
QUIT TRYING TO PROVE SOMETHING, AND GET WITH THE TEAM!
AIEE!!
DON'T EVEN THINK OF HELPING, PAOLO! HE'S TOAST!

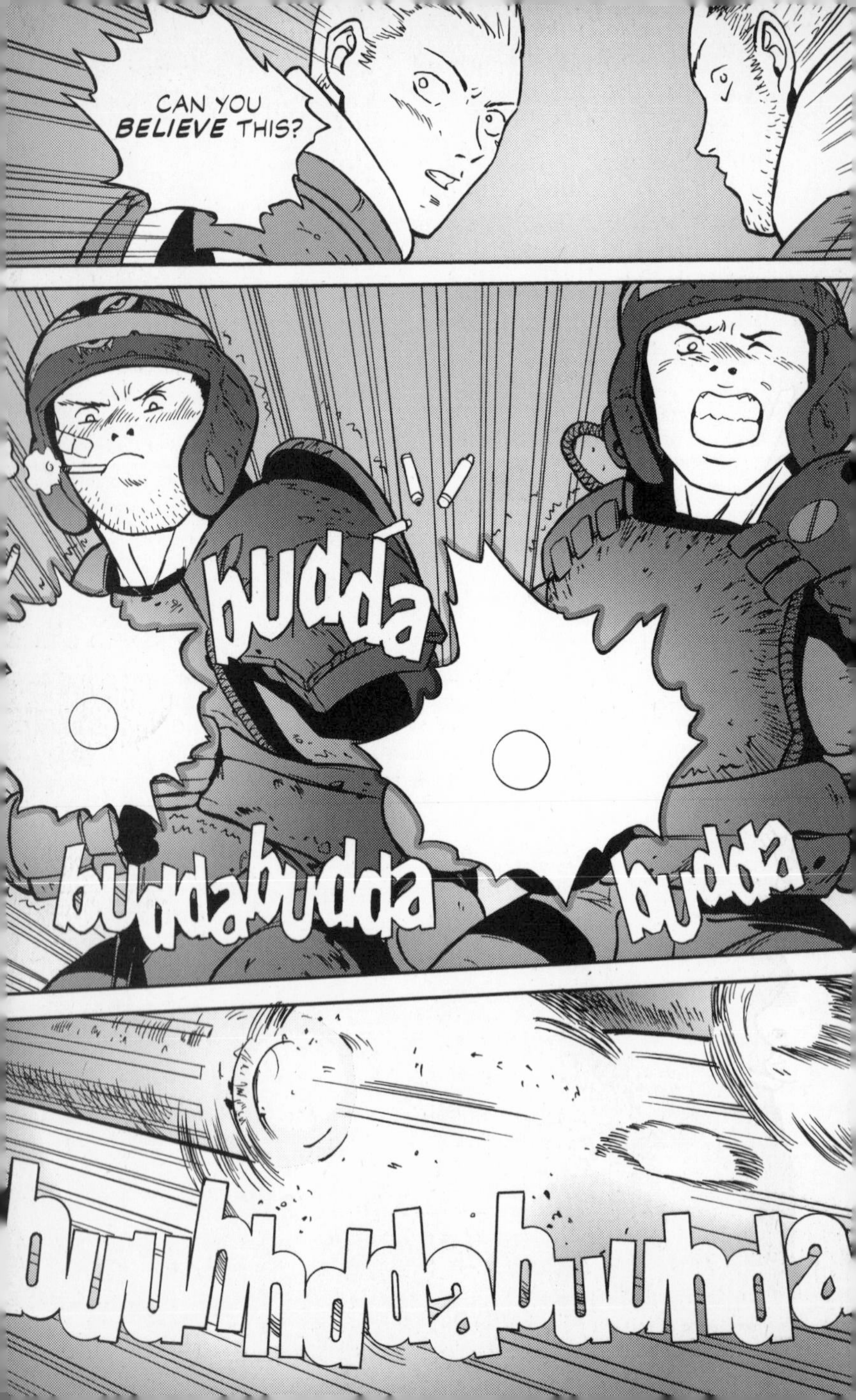
CAN YOU *BELIEVE* THIS?
budda
buddabudda
budda
buuhddabuuhda

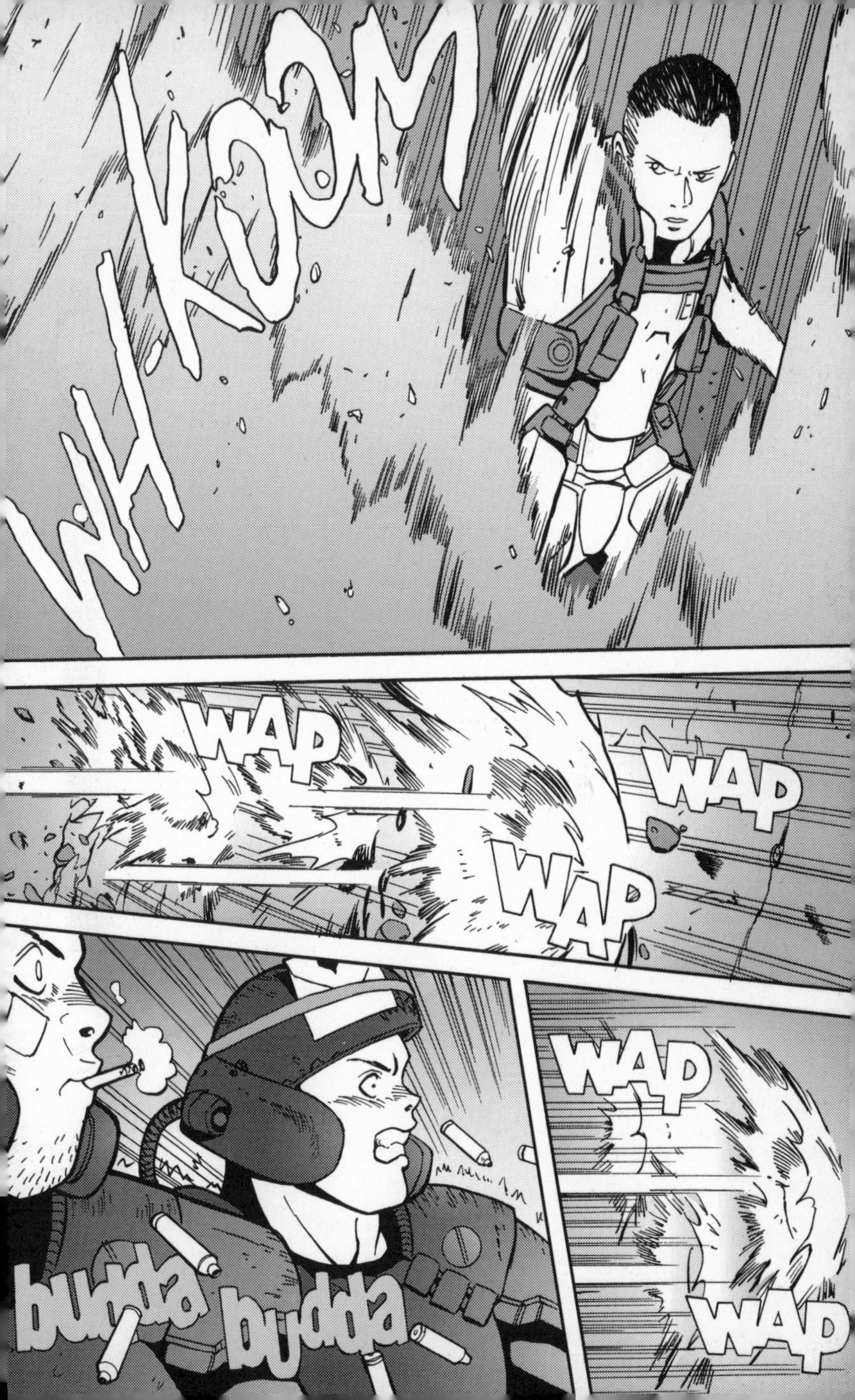
WHKOOM
WAP
WAP
WAP
budda budda
WAP
WAP

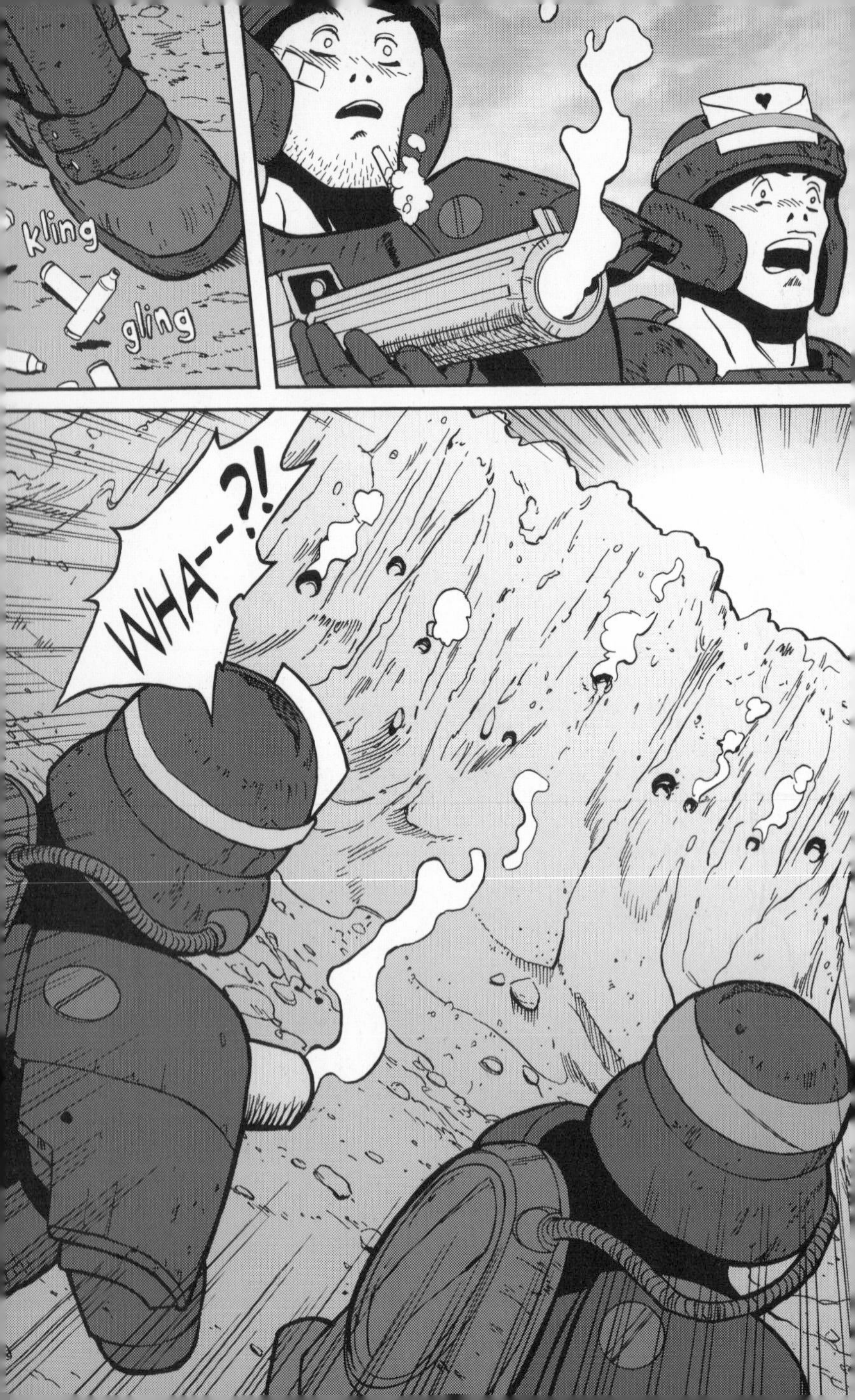
kling
gling
WHA--?!

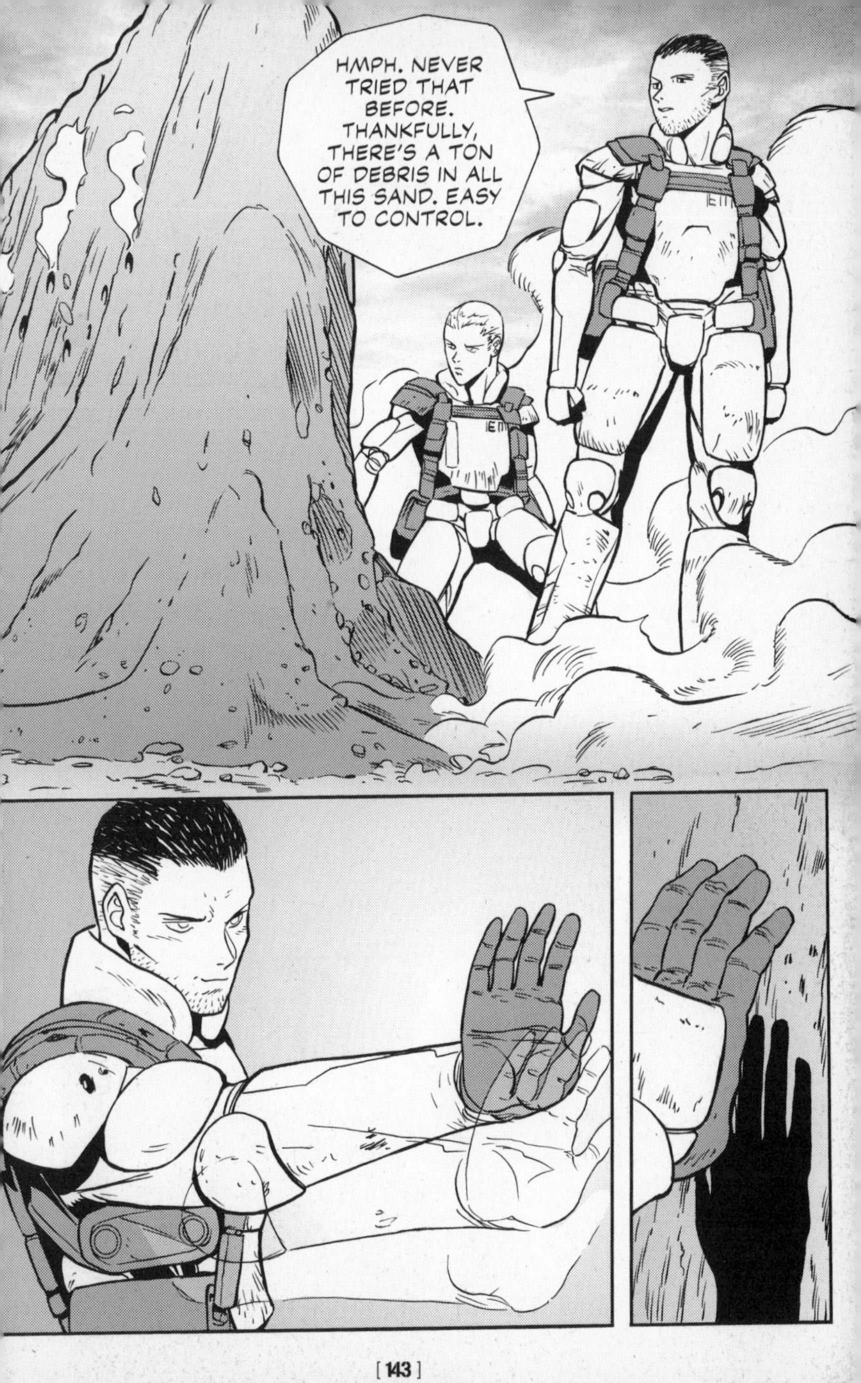
HMPH. NEVER TRIED THAT BEFORE. THANKFULLY, THERE'S A TON OF DEBRIS IN ALL THIS SAND. EASY TO CONTROL.

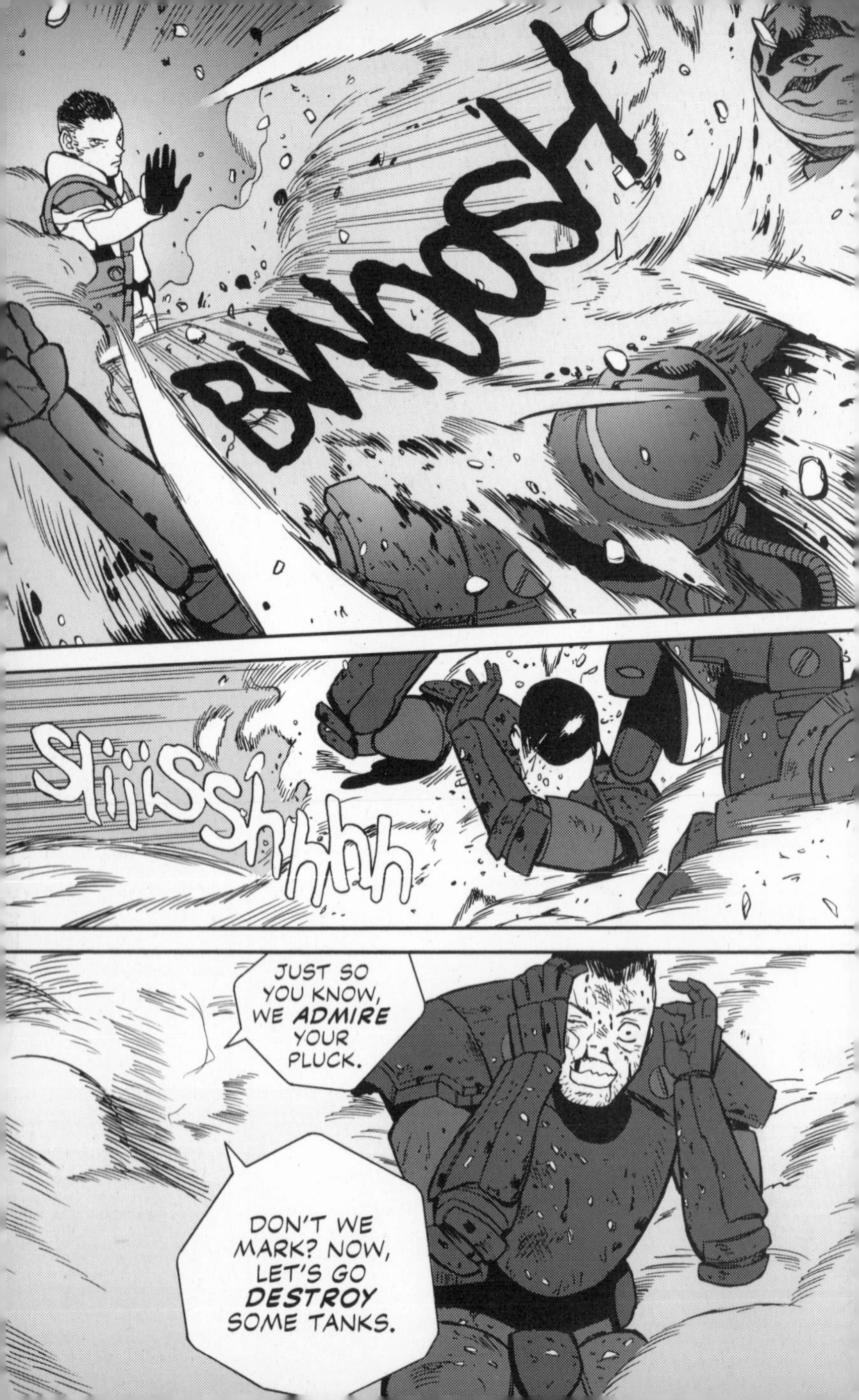
BWOOSH!
SHIISSHHHH
JUST SO YOU KNOW, WE ADMIRE YOUR PLUCK.
DON'T WE MARK? NOW, LET'S GO DESTROY SOME TANKS.

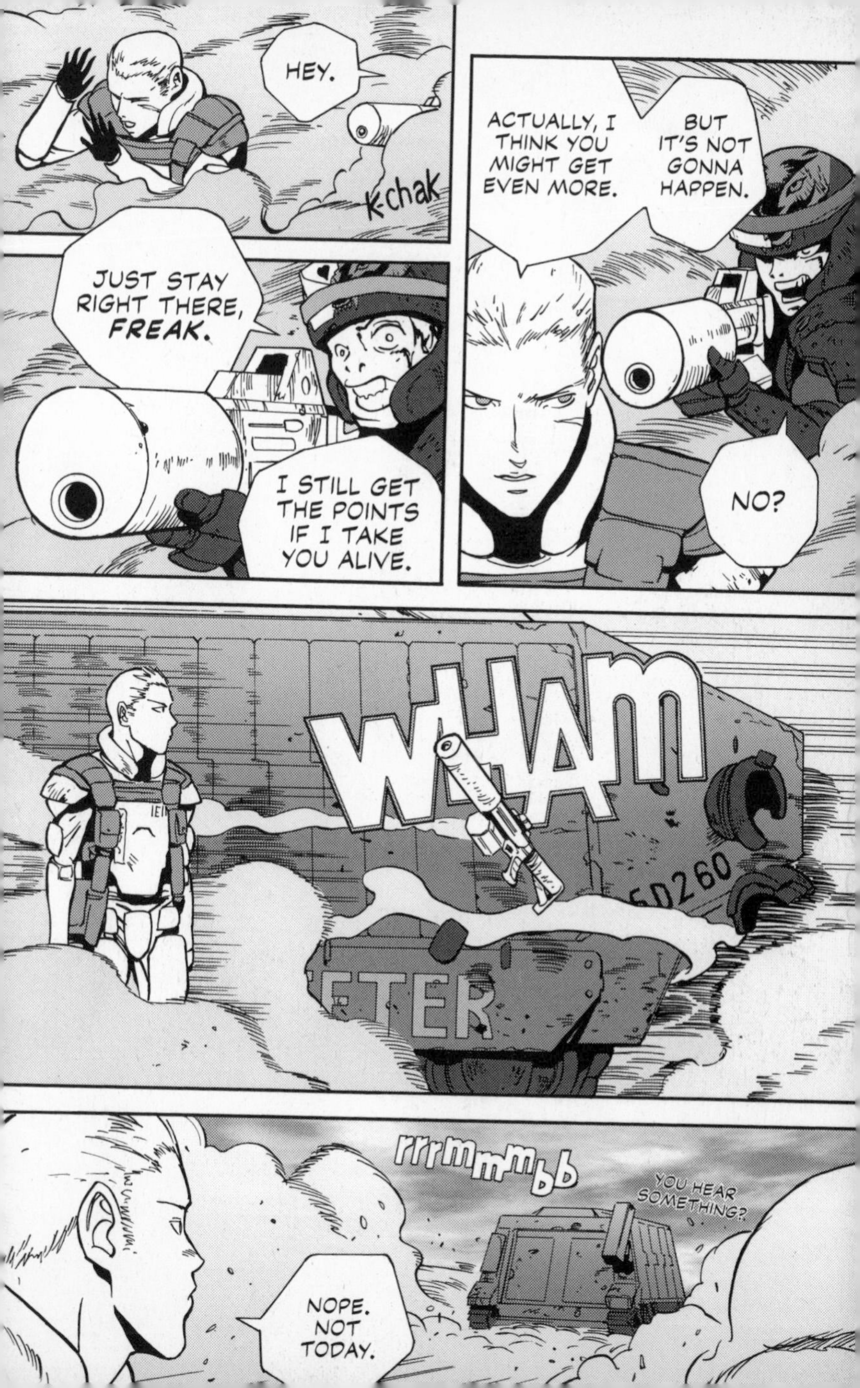
HEY.
K-chak
JUST STAY RIGHT THERE, FREAK.
I STILL GET THE POINTS IF I TAKE YOU ALIVE.
ACTUALLY, I THINK YOU MIGHT GET EVEN MORE.
BUT IT'S NOT GONNA HAPPEN.
NO?
WHAM
SD260
TER
rrrmmmmbb
YOU HEAR SOMETHING?
NOPE. NOT TODAY.

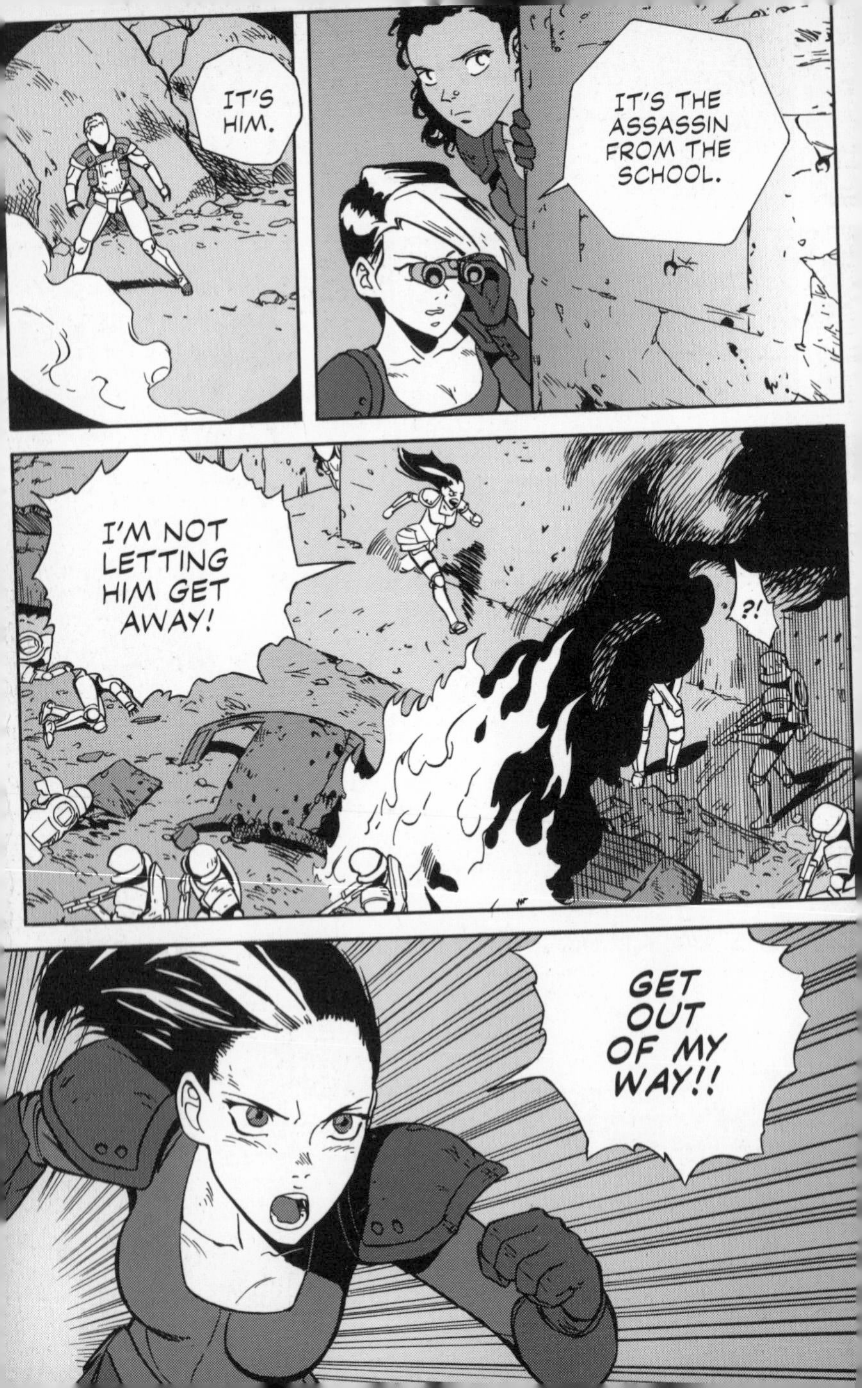
IT'S HIM.
IT'S THE ASSASSIN FROM THE SCHOOL.
I'M NOT LETTING HIM GET AWAY!
?!
GET OUT OF MY WAY!!

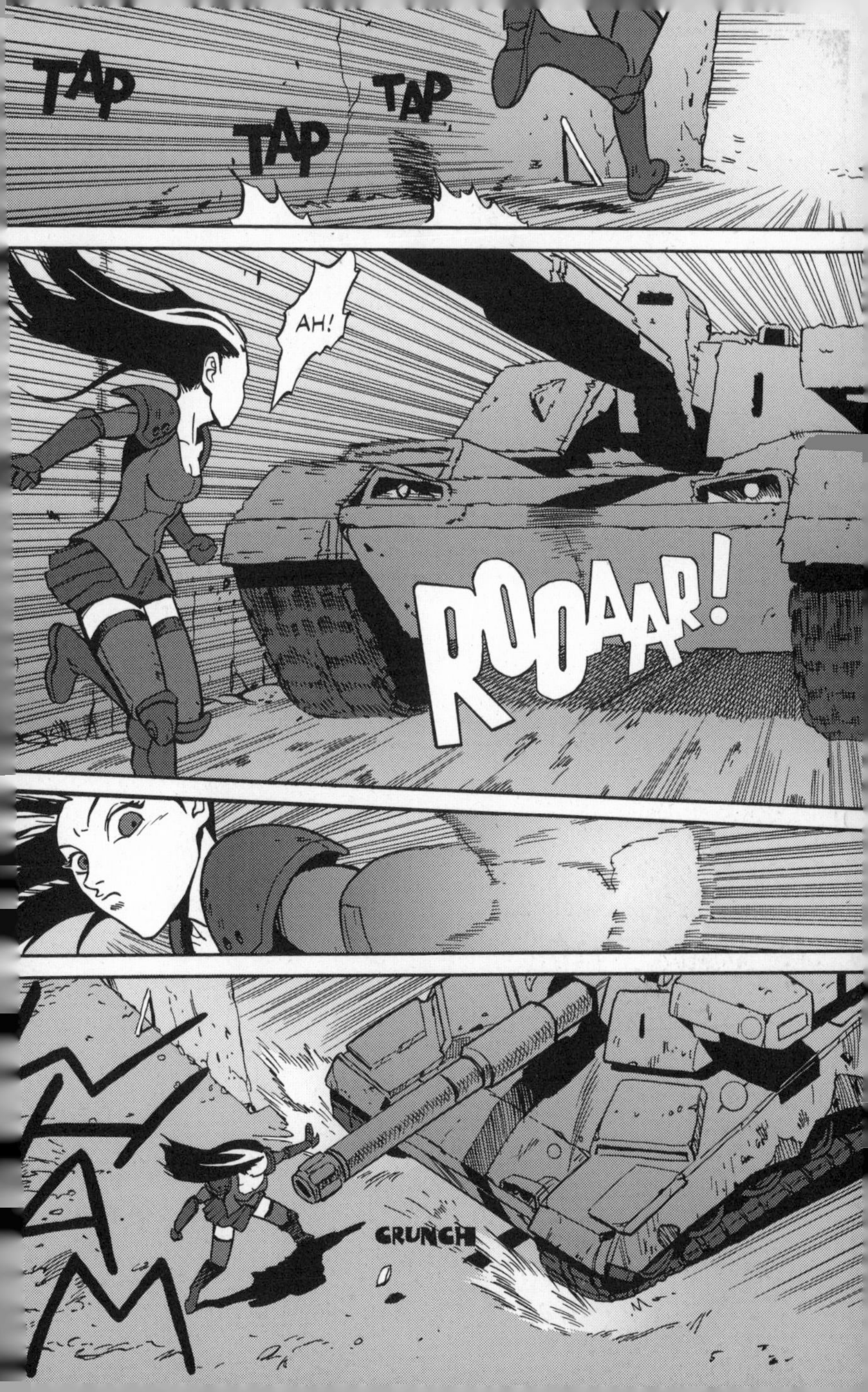
TAP
TAP
TAP
AH!
ROOAAR!
ZAM
CRUNCH

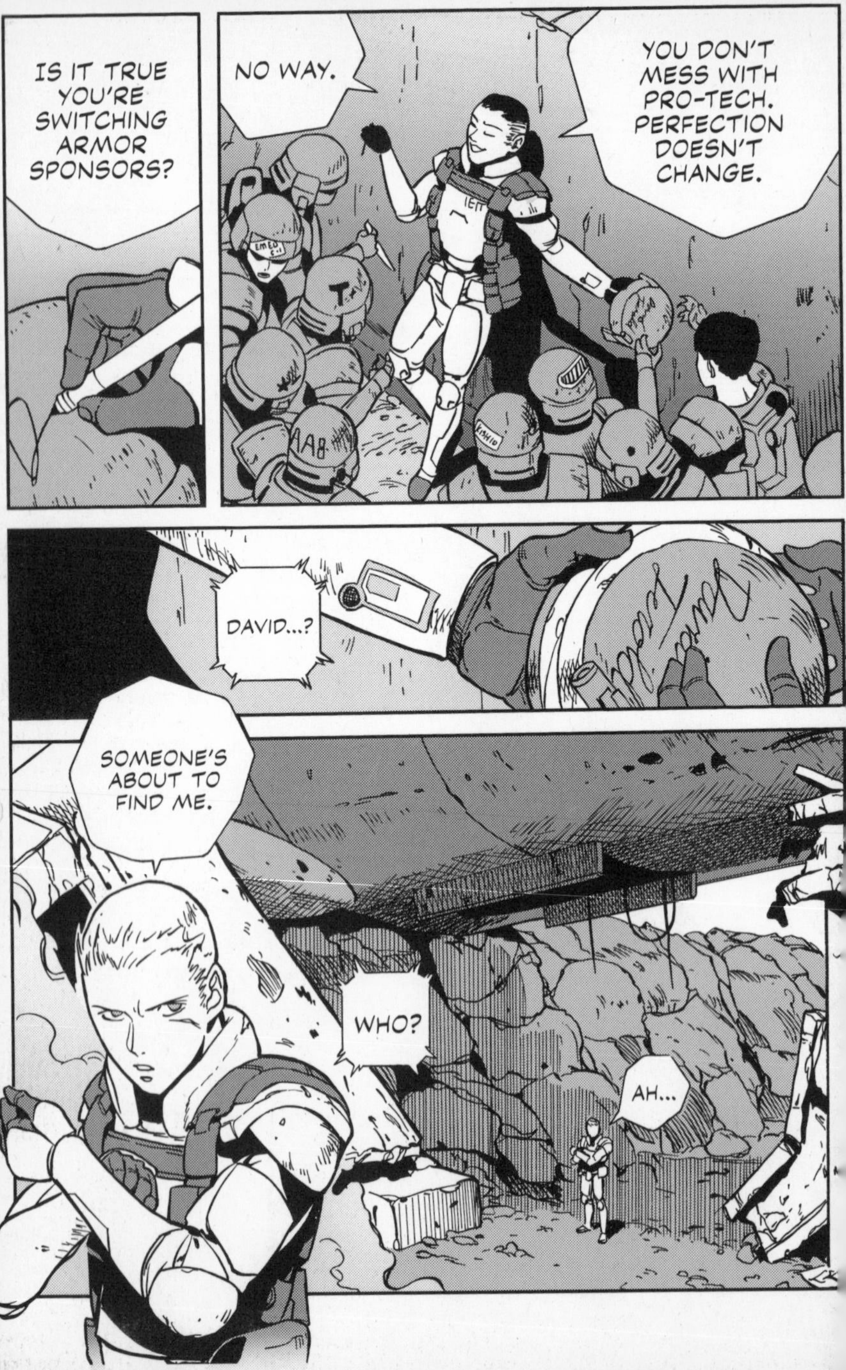
IS IT TRUE YOU'RE SWITCHING ARMOR SPONSORS?
NO WAY.
YOU DON'T MESS WITH PRO-TECH. PERFECTION DOESN'T CHANGE.
DAVID...?
SOMEONE'S ABOUT TO FIND ME.
WHO?
AH...

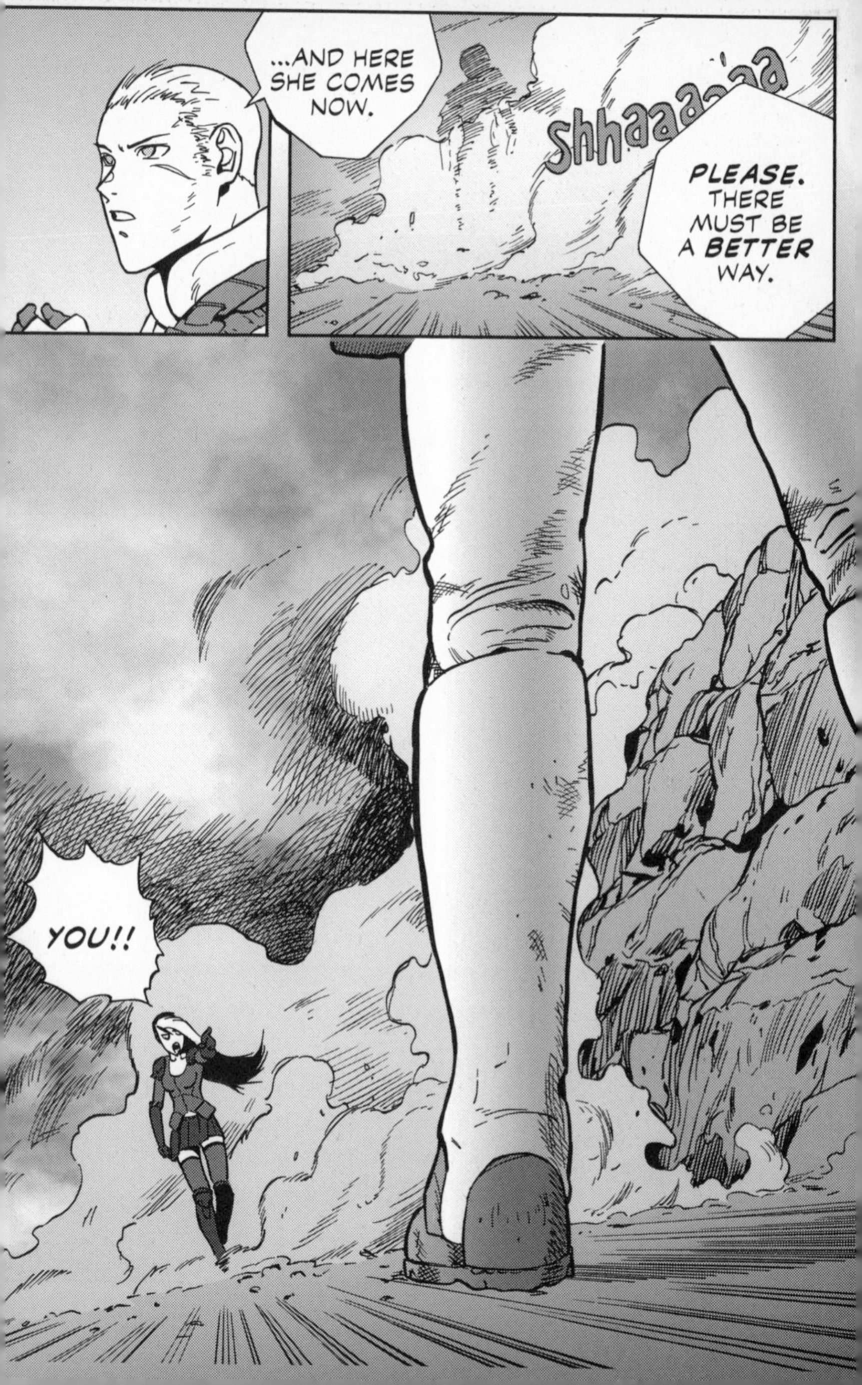
...AND HERE SHE COMES NOW.
Shhaaaaaaa
PLEASE. THERE MUST BE A BETTER WAY.
YOU!!

PSY★COMM

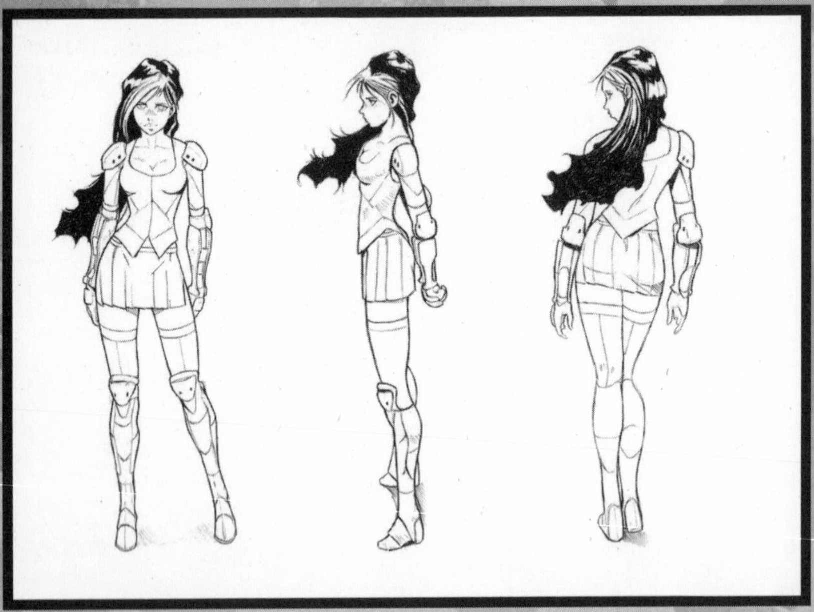

EARLY DESIGN SKETCH FOR SNOW LUCENTE:
HER LOOK HAS REMAINED ESSENTIALLY THE SAME,
WITH THE EXCEPTION OF HER HAIR AND THE ARM-GUARDS

PSY★COMM

CHAPTER [8]

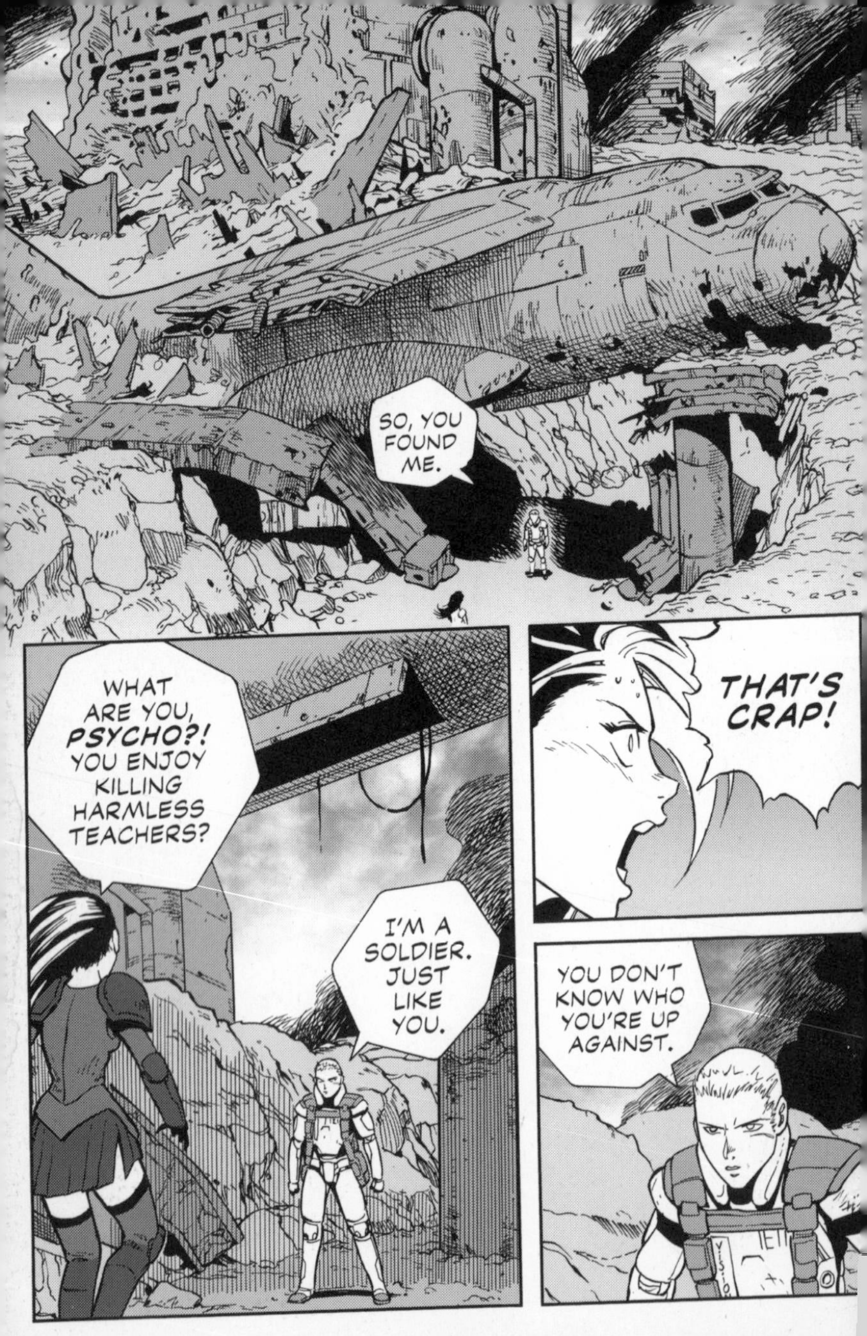

SO, YOU FOUND ME.
WHAT ARE YOU, PSYCHO?! YOU ENJOY KILLING HARMLESS TEACHERS?
I'M A SOLDIER. JUST LIKE YOU.
THAT'S CRAP!
YOU DON'T KNOW WHO YOU'RE UP AGAINST.

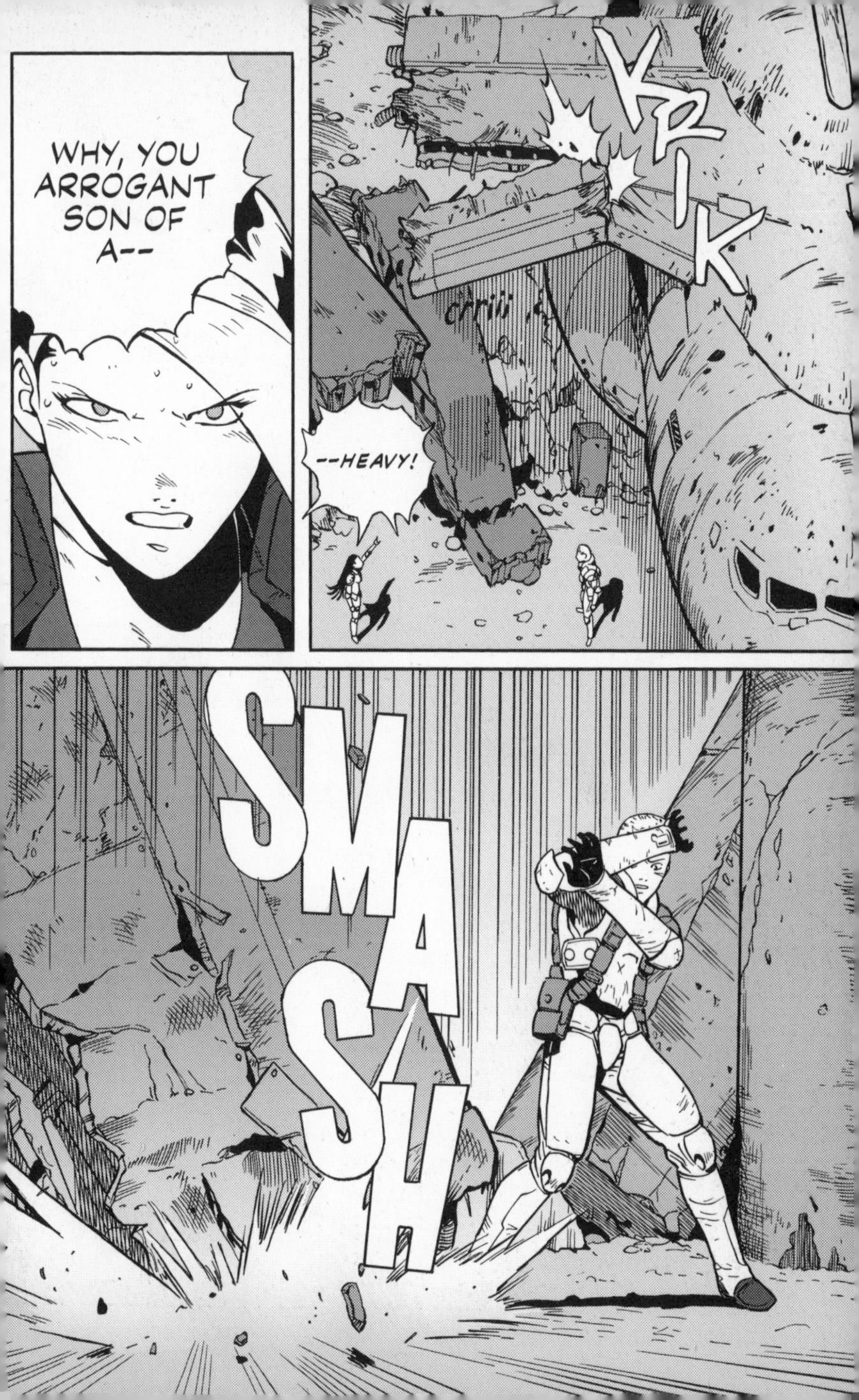
WHY, YOU ARROGANT SON OF A--
KRIK
crriii
--HEAVY!
SMASH

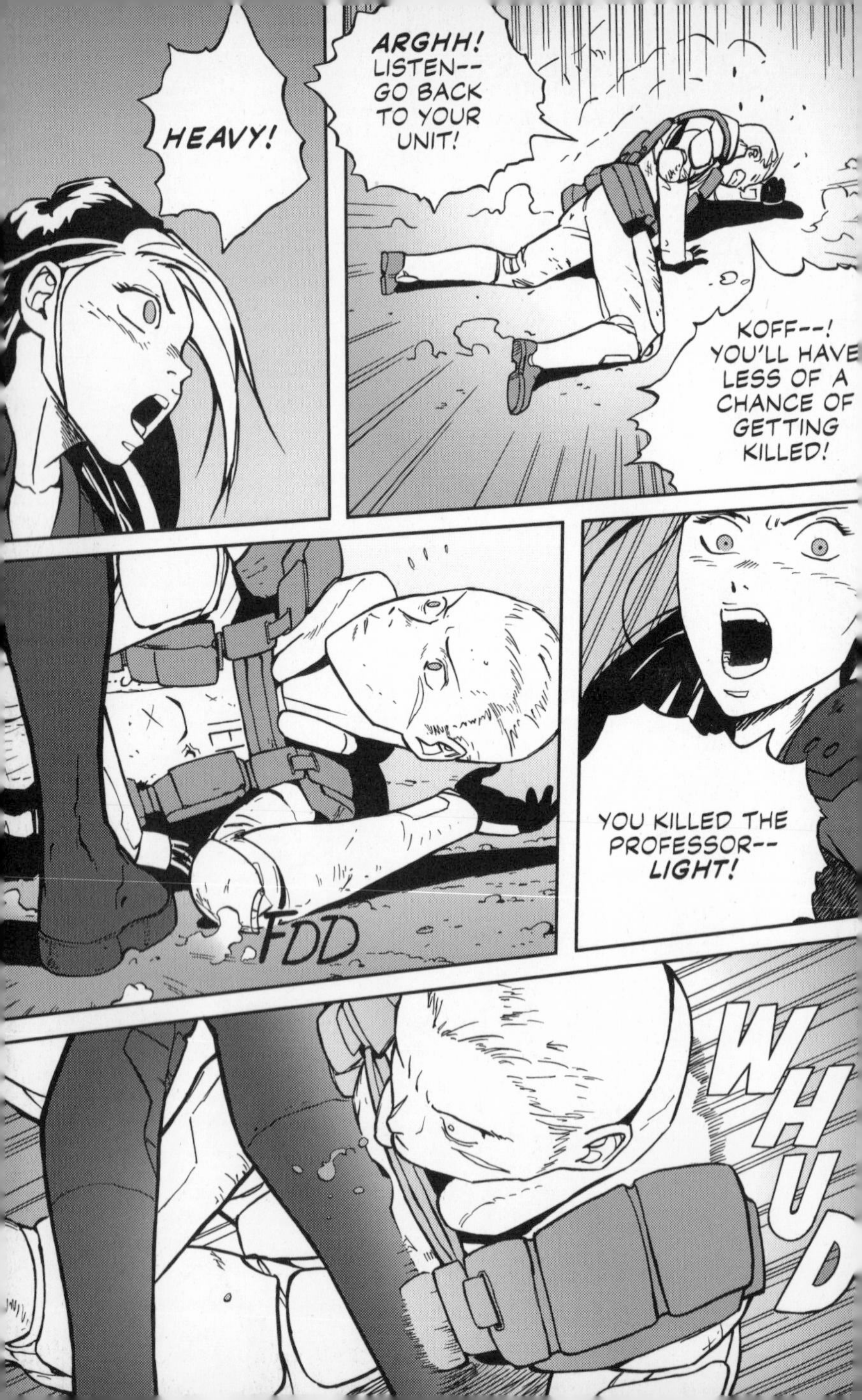
HEAVY!
ARGHH! LISTEN-- GO BACK TO YOUR UNIT!
KOFF--! YOU'LL HAVE LESS OF A CHANCE OF GETTING KILLED!
FDD
YOU KILLED THE PROFESSOR-- LIGHT!
WHUD

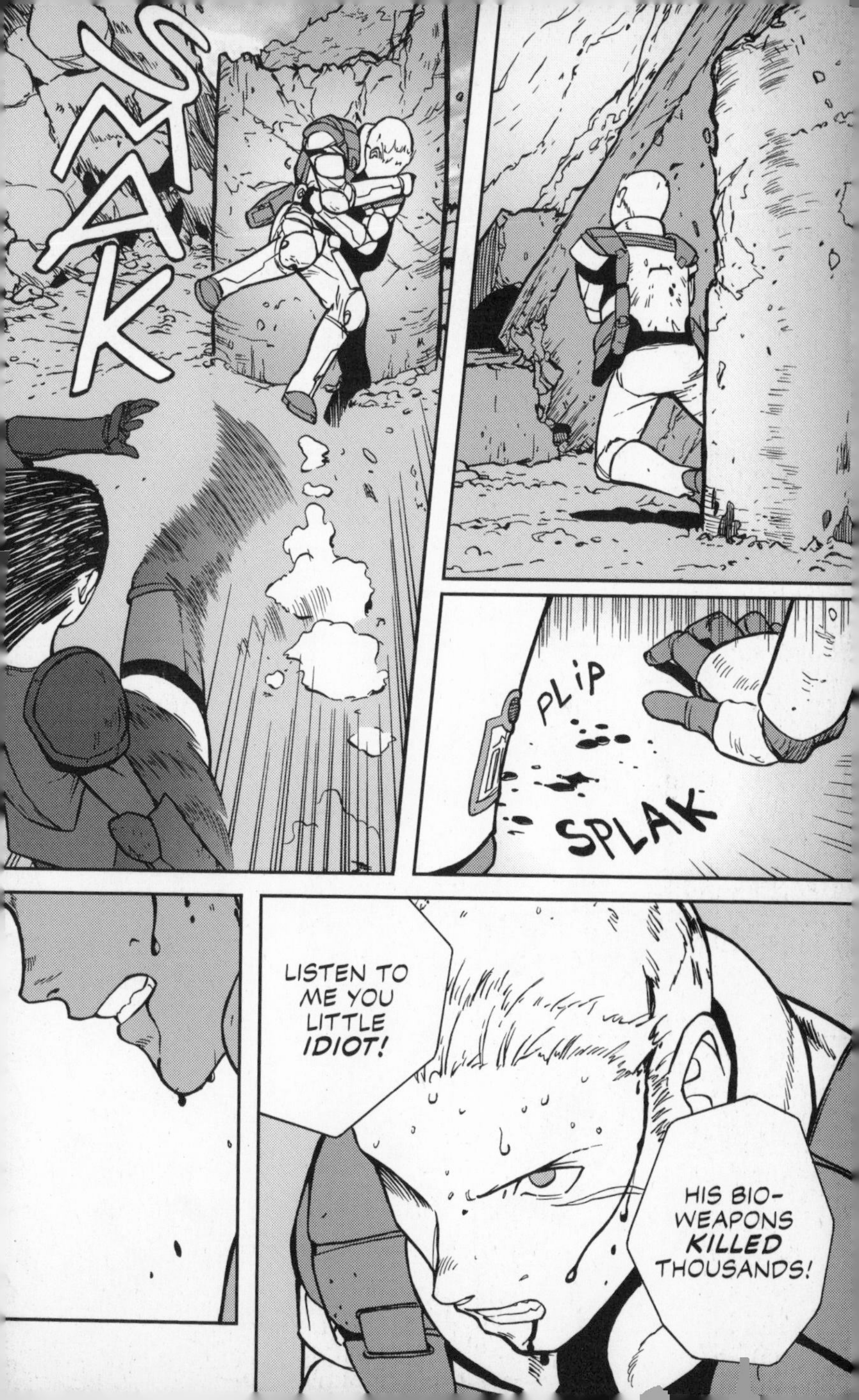
SMAK
PLIP
SPLAK
LISTEN TO ME YOU LITTLE IDIOT!
HIS BIO-WEAPONS KILLED THOUSANDS!

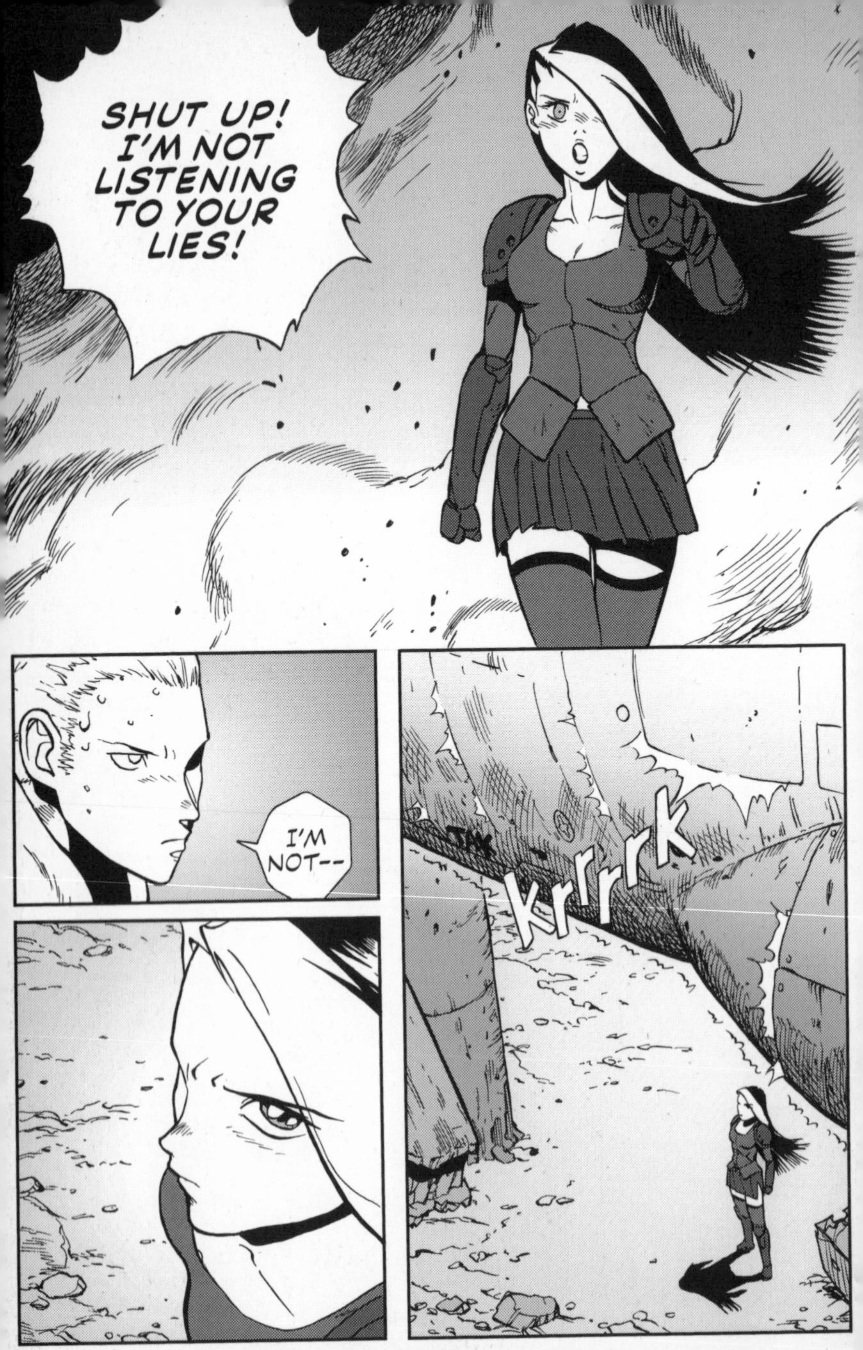
SHUT UP! I'M NOT LISTENING TO YOUR LIES!
I'M NOT--
Krrrrk

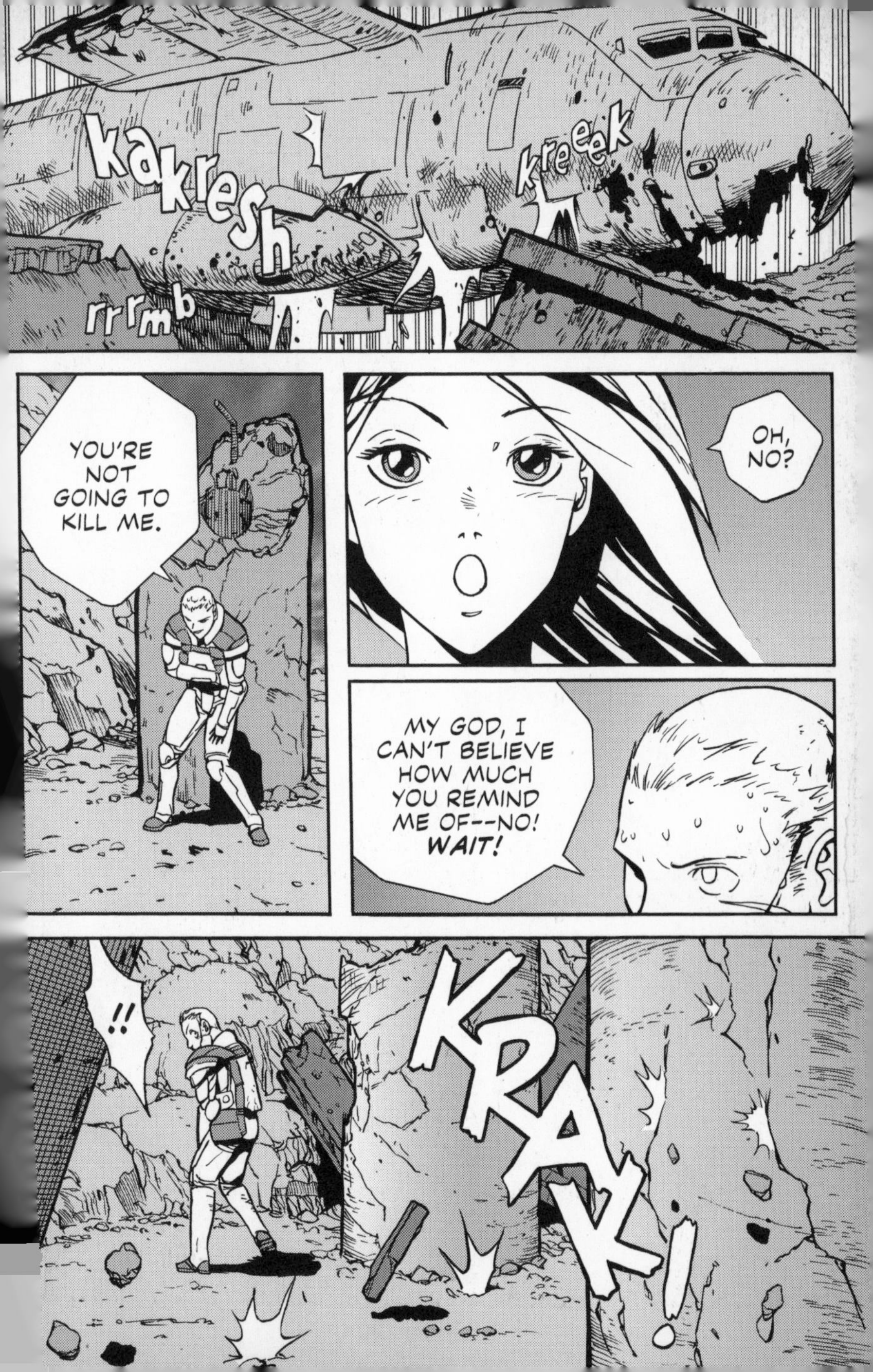
kakresh
kreeek
rrrmb
YOU'RE NOT GOING TO KILL ME.
OH, NO?
MY GOD, I CAN'T BELIEVE HOW MUCH YOU REMIND ME OF--NO! WAIT!
!!
KRAK!

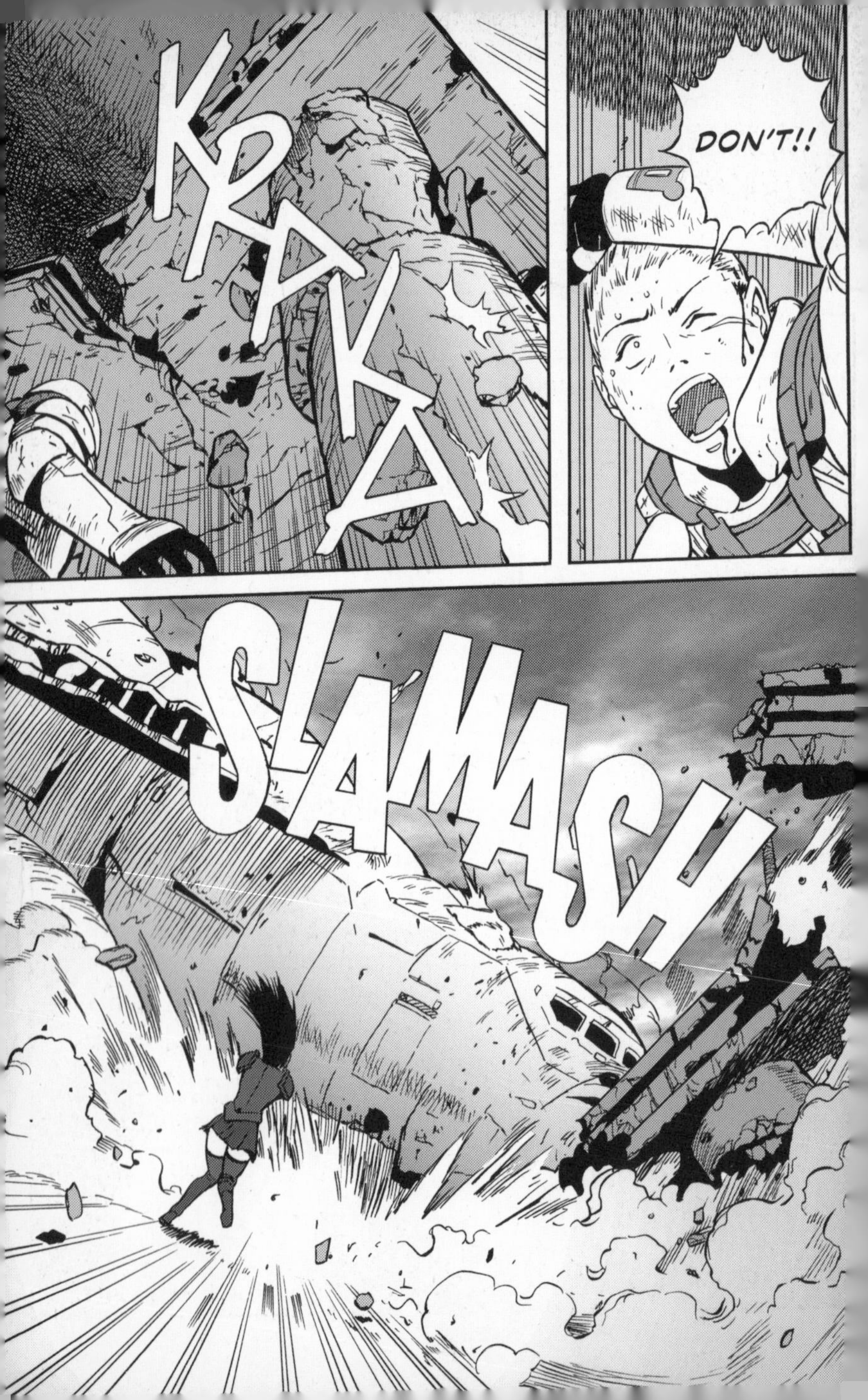
KRAKA
DON'T!!
SLAMASH

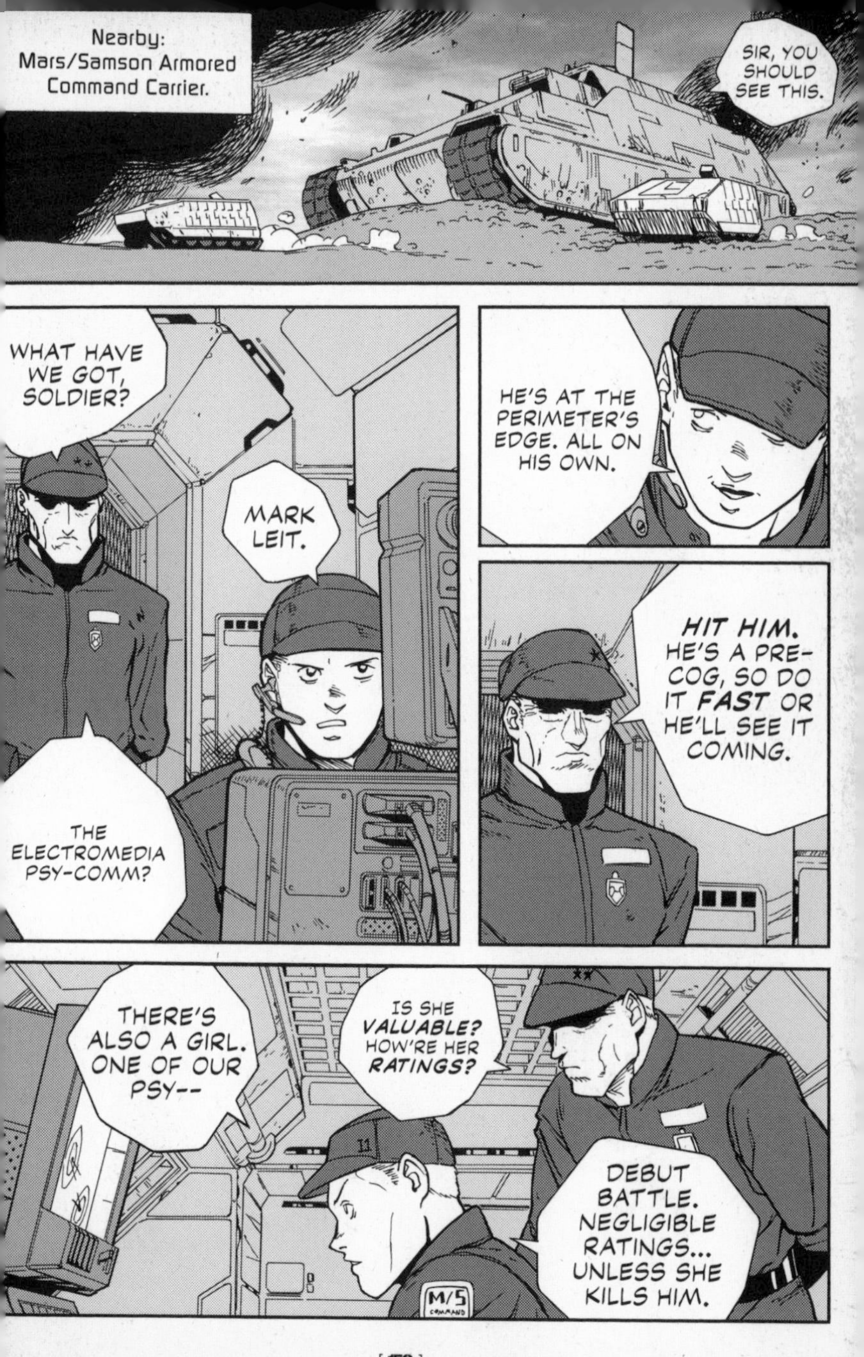
Nearby: Mars/Samson Armored Command Carrier.
SIR, YOU SHOULD SEE THIS.
WHAT HAVE WE GOT, SOLDIER?
MARK LEIT.
THE ELECTROMEDIA PSY-COMM?
HE'S AT THE PERIMETER'S EDGE. ALL ON HIS OWN.
HIT HIM. HE'S A PRE-COG, SO DO IT FAST OR HE'LL SEE IT COMING.
THERE'S ALSO A GIRL. ONE OF OUR PSY--
IS SHE VALUABLE? HOW'RE HER RATINGS?
DEBUT BATTLE. NEGLIGIBLE RATINGS... UNLESS SHE KILLS HIM.
M/5 COMMAND

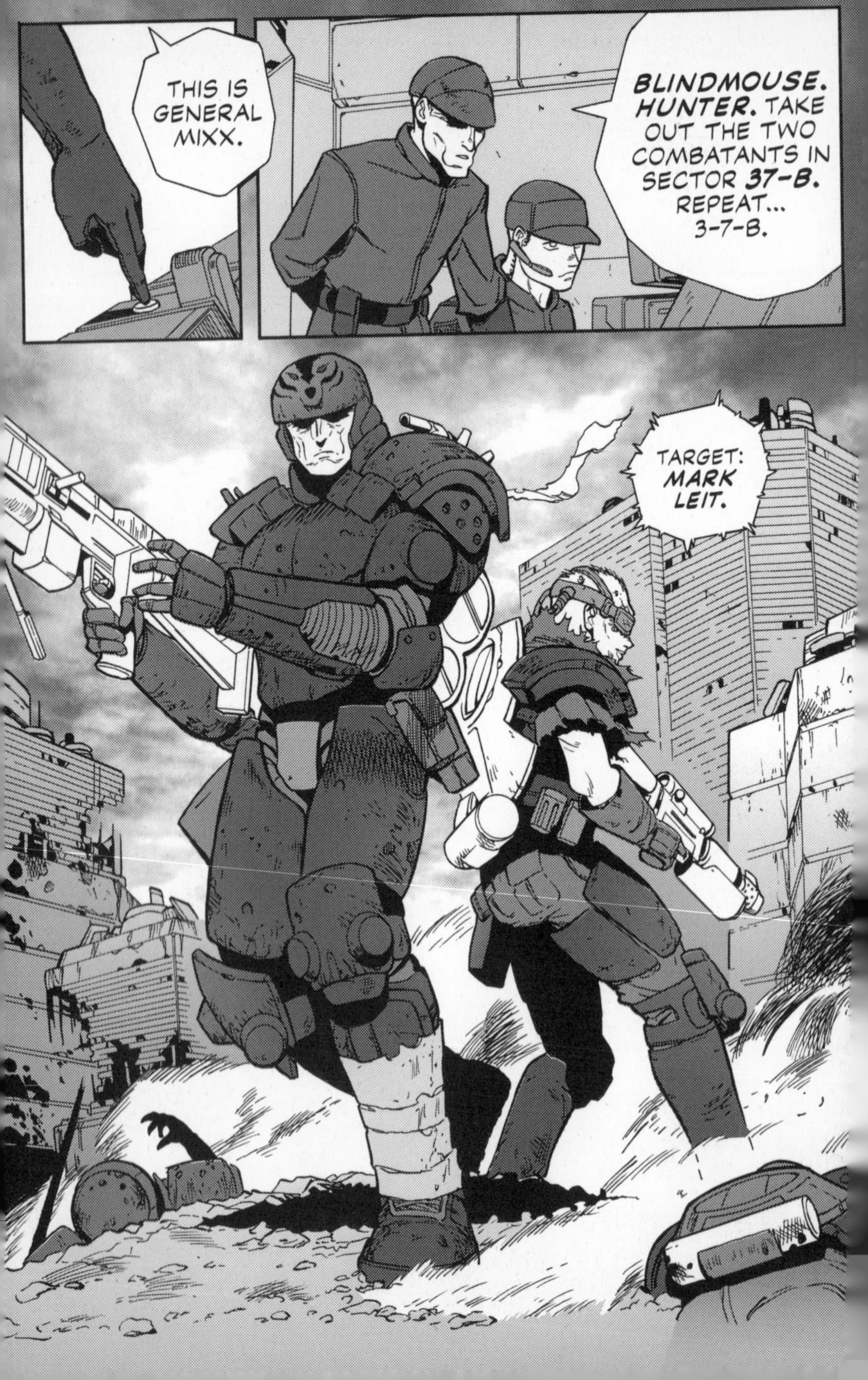
THIS IS GENERAL MIXX.
BLINDMOUSE. HUNTER. TAKE OUT THE TWO COMBATANTS IN SECTOR 37-B. REPEAT... 3-7-B.
TARGET: MARK LEIT.

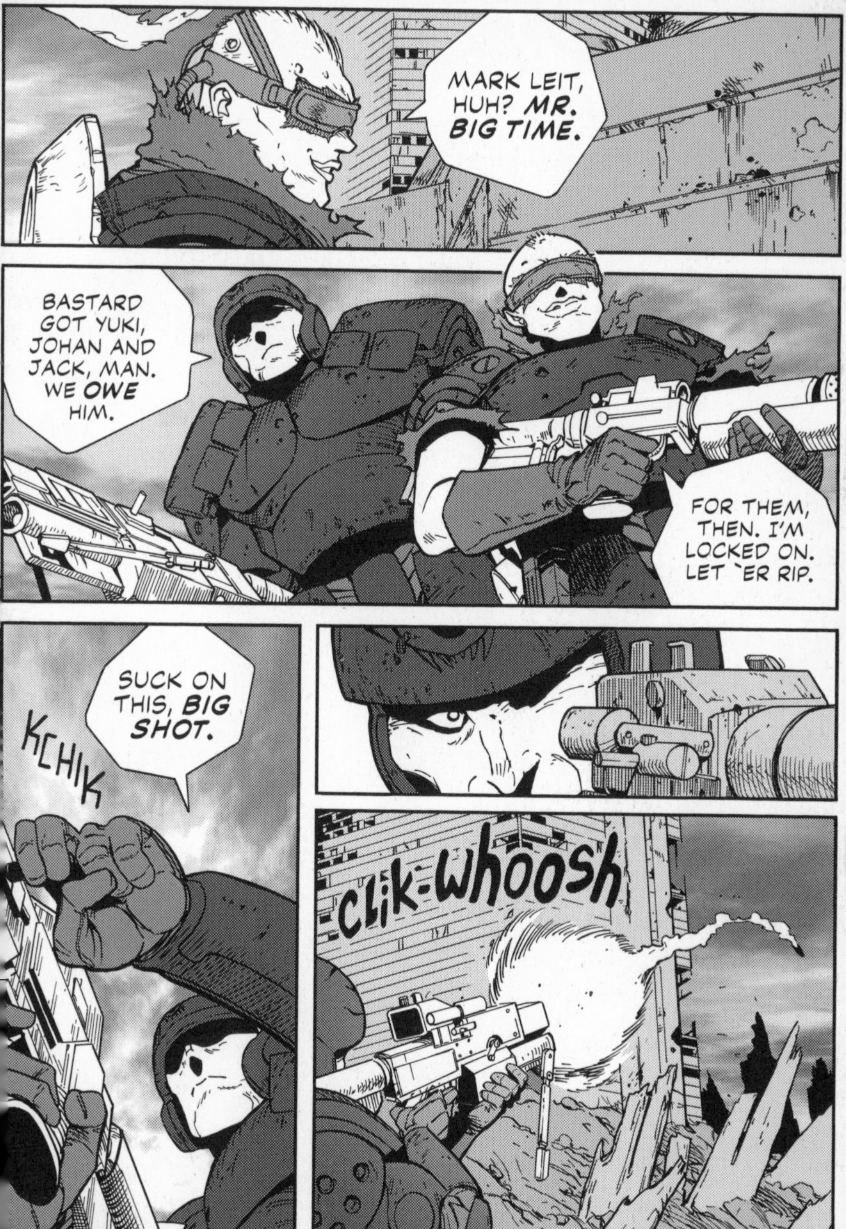
MARK LEIT, HUH? MR. BIG TIME.
BASTARD GOT YUKI, JOHAN AND JACK, MAN. WE OWE HIM.
FOR THEM, THEN. I'M LOCKED ON. LET `ER RIP.
SUCK ON THIS, BIG SHOT.
KCHIK
CLIK-WHOOSH

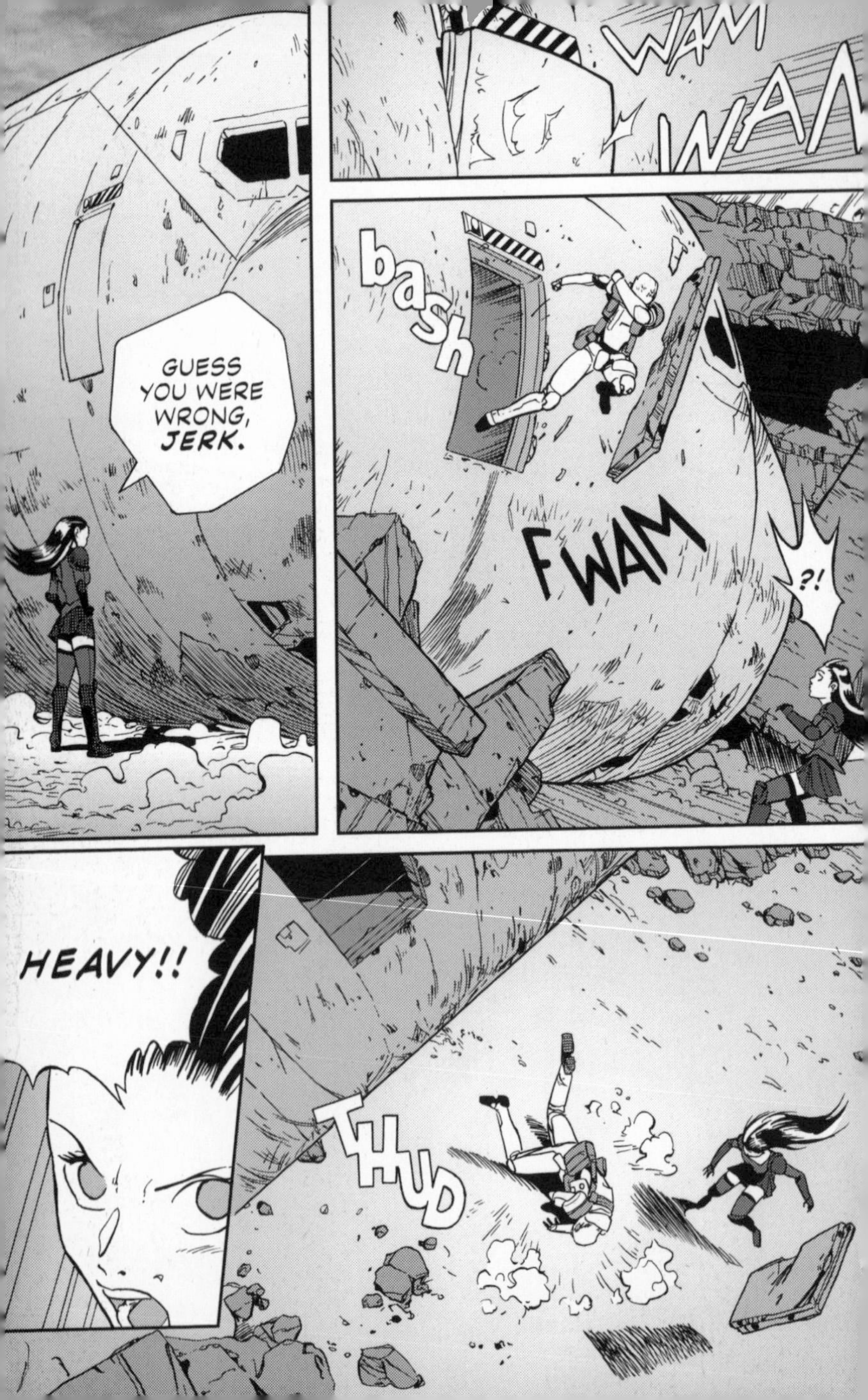
GUESS YOU WERE WRONG, JERK.
WAM
WAM
bash
FWAM
?!
HEAVY!!
THUD

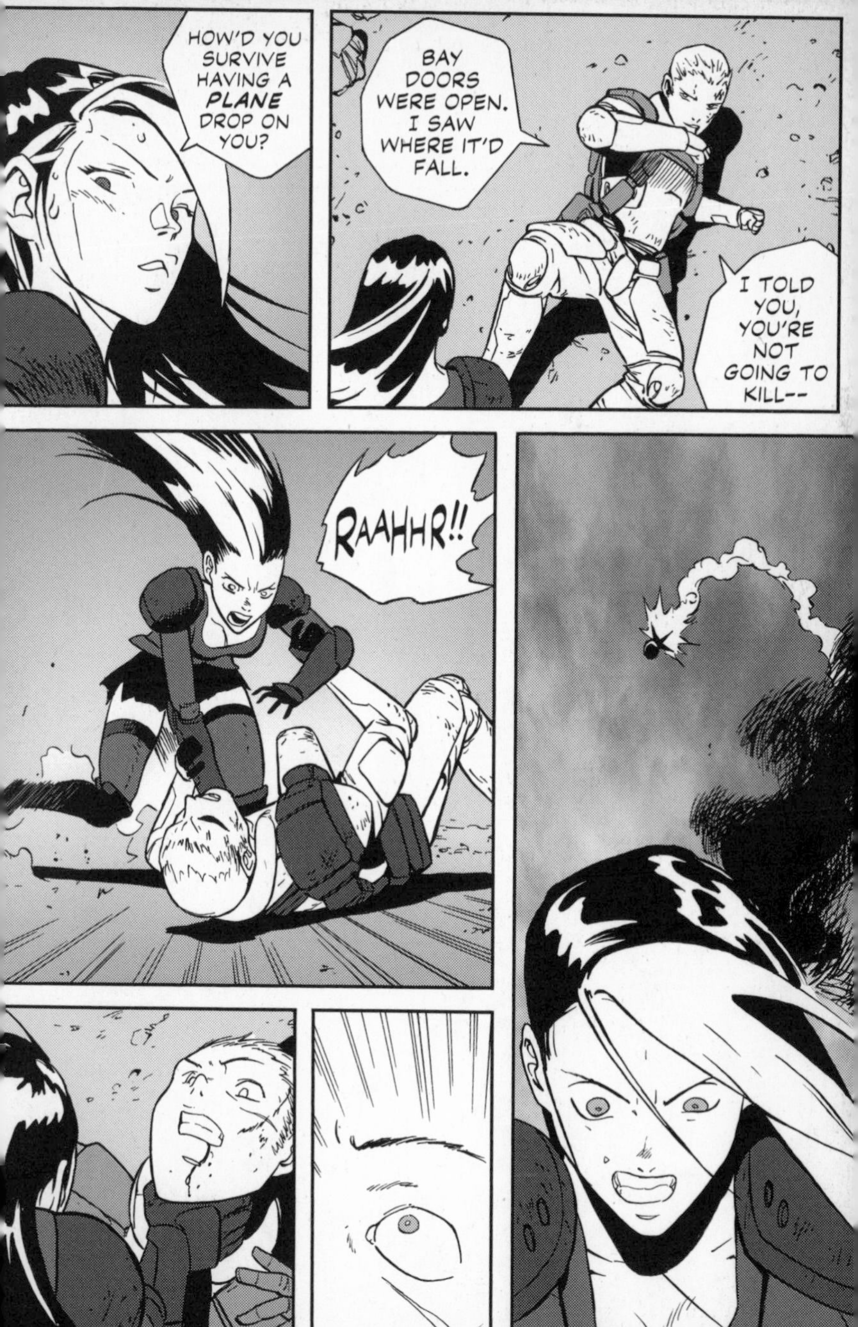
HOW'D YOU SURVIVE HAVING A *PLANE* DROP ON YOU?
BAY DOORS WERE OPEN. I SAW WHERE IT'D FALL.
I TOLD YOU, YOU'RE NOT GOING TO KILL--
RAAHHR!!

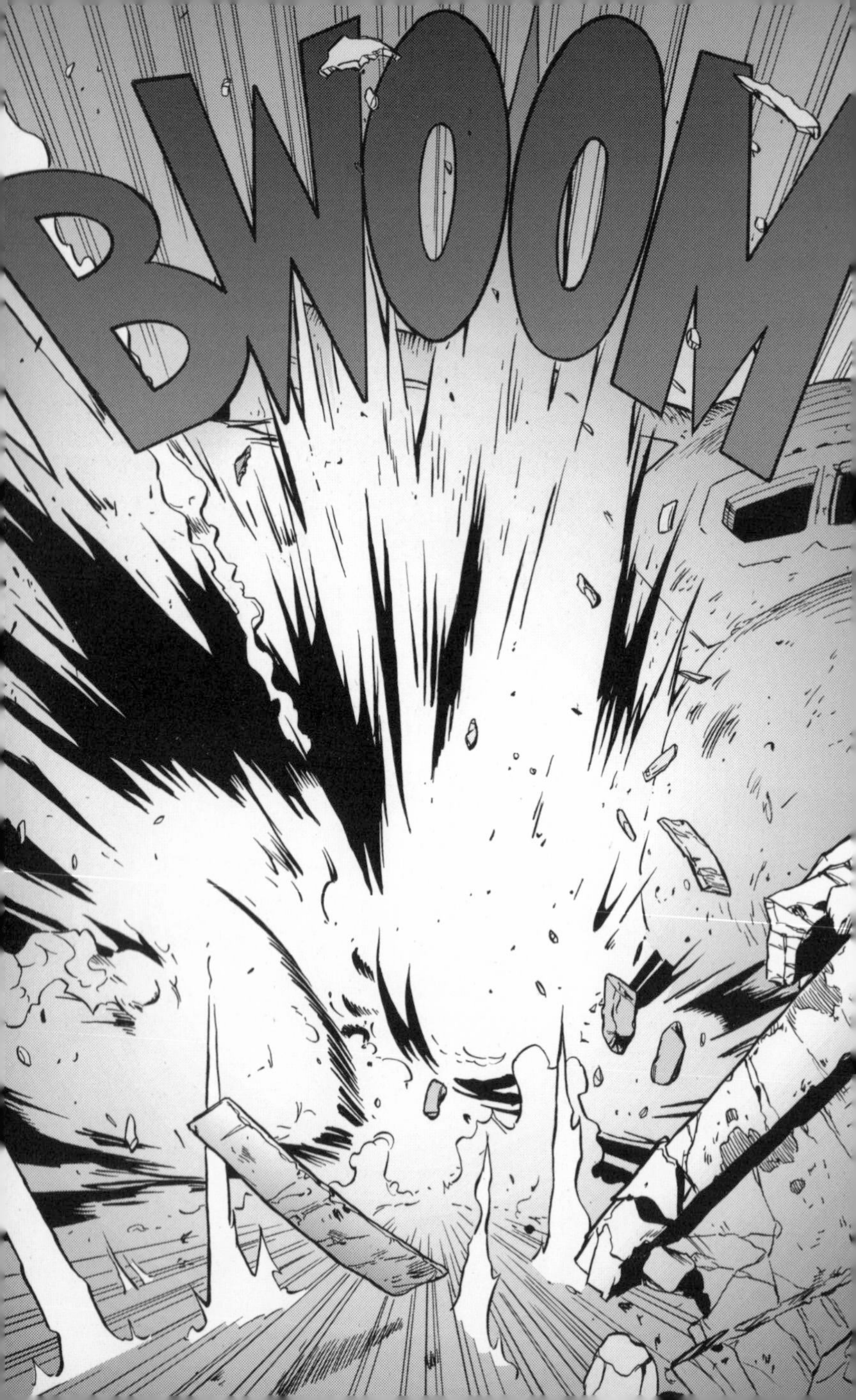
BWOOM

PSY★COMM

CHAPTER [9]

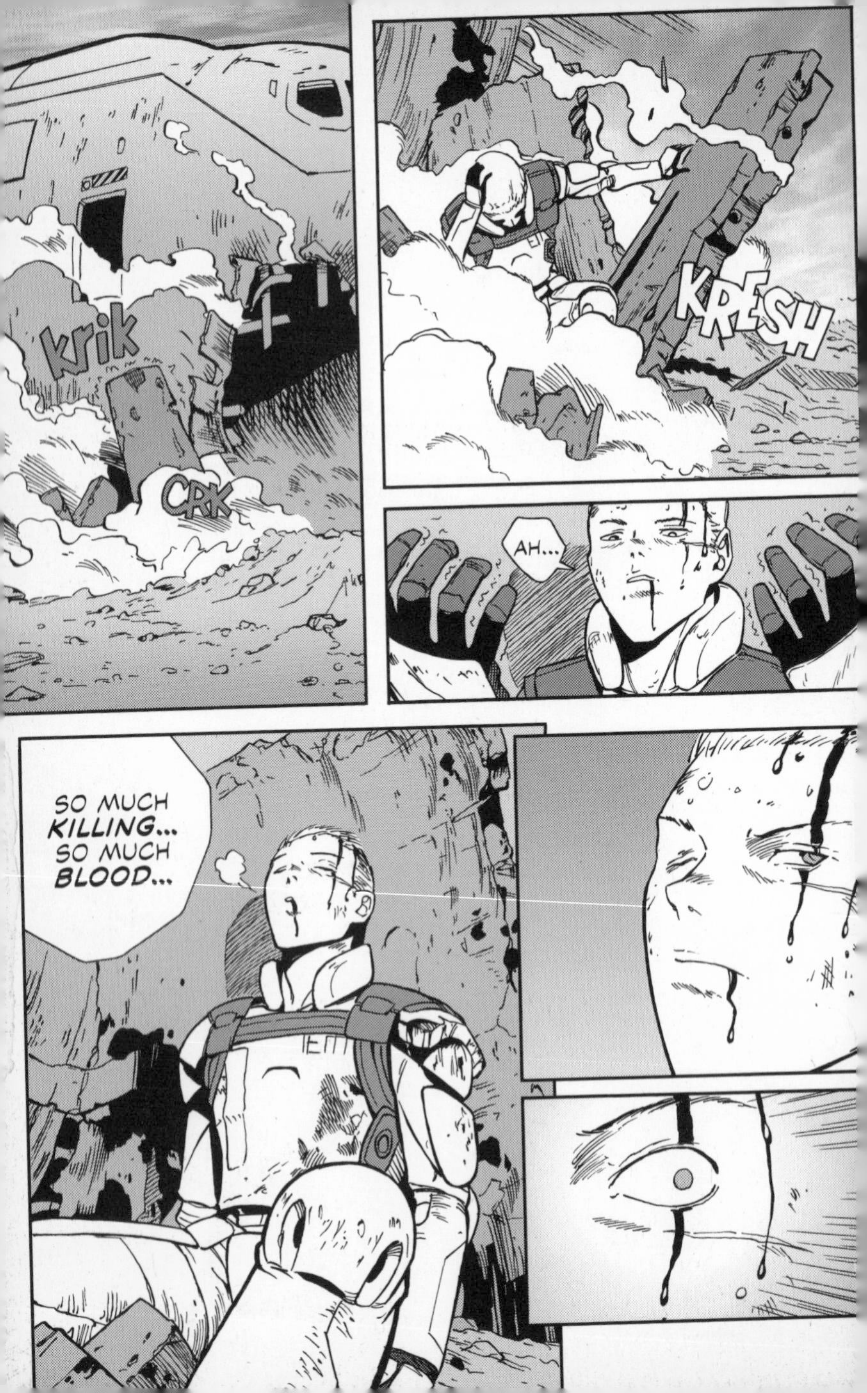
krik
CRK
KRESH
AH...
SO MUCH KILLING... SO MUCH BLOOD...

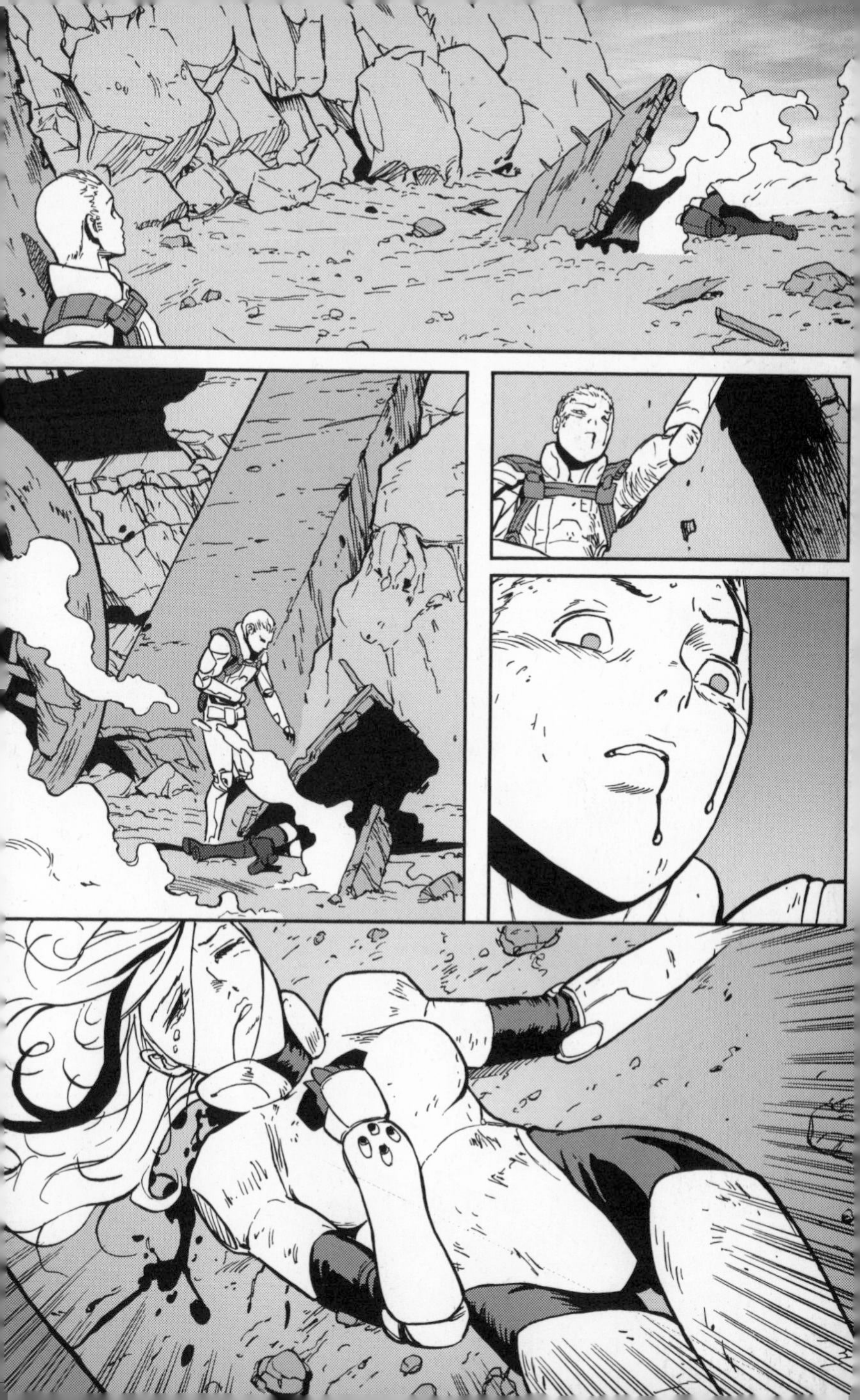

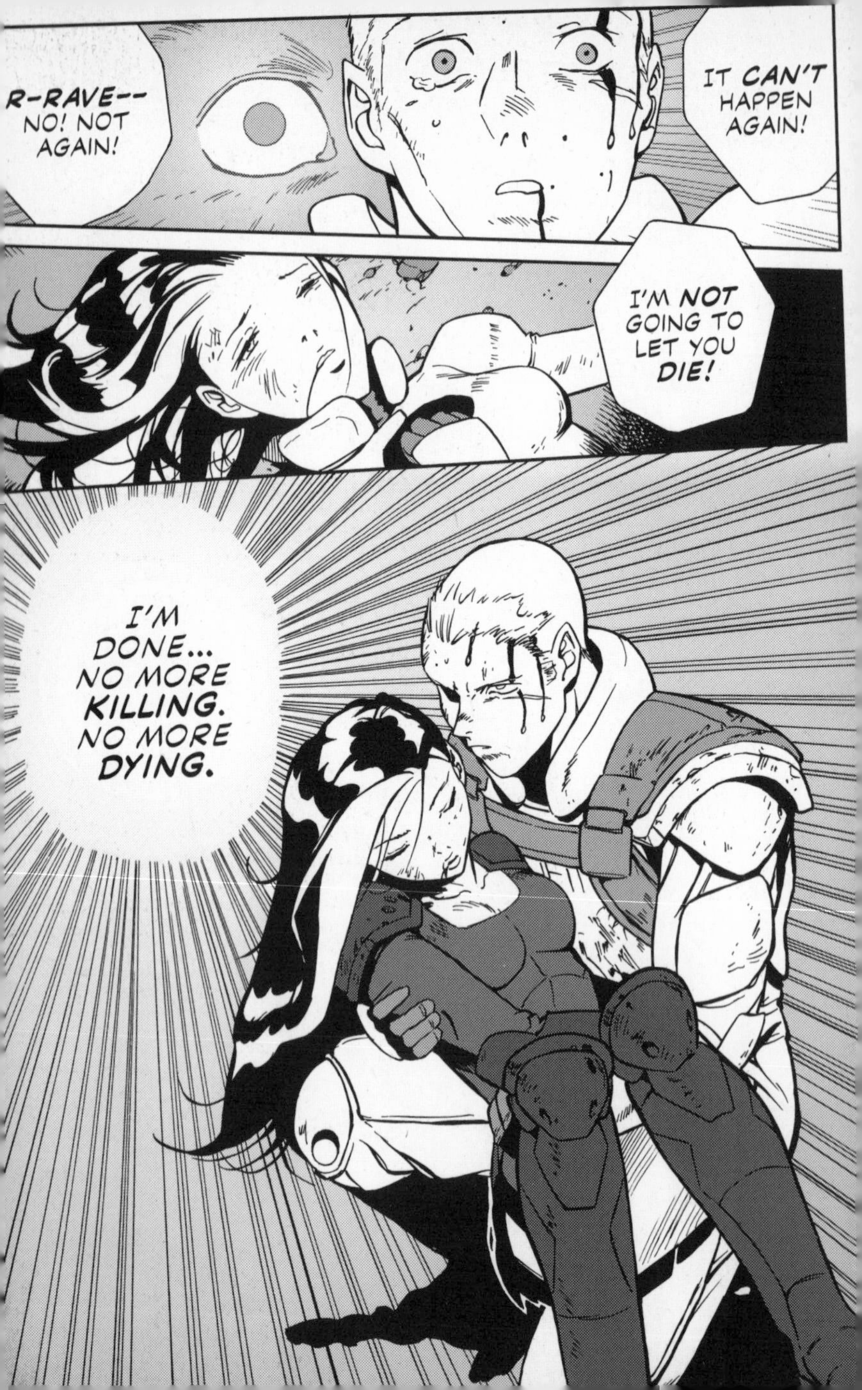
R-RAVE--
NO! NOT
AGAIN!
IT CAN'T
HAPPEN
AGAIN!
I'M NOT
GOING TO
LET YOU
DIE!
I'M
DONE...
NO MORE
KILLING.
NO MORE
DYING.

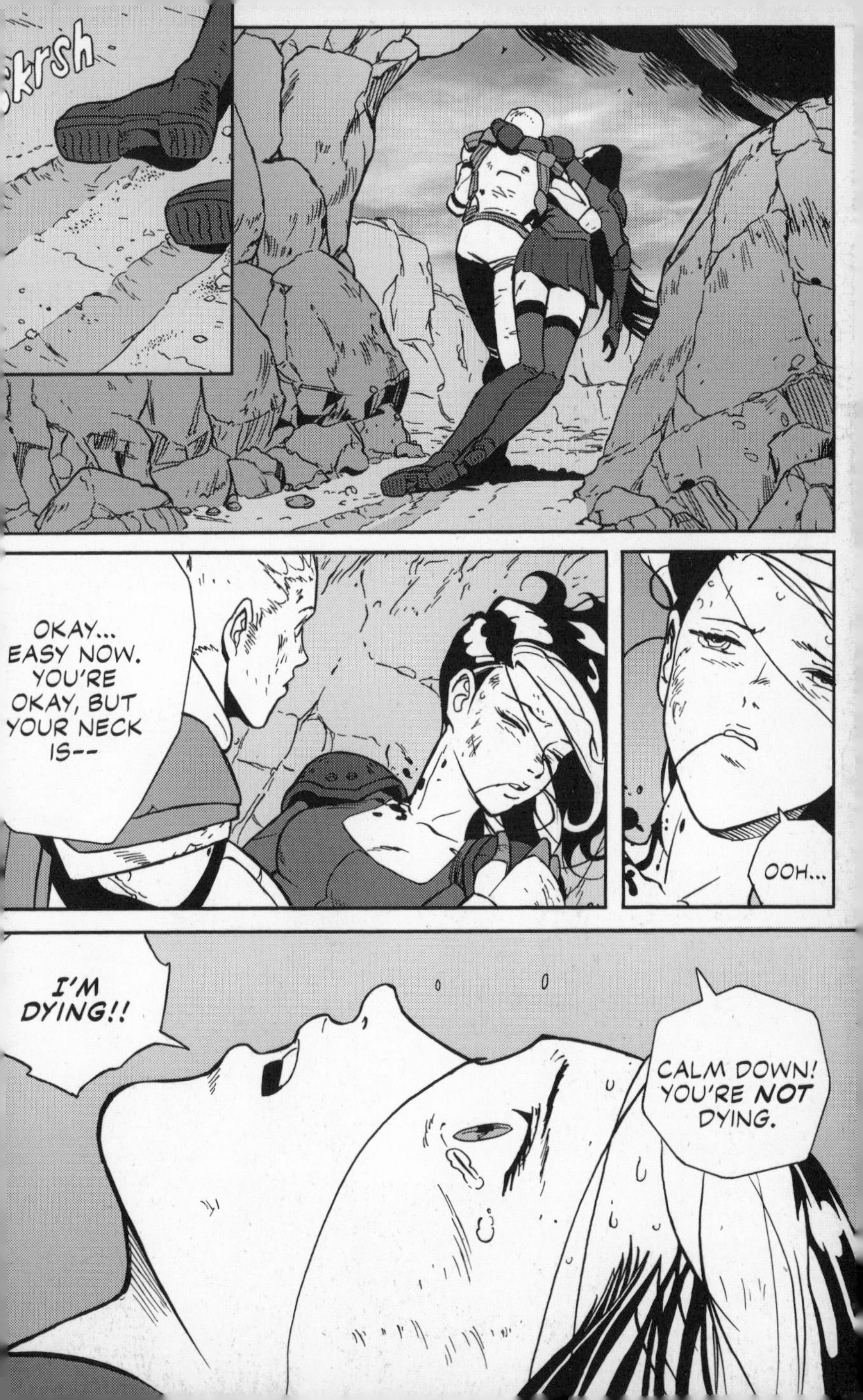

SKRSH
OKAY... EASY NOW. YOU'RE OKAY, BUT YOUR NECK IS--
OOH...
I'M DYING!!
CALM DOWN! YOU'RE NOT DYING.

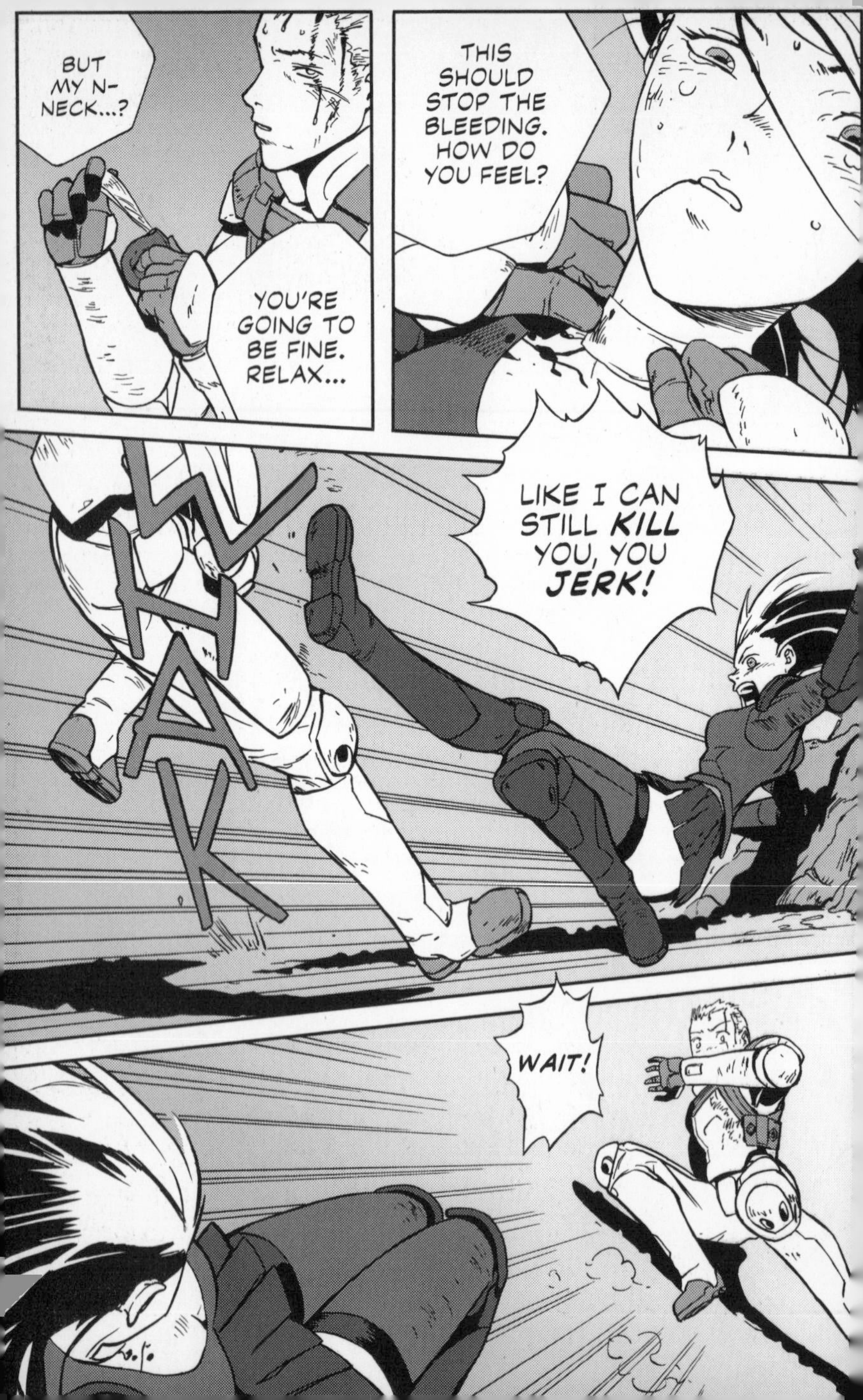
BUT MY N-NECK...?
YOU'RE GOING TO BE FINE. RELAX...
THIS SHOULD STOP THE BLEEDING. HOW DO YOU FEEL?
THWAK
LIKE I CAN STILL **KILL** YOU, YOU **JERK!**
WAIT!

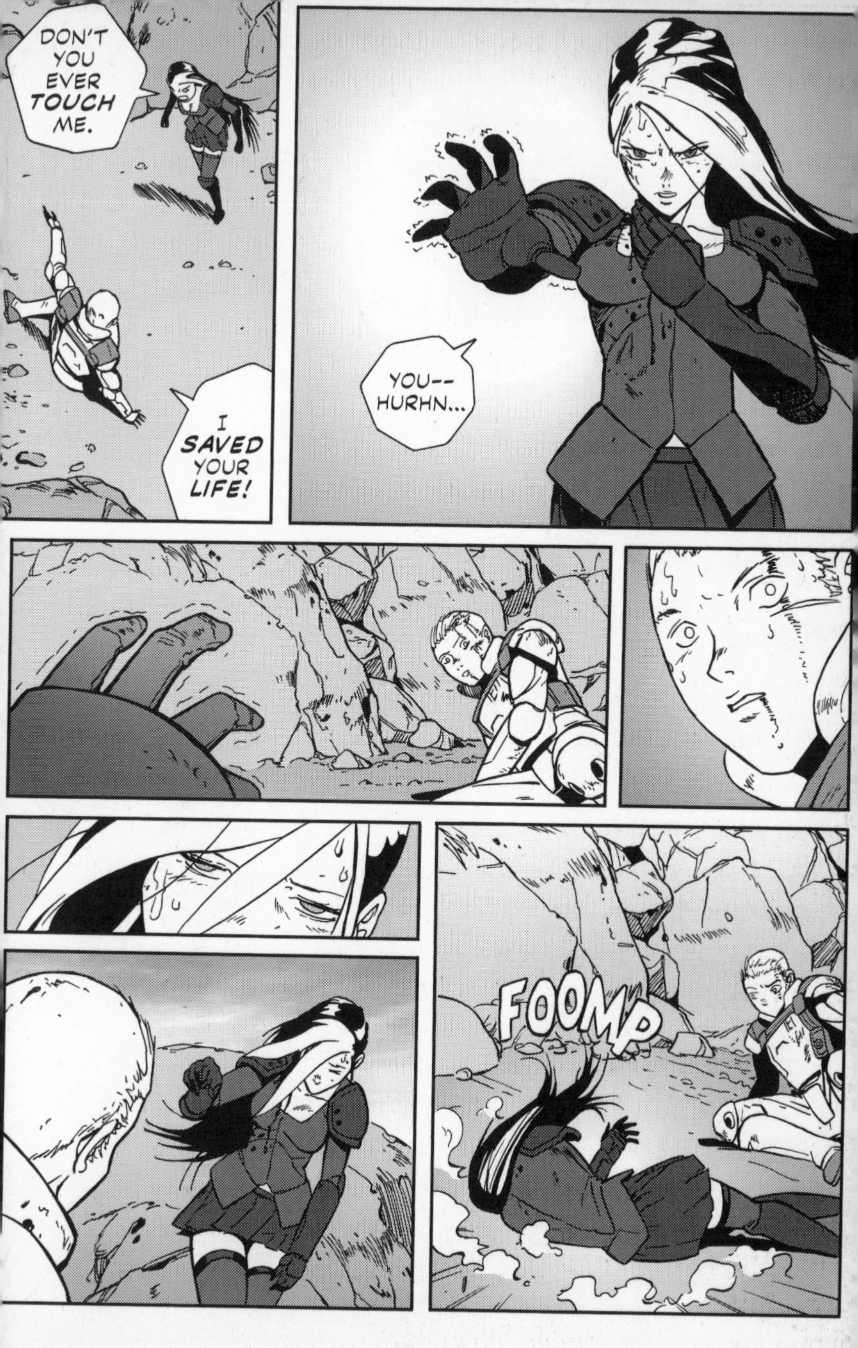
DON'T YOU EVER *TOUCH* ME.
I *SAVED* YOUR *LIFE!*
YOU-- HURHN...
FOOMP

YOU WON'T MAKE IT IF YOU KEEP THIS UP.

WH-WHAT'S *WRONG* WITH YOU?

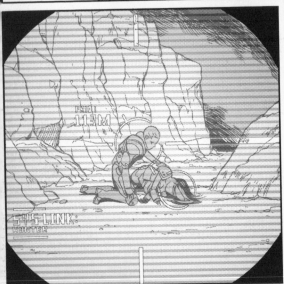

bzzp

beep

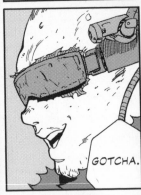

GOTCHA.

boosh

boosh

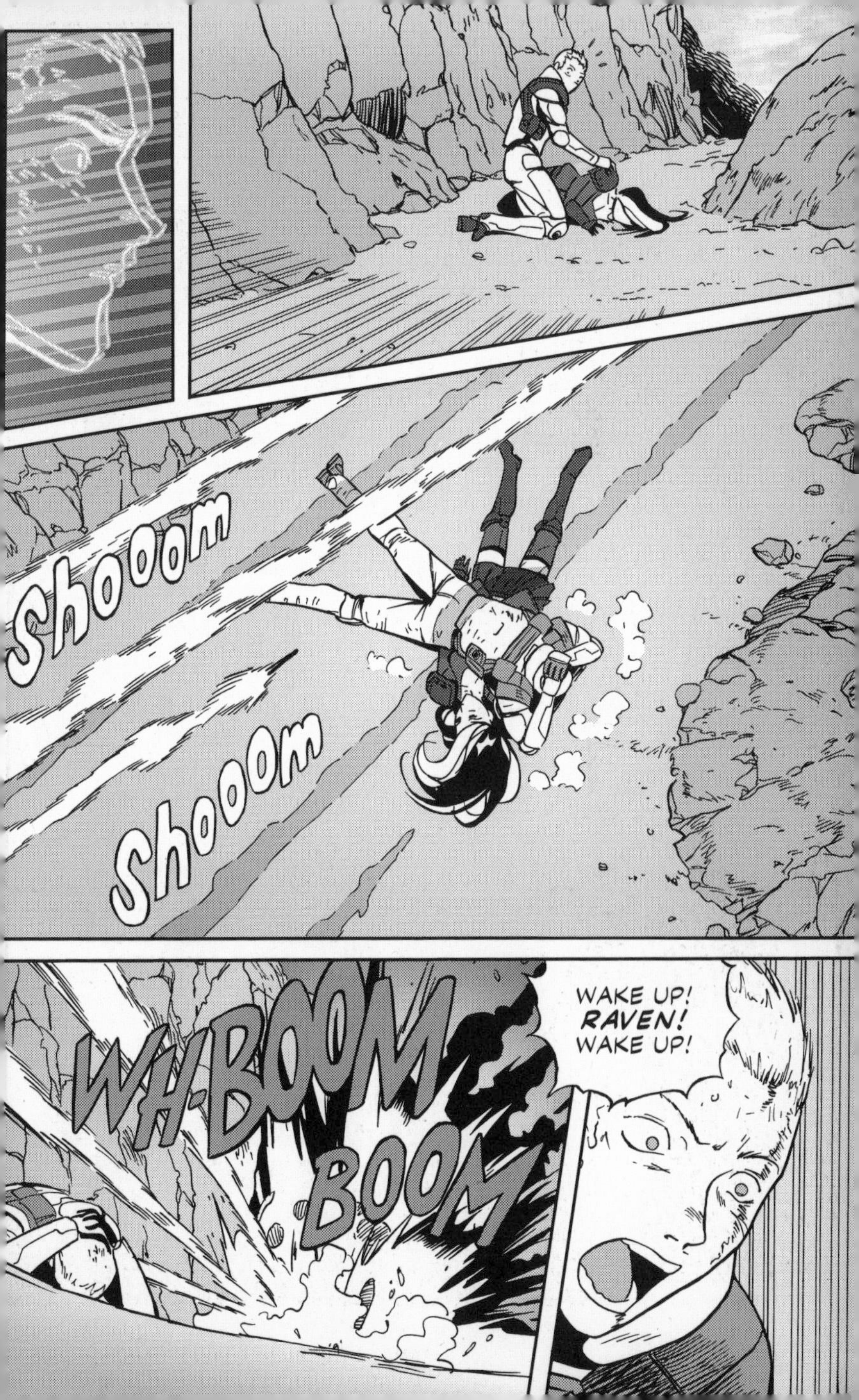
Shooom
Shooom
WA-BOOM
BOOM
WAKE UP!
RAVEN!
WAKE UP!

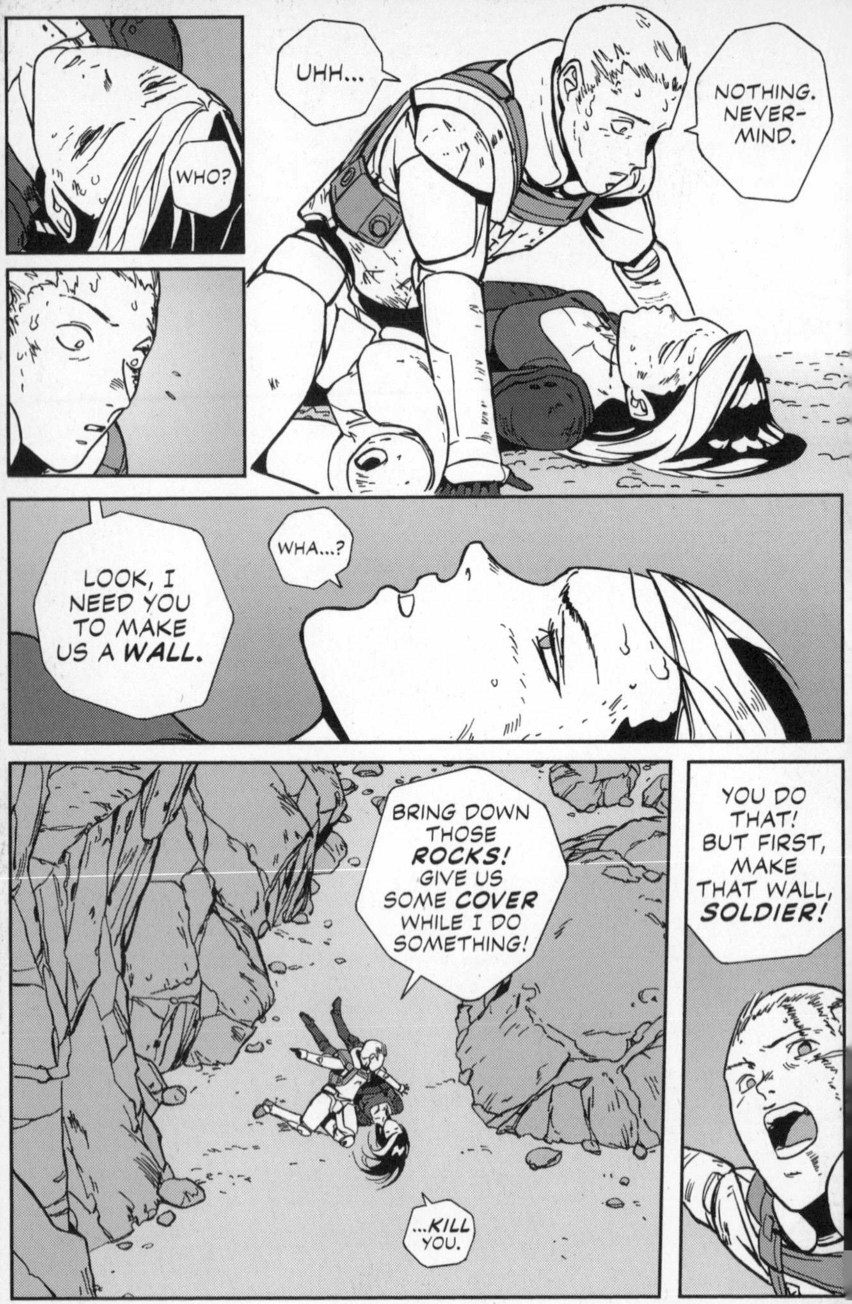
WHO?
UHH...
NOTHING. NEVER-MIND.
LOOK, I NEED YOU TO MAKE US A **WALL.**
WHA...?
BRING DOWN THOSE **ROCKS!** GIVE US SOME **COVER** WHILE I DO SOMETHING!
...**KILL** YOU.
YOU DO THAT! BUT FIRST, MAKE THAT WALL, **SOLDIER!**

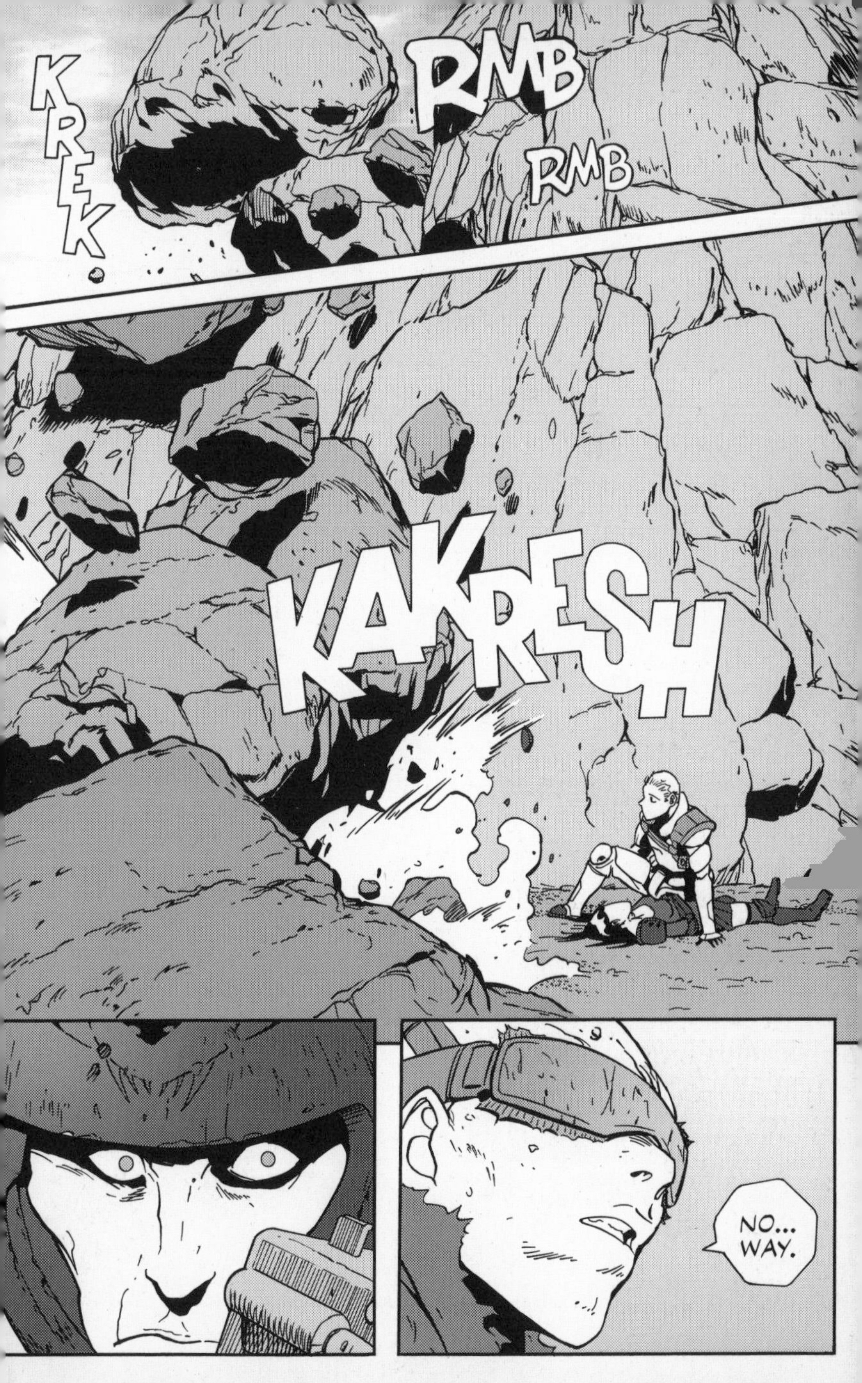
KREK
RMB
RMB
KAKRESH
NO... WAY.

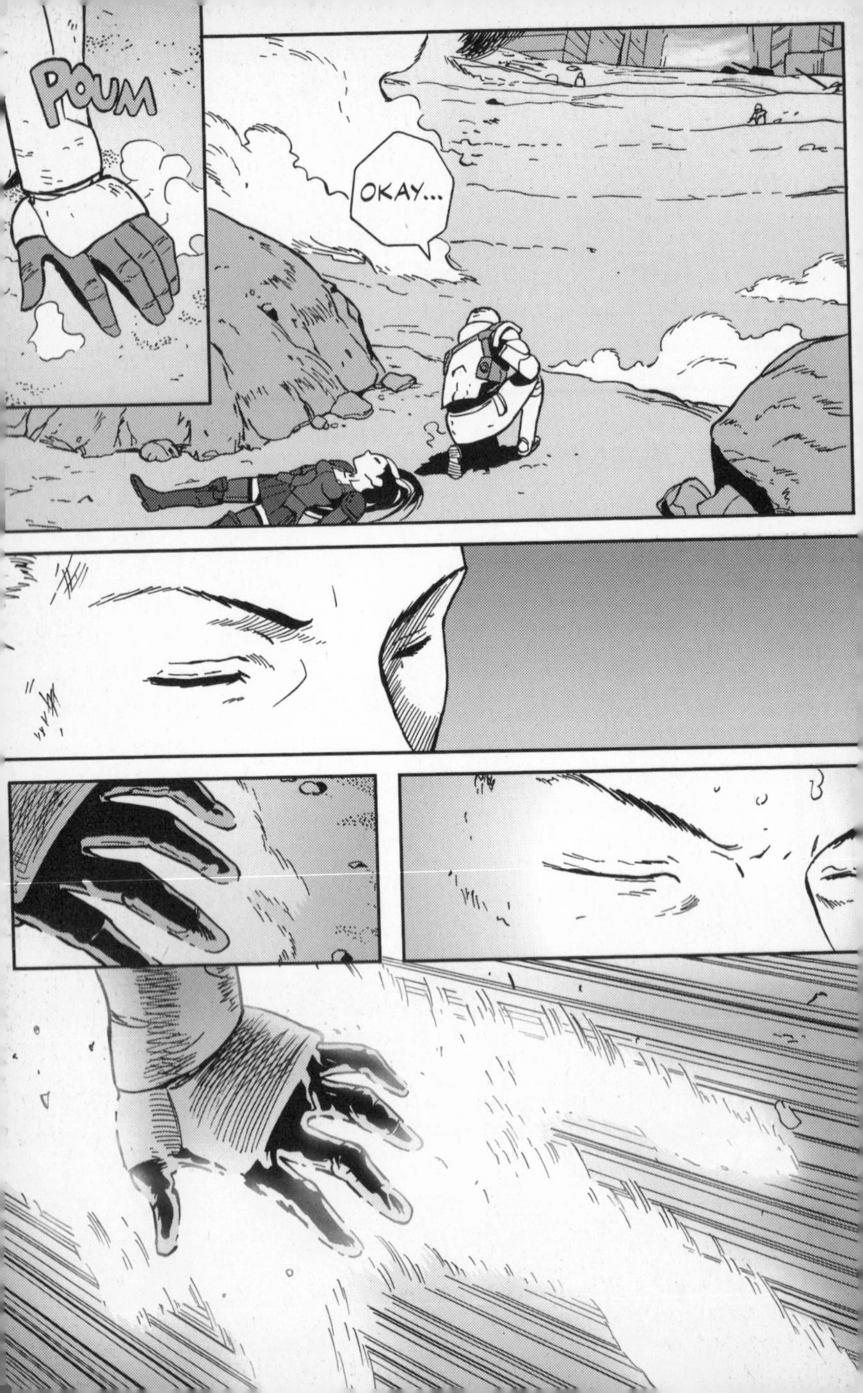
POUM
OKAY...

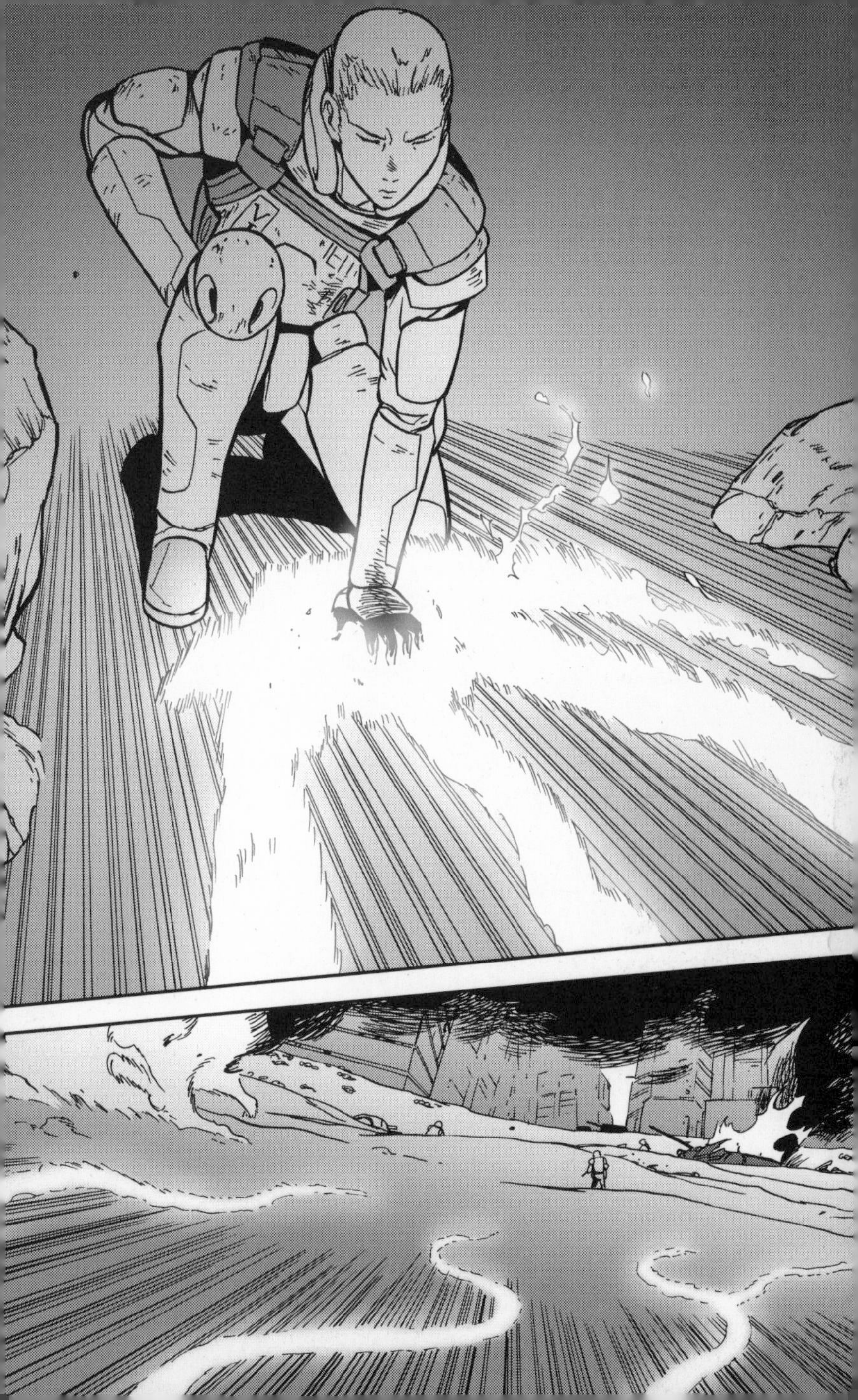

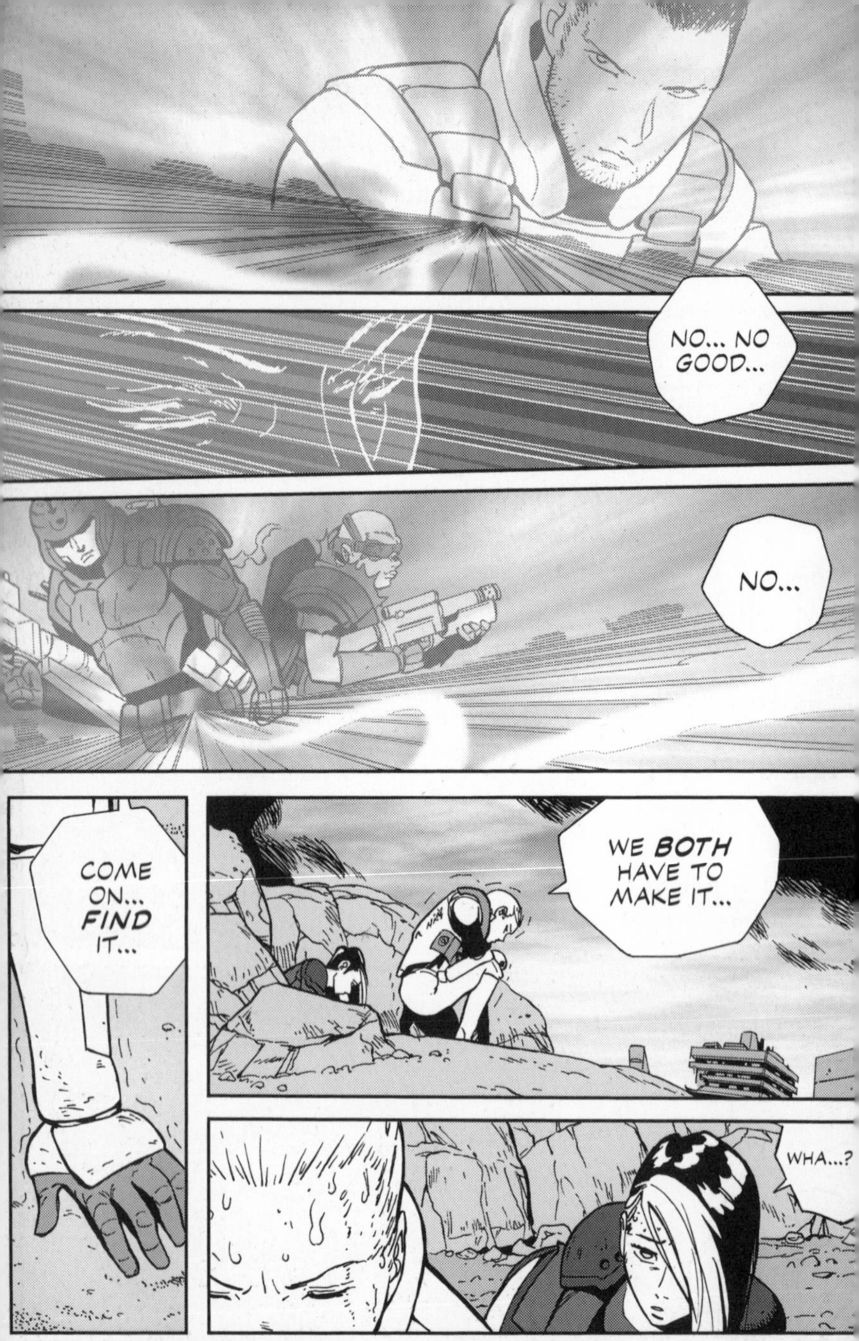
NO... NO GOOD...
NO...
COME ON... FIND IT...
WE BOTH HAVE TO MAKE IT...
WHA...?

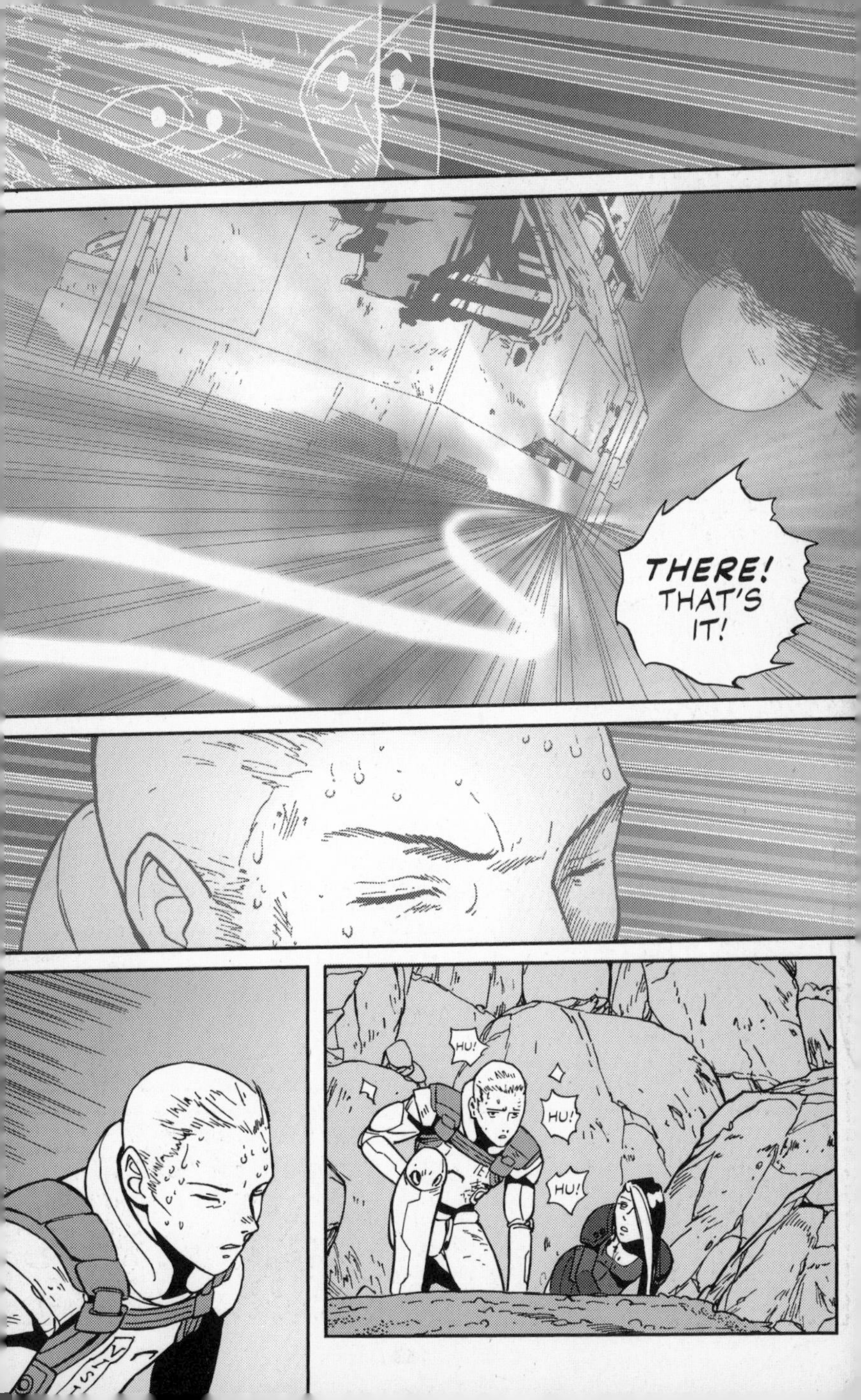
THERE! THAT'S IT!
HU!
HU!
HU!

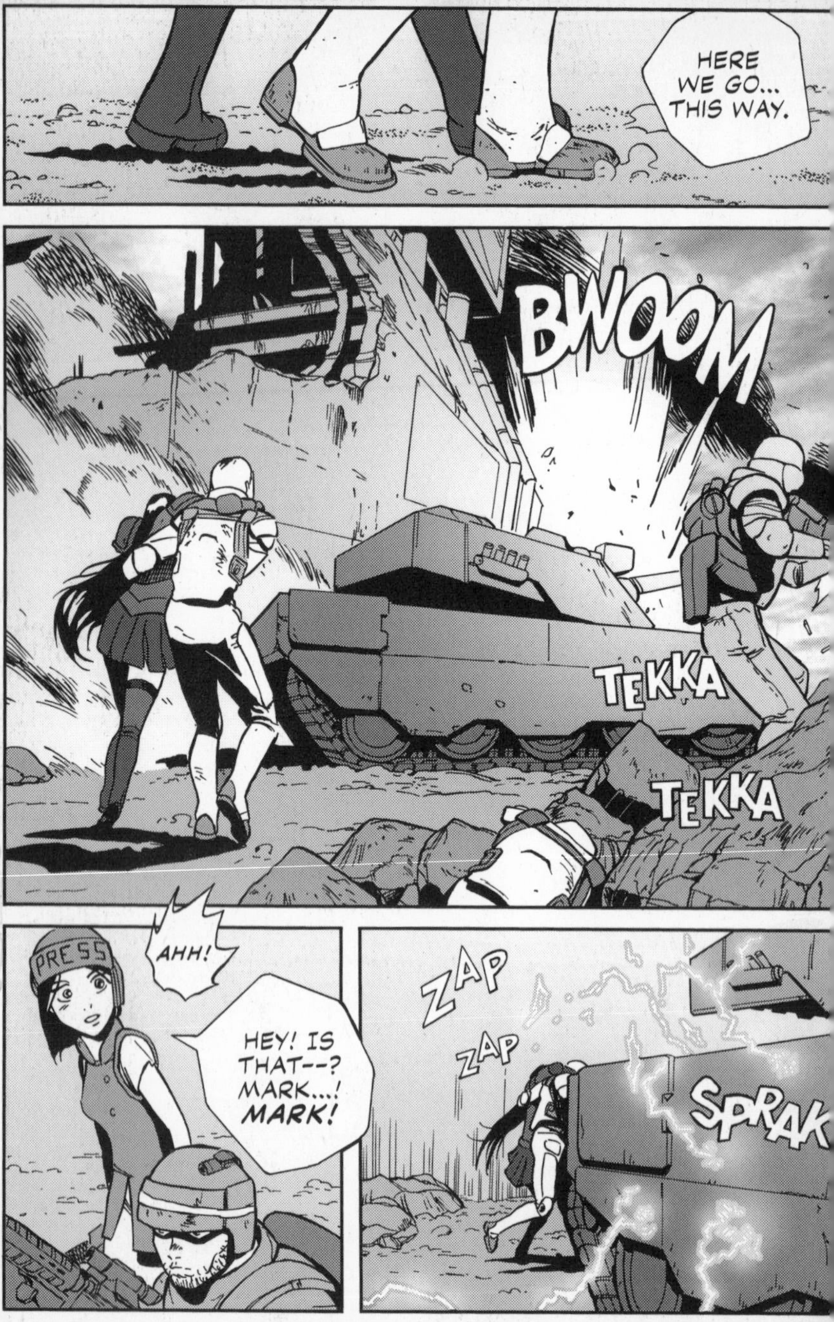
HERE WE GO... THIS WAY.
BWOOM
TEKKA
TEKKA
AHH!
HEY! IS THAT--? MARK...! MARK!
ZAP
ZAP
SPRAK

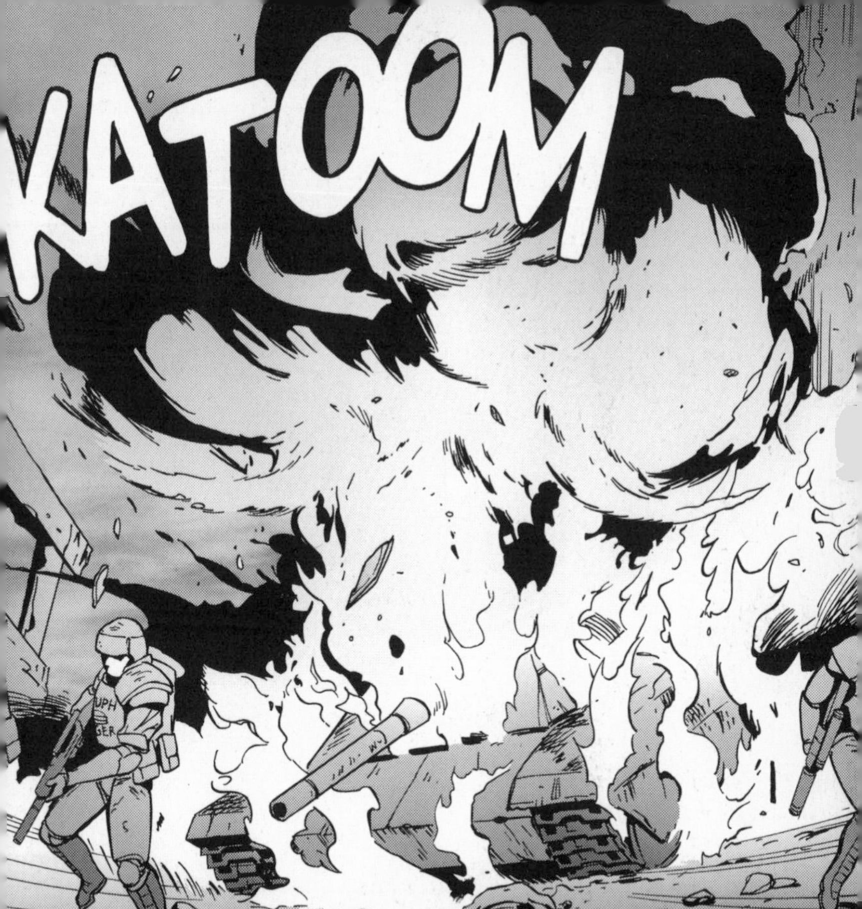
KATOOM

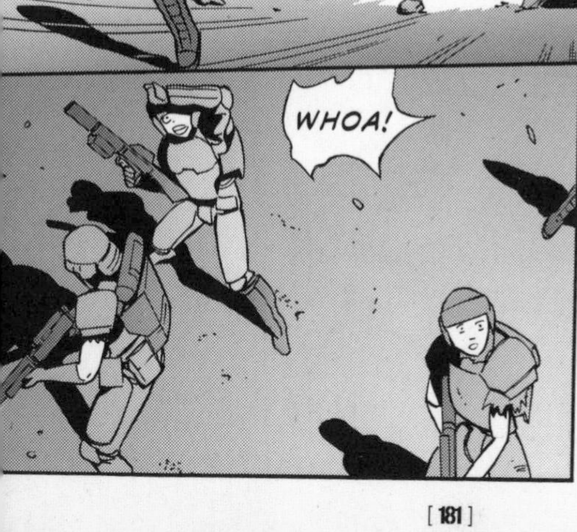
WHOA!

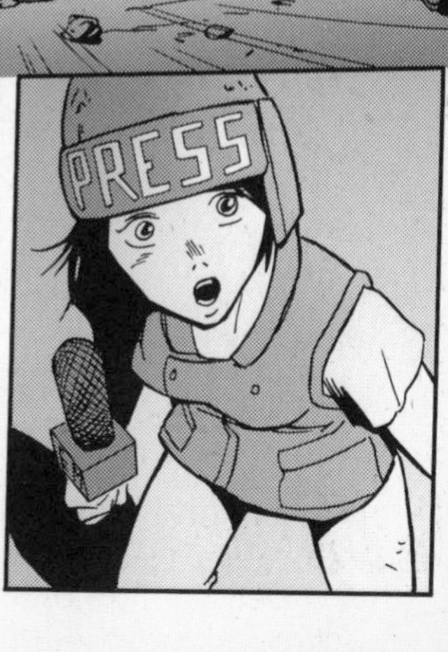
PRESS

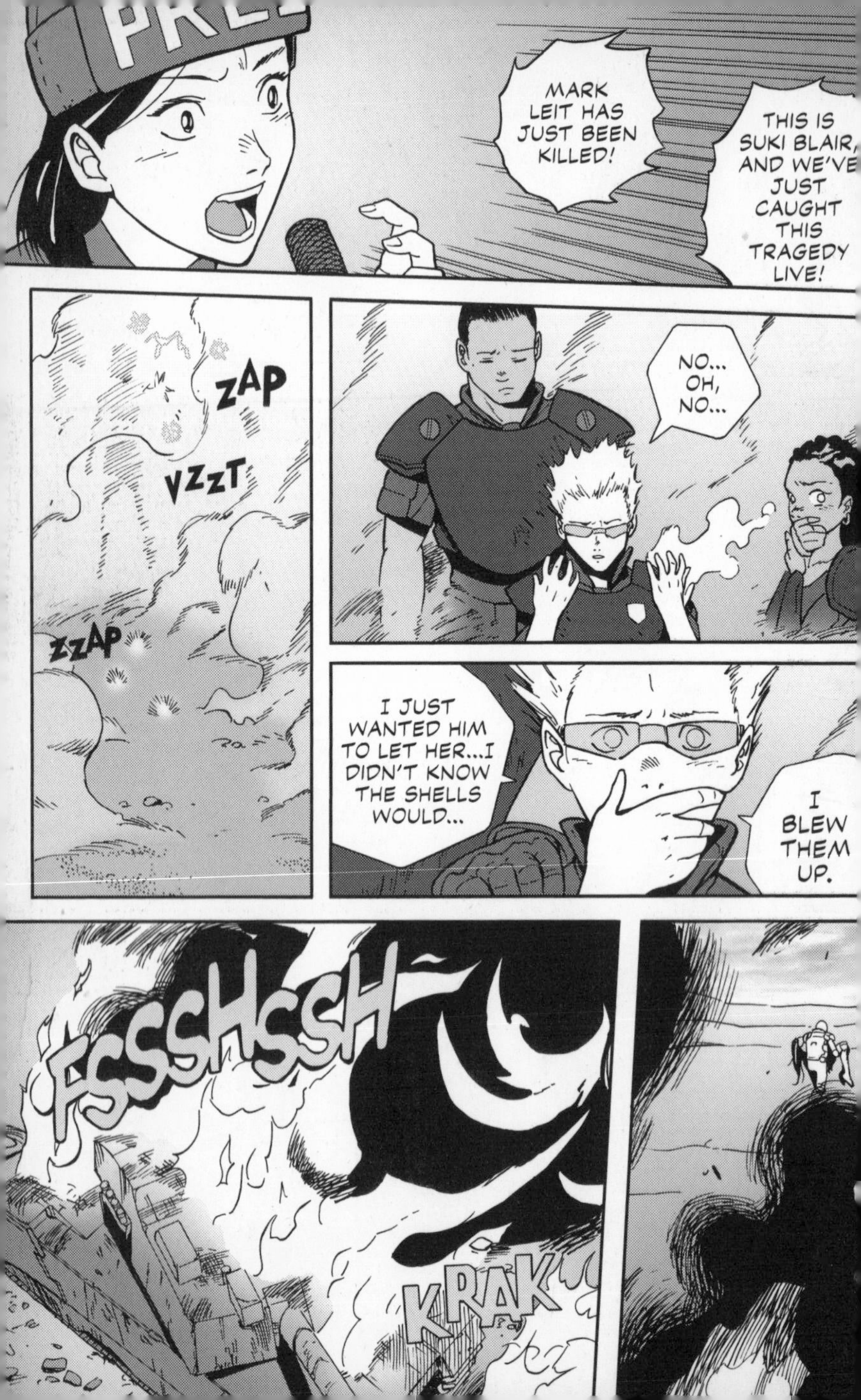
MARK LEIT HAS JUST BEEN KILLED!
THIS IS SUKI BLAIR, AND WE'VE JUST CAUGHT THIS TRAGEDY LIVE!
ZAP
VZZT
ZZAP
NO... OH, NO...
I JUST WANTED HIM TO LET HER...I DIDN'T KNOW THE SHELLS WOULD...
I BLEW THEM UP.
FSSHSSH
KRAK

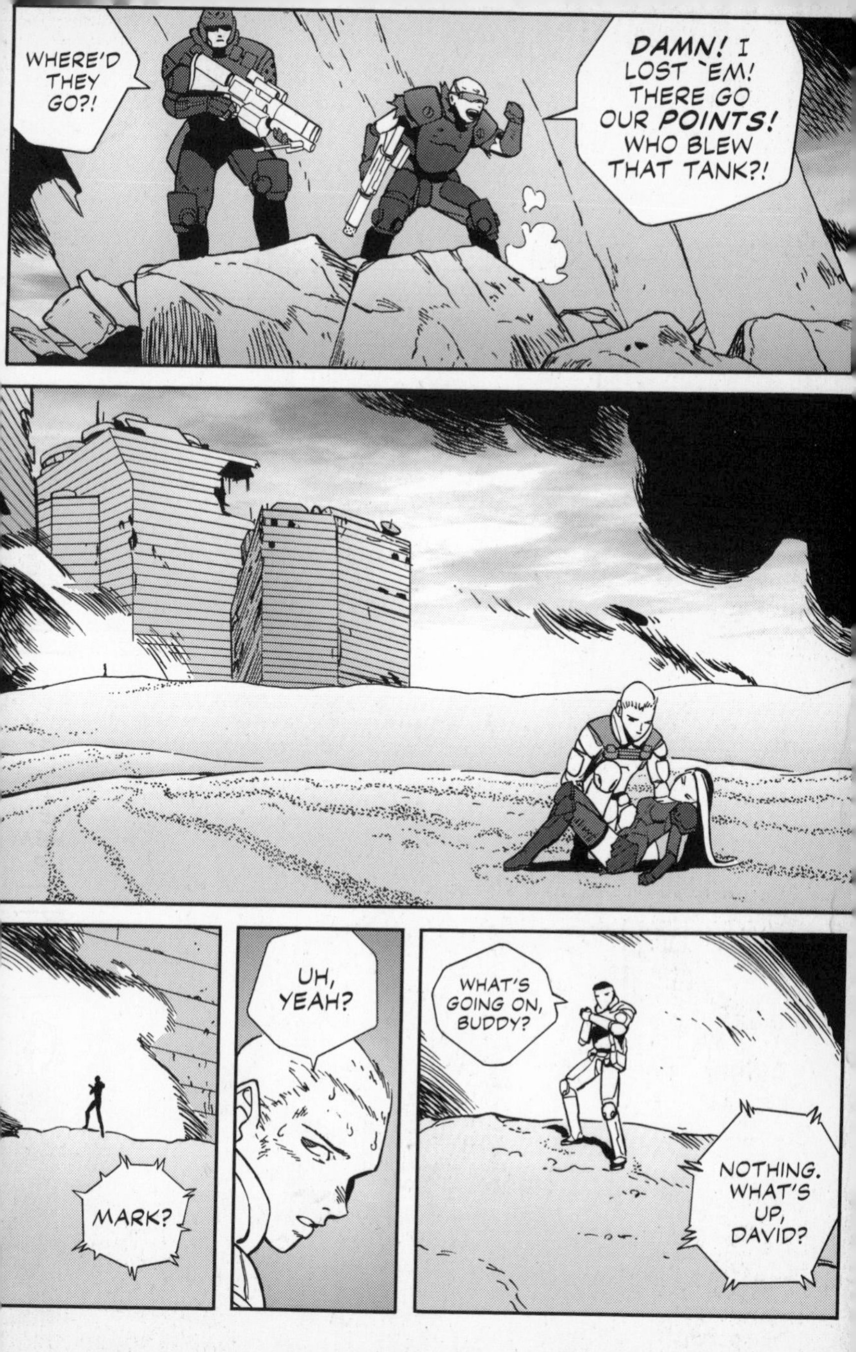
WHERE'D THEY GO?!
DAMN! I LOST `EM! THERE GO OUR POINTS! WHO BLEW THAT TANK?!
MARK?
UH, YEAH?
WHAT'S GOING ON, BUDDY?
NOTHING. WHAT'S UP, DAVID?

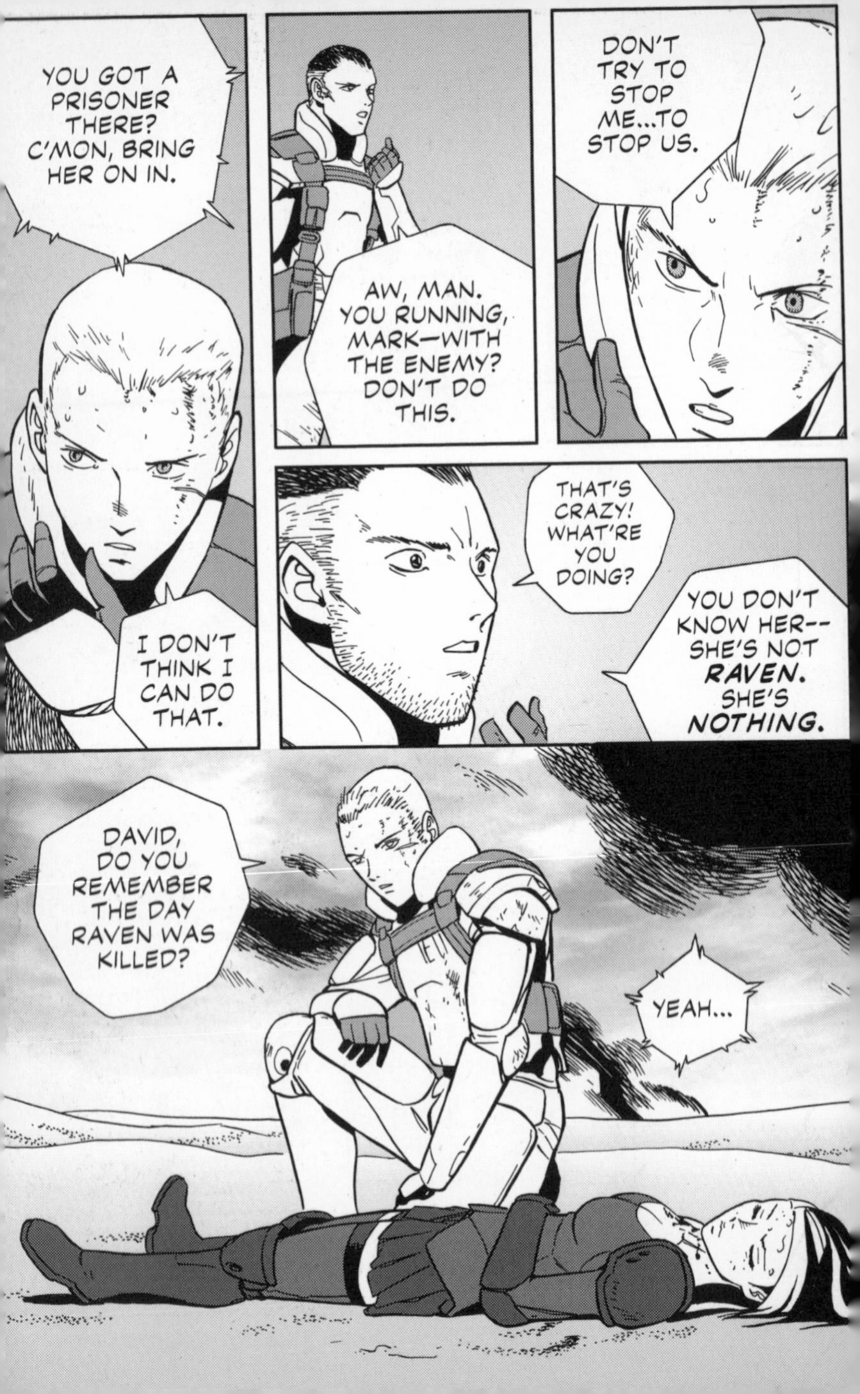
YOU GOT A PRISONER THERE? C'MON, BRING HER ON IN.
AW, MAN. YOU RUNNING, MARK—WITH THE ENEMY? DON'T DO THIS.
DON'T TRY TO STOP ME...TO STOP US.
I DON'T THINK I CAN DO THAT.
THAT'S CRAZY! WHAT'RE YOU DOING?
YOU DON'T KNOW HER--SHE'S NOT *RAVEN.* SHE'S *NOTHING.*
DAVID, DO YOU REMEMBER THE DAY RAVEN WAS KILLED?
YEAH...

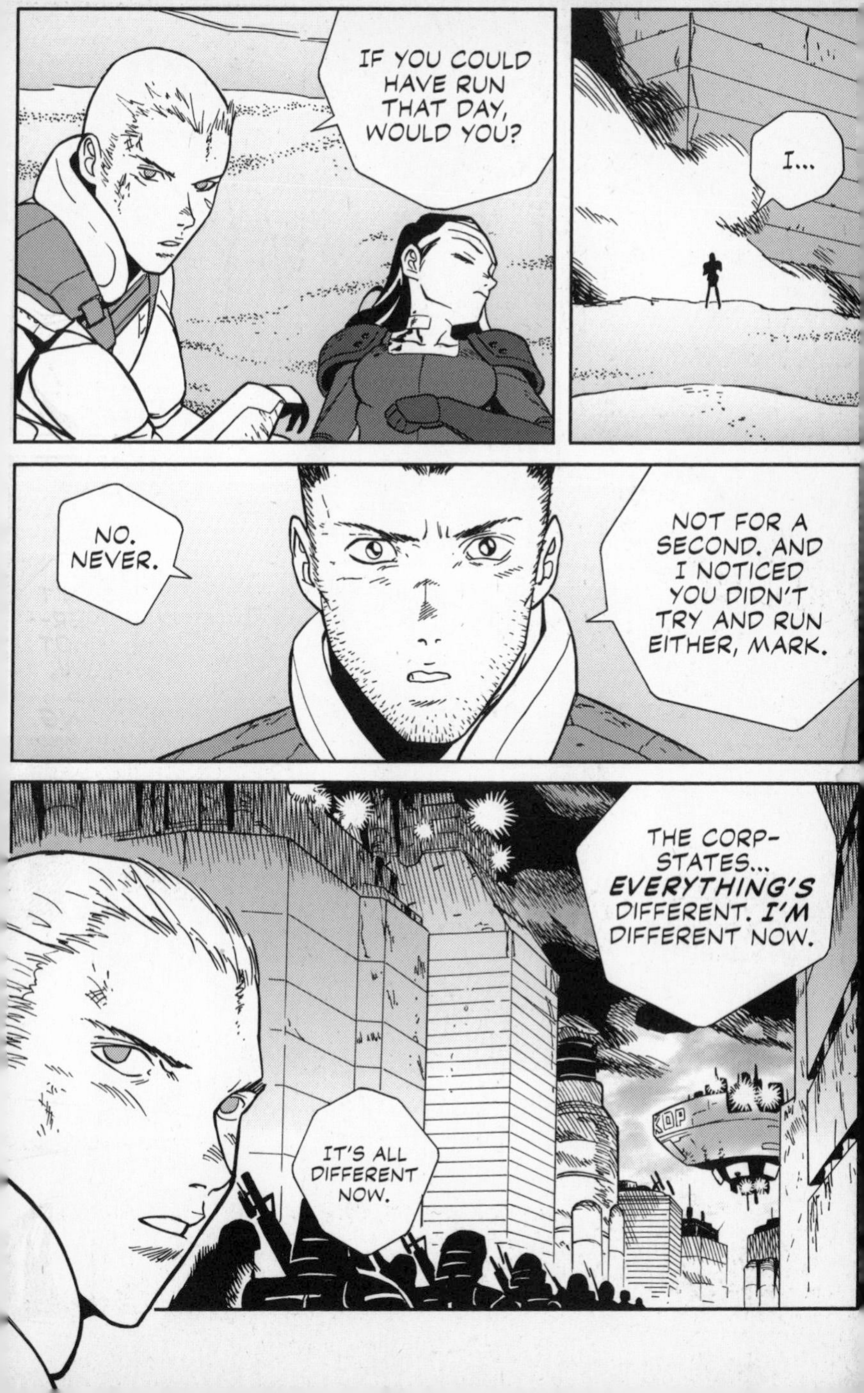
IF YOU COULD HAVE RUN THAT DAY, WOULD YOU?
I...
NO. NEVER.
NOT FOR A SECOND. AND I NOTICED YOU DIDN'T TRY AND RUN EITHER, MARK.
THE CORP-STATES... EVERYTHING'S DIFFERENT. I'M DIFFERENT NOW.
KOP
IT'S ALL DIFFERENT NOW.

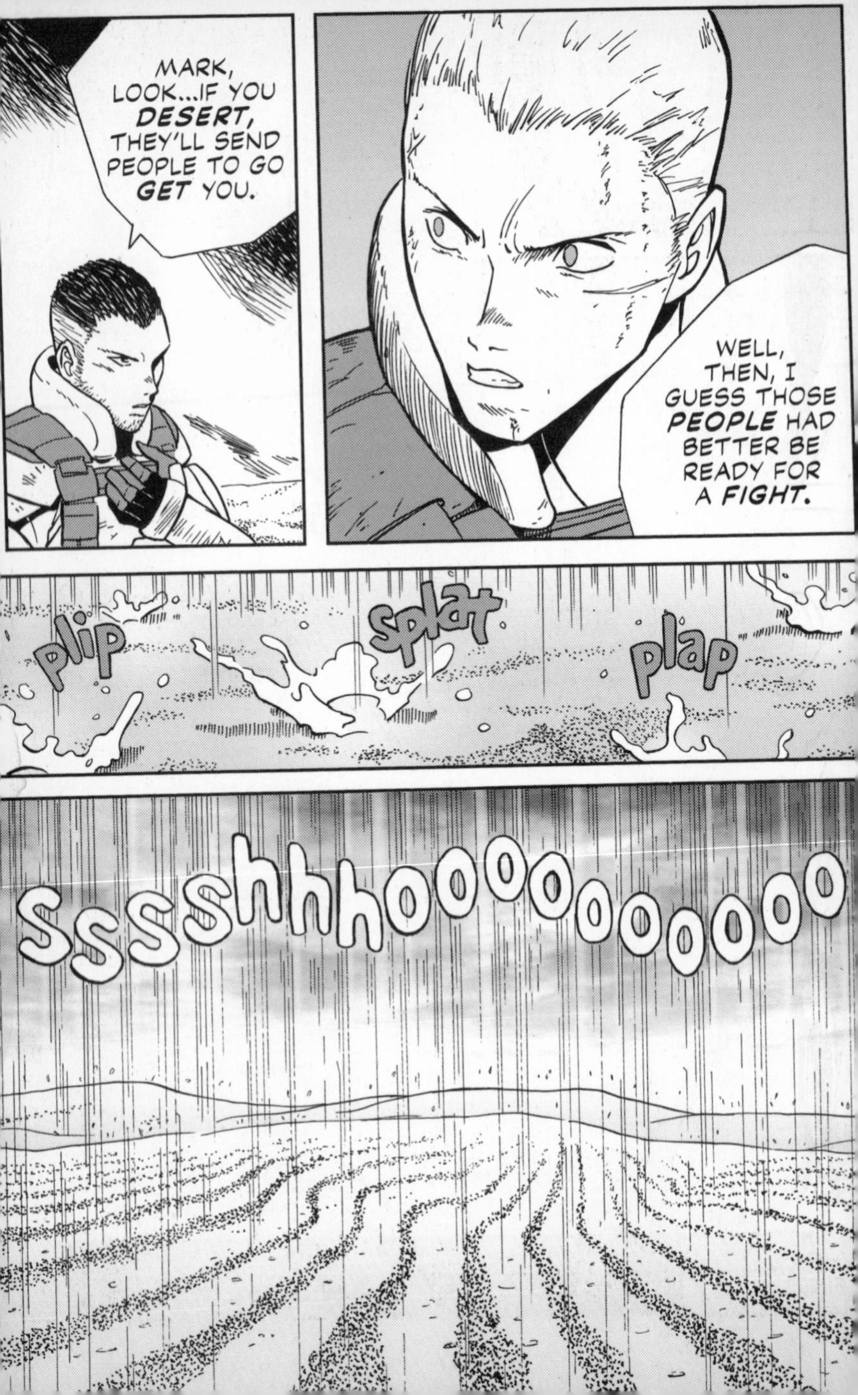
MARK, LOOK...IF YOU DESERT, THEY'LL SEND PEOPLE TO GO GET YOU.
WELL, THEN, I GUESS THOSE PEOPLE HAD BETTER BE READY FOR A FIGHT.
plip
splat
plap
SSSHHOOOOOOOOOO

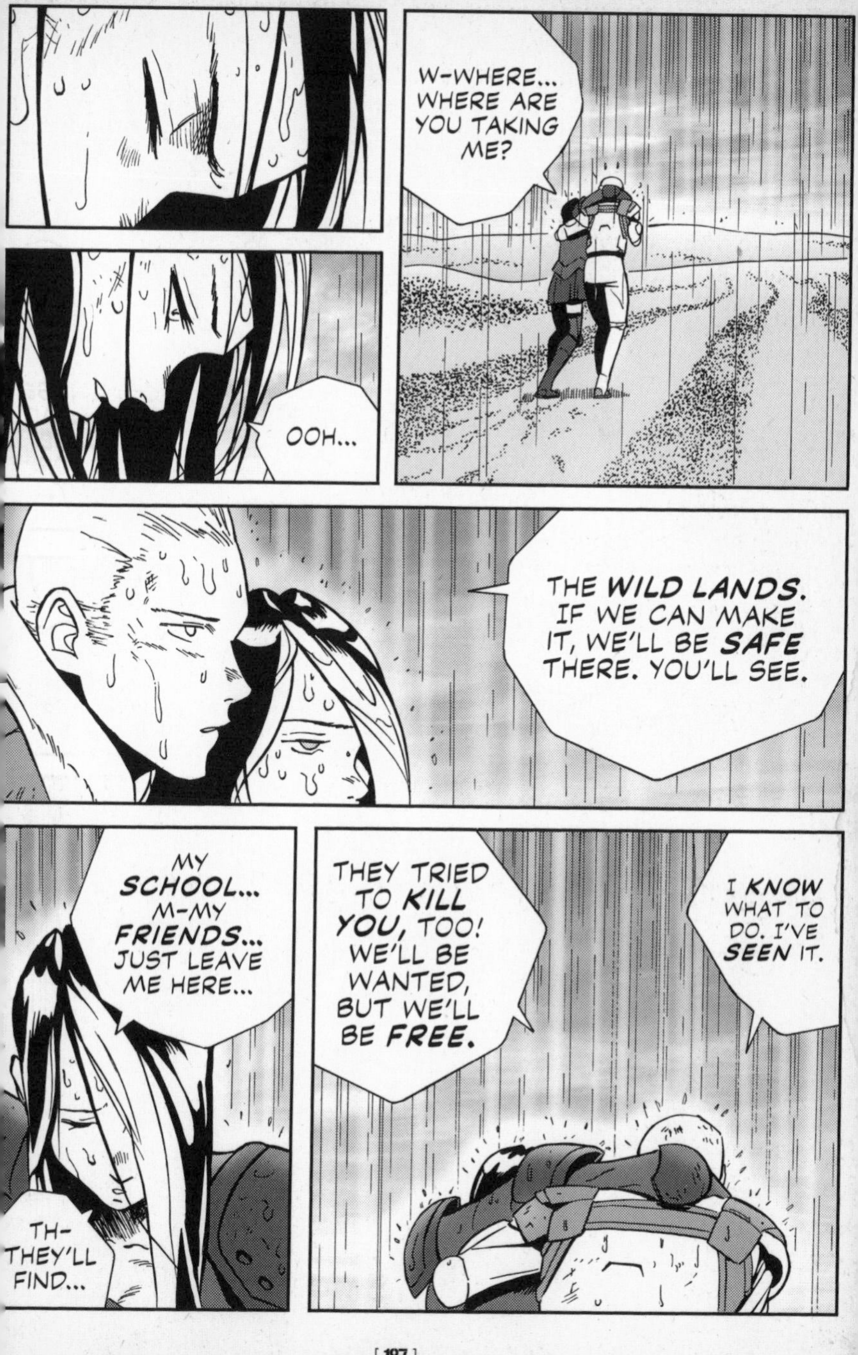
OOH...
W-WHERE... WHERE ARE YOU TAKING ME?
THE WILD LANDS. IF WE CAN MAKE IT, WE'LL BE SAFE THERE. YOU'LL SEE.
MY SCHOOL... M-MY FRIENDS... JUST LEAVE ME HERE...
TH- THEY'LL FIND...
THEY TRIED TO KILL YOU, TOO! WE'LL BE WANTED, BUT WE'LL BE FREE.
I KNOW WHAT TO DO. I'VE SEEN IT.

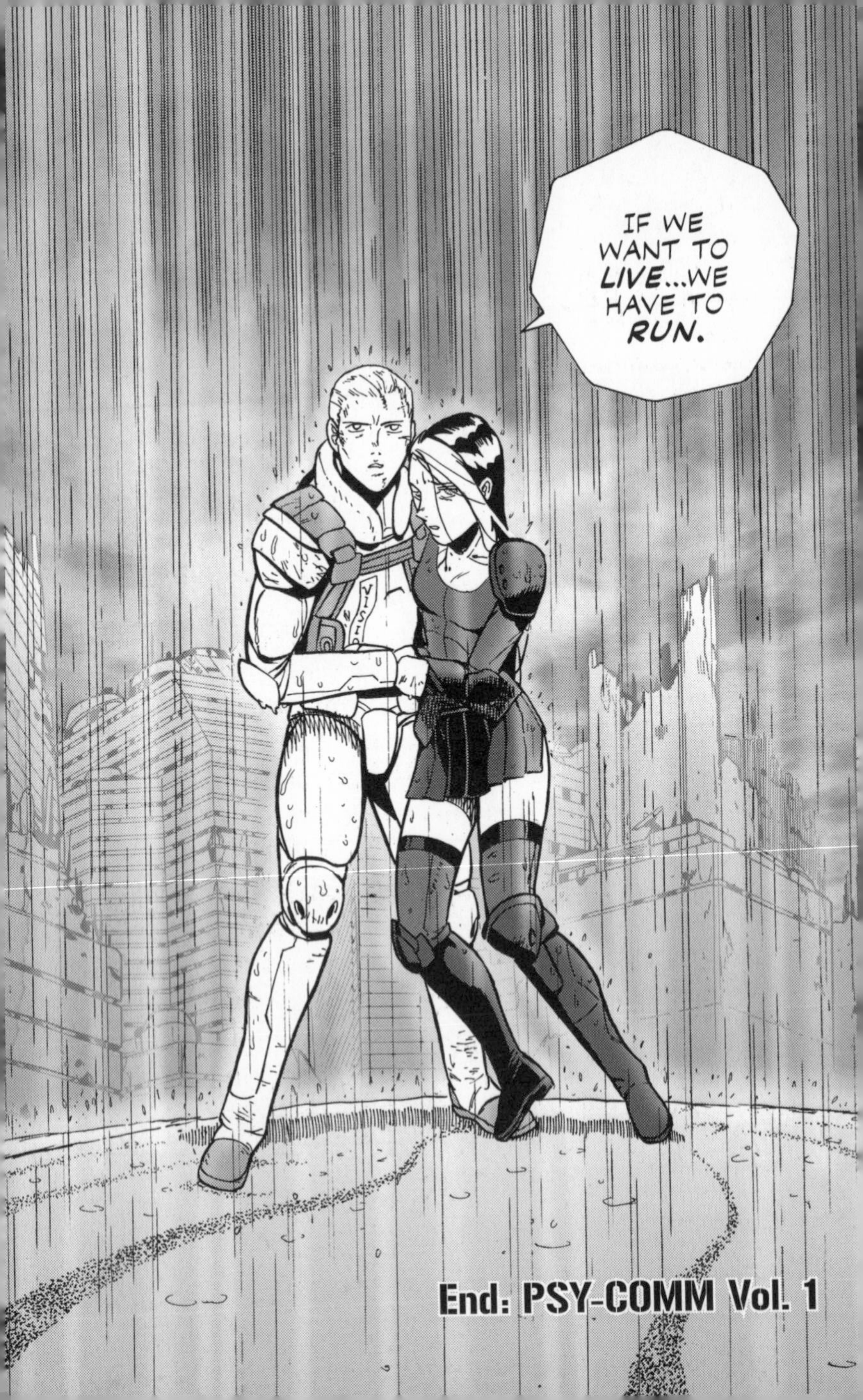
IF WE WANT TO LIVE...WE HAVE TO RUN.
End: PSY-COMM Vol. 1

COMING SOON...

PSY★COMM
VOLUME [2]

Mark Leit's run for freedom and redemption begins, but it won't be without its consequences. His unwilling accomplice, Snow Lucente, still sees her duty quite clearly--kill the enemy. Among their pursuers is David Jerold, who views Mark's desertion as the ultimate act of betrayal--not only of Electromedia Corp-- but of their friendship. Mark's journey will be fraught with danger and deception as he doggedly pursues a utopian ideal that may not even exist...The Wild Lands.

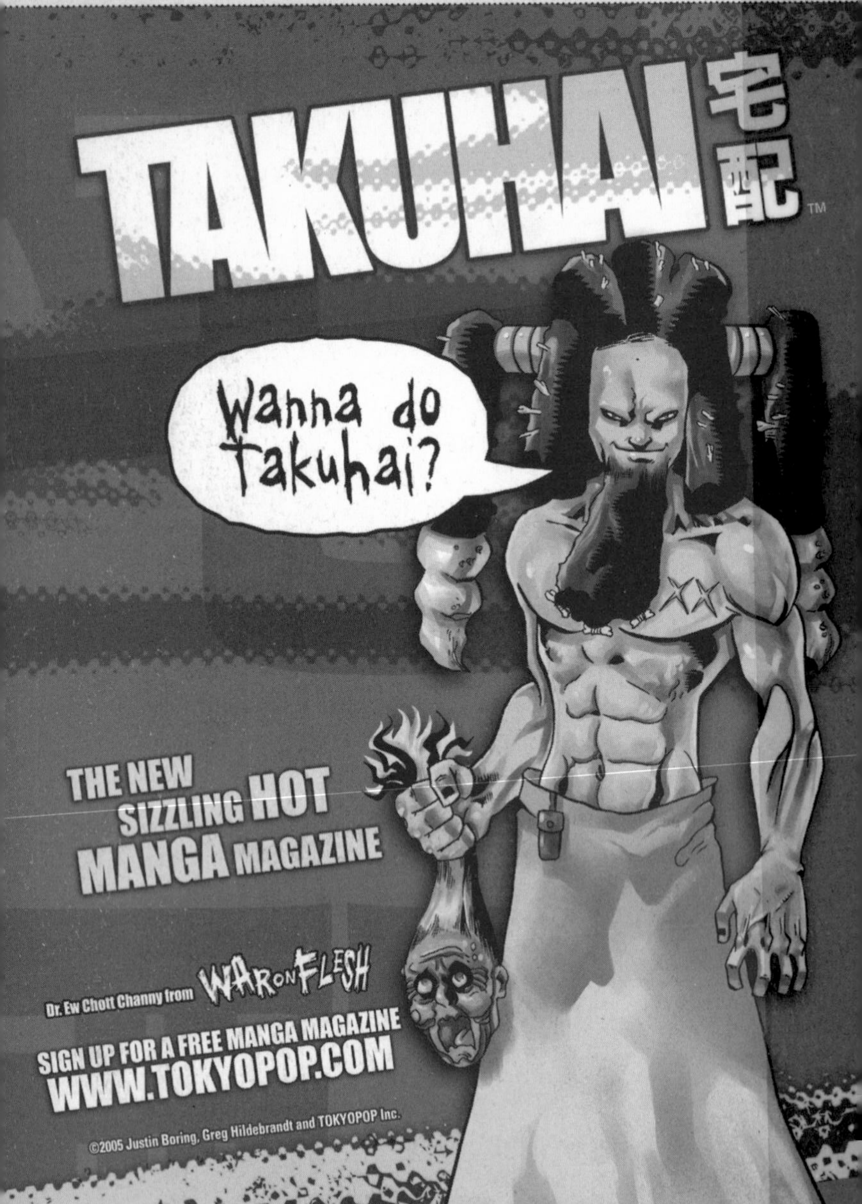
TAKUHAI 宅配 TM
Wanna do Takuhai?
THE NEW SIZZLING HOT MANGA MAGAZINE
Dr. Ew Chott Channy from WAR ON FLESH
SIGN UP FOR A FREE MANGA MAGAZINE
SIGN UP FOR A FREE MANGA MAGAZINE WWW.TOKYOPOP.COM
©2005 Justin Boring, Greg Hildebrandt and TOKYOPOP Inc.

TOKYOPOP SHOP

MARK OF THE SUCCUBUS

BY ASHLY RA

Maeve,
to the h
hone he
things g
her sigh
unmotiva
school. M
has sent
doesn't s
Aiden's
best fr
conspira
lucky to

Here is
in one
known

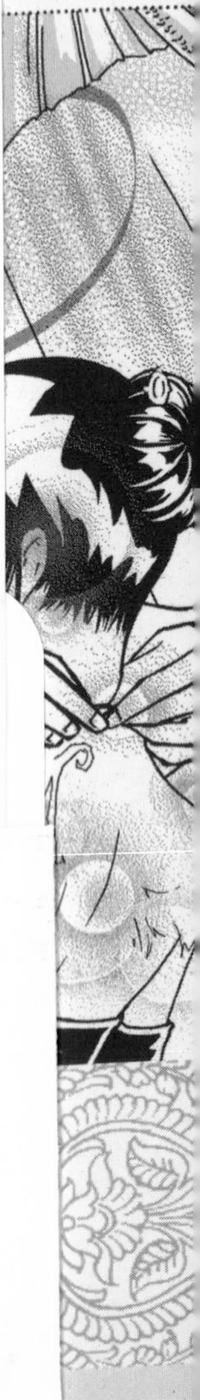